Building Cities That

Building Cities
That Work

EDMUND P. FOWLER

McGill-Queen's University Press
Montreal & Kingston • London • Buffalo

© McGill-Queen's University Press 1992
ISBN 0-7735-0820-1 (cloth)
ISBN 0-7735-1183-0 (paper)

Legal deposit second quarter 1992
Bibliothèque nationale du Québec

∞

Printed in Canada on acid-free paper
First paperback edition 1993

This book was first published
with the help of a grant from the
Social Science Federation of Canada,
using funds provided by the
Social Sciences and Humanities
Research Council of Canada.
Funding was also received
from Glendon College, York University.

Canadian Cataloguing in Publication Data

Fowler, Edmund P. (Edmund Prince), 1942–
    Building cities that work
    Includes bibliographical references and index.
    ISBN 0-7735-0820-1 (bnd)
    ISBN 0-7735-1183-0 (pbk)
    1. City planning. 1. Title.
    HT231.F69 1992   307.1   C91-090618-1

Typeset in Baskerville 10/12
by Caractéra production graphique inc.,
Quebec City.

To Shelly

Contents

Tables and Figures   ix

Preface   xiii

1 Postwar City Building from Above and
Below   3
The New Urban Environment   3
The Areas of the Toronto Study   14

PART ONE   THE LACK OF PHYSICAL
DIVERSITY: ITS CONSEQUENCES

2 The Economic Costs of the New North
American City   29
The Costs of Municipal Services   29
Housing   55
Retail and Manufacturing   65
Conclusions   68

3 The Social Consequences of the New North
American City   70
The Suburbs   70
Likes and Dislikes   74
Friendship Patterns   83
Crime   90

4 Children   99
Belonging to the Environment   101
Socializing   105
Juvenile Delinquency   109

5 Politics and the New Urban
   Environment   115
   Conventional Politics   115
   Authentic Politics   117
   Local Government   118
   The Impact of the New Built Environment
   on Politics   120

   PART TWO   EXPLORING WHY WE
   BUILT THIS WAY: OPENINGS TO
   CHANGE

6 Why Did We Do It? Explanations for the
   Postwar Urban Environment   139
   Economic Explanations   139
   Political Explanations   148
   Culture   168
   Planners and Planning   171

7 Basic Assumptions   178
   Separation from Nature   180
   Economic Institutions   184
   Political Institutions   191

8 Our Cities, Our Selves   199

   Appendix   The Areas and Their Scores on
   Physical Diversity   223

   Notes   229

   Bibliography   269

   Index   291

Tables and Figures

TABLES

1 Office space taken up per office worker, downtown Toronto   7

2 Density gradients, Canadian and US metropolitan areas, 1950–51 to 1975–76   10

3 Population of selected North American cities, 1870–1980   12

4 Annual spending on urban transportation, US and Canada   32

5 Highway spending, transit operation costs, and use density, US cities, 1982–86   36

6 Increase in urban highway mileage, US   37

7 Canadian cities' spending on streets, 1987   38

8 Transit costs per passenger and density – Canadian transit systems, 1987   39

9 Road supply in selected world cities, 1980   40

10 Land in square miles displaced by highways and by bus and rail transit, 1972 and 1980, in US cities over 1 million   44

11 Population and jobs displaced by new urban transportation-facilities planned for the 1970s, US 45

12 Sewage and sanitation operating costs, by use density, US cities, 1985–86 51

13 Sewer and waterworks operating expenditures of Canadian cities, by density, 1987 52

14 Cost of providing public services to one unit, by property type and density 53

15 Additional local government expenditure per resident for leapfrog development 54

16 Changes over a three-year period in the rental housing stock of selected US central cities, different years 58

17 Satisfaction with housing and neighbourhood by type of dwelling 78

18 Juvenile crime and physical diversity 112

19 Crime rates in two Toronto neighbourhoods 113

20 Contrasting economic values 189

FIGURES

1 The density gradient 8

2 Examples of density gradients in three North American cities 9

3 Urban density versus gasoline use per capita adjusted for vehicle efficiency 48

4 Toronto child's picture of his street 81

5 Front porch, downtown Toronto 89

6 Renovated house, stripped of its front porch, downtown Toronto 90

7 "Front yard" of a high-rise 91

8 Public contact among street users 94

9 Suburban street, picture by a ten-year old Toronto girl 104

10 Boy with hockey stick, Toronto suburbs 107

11 Casual surveillance of children 111

12 The Scarlett O'Hara staircase 114

13 Picture by a child of diverse downtown neighbourhood in which she lives 134

14 We get what we deserve 138

15 Choice land: market mentality and the suburban home 146

16 Front view of suburban house, Toronto area 165

17 Front view of downtown house, Toronto 166

18 Scrap metal mural 190

19 Street performer, Queen Street, Toronto 201

20 It's hard to be aware of our daily habits 203

21 Man with his rose garden, Kensington Market, Toronto 206

22 Carved wooden porch, downtown Toronto 206

23 Front yard and its creators, downtown Toronto 207

Preface

This book had as its original inspiration Jane Jacobs' book *The Death and Life of Great American Cities*. Stimulated by her thesis that physical diversity in the city has an important impact on both social and economic activity, I set out to test her ideas systematically in Toronto. More than simply providing support for Jacobs's ideas, my study started me thinking about how the unhealthy lack of physical diversity in our cities perversely reflects some of our deepest values and fondest dreams. In other words, it appeared that we had to recognize not only that the city affects us in ways we do not comprehend; it is also a tangible expression of some of our most basic beliefs.

I have a new sense of urgency about the subject matter now, since it is becoming apparent that these basic beliefs are driving us towards an ecological catastrophe. Our cities are merely the most concrete example of a form of development which is about to wreck the planet. As this book tries to make clear, our own settlement patterns and ways of life are every bit as threatening to our future as the destruction of the Amazon rain forest. The two phenomena are related, and both are symptoms of a rampant materialism which has overwhelmed other dimensions of the human spirit.

And yet the book has a hopeful message. Thousands of men and women in North American cities have seen their way clear of this depressing impasse and started organizing their lives, in cooperation with their neighbours, in ways that transcend the old ways of thinking. I hope the examples given in the last chapter are as inspiring to the reader as they were to me.

Literally hundreds of people have assisted me in this enterprise. Some 322 Torontonians in nineteen different neighbourhoods were generous with their time in answering my questionnaire. Another several hundred businessmen, receptionists, secretaries, storekeepers and workers shared information with me about their businesses.

I am grateful to Inspector Richard Gibson of the Metropolitan Toronto Police Force for allowing me access to patrol-area crime statistics and for arranging interviews with the following officers: Charles Lawrence of 52 Division; Ernie Baker, Jim Bamford, Doug Day, and Gerrard Jones of 51 Division; Bruce Richardson and Henry Polowski of 14 Division; Hugh McConnell of 13 Division; Bill Yates and Bill Aldwych of 31 Division; and Kevin Boyd, Bob Wilson, and Dave Dix of 33 Division. It was a long process, and through it all I felt most appreciative of Inspector Gibson's patience, warmth, and good humour. The patrol officers were frank and easy to talk with. I thank them all.

Municipal officials who gave of their time to discuss the intricacies of local government road finances with me included Ed Gilmour in San Jose; Chip Wood in San Diego; Paul Sachs of the San Francisco Bay area; M. Faysal Thaneen in Baltimore; T.J. Corrigan in London, Ontario; Colin Kerr and Doug Farquhar in Hamilton; Terry McDonough in Toronto; and Brian Lokkesmoe in Minneapolis. I also thank Charles Fitzsimmons and Dave Roberts of the Canadian Urban Transit Association for their help in providing me with data as well as interpreting them for me.

Glendon College Faculty Council's Research Grant Committee provided me with funds for updating much of the data in chapter 2, for which support I am most thankful.

Thanks to Grant McLean for helping me collect data on municipal spending, performing calculations on them, and presenting them in eminently readable form.

I am especially appreciative of the faith shown by Peter Blaney of McGill-Queen's in what I now see as an embarrassingly preliminary draft of the manuscript.

Two anonymous reviewers made numerous helpful suggestions for improving the manuscript.

Claire Gigantes was a knowledgeable and perceptive editor, responsible for numerous improvements to the final product, including both style and substance. Joan McGilvray shepherded me gently through the publication process with forbearance and understanding about missed deadlines. Jan Goodman was invaluable in the final edit.

To Jane Jacobs I owe special gratitude. First, of course, her book lies at the very heart of this project. Second, she has been unfailingly generous with both keen criticism and warm enthusiasm for my endeavours. It has been a privilege to work with such a wise and wonderful woman.

Drafts of the book were read in part and commented on by many loyal friends: Alan Powell, Jon Caulfield, Michael Goldrick, Max Vos,

Jack Klein, and John Sewell. Shoukry Roweis also helped me out when I knew nowhere else to turn for advice. I am grateful to them all.

Florence Knight was a miracle typist at the start of this project: her work was consistently flawless. When she could do no more, Pearl Jaffe and Eric Hellman took over and finished it off professionally, in addition to giving me useful suggestions on style and content.

Rebecca, my daughter, helped me copy the children's drawings into a form which could be easily reproduced – my thanks to her as well.

Finally, my debt to my wife Shelly is limitless. Aside from encouragement, she gave me commentary and criticisms which were brilliant and always suggestive of new perspectives or approaches I never would have dreamed of. In many ways, this book is as much hers as it is mine.

Building Cities That Work

CHAPTER ONE

Postwar City Building from Above and Below

In an astonishing transformation of the landscape, North Americans have built, or rebuilt, an entirely new urban environment since World War II. The title of a 1963 book on urban and regional planning, *Man-Made America*, reflected the spirit of the times. One careful study in Canada found that one-third of the country's dwelling units were less than ten years old in 1975. In 1985 in the US, fifty-three percent of housing had been built since 1960.

This chapter has two parts. The first half outlines in broad terms the nature of the postwar revolution in urban development in North America. The second half is a street-level view of seven neighbourhoods in the city of Toronto. Although Toronto is not a typical North American city on the whole, experiencing bits of it at the street level gives one a good idea of neighbourhood types which can be found all over the continent. The sketches are offered as verbal illustrations of some of the abstractions in the first half of chapter 1 and in subsequent chapters.

THE NEW URBAN ENVIRONMENT

The postwar urban transformation was by no means random, although popular treatments of urban woes used such terms as chaotic, sprawling, messy, and shapeless. The physical characteristics of North American cities are easily identified: they are large in scale, deconcentrated, and homogeneous.

Large-scale projects have become the norm in North American urban development. For instance, instead of one office building, developers build downtown complexes of several towers. While Rockefeller Center, built in New York City in the 1930s, was probably the prototype, by the 1960s dozens of such projects were under con-

struction or on the drawing board in both the United States and
Canada. William Zeckendorf, one of the most successful developers
in North America, proposed Place Ville Marie to the city of Montreal
in 1958, an $835 million (1987 dollars) combination of office build-
ings, shops, and indoor concourses in the centre of town. Once built,
it was an instant success, and Montreal and other North American
cities went on to build many other projects of a similar design. These
developments generally took up two or more blocks of prime downtown land, combined land uses (usually retail and office space, but
sometimes residences as well), and involved the active cooperation of
large developers, large banks, and eager city politicians. In the
United States, large-scale downtown projects such as the Renaissance
Center in Detroit were common, with a seventy-storey hotel and four
thirty-nine-storey office buildings. Philadelphia built Market Street
East: three to four storeys of shops extending three full city blocks.

Office buildings are only one example of the large scale of new
urban development. Residential projects in the center of cities are
now made up of clusters of high-rises – six, eight, fifteen or more
buildings, as many as thirty stories high, are not uncommon. Robert
Moses, who represented the grotesque extreme of North America's
fascination with huge urban developments, played a key role in con-
ceiving and organizing Co-Op City in the Bronx, the largest apartment complex in the United States, with 15,382 units. In his
dedication speech for that project, he proposed a 50,000-unit community called Atlantic Village. (Using village as a label in this context
is not uncommon and shows how we play games with reality in urban
development, as elsewhere.) Another example may be found in
Toronto, where in the middle 1960s a group of developers built St
Jamestown, a $140 million (1987 dollars) high-rise residential com-
plex for 15,000 people. No building had fewer than sixteen storeys
and some had thirty-three. These are just illustrations, but they give
an idea of the scale of individual projects which have been developed.
By contrast, housing projects in larger French cities may not, by law,
have any more than two thousand units.

Large-scale housing has also been packaged in the form of so-called
integrated communities, some with more than 20,000 residents, built
on the fringes of metropolitan areas by large developers. Perhaps the
most famous of these communities were the Levittowns in New Jersey
and Bucks County, Pennsylvania, and on Long Island, New York.
Built in the late 1940s and the 1950s by Abraham Levitt and his sons,
these developments usually had 25,000 residents or more. All of the
homes were single-family detached houses, with only a modest range

in price. A shopping centre would be built at the edge of the community, but in general there were few other community services.

In Canada, E.P. Taylor developed a suburb called Don Mills in the early 1950s, and it had similar characteristics to the Levittowns'. It was planned well in advance to include job opportunities for residents as well as shopping and recreational facilities; it provided housing for over 25,000 people in a mixture of single-family homes, duplexes, and apartments. To the immediate south of the housing area was a 300-acre industrial site, employing 4,500, although fewer than five percent of these workers ended up living in Don Mills. Larger and larger communities of this sort were planned and built in the 1960s; Meadowvale, in Mississauga, Ontario, for instance, was planned to house 65,000.

While monopoly of suburban house building was more pronounced in Canada than in the United States, big builders in the latter were constructing Levittown-type communities from the 1950s onward. In this regard, says Barry Checkoway in his history of postwar building,

Levitt was the largest but not the only builder of his kind. Large builders were increasing in number and production outside every major city. Among them was [sic] John Mowbray outside Baltimore, Waverly Taylor outside Washington D.C., Don Scholz outside Toledo, Maurice Fishman outside Cleveland, Irvin Blietz outside Chicago, J.D. Nichols outside Kansas City, Del Webb outside Phoenix, Carl Gellert and Ellie Stoneson outside San Francisco, and Dave Bohannon, Fritz Burns, and James Price outside several cities. They symbolized a revolution in housebuilding and were instrumental in postwar suburbanization. [It was] said of them: "These are the new giants in an industry once populated by pygmies. Here, at the very peak of their housebuilding pyramid, are the leaders of construction who are not content merely to build houses. They construct communities."

In addition to office-building complexes, apartment clusters, and suburban communities, the new urban development has been characterized by vast new industrial sites. As early as the 1890s Chicago realtors were packaging industrial districts with railroad sidings, far from the centre of town. Some manufacturing firms found that the best way to achieve economies of scale* was to build huge plants on

---

* Politics as well as economics have played a role in the manufacturers' move to the suburbs: they have seen it as a way to escape the noxious influences of urban leftwing ideas on workers. See chapter 7.

cheaper land at the edge of the city. The prototype was Henry Ford's River Rouge plant outside Detroit, which employed tens of thousands of auto workers over hundreds of acres. But there were many others. Bethlehem Steel's Sparrows Point plant, twelve miles southeast of Baltimore, employed as many as 28,000 workers and produced six or seven percent of all the steel in the United States in the late 1950s. The steel plant, including housing for over 6,000 workers, also took up hundreds of acres of land.

This brings us to the second characteristic of urban development in postwar North America. These large-scale features of the urban environment have not (with the exception, perhaps, of office towers) been placed close together, but have sprawled out over more and more square miles of land. Cities have become decentralized and deconcentrated. Even high-rise apartment towers are surrounded by hundreds of square feet of landscaping, to increase the amount of "open space" in high-density developments.

Workplaces are taking up more urban acreage. E.P. Taylor's Don Mills has industrial sites where the floor space index is only about .2. This means that for every square foot of building there are four square feet of parking lots, roads, grass, and trees. One reason for this demand for less dense industrial space was the development of the continuous-material-flow system of production, whereby conveyor belts hundreds of yards long take mushrooms or refrigerators through a complete processing on a single level; the finished product emerges, all packaged, ready to be loaded on a truck. This process, whether it involves cars or apricots, takes a great deal of space, and the effects on land requirements have been dramatic: "Surveys indicate that the amount of plot space per worker in the postwar suburban plants of the [New York] region is over four times as great as in suburban plants built before 1922. In the new plants more than an acre of land is used for every ten workers." The geographer A.J. Scott cautions against assuming spread-out plants as a consequence of deconcentration; their technology, he suggests, could have come along because firms had already decided for other reasons to move out where land was cheaper. At this point, however, the goal is simply to note that manufacturing is using more space per worker.

Modern capital has also discovered the value of "disintegrating" large firms, which means subcontracting many manufacturing and service functions to small companies which are less likely to be unionized and more likely to be operationally flexible. The new locations for groups of large and small companies which work together this way are now more likely to be sprawling out through, say, Orange County south of Los Angeles, than to be shoehorned into an intense

Table 1
Office space taken up per office worker, downtown
Toronto

Year	m^2 per worker
1960	19.2
1970	21.5
1975	22.5
1980	25.0
1985	26.0
1988	25.2

Source: City of Toronto Planning Department, Cityplan '91,
Report #5 Central Area Trends Report, Feb. 1990; Table 3, 22.

downtown industrial district, where workers are less malleable and
have more employment options nearby.

Even in office buildings, more space is being used per white-collar
worker. For instance, the average space per office worker in New York
City buildings increased by about twenty percent between 1947 and
1958. Not only is the average Toronto office worker presently being
allotted more space in the core of the city (see Table 1) but his or
her counterpart in the next ring of office buildings (the "Outer
Core") has forty percent more space still. Recent office-space growth
in Vancouver was characterized in a planning report as providing
more spacious offices rather than evidence of more jobs. Or, sometimes the additional space is related to the additional use of office
machines.

None of this deconcentration of office and factory space
approaches the use of land for the new low-density residential development, however.

It was and is the North American ideal to escape the noisy, crowded
city and find space – a front lawn and backyard, places for the children to play and for parents to garden. This ideal came within reach
of vast numbers of Americans and Canadians in the 1950s and
1960s; they took advantage of the opportunity, so that by 1970 more
people lived in the suburbs than in either the central cities or the
countryside. The densities demanded by these suburbanites were
extremely low. Writing in the late 1950s, Hoover and Vernon noted
that, with respect to New York City, "Whereas a homesite of about
one sixth of an acre was representative of 'middle income' suburban
developments in the region a generation ago, buyers in the corre-
sponding category today are generally demanding one third of an
acre." The result writ large was that dwelling units per acre of developed land went from 25.7 to 3.2 as one travelled from the zone closest

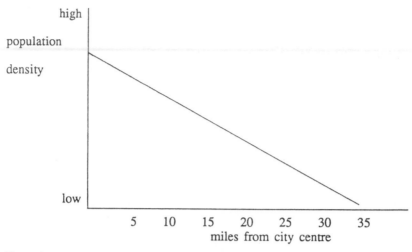

Figure 1
The density gradient

to Manhattan to the farthest zone. Kenneth Jackson, author of a history of American suburbs, reports: "Between 1950 and 1970, for example, the urbanized area of Washington grew from 181 to 523 square miles. Such sprawl results from the privatization of American life and the tendency to live in fully detached homes. Of the 86.4 million dwelling units in the United States in 1980, about two-thirds, or 57.3 million, consisted of a single family living in a single dwelling surrounded by an ornamental yard."

Canadian suburbanization was similar. One researcher wrote that "by 1955, Canada's average suburban development was putting not more than fifteen people to the acre, and the big metropolitan centers of Montreal and Toronto with 1,000,000 people or more each, occupied a land area that in Tokyo or London would hold ten times that number." In Montreal, each additional thousand people were taking up fifty acres in 1952; by 1964, the same population increment was claiming ninety-six acres for its activities. Canadian cities are not as deconcentrated as American cities, but the former are far less concentrated than cities in Europe.

If one were to imagine population density on a graph so that the higher the line, the greater the density, then one could picture the relationship between population density and distance from the city centre as in Figure 1 – different cities will have lines with different slopes, of course. We know that American cities have been more spread out than Canadian cities, and bigger cities more spread out

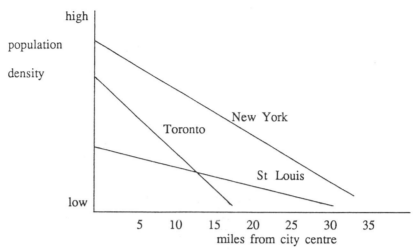

Figure 2
Examples of density gradients in three North American cities.
Data are not precise. Compiled from Yeates and Garner, *The North American City*,
Third Edition (New York: Harper and Row 1980), 226, 234.

than smaller ones. This might be represented by comparing three
typical cities as in Figure 2. The steeper the slope of the line (say,
Toronto's), the more concentrated a city is, and therefore the larger
the *density gradient*, as it is called. The dramatic decrease in concentration in us and Canadian cities in the postwar period, represented
by decreases in density gradients, is shown in Table 2. In the late
1970s, the trend began to reverse somewhat as land in the suburbs
became extremely expensive, mostly because of profit taking by
developers. Kenneth Jackson notes that by 1980 the population of
the city of Los Angeles, the quintessential example of urban sprawl,
had increased by forty percent since 1950.

But the vast amount of suburban development was a response to
the low-density aspirations of Americans and Canadians; and, once
built, these density patterns have, say Hoover and Vernon, been
"stubbornly resistant to change."

A final example of deconcentration of the city is tied up with
highways, streets, and parking lots. Because the density of development in many cities is too sparse to permit the use of public transit,
the private auto has become indispensable to most suburbanites and
even to many residents of the central city. The financial implications
of this will be considered in chapter 2; the physical significance of
making room for the car is startling, however. The Economic Council
of Canada has put it this way: "It has been estimated that for Amer-

Table 2
Density gradients, Canadian and US metropolitan areas, 1950–51 to 1975–76

Year	Canada	USA
1950/51	0.93	0.76
1960/61	0.67	0.60
1970/71	0.45	0.50
1975/76	0.42	0.45

Source: Barry Edmonston, Michael A. Goldberg, and John Mercer, "Urban Form in Canada and the United States: An Examination of Urban Density Gradients," *Urban Studies* 22 (1985): 209-17.

ican cities the average journey to work by private car travelling about 20 miles an hour requires roughly six to forty-five times as much road space per person as by transit bus, the range depending upon assumptions concerning the average number of passengers per vehicle." An urban expressway takes up ten acres a mile and thirty acres an interchange, and each car needs 280 square feet of parking space, which works out to 173 cars per acre. Spread-out housing makes cars more necessary, of course, but the new retail patterns of development bring the amount of space devoted to cars to comic proportions: 130,000 square feet, or about two acres, of shopping surrounded by forty acres of parking. In the downtown, cities are finding themselves in the dilemma posed by planning consultant Victor Gruen, that the more space provided for cars – both moving and parked – the less concentrated the downtown, and the greater the need for *more* cars. Gruen's own calculations were that easing congestion in downtown Fort Worth would require an increase in roads alone from five million square feet to sixteen million square feet. New cities, such as Los Angeles, devote up to two-thirds of their downtown land to parking and roadways.

The car contributes to the deconcentration of the city as well, then, not only by making deconcentration possible but by the car's own need for space.

Homogeneity is the third distinctive feature of the new urban environment. In many ways, of course, homogeneity is a subjective experience, particularly when it is applied to architecture: what is boring and repetitive to one eye can delight another with hundreds of variations. It is undeniable, however, that sameness has been produced by historical events. Building booms, responding to population pressure or great fires, have been responsible for block after block of the same kind of architecture. Such building booms have not been restricted to the postwar era. In the last two decades of the nineteenth century and the first decade of the twentieth, North American cities experienced phenomenal growth. Some examples are given in Table

3. Canadian urbanization took place later in the era, but the patterns are the same. Whole new sections of cities were built in the space of two or three years during this growth, with the help of new transportation technologies. Harlem and the South End of Boston had sections which were all built simultaneously, towards the end of the last century, as the streetcar enabled people to commute farther to work. Table 3 also gives some concrete examples of the shape of postwar urban growth: central cities declined, but metropolitan areas doubled in many cases.

The point is that even if we wanted to build different-looking buildings during the same era, it would be very difficult. This is a simple outcome of the state of architectural fashions and building technology at a particular time. The historical similarity need not be overwhelming, unless one is constantly enveloped by buildings which are all from the same period. This experience is becoming more common, however, both because of the unprecedented numbers of new structures built after World War II, and because of their concentration into bigger and bigger clumps.

The new North American city is homogeneous not only with respect to architecture but also with respect to land use. This dimension of homogeneity is ultimately tied to scale and concentration, the two other features of postwar North American cities. For instance, as the scale of the projects increases, and as they become more spread out, one must walk or drive some distance to experience a different kind of economic activity. The city's land uses have been allocated to large – sometimes huge – functionally homogeneous areas like Co-Op City, Levittown, Place Ville Marie (which, admittedly, mixes shops with offices and hotel space), and industrial parks. Even in "integrated communities" where industry and shopping are included in the same development, the scale of integration is so immensely coarse that the effect is one of land-use segregation. Here, one finds mostly offices with no industrial or residential use and just a smattering of retail stores; there, a shopping centre with nothing but retailing; and over here, acres and acres of suburban high-rise or single-family housing.*

* Most of this functional homogeneity is held together by zoning, which was introduced early in this century to prohibit certain kinds of land uses in some areas. The goal was to protect certain residential areas from invasions by noxious industries, to say nothing of noxious residents. By allowing only dwellings, or certain kinds of dwellings, such as detached single-family homes, a zoning by-law can have a powerful effect on the diversity of a neighbourhood, socially as well as physically. By the same token, some zoning ordinances forbid the building of homes in areas of primarily industrial use, thus preserving homogeneity of another kind. More on zoning in chapters 5 and 6.

Table 3
Population of selected North American cities, 1870-1980[a] (in thousands)

	1870	1880	1890	1900	1910	1920	1930 1941[b]	1950	1960	1970	1980
New York	1478	1912	2507	3437	4767	5489	6930	7892	7782	7895	7035
Chicago	299	503	1100	1699	2185	2672	3376	3621	3550 (6221)	3367 (6093)	2970 (6060)
Philadelphia	674	847	1047	1294	1549	1915	2072	2003	1949 (4432)	1680 (4824)	(4717)
Detroit					466	760	1569	1850	1670 (3762)	1514 (4554)	1204 (4488)
Montreal		141		268 (415)	(616)	619 (796)	903 (1216)	1191 (1539)	(2216)	980 (2743)	(2828)
Toronto		86		208 (303)	(478)	522 (686)	667 (1002)	(1262)	672 (1919)	(2628)	599 (2999)
Winnipeg		8		42 (48)	(157)	179 (229)	222 (302)	(357)	265 (477)	(540)	564[c] (585)
Edmonton				3 (15)	(48)	59 (87)	94 (136)	(193)	281 (360)	(496)	532 (657)
Vancouver				26 (43)	(115)	117 (224)	275 (394)	(588)	385 (827)	(1082)	440 (1268)

Sources: US Census, various years; and Statistics Canada, Census of Canada; also N. H. Lithwick, Urban Canada: Problems and Prospects (Ottawa: Central Mortgage and Housing Corporation 1970), 73. The figures in parentheses are the population of metropolitan areas – Standard Metropolitan Statistical Areas (US) or Consolidated Metropolitan Areas (Canada).

[a] Canadian census figures are collected in 1901, 1911, etc., and US figures in 1900, 1910, etc.

[b] US figures for 1930; Canadian figures for 1941

[c] Winnipeg consolidated its metropolitan area into a single city in 1972.

The experience of having to walk or drive further to get a change of scene highlights the importance of space to the idea of homogeneity, or to its opposite, diversity. Any area can be called homogeneous if its boundaries are small enough, or diverse if its boundaries are big enough. My point is simply that if one took the same arbitrary unit of area (an acre, a square mile) and measured the degree of land-use mix within that area over time in urban North America, one would find greater homogeneity now than previously.

Thus, the essence of this physical transformation of the North American city is made clearer if we leave behind terms like suburbanization or urban sprawl. Suburbs have been around for thousands of years, and numerous studies have already exposed the emptiness of stereotyping them as middle class, residential, or homogeneous. Urban sprawl is simply a derogatory name for deconcentration and in any case refers to only one dimension of what has been happening to our cities.

What *has* been happening is an increase in the scale of developments, a decrease in concentration of land use, and homogenization. The significance of scale lies not just in big buildings but in the production of large areas of the city with the same land use. In addition, so much has been built in the last three decades that the result has been mile after mile of new development.

In Jane Jacobs' "attack on city planning," *The Death and Life of Great American Cities*, her central thesis is that it is just these factors which, along with block length, determine how much physical diversity, and therefore vitality, a city has. She argues that a city's vitality is nurtured by (1) a mixture of land uses, (2) a concentration of uses (not just residential but commercial, recreational, and industrial uses as well), (3) a mixture of old and new buildings, and (4) short blocks. The reason for short blocks, says Jacobs, is to maximize the number of path crossings. At such crossings, there is more activity, more interaction, commercial as well social – street corners are always considered more desirable for business. Long blocks, on the other hand, reduce an area's vitality, Jacobs argues, by minimizing the number of path crossings and isolating one street from the next. Jacobs, it can be guessed, is not enamoured of recent trends in city buildings.

Neither am I. Today's urban development is unbelievably expensive and it is destroying us along with our planet.

In fact, Jacobs has inspired me and many others to delve more deeply into the truly damaging effects of North America's urban transformation and to explore ways of turning things around before it is too late.

My first project was to test systematically Jacobs' thesis that physical diversity is connected to urban vitality. This project involved collecting data on nineteen different Toronto areas and, with my wife Shelly, interviewing their residents and business people. The general findings of this study are presented throughout the book in various chapters. What follows are personal and subjective descriptions of seven of the areas. Two of them could be characterized as pure examples of postwar citybuilding; the others have varying amounts of old and new development in them. The descriptions give the reader a human-scale perspective on mixture of land use, scale and age of buildings, and block length; they also illustrate that cities are in a real sense defined by the daily life of people in neighbourhoods.

THE AREAS OF THE TORONTO STUDY: PLEASE NO DOGS

"No canvassing permitted: please no dogs," it said on the front window pane of the apartment-house lobby. Although Shelly and I had ignored that sign many times before, it always added to the psychological hurdle of tackling another building. This one was rather small, not busy enough; in the large high-rises at 7:00 P.M. it is easy to slip into the stream of people going in and out. And from experience we knew that the superintendent would be indignantly protective of the tenants' privacy. As we stood hesitantly, a nine- or ten-year-old boy walked up to us.

"You want to get in? I have a key. Come on," he urged, and opened the front door for us. We wondered if he was going to ask us whom we wanted to see. He didn't. We headed upstairs as he ran out to play.

We started interviewing on the sixth floor and worked our way down. On the third floor, an Italian lady opened the door in response to our knock, and right behind her was the same little boy. She was very negative.

"No. No time. No speak English." The boy said something to her. She ignored him. "No. Not today." She shut the door. We worried that she was going to call the super. The next door on this hall was opened a crack by an old lady with a quavering voice, the door-chain held taut at eye-level. But within moments she had opened her door all the way and was talking animatedly to us. As the interview came to a close, the door down the hall opened, and the Italian lady who had just refused us came marching over with a steaming plate of food and handed it to the old woman we'd been questioning. "Good appetite!" she said with a smile at our respondent.

How does one generalize from this kind of experience? It illustrates how many conflicting stimuli each neighbourhood provided.

Reading over the descriptions gives the impression of incredible diversity, even in those areas which were physically quite monotonous. This impression is hard to escape, for we spent so much time in each area and had so many interesting experiences; naturally, it is those experiences which are stressed in the descriptions. The reader would get a sense of balance by referring to the Appendix, which summarizes the elements of physical diversity in each of the nineteen areas.

A good deal of time was spent walking, interviewing at different times of day, having coffee in restaurants while we discussed the area with proprietors or observed their clienteles. Out of these experiences the following impressions emerged. While slanderous statements are avoided, some areas were obviously more attractive to me than others, and I apologize in advance to residents (especially those we interviewed) who feel that my description of their area is inaccurate or unflattering. Much has changed, in any case, since the interviews were conducted in the late 1970s. It should be stressed again that these descriptions are simply to give the reader a feel for the subject matter of the Toronto study; they are not the actual data from which any statistics were computed. Not all the areas are included in these descriptions. See the Appendix for a complete list of areas.

AREA 1   Niagara Street and Walnut Avenue from King Street to Richmond Street (6.3 acres)

"The Portuguese are the best you can find" (Ukrainian homeowner).
"Too many bums around here" (long-time resident).
"Nobody bothers me – if it doesn't touch me I don't care" (Portuguese homeowner on King Street).
"The Portuguese move in and out but the Canadians stay"
   (eighteen-year-old high-school student).
"I don't feel safe anywhere. Once, I used to go out, two, three in
   the morning; now I'm alone I'm more scared" (widow, homeowner in area for thirty-seven years).
"We're used to industry, but there are some pretty stinky sites"
   (member of Niagara Neighbourhood Improvement Group).

This area had one of the highest scores on the diversity scale. It was so far downtown that a few years ago it was designated as industrial land and no new residential buildings were allowed on it. That designation has since changed, and in the last few years the city has organized a program whereby residents have been helping each other fix up their houses: local residents donate their labour, while the city aids in the purchase of building materials. New housing has also been built just to the north, between Richmond and Queen Streets.

Niagara Street was chosen especially for its mixed land uses. Numbers of old houses were interspersed with warehouses and businesses. There were a couple of printing firms, a janitorial service (since moved), and a trophy manufacturer. There was also a cotton-felt manufacturing plant, owned and run by a sixty-three-year-old lady who loved the neighbourhood. She'd had a business here most of her life, and she told us, "It's never been better and cleaner, mainly because of the Portuguese and Italians." This was in sharp contrast to Bathurst and Queen, only a few streets away, which according to everyone, including the police, was an extremely rough neighbourhood. The lady's assessment also differed from that of a study completed a few years before (when, admittedly, the area might well have been different), which treated the general region as an out-and-out slum.

The people living in the area were mainly Italian, Portuguese, and Ukrainian. Many of them were long-time residents – i.e., they had been there over twenty years. In fact, while there seemed to be a number of people who were essentially short-term, transient tenants, there were just as many who had no intention of moving. Mostly working class, they were very friendly and willing to talk about their part of the city. Relative to the size of the area, the population was quite small.

Most of the houses were single-family units. Many of them had been fixed up and were in good shape at the time of the interviews. Although it was by no means a high-class neighbourhood, it was obvious that people took pride in the condition of their homes. Most of the businesses were housed in newer or larger buildings.

On one side of the area, across Walnut Avenue, was Stanley Park, the scene of a number of disturbances in the past, but both the police and the residents told us that things had quieted down considerably. On the other side of Niagara Street were the Niagara Street Public School and the Buntin Reid Paper Company, whose large trucks were constantly backing in and out. Since these trucks went, as a rule, directly onto King Street, they didn't seem to bother the residents.

AREA 2   Wellesley and Maitland Streets from Church Street to
Jarvis Street; Alexander Street from Church to Mutual Street
(11.3 acres)

"I've heard from people who've lived in Toronto all their lives that
    this is a really nasty neighbourhood" (taxi driver in low-rise
    apartment).
"All I can say is I'd rather lose my wallet here than in Rosedale"*
    (construction worker, homeowner for twenty years on Alexander
    Street).
"When you're in the Lodge [knitting for crippled children] you
    don't have time" (widowed homeowner on Wood Street, after
    being asked whether she had any personal friends in the area).
"I do not like high-rise life, but I had to live some place" (woman
    in high-rise).

This area had the highest score on the diversity scale. A number
of new high-rises combined with remodelled and well-kept-up old
houses have given this part of the city a high population density.
There were also two or three very run-down and uninviting low-rise
apartment houses whose tenants and superintendents were equally
inhospitable. These buildings seemed to house the most transient
residents of the area.
   Only one block away from the city's main north-south street and in
the heart of busy midtown Toronto, Church and Wellesley were lined
with a large office complex (the Canadian Red Cross) and interesting
specialty shops and restaurants. The National Ballet School and its
dormitories were on Maitland Street; across Church were some Canadian Broadcasting Corporation offices; and across Jarvis Street (a
major north-south artery) was Jarvis Collegiate Institute, a high
school with one of the most heterogeneous student bodies in the city,
its pupils coming from upper-class Rosedale as well as from the working-class east end.
   The residents of this area were as diverse as its other users. Among
those interviewed were a taxicab driver who had lived there for one
week, a single businessman who had lived in the same high-rise for
three years without speaking to anyone in the building, and a construction worker who had owned his own home since World War II.
The area was known as a meeting place for Toronto's gay community.
The ethnic mix included small proportions of Koreans, Chinese, and

---

* A nearby, high-income residential enclave (Area 16).

Pakistanis, but not many Europeans. Our reception as interviewers here was somewhat more guarded than average, although that might have been because it was the first area done, and our own nervousness might have rubbed off.

Along Church Street there were two interesting stores – a bakery and a butcher's. They both catered to Dutch people from all over Toronto. Although the bakery had originally been run by a Dutchman, it was now run by a friendly German couple who were pleased to continue in the tradition started by their predecessor. The shop was open from lunch until 7:00 P.M., serving snacks and sandwiches at a number of minuscule tables in the back. The place was wildly successful. Further down Church Street we found a fancy Japanese restaurant, an occult bookstore, one or two other restaurants, and a print shop. There were many, many restaurants to serve the large numbers of office workers in the neighbourhood.

The blocks in the area were quite short, although Wellesley Street from Church to Jarvis goes six hundred and fifty feet without a cross street. The traffic on Wellesley, Church, and particularly Jarvis was quite heavy. Jarvis was also wide, so it was a real barrier to pedestrians. However, the pedestrian traffic on Church and Wellesley was considerable. Despite the fact that it was a very busy area with a number of large-scale buildings, the small shops on Church Street and the houses on Maitland and Wood made one feel quite comfortable.

Of all the areas, this one had changed the most by 1990. The large Red Cross office building had been replaced by a larger office building, and most of the stores referred to were gone.

AREA 3   Margueretta Street between Bloor and College Streets (22.3 acres)

"The traffic *flies* down here all during the night" (homeowner, widow).

"When there's a long street, they're not as sociable" (homeowner, forty-two years on the street).

"People are nice on this street" (factory worker, grandfather).

"My friends all went to the suburbs years ago" (all Anglo-Saxons on the street).

"My friends all went to the suburbs years ago" (all Italians on the street).

"I've lived in this area since 1922. I want to get the hell out. The kids are too saucy" (engineer, owner of two homes on the street).

"This is home. I was born and raised here. But I wish there were
more friendly people. If you said hello they think you are crazy"
(father of seven).

"Unfortunately, thirty years. I'd move, except for my mother. The
kids are too noisy. The Europeans never spend any money, and
buy up all the houses" (Anglo-Saxon woman, about 50 years old,
having been asked how long she'd lived there).

Margueretta Street was chosen because it must be one of the long-
est unbroken blocks in Toronto – about half a mile between Bloor
and College. There were quite a few trees and well-kept lawns. At the
time of our interviews the road was being repaved and children were
playing delightedly over the idle construction vehicles. Almost without exception, the dwelling units were single-family detached dwellings and duplexes. The only businesses nearby were on Bloor Street,
a major shopping street to the north, a variety store half-way down
the block, and a few stores on College Street, another major east-west
route. Most of the houses and stores were built around the same time,
during the first twenty years of this century.

The ethnic mix was surprisingly diverse. We had expected mostly
Italians and Portuguese, but respondents to the questionnaire
included a number of Anglo-Saxons, two old Macedonian sisters, and
Ukrainians. It must be stressed, though, that despite its ethnic diversity the area was physically monotonous.

The attitude of the Anglo-Saxons, most of whom had lived there
for many years, was one of hostility towards the newcomers; the old-
timers who stayed behind (most of their friends having moved away)
were obliged to do so for one reason or another and clearly resented
it. The refusal rate on this street, either because of the language
barrier or because of the xenophobia of the Anglo-Saxons, was higher
than in most areas. We had started an interview with one elderly lady
when her son came out on the porch. He was quietly belligerent and
his manner frightened us thoroughly. "What do you want? Who are
you? What are you selling?" Without giving me time to answer, he
turned to his mother, saying, "I want you to go inside and stop talking
to strangers." And to us: "Get the hell off this porch." Although there
were a number of open and friendly people, the interviewing turned
up at least two extremely hostile characters such as this one. Their
behaviour made it difficult for us to come away with a pleasant feeling
about the neighbourhood.

The shopping area on this particular section of Bloor Street was
less interesting than the stretches further along, either to the west or
to the east. Most of the stores served a very local clientele. This was

even more true of College Street, where at the intersection with Margueretta, some of the houses had not yet been converted into stores.

AREA 6   Veery Place and Ternhill Crescent, Don Mills (11.3 acres)

"They keep moving – we stay put" (real estate broker, asked
  whether he/she had any personal friends in the area).
"Houses four to six in a row, I don't like those" (ten-year-old boy on
  Veery).
"There's no traffic, it's nice and quiet, great for kids" (everyone).
"I would like to get out of the city, if I had my choice, but it's a
  good place to grow up if you have to live in the city" (twenty-one-
  year-old man).
"We're anti-social; people aren't our age on this street, and nobody
  has kaffeeklatsches – I like that" (young father).
"Don Mills is great for kids until they are teenagers" (mother of
  three teenagers).

Don Mills, as noted earlier, was a planned community from the
start. With a small city centre, a post office and a police station near
the centre, churches and schools scattered judiciously around the
development's four quadrants, and a number of clean industries
around the edge, some of the people there felt quite at home never
leaving the place – they worked, shopped, and played right in the
area, seldom going anywhere. Such a description gives the misconception that land uses had been mixed in Don Mills; in fact, with the
exception of the Foxden Road area (Area 19 in this study), residential
areas are carefully segregated from the industrial and retail land
uses. Thus, Area 6 scored low on land-use mix. Its overall score on
diversity was the lowest of any of the areas.

Very few people disliked living in Don Mills. Residents liked the
quiet streets with no traffic, where kids could run loose. And there
seemed to be genuine satisfaction with the friendships formed with
neighbours. While we expected to find mostly Anglo-Saxons in Don
Mills, a surprising number of other nationalities were found – Eastern European, Asiatic, and West Indian.

Veery and Ternhill were two dead-end streets in the southwest
quadrant of Don Mills. Ternhill was lasso-shaped, while Veery was a
simple elbow. The dwellings were detached on Ternhill, semi-
detached on Veery. A good half of the residents had moved in when
the area was first built up in the early fifties, so the neighbourhood
appeared to be quite stable. While everyone felt that Don Mills was
as "safe" as it could be, most mentioned a number of break-ins over

the last few years; however, it appeared that all these activities were carried out by one gang of teenagers from the other side of Don Mills.

One persistent complaint was that the quality of the service and of the merchandise at Don Mills Plaza was consistently bad. However, most residents had accepted this philosophically: if you wanted better, you would have to drive farther afield for it – and many did.

AREA 8   St Jamestown (11.0 acres)

"It's too bloody big" (bus driver on the fourteenth floor).
"You always smell cooking food – everyone's making supper; you
    know, it's too congested, too many people" (fashion-wear designer
    on the fourth floor).
"I like the racial mix" (white security guard, about thirty-five).
"I love the area, but I hate St Jamestown; I'm petrified to get in
    the elevator by myself. The express elevator doesn't stop between
    one and eighteen" (teenage girl, twenty-third floor).
"Too many blacks" (young white single mother).
"In Montreal, if you went for a walk in the park, people would
    nod and say, 'Good Morning' – black, white, yellow. Here, every-
    one keeps to himself" (young black man living in low rise
    apartment).

St Jamestown was a block of a dozen or more huge high-rises, many over thirty stories, in downtown Toronto's east end. Three of the buildings were low-income housing owned by the Ontario Housing Corporation (OHC). There were a couple of large chain stores – a supermarket, a drug store – and several smaller stores on the first floor of one of the buildings. All around St Jamestown, blocks of mostly single-family working class homes could be seen. But working-class families were being rapidly displaced. On the one hand, the middle class was moving into the area, buying up the houses and renovating them. On the other hand, "West of St Jamestown" and "South of St Jamestown," two more high-density developments, had claimed more working-class homes in the indicated directions from the original version.

St Jamestown was the area in the study most disliked by its users, even taking into account that half of those interviewed lived in OHC accommodation, which is normally liked less than other housing.

The area was run down in outward appearance. The non-OHC buildings were poorly kept up; they lacked light bulbs in the halls, displayed enough graffiti to fill a book (a rather interesting book, in fact) and reeked of offensive smells. The OHC buildings were worse. Everyone had stories about break-ins, rapes, thefts, and vandalism. One respondent had had her apartment broken into twice in the previous two months.

Unlike the purely ornamental grounds surrounding many high-rises, the land around the St Jamestown buildings was obviously well used, if only for through pedestrian traffic. This might have been simply a function of high density. The buildings all had entrances on the streets surrounding the superblocks, and in the interior was a mall and an overused playground. The benches in this area were filled with senior citizens from the OHC building, even on an unseasonably cool evening in summer.

Almost everyone complained about the abysmal merchandise at the supermarket in the centre of the project, although most people shopped there because it was "convenient." In fact, convenience to downtown jobs, shopping, or entertainment was candidly given as the main reason for living in St Jamestown and for tolerating its drawbacks. The OHC tenants, of course, had no choice about moving, but evaluations of the area by others seemed little better.

A number of organizations softened the high-rise harshness of the project. Some people mentioned ethnic friendship societies, the YMCA, and choral groups with which they were involved. But the police reported that St Jamestown people used recreational facilities less than people in other areas. On the whole, very few personal relations seemed to flourish in the neighbourhood.

AREA 11   Adelaide and Front Streets from Ontario Street to Sherbourne Street (9.1 acres)

"If you break into one of these old buildings, you've broken into everything in the building" (police officer).
"We've had only one break-in in thirteen years, by an irate employee who had gone over the brink" (owner of a business at Adelaide and Sherbourne).

This area scored low on overall diversity because it had only one use and because the concentration of use was rather low. Nevertheless, it was a fascinating district, close to the part of Toronto which was first settled in the early 1800s. I went in one door on King Street and found myself in a small room with bare walls and no furniture except a couple of tables and chairs; an old man and an old woman were hand-rolling cigars.

One corner of the district rocked to loud music because of a building which rented out practice rooms. The area had costume rentals, a motorcycle shop, a leather tanner, an establishment which recharged fire extinguishers, a distributor of automatic doors, a single old man who worked as a welder in a store front, a maker of rubber stamps, a food-discount warehouse, a popcorn manufacturer, and a number of novelty companies.

These enterprises were housed in old, four- and five-storey warehouses, many of which had unused space. While the police were contemptuous of the security in these old, even partly deserted buildings, very few break-ins were reported by the businessmen themselves. None of them spontaneously praised the area's ambience, but they all seemed satisfied with its low rent, as well as with its location. An employee of one of the firms, specializing in emergency repairs of elevators, pointed out that it would be ridiculous for them to be in the suburbs when they were usually needed very quickly somewhere downtown.

Only one new building had been put up in the last twenty years, and it hardly looked as though it had started a trend. On the other hand, it was doubtful whether the area was losing its economic vitality.

AREA 13   Spadina Avenue, Huron and Ross Streets from Cecil Street to College Street (12.8 acres)

"The people here are friendly, they're good; we leave our doors open" (housewife on Ross Street, mother of eight).
"People move in and out a lot, it's hard to keep a friend" (carpenter, homeowner for twenty-one years).
"It's really convenient to things – if you're broke you can walk. And there's a great ethnic mixture" (tenant, an "overeducated and underskilled" artist).
"We like it because the same kind of people live here" (Chinese cook).
"I feel safe here. There's no rich people. It's not spic and span. I can't handle the suburbs" (tenant, craftsperson in low-rise apartment).

This area was close to Kensington Market and to an area of dry-goods jobbers in downtown Toronto. There were mostly houses, but one or two small apartments as well. College and Spadina were lined with store fronts. On Spadina many of these spaces seemed to lead a rather precarious existence. While some firms had remained for years because they didn't depend on business from passers-by (like the tombstone maker), other enterprises came and went with the seasons; there were always two or three stores for rent. Nevertheless, there also seemed to be someone to step in and take them. College Street featured one or two large enterprises, the most prominent of which were a burlap-bag company and a distributor of dental equipment. A number of restaurants could be found along here as well. The Dora Hood Book Room, which specialized in old Canadiana, was on Ross Street, just off College.

The residential streets of this area were very quiet. The main noise, almost everyone complained, was made by the garbage truck which, at two in the morning, twice a week, ground its garbage behind one of the small apartment houses. The effect was ear-shattering. Both the police and the storeowners along Spadina, however, had a different story. It was quite rough here, and at least one shopkeeper had left because he'd had too many break-ins. The police reported trouble with drunks as well.

A variety of nationalities lived in the area. Among those interviewed were Chinese, Ukrainians, Anglo-Saxons, and one Hungarian. In future the proportion of Chinese would increase, for Dundas and Spadina were rapidly becoming a new focus for Toronto's Chinese community, which was being squeezed out of its old location near Bay and Dundas. A number of students lived in the apartments, since the University of Toronto was only a couple of blocks away. Being close to Kensington was a decided plus for most residents, who shopped there regularly. They could find a far wider range of foods, at lower cost than at any supermarket. This area was the first home of Pat and Stewart's second-hand clothing store, Courage My Love, which I shall return to in chapter 8.

Most of us are living and working in some sort of neighbourhood. Our own daily activities weave imperceptibly into buildings and streets which are the physical fabric of the city and its suburbs. A large proportion of these buildings and streets, as familiar as they are to us, are of recent design and represent the pattern of development described in the first half of this chapter.

This book springs from a desire to counteract the tendency to accept this contemporary urban development as normal. It is most definitely not. It is a perverse and unnatural way to build; but like the (unhealthy) air we breathe, we have become unconscious of it, and of how it is ruining us and our environment.

Part One of this book is an examination of the economic and social costs of the new form of development. It will become obvious that these costs have been incurred in part because of our own narrow views of the nature of economics and the nature of society and politics. Thus, chapter 2 starts from a conventional perspective on economics; but questions are raised about the desirability of pursuing some values energetically and suppressing our desire to seek others, and these questions undermine the usual assumptions of economic analysis. In chapter 5 it is made clear that it is our own personal values that are allowing land-use patterns which discourage political involvement.

Part Two provides some explanations of how we got into building cities this way, and explores the idea that the physical environment we build reflects our own insecurities and strengths in embarrassingly direct ways. The positive message is that our cities can be expressions of the best of what humans have to offer – imaginative modes of cooperation, creative responses to the planet's needs, and a culture and spirituality which embrace all life.

One final note: Michael Goldberg and John Mercer have made the important point that Canadian and American cities differ in physical form, socio-economic characteristics, and politics. This is certainly the case, although cities within both countries differ from each other as well. The reader will intuit, however, that the broad physical features I am dealing with characterize all North American cities. Also, while society, politics, and economics do vary across as well as within national borders, this book will make it clear that the relationships *between* physical features, and socio-economic and political variables, are similar in the two nations.

PART ONE

The Lack of Physical Diversity: Its Consequences

The Economic Costs of the New North American City

As succeeding chapters will show, costs need not be measured in dollars. But North Americans love dollars and they are easy to count, so costs are more likely to be measured in dollars than in anxiety units or pounds of garbage. Although I hope to transcend narrow fascination with economic causes and effects (often called economism), this chapter considers some of the economic costs of the new urban environment in conventional economic language. The point is to show that even through the economic lenses with which we usually view – and justify – our urban environment, it is an awesomely expensive form of development.

These huge expenses can be traced quite clearly to the features of the new North American city outlined in chapter 1: deconcentration of use, unmixed land use, long blocks, and an absence of a mixture of old and new buildings. While the suburbs will be discussed, and while they may contain most or all of these features, it is not the suburbs *per se* which are the focus of this and of subsequent chapters; rather, the focus will be on physical features of which the suburban stereotype happens to be such a good example.

In the first half of this chapter, evidence is drawn from many sources to show how low density and land-use specialization make municipal services more expensive. In the second half, it is shown that our housing and the goods we buy are also costing more because of our form of urban development.

THE COSTS OF MUNICIPAL SERVICES

Building and Servicing the Transportation System

Servicing urban development since World War II has required an elaborate and costly transportation network. Worldwide, municipal governments spend fifteen to twenty-five percent of their budgets on transportation systems. Not only are they funding longer and more complex networks but transportation facilities have become physically larger so that they themselves produce economic dislocations.

Transportation costs for postwar urban development are high not just because that development is deconcentrated but also because its land use is segregated, which ensures that our activities are geographically separated. Separation of economic activities makes possible such putative benefits as exclusively residential neighbourhoods, large-scale shopping centres with great breadth of product choice, and removal of unsightly and noxious industries from the course of our normal daily experience. But it also makes necessary urban transportation.

In fact, urban transportation is something of an anomaly. The essence of a city is that it is a place where people get together for commerce, for culture, for companionship. Why take a trip when we are already there? It is like taking a bicycle from the living room into the kitchen.

In chapter 1, part of the answer was hinted at in terms of capital's restructuring of the workplace. Another part of the answer has social and political dimensions and is dealt with later, in chapter 6. All that is needed here is a rough sketch of how the shape of economic activity, symbiotically with changes in transportation technology, partially explains our deconcentrated and segregated cities.

One basic factor in the rise of urban transportation has been a basic change in the scale of activity clusters, a change pre-dating the adoption of new processes in manufacturing such as those outlined in chapter 1. In the medieval city, work, recreation, and sleep often took place under the same roof. But after the sixteenth century, says the urban historian Lewis Mumford, "large-scale industrial areas" started to be "set apart from the mixed uses of the ordinary medieval city." Functional precincts were set off from each other, for instance, so that some areas would be reserved for religious activities, others for financial or political activities, still others for heavy industry. It needs to be stressed that these uses were separated by virtue of the larger scale of the given commercial enterprises and industries.

This kind of separation necessitated the journey to work, if at first only on foot. Markets became larger, too, no longer a step or two from one's residence. These developments went hand in hand with changes in transport technology. Improvements in carriage wheels as early as the seventeenth century in England created pressures for better streets in the city. Increased mobility then made it possible for merchants to live out of town instead of over their warehouses.

Whichever came first, improvements in transportation or increases in the scale of enterprises, the cities of the eighteenth and nineteenth centuries were explosions in geographical scale: huge public monuments and boulevards, and, gobbling up territory at a growing rate, the suburbs. The inner city residential neighbourhoods were constantly being displaced by commercial and industrial uses as more and more people moved to the periphery. The workplace and the home started to become increasingly separate from each other.

Transportation technology continued to play a crucial role. First there were "streetcar suburbs," then subdivisions accessible only by car, and finally industrial parks and shopping plazas serviced by superhighways, all helping the city burble out over the countryside, with urban functions sprawled over hundreds of square miles. (For a number of reasons, also discussed in chapter 6, this process was more dramatic in North America than in Europe.) In southern Ontario, for example, the rural landscape – rolling fertile farmland which meets the rugged pre-Cambrian Shield to the north – conceals a number of one-, two-, or ten-member firms designing and manufacturing highly sophisticated speaker and sound systems for rock groups and theatres; also scattered around are very large-scale manufacturing plants, miles from the nearest city or town ... where is the boundary between urban and rural functions?

Apart from this dynamic between scale, land-use separation, and transport, another process was at work. Land was being turned into a commodity. It could be bought and sold to the highest bidder. Some land uses could offer much higher prices for land than others. The uses that could offer the most money, therefore, would push out other uses. Banks and offices, for instance, wanted core-area land and could afford to outbid anyone else for it. A slightly less central area might interest retail stores more than banks; the stores, however, could outbid people who wanted to live downtown. Thus, the land market sorted out users according to what they were able and willing to pay and concentrated different uses in different parts of the city. Why we accepted this system is another question, taken up in chapters 6 and 7.

Thus we ended up with modern cities where we sleep *en masse* in huge residential complexes and work *en masse* in huge retail or industrial developments – and spend our lives travelling between them, from living room to kitchen, so to speak.

It is a bit anomalous: the more extended a city, and therefore the city's transportation system, the harder it is to find the city. The more we have urban transportation, in a sense, the less we have a city. We have grown used to what is, in fact, a very strange way of building

Table 4
Annual spending on urban transportation, US and Canada,
selected years*

Expenditure Item	Total (millions)	Spending per capita	Year
US highways			
operating and capital	US $16,903	US $98.09	1985–6
US transit – operating	US $11,751		
– capital	4,200#		
Total	15,951	US $115.92	1986
Canadian highways			
operating and capital	CAN $3,840	CAN $153.74	1984
Canadian transit – operating	CAN $2,279		
– capital	401		
Total	2,680	CAN $192.22	1987

Sources: US Bureau of the Census, *County Government Finances, 1985-86* (Washington, DC: US
Government Printing Office, 1988) and *City Government Finances, 1985-86* (Washington, DC: US
Government Printing Office, 1988); Statistics Canada, *Local Government Finances* (Ottawa:
Ministry of Supply and Services, 1988); US Dept. of Transportation, *National Urban Mass Transit
Statistics: 1986 Section 15 Annual Report* (Washington, DC: US Dept. of Transportation 1988); The
Canadian Urban Transit Association, *Operating Characteristics of Member Systems, 1987-88* (Toronto
1989).
#This is an estimate: only 373 of 432 systems reported, giving a total of $3,833 million in capital
expenditures. Most non-reporting systems were small ones.
*Canadian highway figures are for all local governments; thus, they are divided by the total
population of Canada in 1984. Transit figures are divided by the urban populations served in
Canada – 13,942,202. A similar procedure was adopted for US figures; US transit-service
population was 137,601,000.

things. For the moment, let us consider the economic costs of the
transportation network required by this strange urban form.

To get an idea of what US and Canadian cities were spending on
transportation in the 1980s, I collected some census data from both
countries and from city budgets. It is difficult to imagine the morass
of inconsistent criteria, overlapping boundaries, and frustrating gaps
of information that such a foolish project entails. A few of these
difficulties will be mentioned as the data are presented.

The total amount of money spent by North American local governments (counties and cities) on highways and transit in a single
year is shown in Table 4. The figures are both approximate and
understated, because they do not include US federal government
spending on interstate highways, which slice through all American
cities, and Canadian provincial spending on major provincial highways, which often become urban expressways just like the interstates.

The table shows two kinds of spending for city highways and public transit. The first kind involves expenses for building new roads, sidewalks, tracks, and transit stations, or buying buses, subway cars, and land for transportation corridors. These are called capital expenses and are usually too great for a municipality to afford out of its annual operating budget; instead, the city borrows money to pay for such projects and includes repayment costs, including interest, in its annual budget. The second kind of spending involves operating expenses to maintain the existing system: repairing potholes, paying bus drivers, keeping transit vehicles in good running order, and clearing streets of dirt and snow.

Capital expenditures tend to vary from one budget-year period to the next. A city may undertake a major roads project one year but concentrate on several smaller community centres the following year. Thus, taking an average of capital expenditures for one item over a number of municipalities or over several years provides a more accurate picture than using a single year's figures for a single city. In Table 4 the unevenness is smoothed out because the spending of all cities is considered.

However one slices it, the message is pretty clear: North Americans were spending billions of dollars to build and maintain city streets and public transit systems. It will be shown that this is only part of the actual cost of the transportation system, but it could be considered as the base figure.

As important as it is to see the total amount spent in this way, the main point of this exercise is to show how cities with large-scale, deconcentrated, and homogeneous urban development – or, more generally, cities which had their most dramatic growth after 1950 – are spending more money to build and maintain transportation systems than older, more compact cities with mixed land use. In the US and Canada, the range of densities is not that great when compared to cities worldwide; but urban form does vary, as much within the two countries as between them. Thus, the cities of the North and East, large sections of which were built before the advent of the automobile, still have downtowns which are considerably denser than cities of the West. Midwestern cities tend to lie somewhere in between.

Overlaid on top of this general tendency are a few complicating factors. One is that southern and western cities extend their boundaries as a matter of course to ensure their tax base is not eroded by suburbanite use of central city services. The further east one travels, the more difficult this option has become in North America: it is more likely that a city will be surrounded by previously incorporated towns. In the words of Kenneth Jackson, the historian of the US suburbs,

the first really significant defeat for the consolidation movement came when Brookline spurned Boston in 1874. Starting in 1868, The Hub doubled its area by annexing, in turn, the cities and towns of Roxbury, Dorchester, Charlestown, West Roxbury, and Brighton. But Brookline, the self-styled "richest town in the world," voted against union by a vote of 706 to 299. They were not rejecting growth or development, but were expressing a determination to control the physical and social environment in which they lived.

After Brookline spurned Boston, virtually every other Eastern and Middle Western city was rebuffed by wealthy and independent suburbs – Chicago by Oak Park and Evanston, Rochester by Brighton and Irondequoit, and Oakland by the rest of Alameda County.

The general pattern which has emerged for cities in the North and East in both the US and Canada is to have a smaller, densely used central city surrounded by spread-out postwar suburbs, which were serviced by independent town and county governments; in the South and West of the US and in western Canada, "central cities" are larger and much less dense, surrounded by even vaster and more sparsely populated suburban and exurban counties. In Canada, this pattern is compromised by the more dominant role taken by provinces in municipal reorganization. In addition, the authoritarian and powerful Mayor Jean Drapeau continued the annexation process for Montreal as late as 1983 by adding Pointe-aux-Trembles to the City of Montreal, with the blessing of fifty-nine percent of Pointe-aux-Trembles voters. But in fact the whole meaning of central city is different for, say, Boston (47 square miles) or Toronto (38 square miles) than it is for San Diego (329 square miles) or Houston (573 square miles). Any demographer trying to compare the urban forms of such cities would have to be cautious about using raw census figures when "central cities" have such different personalities.

Yet while the political boundaries have had varied histories resulting in different bases for collecting population data, our poor demographer would be blind not to see that Houston is far more dispersed and automobile-oriented than Boston or Toronto. By the same token, as shown in chapter 1, it is obvious that all North American cities, including Boston and Toronto, have spread out dramatically over their surrounding countryside since World War II. In this spirit, I put the cities in both countries into what seemed to be three or four natural groups, on a rough scale of increasing density. No pretense at scientific precision is being made. In the US, the census had information readily available on the number of jobs in each jurisdiction, so a "use density" of residents-plus-employment was calculated, although it made little difference in the overall grouping of the cities, so crude are the data. Since jobs tend to displace residential use at the city's core, however, use density gives a clearer picture of the degree of concentration than residential density by itself.

The results of my labours can be found in the following few tables. Table 5 ranks US cities according to density of both residents and jobs and then lists how much it costs them to maintain their streets and highways and to run their transit lines. It is obvious that there is tremendous variation, especially in spending on roads, which is caused by factors other than density. Aside from variations in labour costs and labour efficiency, northern cities spend millions of dollars on snow removal as well as on simple repair of the ravages of winter weather on pavements. San Francisco's streets are famous for being hilly, but that also makes them costly to build and maintain. In addition, they are regularly damaged by earthquakes and must be repaired; ten to fifteen percent of them are built with Portland cement as a prevention measure, and this is very expensive. Hills are one thing; but the earthquake factor seemed so unusual that I decided to leave San Francisco out of the group average. While San Jose's city councillors have a tradition of maintaining the best streets in the Bay area, San Diego, which is out of earthquake country and enjoys an extremely moderate climate, can afford to spend far less and still have good roads. The city of Baltimore decided long ago that it wanted to have complete responsibility for all streets and highways within its boundaries. It is unique in that it builds and maintains even federal and state highways within its jurisdiction. For that reason, its spending figures on roads were also excluded from the averages. Finally, it must be noted that not only do cities vary in the priority they give to their roads within their budgets; they also have varying amounts of money to spend because of different tax bases or political will. For example, Dallas and San Jose were both spending about $585 per capita in 1985, but Dallas put eight percent of its budget into highways while San Jose put almost twenty-one percent. (San Francisco's expensive street building program was helped out by the city's budget of $1,806 per capita.)

It was a bit surprising, therefore, that although the trend is modest, more compact cities in the US seem to be spending less money maintaining their streets, even though these cities tended to be in the North and East where the urban infrastructure is older and subject to more wear and tear. The implication is that if some of these other factors were equalized, the trend might be more obvious. Unfortu-

Table 5
Highway spending, transit operating costs, and use density, us cities, 1982–86

City	Central-city use density, 1982	Central-city per capita spending on roads, 1984–85			Operating cost per passenger – motor bus transit, 1986	
Kansas City	2570	us $83.70	(9.7)[a]		us $1.81	
Dallas	3454	46.10	(7.9)		1.54	
San Diego	3976	29.80	(6.0)	60.03[b]	2.56	1.96
Houston	4011	32.60	(6.5)	(9.3)	2.28	
Atlanta	4657	46.50	(4.7)		1.03	
San Jose	4885	121.50	(20.8)		2.56	
Seattle	5712	30.50	(3.9)		1.77	
Denver	6347	56.10	(4.2)		1.90	
Cincinnati	6687	59.50	(6.6)		1.43	
New Orleans	6946	92.20	(9.0)		.86	
Minneapolis/						
St Paul	8267	95.98	(8.6)		1.30	
Milwaukee	8533	76.50	(10.8)		.86	1.57
Los Angeles/				69.88		
Long Beach	8736	32.65	(5.1)	(7.6)	1.62	
Cleveland	9874	52.70	(7.2)		1.28	
St Louis	10260	70.30	(6.5)		1.69	
Detroit	10520	110.70	(10.5)		1.57	
Pittsburgh	10604	91.60	(11.6)		1.36	
Baltimore	12079	(200.30)	(12.8)		1.69	
Miami	13953	37.50	(6.2)		1.58	
Philadelphia	15234	45.90	(4.1)	49.98	.90	
San Francisco	15899	(144.50)	(8.0)[c]	(5.7)	.96	1.11
Chicago	16549	60.90	(9.2)		.77	
Boston and						
Suffolk	16780	55.60	(3.4)		1.36	

Source: us Bureau of the Census, *County and City Data Book* (Washington: 1988) and us
Department of Transportation, *National Urban Mass Transit Statistics: 1986 Section 15 Annual Report*
(Washington: 1988). Use density is the sum of residents and employees per square mile. Capital
spending on roads not included.
[a]   Percentage of budget spent on road maintenance
[b]   Average of group of cities
[c]   Baltimore not included in group average of road spending because its figure is for all federal,
     state, and county highways within its borders. San Francisco not included in group average
     because of special earthquake-related factors. See text.

nately, however, since the younger cities with more deconcentrated
and segregated land use are in the sunny and snowless South and
West, it is difficult to make a clear inference.

It should be pointed out that Table 5 shows only spending for city
streets. County roads are often part of the city's network of roads, as

Table 6
Increase in urban highway mileage, US

	1956	1969
Urban highway mileage, total	36,222	55,980
Percent	100	100
(a) State primary system, 4-lane divided	2,596	13,112
Percent	7.2	23.4
(b) State primary system, full-access control (no grade crossing)	355	6,247
Percent	1.0	11.2
(c) Remaining urban highway mileage	33,271	36,621
Percent	91.0	65.2

Source: Eugene Lewis and Frank Anechiarico, *Urban America: Politics and Policy, Second Edition* (New York: Holt, Rinehart and Winston 1981), 247.

are state and federal highways. By 1969, state and federal highways made up 34.6 percent of urban road mileage (Table 6). The jurisdictional responsibilities and the way those responsibilities were shared varied so much from state to state that estimating total spending on highways by all governments within the cities in Table 5 was too much for me. But the point is that a city's expenditures on its own streets are but a fraction of the total spending for highways within its borders. What needs to be noticed in Table 5 is the trend more than the actual amounts, which underestimate total spending considerably. Capital expenditures have been omitted from all these figures, as well.

A more standardized comparison of the US cities' transportation networks may be found by looking at their transit systems. Although data were available for rapid transit, streetcars, and trolley cars and buses, it seemed most logical to compare the efficiency of the cities' motorbus fleets (even though they might be deployed differently) since motorbuses could be found in every city. As Table 5 shows, every time a passenger boarded a bus in 1986, it cost the system $1.11 in the more compact cities, while in the decentralized cities the system would often be paying over $2.00. (Streetcars and rapid-transit lines in the cities of the North and East also had costs per ride which hovered around the $1.00 mark. The Bay area's rapid-transit system, on the other hand, was costing $2.31 a passenger, which was actually an improvement over the 1970s. Here is a good illustration of the wastefulness of the postwar urban form.)

With respect to winter weather, Canadian cities might be expected to offer a more homogeneous sample. Unfortunately, this is not the

Table 7
Canadian cities' spending on streets, 1987

City	City density pop./sq. mi., 1986	City spending per capita on streets	
Edmonton	2218	CAN $116.19	
Winnipeg	2656	85.98	
Saskatoon	3476	69.11	111.92[a]
Windsor	4171	204.23	
London	4299	84.11	
Scarborough[b]	6685	105.08	
Ottawa	7060	125.54	
North York[b]	8137	111.86	98.88
Metro Toronto	9007	99.66	
Vancouver	9889	52.25	
Montreal	14867	99.55	
York[b]	15112	80.43	91.65
Toronto City[b]	16328	94.98	

Sources: Financial reports and budgets of individual cities; conversations with civic officials of individual cities (see notes to text).
[a]   Average of group of cities.
[b]   These are constituent municipalities of the Municipality of Metropolitan Toronto, which looked after major roads in its jurisdiction at a cost of $30.58 per capita in 1987. This latter sum was added to each constituent municipality's spending for local streets to arrive at the figure given. Metro's figure is $30.58 plus a weighted average of street spending by constituent municipalities ($69.08). Thus, the cases overlap and are not totally independent of each other; however, it should be noted that North York and Scarborough are the newer and more deconcentrated municipalities.

case: it cost Montreal $46 million of its $100-million 1987 roads budget just to clear the snow. By contrast, London, Ontario, which is hardly in the sunny South, spent only about $2.9 million for snow clearance out of a total roads budget of $22.6 million.

Nevertheless, the more spread-out Canadian cities (which include London) tended to spend more money per capita on maintaining their road system than the more concentrated cities.

Once again, the trend is clearer when one looks at the costs of operating a transit system over sparsely populated areas. Canadian transit systems, as Table 8 shows, are up to one-and-half times more costly to run when they try to service deconcentrated settlements, although the trend is not quite as dramatic as in the US. (Since transit systems usually serve much more than just the central city, and since the Canadian data included density for the whole transit service area, "dense" cities in Table 8 may not be the same as "dense" cities in Table 7.)

Table 8
Transit costs per passenger and density – Canadian transit systems, 1987

City	Density of service area in square miles	Operating cost per passenger		
Halifax*	1489	CAN $1.23		
Laval	1874	1.89		
Vancouver	2162	1.74	1.51	(1.68)
Victoria*	2307	1.27		
Hamilton	2423	1.41		
Quebec	2781	1.65		
Calgary	3179	1.59		
Winnipeg	3342	1.09	1.37	(1.42)
Saskatoon*	3345	.92		
Mississauga	3464	1.61		
Ottawa	3956	1.28		
London	4096	1.09		
Regina*	4119	1.32	1.32	(1.32)
Windsor	4207	1.14		
Edmonton	4435	1.79		
Toronto	8984	1.06	1.11	
Montreal	9093	1.15		

Source: Canadian Urban Transit Association, Operating Characteristics of Member Systems, 1987-1988 (Toronto: 1989).
*These are the smallest systems in the sample and exhibit many idiosyncrasies. Leaving them out of their groups results in the averages shown in parentheses.

Now it is time to lengthen the perspective. I have been showing how within the us and within Canada there is some indication that the newer urban development with deconcentrated and segregated land use is more expensive to travel around. For various technical reasons, it is difficult to make a precise or detailed comparison of the us with Canada, except to note that it looks as if Canadians and Americans in general spend roughly comparable amounts on streets per inhabitant in the larger cities – this is evident from looking at Tables 5 and 7. However, Canadians have invested more in public transit. For example, Michael Goldberg and John Mercer, who have written an entire book to highlight how different the two nations' cities are, show that in the 1970s Canadian cities had about twenty-one miles of transit service per city resident, while us cities had less than nine miles. By 1986, the us transit systems were providing fif-teen-and-a-half miles per resident, while Canadian networks had grown to twenty-four miles per resident in 1987.

Table 9
Road supply in selected world cities, 1980

City	Metres of road per capita		City	Metres of road per capita	
Adelaide	9.1		Amsterdam	2.1	
Brisbane	6.9		Brussels	1.7	
Melbourne	7.9	8.7*	Copenhagen	4.3	
Perth	13.3		Frankfurt	2.0	
Sydney	6.2		Hamburg	2.2	
			London (UK)	1.9	2.1
Boston	5.2		Munich	1.7	
Chicago	5.0		Paris	.9	
Denver	9.4		Stockholm	2.3	
Detroit	5.8		Vienna	1.7	
Houston	10.6	8.4	West Berlin	1.5	
Los Angeles	4.5		Zürich	2.6	
New York	4.7				
Phoenix	10.4		Hong Kong	.23	
Toronto	2.7		Moscow	.4	.9
Washington	5.1		Singapore	1.0	
			Tokyo	1.9	

Source: Peter Newman and Jeffrey Kenworthy, *Cities and Automobile Dependence* (Brookfield, VT: Gower Publishing Co., 1989).
*Group average

If Canada and the US show differences in urban form and transportation, then it is reasonable to expect that cities in other nations might provide an even greater contrast. Peter Newman and Jeffrey Kenworthy, two Australian geographers, have collected data on urban density and automobile use for thirty-two cities around the world, including some of the North American cities examined in this chapter. While their information did not include spending on highways and transit, they found a clear connection between density, automobile use, and urban-transit facilities. Broadening the focus beyond the US and Canada is instructive. In terms of road supply, for example, the cities of North America and Australia stand out as urban freaks. Look at Table 9. In North America, we have four times as much roadway in our cities as European cities do, while they in turn have double the rest of the world's (admittedly thinly represented here). Needless to say, Newman and Kenworthy find very strong relationships between road supply and urban sprawl. I shall have more to say about this later.

From this perspective, it sounds less exaggerated to say that the amount of resources used to build and maintain North American city highways and streets is truly enormous. Most of us have grown up with all these roads and think of them as normal and natural; but they are not. All North American cities, including Boston and Toronto, have sprawling, expensive road systems, systems which are hardly necessary for a city to work.

It must be underlined that it is not simply deconcentration of land but lack of land-use mix which causes spending to escalate. Land-use mix is difficult to measure at a grand level, but it can be done at the level of individual experience. William Michelson, an urban sociologist, studied the transportation habits of people who had recently moved to a new residential environment. He found that suburban homeowners travelled much further for food, clothing, and sundries than downtown homeowners or than suburban apartment renters who often have shopping centres built across from their housing – usually by the same developer, who has seen the sense of holding a market captive. Suburban single-family housing developments seldom mix land uses, however, and suburban homeowners use the car much more than anyone else. They are spending more of their money on urban transportation because of urban land-use segregation, not just because of deconcentration.

More evidence of how segregated land uses raise transportation costs emerged in the research I conducted in Toronto, in which I classified the different two- or three-block areas according to their mixture in land use. Residents in each of these areas were asked whether they walked to work or to do their shopping. As might be expected, a larger percentage of residents walked in areas of mixed land use than in areas of purely residential land use. Even the quality of the land-use mix varied. Toronto's biggest high-rise complex, St Jamestown, had a number of large stores in its centre that attracted a good share of residents, many of whom were senior citizens in rent-subsidized apartments, yet the low quality of the shopping facilities – the half-heartedness of the use mixture – had pushed many in this project to drive or take transit to other parts of the city in order to shop. St Jamestowners were less likely to walk for shopping than residents of mixed-use low-rise downtown neighbourhoods a mile or so away.

Unfortunately, there is no systematic inventory of how mixed the land use is in different cities across North America. The evidence given by the behaviour of individuals in different milieux certainly suggests, however, that the more a city mixes its residential and commercial land use, the less money the government and its citizens will have to spend on transportation services.

The Indirect Costs of Urban Transportation

To this point, the emphasis has been on how deconcentrated and segregated land use results in an expensive urban transportation system which costs both governments and individuals more money. The costs of building and maintaining the system are only the beginning, though.

Another reason why urban transportation is expensive is that expressways, streets, parking areas, and rapid-transit lines are a significant form of land use. In the downtown of a car-oriented city like Los Angeles or Indianapolis, streets and parking lots can take up two-thirds of the land, despite the presence of high-rise office buildings. When one considers that land in the central core of a big city is often valued at hundreds of dollars per square foot, using several hundred square feet to park one car takes on an aura of unreality. Yet governments build thousands of parking spaces and hundreds of big, wide streets downtown. One reason for this anomaly is that public authorities, when considering investments in transportation, only take into account the private benefits (i.e., parking convenience and shorter trips for commuters) of such investments, not social costs. Land immediately surrounding the downtown core tends to be devoted to transportation because it is undervalued by governments, governments which make important but often uninformed decisions about land use. They habitually turn over extremely valuable downtown land in urban North America to automobile transportation (including parking), depriving citizens of millions of dollars of possible land development. (Land right at the centre and farther out, in turn, tends to be overvalued.)

Whatever the reason for using so much valuable downtown land for transportation, and especially for cars, the loss in terms of potentially developable land is enormous, and this must be treated as one of the costs of our urban transportation system. The National Transportation Survey indicates that Atlanta, for instance, had forty-two square *miles* of land in highways in its downtown in 1972. In its central business district (usually called the CBD) it had more than 33,000 parking spaces, which at 280 square feet per space, works out to about 212 acres of prime downtown land – millions of dollars' worth.

Martin Stern analyzed the impact on land values of adding more cars and widening roads to accommodate those cars. This he did in two ways: he computed the value of land taken by widening the roads sufficiently to accommodate one more car with the same congestion; he also calculated the cost to downtown vitality of decreasing the amount of land devoted to business – reduced synergy, he called it. Together, these costs worked out to between US $1,875 and $2,800 (expressed in 1987 dollars) per car, which, Stern noted, "clearly outweigh those of road installation." He went on to argue that the additional car represented "growth" for the city in an economic sense, and that this growth could be expressed by an increase in land values of anywhere from US $7,384 to $12,556 (1987 dollars). If every additional car indeed represented a net increase in business, this would be a reasonable assumption. However, that car could just as easily belong to someone who had switched from transit because he or she had started earning enough money to buy a car, or moved out of reach of transit and kept the same job, or started commuting by car because the road system improved. Stern simply called the $1,875 to $2,800 cost of road widening to reduce congestion "an unpriced subsidy bestowed by the CBD on the automobile-using commuter." This subsidy can be justified by decision makers, he continued, only if congestion gets really bad. By really bad Stern meant that the time lost to congestion (about US $9.35 per hour in 1987 dollars) would start to be worth more than the land costs. This happens, he said, as cities grow past three million. But if land in the core area is worth a hundred dollars per square foot, which is less than in many North American cities in the early 1990s, and the car is taking up three or four thousand dollars' worth of parking space in addition to the above costs, the whole exercise becomes outlandish: there is no way one could justify, financially, making room for more cars in any downtown core. In other words, Stern probably underestimated the cost of the automobile.

Although the costs of making room for cars are dramatic, considering transit as an alternative makes them even more so. Table 10 shows the amount of land displaced in the US by highways, bus transit, and rail transit, both in 1972 and 1980. It is clear that highways use hundreds of times more land than transit. Adding a transit commuter will obviously not have the same impact on land supply as adding another car. This does not mean that transit is a panacea, for land-use patterns in the postwar North American city often make it an unrealistic alternative. Evidence has already been presented that it costs too much to service most postwar development. Even office development, symbolized by the high-density towers of downtowns, has been moving to the suburbs, becoming almost inaccessible to the public-transit rider.

Stern's calculations underestimated the cost of the car in another way. He assumed that seventy percent of the city's core, on the average, can be built upon, while the rest can be used for streets, side-

Table 10
Land in square miles displaced by highways and by bus and rail transit,
1972 and 1980, in us cities over 1 million

	Land in square miles displaced	
Transportation mode	Cities with population over 2 million	Cities with population 1–2 million
Highways, 1972	1425	488
Projected highways, 1980	1617	553
Bus transit, 1972	1.7	3.7
Projected bus transit, 1980	4.5	5.7
Rail transit, 1972	2.2	.2
Projected rail transit, 1980	3.7	5.9

Source: us Department of Transportation, Urban Data Supplement of 1974, National Transportation
Report (Washington, DC: May 1976).

walks, and surface parking. Although this figure sounds "typical for
... Central Business Districts of good-sized cities (population one-
quarter million to ten million)," there is evidence that it is not.

For instance, in 1973, 34 percent of Toronto's downtown land was
public streets and lanes, while another 8.6 percent of its surface area
was devoted to parking. Back in 1963, Boston's downtown had roads
and parking which took up 26.5 percent and 8.3 percent of its land
area, respectively. This works out to be close to 30 percent, but it
must be remembered that Boston is an older northeastern city, with
fewer people in the centre driving to work. Eighteen percent of Boston city residents bike or walk to work. The probability that someone
from a four-person Boston household, living in a detached house,
with average income, drives to work if the house is downtown, is .33;
in Phoenix, the probability is .84 for the same kind of person (3.4
percent of Phoenix city residents bike or walk to work). While Los
Angeles, with 67 percent of its downtown used for streets and parking, may not be typical of North American cities either, 30 percent
does seem like an unrealistic assumption on Stern's part.

The implication of changing Stern's assumption is that adding one
new car to rush-hour traffic would cost quite a bit more in terms of
land than he calculated.

Thus, the indirect economic cost of urban transportation – especially automobile transportation – as expressed in acres of land it
takes up is considerable. (It must be remembered that buses, streetcars, and taxis also use city streets.) But this is only one of several
indirect costs which stem from the fact that transportation facilities
are an important urban land use. Everyone has an idea of how con-

Table 11
Population and job displaced by new urban transportation facilities planned for the
1970s, US

	City Size	
	2 million +	1–2 million
Jobs displaced by highways	11,961	13,670
Population displaced by highways	40,491	42,793
Jobs displaced by bus transit	244	120
Population displaced by bus transit	0	18
Jobs displaced by rail transit	150	5,540
Population displaced by rail transit	2,763	6,100

Source: Same as for Table 10.

struction of a new building disrupts the life of a street. This disrup-
tion cannot compare to that created by the building of a
transportation facility such as an urban expressway. In fact, urban
expressways financed under the US government's 1956 Interstate
Highway Act had such a catastrophic impact on some inner-city
neighbourhoods during the 1960s and 1970s that in a few cases
highways were simply stopped by local political opposition.

Table 11 gives an idea of how many jobs and homes would be
destroyed by cities' transportation projects in the US in the 1970s.
Figures are impersonal, however, as one graphic example will show.

Robert Moses' plans for the Cross Bronx Expressway in New York
City were opposed by numerous citizens' groups, but he was sympathetic to no one; and, like many urban freeways, the Cross Bronx
was built nevertheless. Robert Caro, in his massive biography of
Moses, described the literal death and destruction which accompanied the building of this road through East Tremont. First, one must
consider the expulsion of thousands of families, whose sufferings
could never be measured, but whose wanderings in search of new
homes were pitiful and often fruitless. In search of harder data, the
cost-benefit analyst would be intrigued by the wide range of costs
imposed by the expressway on the fifty-five thousand residents who
were not actually kicked out, but who had to live with the expressway
during its construction and in its completed state. Huge masses of
dynamite were used to blast away the hills of East Tremont; the result
was that the whole neighbourhood shook: "Mortar and brick were
jarred loose from one end of the neighborhood to the other. As
apartment houses settled or were pushed up as the earth beneath
them heaved, huge gaping fissures began to appear in their walls
and ceilings … One of the by-products of blasting or drilling in solid

bedrock is rock dust, an extremely fine-grained abrasive grit. 'If you closed your windows' [one resident recalled] 'and put towels in to seal them up, it was there anyway ... You got up in the morning and you felt like you had slept in dust.'"

Things got so bad that people began to move out – not just the ones who had been evicted. Shopping became almost impossible; for although overpasses would be built after the road was finished, getting groceries in the meantime was like trekking to Brooklyn five miles away. Many local merchants simply went out of business because half their clientele was cut off from them. The area became intolerable to all but the most destitute, who moved into the unwanted apartments. Vandalism and street crime quickly worsened: "The slaying in Cohen's butcher shop at 164 E. 174 St Monday night was no isolated incident, but the culmination of a series of burglaries and holdups along the street ... Ever since work started on the Cross Bronx Expressway across the street some two years ago, a grocer said, trouble has plagued the area ... Stores which once stayed open to 9 or 10 o'clock are shutting down at 7 P.M. Few shoppers dare venture out after dark, so store-keepers feel the little business they lose hardly justifies the risk in remaining open late."

Still other costs, harder to pin down than that of rehousing urban residents, can be laid at the door of expressways and subways. Certain land uses in cities affect other land uses nearby: a factory may keep some land in shadow most of the day, or a new movie theatre may generate both parking problems for local residents and more business for the corner variety store. Urban expressways impose economic costs, once built, by creating noise. Noise from expressways has been shown to decrease property values by up to 6.7 percent. Another cost may be traced to the cutting off of circulation. Jane Jacobs calls this phenomenon a border vacuum. The through-transportation route is a barrier creating dead-end streets and cul-de-sacs, robbing areas of traffic which feeds social as well as economic life. How many stores does one see on a dead-end street? Even the most rudimentary knowledge of retailing would steer a shop-keeper clear of such locations. Unfortunately, a rapid-transit line or expressway can turn a good location into a bad one. This is what happened to dozens of stores in the vicinity of the Cross Bronx Expressway.

Building our cities so that automobiles are required takes an awesome toll in human life. In the United States alone, about fifty thousand lives are lost each year in car accidents. Simply by laying out our cities differently we could reduce the use of cars and literally save thousands of lives. The problem is that we are so used to this particular cost of the automobile that we seldom think of it in this way – as a killer.

One final cost of North America's car-oriented system of urban transportation is pollution. The cars we use to get around our cities consume vast oceans of fuel. The transportation sector of the US, a large percentage of which consists of travel within cities, uses sixty-three percent of all the nation's oil. Much of that oil goes into cars, of which there were 135 million in the US in 1986. That works out to a ratio of 1.8 people to a car, the lowest ratio in the world. Canada, with 11 million cars in 1985, was second lowest with 2.3 people per car. Each car burns 700 to 800 gallons of gas each year.

Two Australian geographers, Peter Newman and Jeffrey Kenworthy, have made a direct connection between the density of cities and gasoline consumption. They measured density of jobs as well as of residents because they found that only when the two were sufficiently high could an efficient transportation system be designed. In other words, having a high density of jobs (say, in office towers) without residents is land-use segregation, which still requires people to travel some distance to work. This is the way many cities in North America with "dense" downtowns are set up.

The very strong relationship between gasoline consumption and use density is illustrated in Newman and Kenworthy's graph, Figure 3. The cities with more roads (see Table 9) and less use density are using more gasoline. For example, gas consumption per capita in Houston is 546 gallons; it has one-quarter the use density of Chicago, whose per capita consumption is 353 gallons. Since each car emits about a ton of carbon into the atmosphere every year, Chicago's denser urban form means that, for that one city, far fewer thousands of tons of carbon are going into the atmosphere annually. And Chicago is hardly a compact city by world standards.

It should be noted that Toronto comes off rather well in Newman and Kenworthy's research because they used the Municipality of Metropolitan Toronto, with its population of about 2.2 million, as the source of data for their definition of the metropolitan area; in fact, by 1990, the Toronto-centred region had well over 3.5 million people, not including Hamilton (forty miles away), and had spread out over the southern Ontario landscape in a most American way.

The result of this gasoline-consumption pattern means that cities like Houston and Los Angeles are not only doing more to kill their own residents with air pollution; they are doing more to kill the planet. Michael Renner of the Worldwatch Institute spells it out:

Researchers at the University of California estimate that the use of gasoline and diesel fuel in the United States alone may cause up to 30,000 deaths every year ...

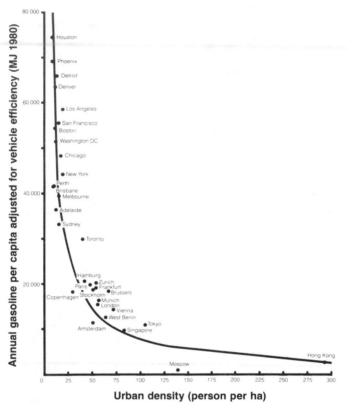

Figure 3
Urban density versus gasoline use per capita adjusted for vehicle efficiency.

Cars, trucks, and buses play a prominent role in generating virtually all the major air pollutants, especially in cities. In OECD member countries, they contribute 75% of carbon monoxide emissions, 48% of nitrogen oxides, 40% of hydrocarbons, 12% of particulates, and 3% of sulfur dioxides. Worldwide, the production and use of automotive fuels account for an estimated 17% of all carbon dioxide released from fossil fuels. Transportation is also the primary source of lead pollution. The adverse health effects of these pollutants are fairly well established.

Perhaps the best known and most pervasive synergistic effect of these pollutants is photochemical smog – the brown haze that causes such health disorders as bronchial diseases and lung damage, dramatically restricts visibility, and erodes buildings and monuments.

Ozone and acid rain from automobile emissions are helping to destroy the forests of Appalachia and eastern Canada, to say nothing of crop losses in the US of \$1.9 to \$4.5 billion in corn, wheat, soybeans, and peanuts. Of course, it is one thing to talk about all this, and another to see it: a vacation in the Eastern Townships of southern Quebec or a hike anywhere along the Green Mountains of Vermont or the Great Smokies in North Carolina will disclose acres and acres – whole mountainsides – of dead and dying trees. It is important to understand this as an outcome, at least partially, of the way we build our cities.

To call these deaths, of both trees and humans, an economic cost of the postwar shape of urban development is a massive understatement, since our survival as a species is probably at stake and since urban form is only part of the reason. But to ignore the economics of it would not be smart.

Renner goes on: "The most serious long term consequence of automotive emissions, however, is the atmospheric buildup of CO_2 and other greenhouse gases – nitrous oxide, methane, and ozone. There is now virtual consensus among scientists that if the concentration of CO_2 in the atmosphere doubles, a substantial increase in global temperature would occur. Indeed, recent research indicates that a rise in temperature is already underway. The impending climate change could shift global precipitation patterns, disrupt crop growing regions, raise sea levels, and threaten coastal cities worldwide with inundation." Coastal cities are not isolated outposts. Some thirty percent of the world's economy and thirty percent of its population lie within one and a half metres of sea-level. As we saw above, the production and use of automobile fuel produces seventeen percent of all carbon dioxide released into the atmosphere.

While I have not attempted to give a total dollar sum of the economic costs of the North American city transportation system, it must surely be clear that the sum is appallingly large, even aside from the US \$5,000 to \$6,000 it costs the individual out-of-pocket to drive around a city for a year. In addition to dollars, the costs can be measured in jobs, human lives, housing units, and environmental degradation. From the transportation point of view alone, the pattern of deconcentrated and segregated land use is unacceptably expensive. However, there are other costs as well, and of these a tally must be made.

The Direct Costs of Other Municipal Services

Deconcentrating and separating our activities makes other municipal services more expensive. For instance, while we tend to think of transport in terms of carrying people and goods from place to place, many other things are being transported around a city. One of these things is water – clean water is delivered to homes and to industries, waste water is carried away. When land use is desegregated and deconcentrated, the cost of providing those water and sewage services is greater. Data on what city governments spend on sewage and sanitation were collected from the US *County and City Data Book* for the years 1985–86 to illustrate this point. The cities were grouped according to use density, as in Table 5.

As with roads and highways, the figures are weird and wonderful. Had time permitted, it would have been intriguing to ask the St Louis and Detroit city fathers to explain to each other why St Louis spends 2.6 percent of its budget, or $28.10 per capita, on sewage and sanitation, while Detroit (with the same density as St Louis) sees fit to spend 15.3 percent of *its* budget, or $161.30 per capita, on the same services. I have already said that earthquake-prone San Francisco, one of the densest of North American cities, needs to spend considerably more money on its public works, and sewage is no exception. Its outlays were excluded from its group's mean. In general, it should be noted that, San Francisco aside, the newer, spread-out cities are spending more money, and a larger proportion of their budgets, on sewage and sanitation (Table 12).

Canadian cities exhibit a similar pattern: the denser the settlement, the cheaper it is to maintain sewers and to provide water (see Table 13).

More comprehensive efforts have been made to illustrate the costs of servicing different settlement patterns. Table 14 takes into account both capital and operating expenses for police, fire, sanitation, schools, water supply, storm drainage, and sanitary sewage. Almost every urban service gets steadily cheaper as residential density increases. The only apparent exception is that fire protection is costlier for high-rise buildings.

Urban services are not priced according to Table 14, of course, so that in effect, spread-out development is being subsidized by everyone. Residents are seldom aware that they are being subsidized in this way, however. As Newman and Kenworthy point out, "recent calculations on Melbourne estimate that for each additional household located in central Melbourne, rather than on the urban fringe, the community saves over $A 40,000 in the cost of public infrastructure such as roads, water, sewerage, electricity, education, police, fire, childcare facilities and in individual costs such as getting to work ... The trade-off between urban space and government costs is generally not perceived by the ordinary person seeking a new home in a new suburb." This lack of awareness among consumers is an extremely important part of why our cities do not work. It will be considered further in chapters 3 and 6.

Table 12
Sewage and sanitation operating costs, by use density, us cities, 1985–86

City	Central-city use density	Central-city spending per capita on sewage and sanitation, 1985–86		
Kansas City	2570	us $72.50	(8.4)[a]	
Dallas	3454	76.40	(13.1)	
San Diego	3976	70.90	(14.3)	96.87[b]
Houston	4011	105.40	(17.8)	(14.1)
Atlanta	4657	181.20	(18.3)	
San Jose	4885	74.80	(12.8)	
Seattle	5712	103.90	(13.3)	
Denver	6347	105.60	(7.9)	122.16
Cincinnati	6687	131.70	(14.6)	(12.6)
New Orleans	6946	147.50	(14.4)	
Minneapolis/St Paul	8267	92.30	(8.6)	
Milwaukee	8533	122.50	(17.3)	
Los Angeles/Long Beach	8736	42.40	(10.8)	
Cleveland	9874	57.80	(7.9)	85.24
St Louis	10260	28.10	(2.6)	(9.5)
Detroit	10520	161.30	(15.3)	
Pittsburgh	10604	40.30	(5.1)	
Baltimore	12079	137.70	(8.7)	
Miami	13953	69.50	(11.5)	
Philadelphia	15234	105.20	(9.4)	74.23
San Francisco	15899	(171.60)	(9.5)[c]	(8.2)
Chicago	16549	47.00	(7.1)	
Boston	16780	75.20	(4.6)	

Source: us Bureau of the Census, County and Cita Data Book (Washington: 1988).

[a] Figures in parentheses throughout the table are percentages of total spending on operations
    that sewage and sanitation spending represents

[b] Average for this group of cities

[c] San Francisco not included in average for its group because of earthquake-related factors. See
    text.

Precise figures such as those in Table 14 cannot be given for the costs of segregated land use. However, some interesting efforts have been made in this direction. For instance, David Nowlan, an economist at the University of Toronto, submitted a report to the Toronto Planning Department in 1989 which indicated that it would cost the city far less to build housing for office workers in the downtown core (normally reserved exclusively for office space, which can afford to pay more for land on the open market) than it would to pay for the transportation infrastructure to bring workers in and out.

Table 13
Sewer and waterworks operating expenditures of Canadian cities, by density, 1987

City	Density pop./sq. mi.	Spending on sewers per capita		Spending on waterworks per capita	
Edmonton	2216	CAN $61.21		118.87	
Winnipeg	2656	49.77		58.23	
Calgary	3078	88.12	68.15[a]	116.87	81.02
Saskatoon	3476	41.76		69.20	
Regina	4119	49.88		74.79	
Windsor	4171	118.14[b]		48.13	
Ottawa	7060	40.76[c]		[d]	
Vancouver	9889	17.29	36.12	[d]	
York	15112	43.12[b]		46.18[b]	
Toronto City	16328	43.31		45.75	

Sources: Same as for Table 7. As in Table 7, Metro's costs on sewers and waterworks were added on to York's and Toronto's.

[a]   Group average
[b]   1988 figures
[c]   This may be an underestimate; Ottawa Carleton Regional Governement spending not included
[d]   Data unavailable

Roy W. Bahl and J. Michael McGuire conducted a study which makes somewhat clearer the implications of dividing cities into exclusively residential, commercial, and manufacturing areas. They computed the incremental costs of a 200-acre leapfrog* residential development in terms of utilities such as water, gas, electricity, and telephone; fire, police, and garbage services; and commuting, public transit, and delivery services. Of the additional costs, sixty-three percent were traced to automobile commuting, paid for by residents of the subdivision. Even though the residents themselves ended up paying a large proportion of the additional costs – at least as measured in this study (any reader of this chapter could suggest more) – they were being subsidized by local government with respect to services other than transportation. The figures in Table 15 show that the government service bill to residents of the subdivision would have been twenty-eight percent greater had the actual cost of these services been paid.

This example is illuminating because the subdivision is not only an example of urban sprawl; it is also a residential community separating itself from the rest of the built-up area of the city, yet receiving city services. It is an example of segregation of land use as well

---

* A leapfrog development is a residential subdivision which does not border on any previously built-up area.

Table 14
Cost of providing public services to one unit, by property type and density

Services	Single-family homes 5 per acre	Townhouses 10 per acre	Walk-up apartments 30 per acre	High-rise apartments 30 per acre	High-rise apartments 60 per acre
Capital costs					
Police	us $269.74	268.21	265.14	265.14	265.14
Fire	188.58	135.50	135.50	135.50	167.47
Sanitation	59.19	54.33	44.46	40.42	37.91
Schools	13694.46	11608.61	11608.61	4210.90	4210.90
Water supply	4449.28	2975.34	1241.40	1449.85	856.37
Storm drainage	2732.07	1817.84	591.59	727.88	301.03
Sanitary sewers	2080.68	1519.50	1263.86	882.66	702.20
Total capital	23473.97	18379.36	15058.74	7744.35	6539.48
Yearly capital	2017.60	1579.85	1263.86	675.36	569.03
Operating costs					
Police	142.28	133.20	118.05	118.05	108.97
Fire	145.58	106.39	106.39	139.97	139.97
Sanitation	71.06	65.15	53.10	48.22	45.12
Schools	2988.41	2528.66	2528.66	689.64	689.64
Water supply	81.40	77.00	77.00	65.33	65.33
Storm drainage	–	–	–	–	–
Sanitary sewers	78.27	71.68	68.25	58.40	57.50
Yearly operating	3506.99	2982.06	2948.89	1119.59	1106.51
Non-educational capital cost	9779.52	6770.74	3450.13	3533.44	2328.57
Non-educational yearly operating	518.58	453.41	420.23	429.95	417.13

Source: Paul Downing and Richard Gusteley, "The Public Service Costs of Alternative
Development Patterns: A Review of the Evidence," in Downing, ed., *Local Service Pricing Policies
and Their Effect on Urban Spatial Structure* (Vancouver: University of British Columbia Press 1977):
63–85. Prices have been adjusted to 1987 dollars.

as of deconcentration. Exclusively residential suburban communities
are almost totally dependent on the outside. They produce none of
their own goods and services but require them to be imported, at
considerable cost not only to themselves but also to governments and
to the environment. A new suburban development of ten thousand
people, for example, needs an extra 9.8 billion btus of energy a year
just to supply it with milk, 42.8 billion btus to supply it with apples,
and 7.6 billion btus for water. Altogether, this suburb needs 700,000
gallons more of diesel fuel per year to service it, just because it is
homogeneous and segregated.

The office districts and factory districts present the other side
of the coin. Humming with activity during the day, they are silent at
night – and so are the city services. By segregating work activities

Table 15
Additional local government expenditure per resident for leapfrog development

Function	Incremental cost per resident of leapfrog subdivision	Total metro-politan area expenditures	Incremental cost as per-cent of total
Sanitary sewage	US $26.97	$60.96[a]	44.25
Refuse collection	1.93	17.92[b]	10.76
Fire protection	.63	30.83	2.04
Police protection	22.22	29.64	74.97
School-bus service	2.19	217.22[c]	1.00
Total	54.02	193.25[d]	27.95

Source: Roy W. Bahl and J. Michael McGuire, "Urban Sprawl: Policies for Containment and Cost Recoupment," in Paul Downing (ed.) *Local Service Pricing Policies and Their Effect on Urban Spatial Structure* (Vancouver: Univ. of British Columbia 1977), 253. Amounts converted to 1987 dollars.
[a]   Including capital outlay
[b]   Sanitation other than sewage
[c]   Total education
[d]   Other than capital outlay

from residential and recreational activities, we have made it necessary to build a special, and specialized, set of urban services for each activity. The names of the establishments proclaim our ambitions: Food City, Drug Town, Shoppers' World, Industrial Park. There is a special, set-apart world for industry, for shopping, and, of course, for residing.

Finally, although the costs of roads, sewers, utilities, and so forth are vastly more expensive for the segregated, deconcentrated, and large-scale city, one must not forget that those costs represent only first-time construction plus maintenance. There are miles of high-ways, underground pipes, bridges, and other parts of the urban infrastructure which will eventually have to be rebuilt. The immensity of such a project is just beginning to dawn on policy makers in both the US and Canada. For example, during the frenzied city growth which occurred at the turn of the century, thousands of miles of water and sewage pipes were built underground to service the new development. Many of those pipes are beginning to show their age, necessitating capital-works programs to replace them. The amount of money this will cost will be a fraction of the outlay required to replace similar pipes in our deconcentrated, decentralized cities. In the US, although estimates vary and are open to question, there is consensus that such a rebuilding program will run to hundreds of billions of dollars. Surely, by itself this should deter us from blindly continuing the pattern of development we have been following since World War II.

HOUSING

Municipal services are not the only things which cost more in North America's postwar cities. Housing, which represents a significant proportion of the spending and assets of the entire economic system, is also more expensive because of this form of development: it is all brand new; it is deconcentrated; and it is segregated from other uses, partly because of land use and partly because of the scale of development, as explained in chapter 1.

Housing in the postwar North American city is incredibly new. In 1975, one-third of Canadian dwellings were less than ten years old. In 1985, 36.5 percent of US housing had been built since 1970. This represented about 36,000,000 units. In the same period, from 1970 to 1985, the number of households had increased by only about 23,000,000. What this implies, of course, is that millions of units of new housing were built not to house newly formed families, but to replace older housing. A similar process has been going on in Canada.

The evidence that new housing is deconcentrated can, of course, be inferred simply by looking at the way North American cities have spread out over the countryside since World War II. The density gradients discussed in chapter 1 show how dramatically this happened in both the United States and Canada. Another suggestive piece of indirect evidence comes from the proportion of new housing that was built as single-family dwelling units (SFDUS). In the early 1970s in the US, SFDUS made up about 55 percent of total units being built, but that percentage had soared by 1975 to 76.2 percent. After subsiding to the low sixties in the early 1980s, the percentage reached 70.6 in 1987. For years, Canada was building more multi-family dwellings than SFDUS, which set it off somewhat from the US; however, starting in 1983, it too was building more single-family homes than other types of housing. In 1988, 54 percent of Canada's new housing consisted of single-family homes. This type of housing takes up much more room, of course, than multiple-family housing, so it is not unreasonable to infer that the newer housing is responsible for growing amounts of urban sprawl.

The segregated nature of North America's new housing, again, can only be inferred from observing the proliferation of suburban development, such as that pioneered by Abraham Levitt and E.P. Taylor, and of large high-rise residential buildings, first as low-income public housing and then, increasingly, as luxury condominiums. As pointed out in chapter 1, the large scale of these two types of development was an inherent part of their lack of land-use mix. Surprisingly, as I shall show, it also guaranteed their costliness.

The newness of North American urban housing development is expressed in two ways: urban renewal, or replacing older buildings with new ones, and greenfields development, or taking up previously undeveloped land with new housing.

The decisions to tear down whole sections of the city in the 1950s and 1960s did not reflect an innovative current in urban-planning theory. Baron Haussman destroyed huge sections of Paris in the nineteenth century in order to construct the Boulevard St Michel and the Champs Élysées, and in the 1920s the architect Le Corbusier proposed even more massive razing to make way for his radiant city of high-rises. In fact, Le Corbusier and his followers were extremely influential among American and Canadian architects and planners right through the 1950s and 1960s. This can be seen by comparing the French architect's drawings of ideal cities in the 1920s with what was actually built in the fifties and sixties.

But turning Le Corbusier's wispy drawings into a massive concrete reality required money, large private and public developers, an authoritarian attitude towards city building, and an insensitivity to the social, cultural, and psychological meanings of older neighbourhoods and their buildings. North Americans had all these things. The extra costs – those over and above actual construction costs – included the following.

Jobs.   Sections of older housing that were torn down almost invariably were part of a mixed land-use pattern so that numerous small businesses, often paying low rents, were combined with the dwelling units. Destroying the whole area, of course, destroyed many of these jobs, which could not be supported in a higher rent district. In general, rents for businesses in new areas were much higher than rents in the old district. If the new development had stores in it, the rents were often too high for, say, unique clothing stores or specialty bookstores, whose business depended on recognition rather than fast turnover. The cost of all this in terms of jobs cannot be determined in any precise fashion, but it has been estimated that anywhere from one- to two-fifths of otherwise stable businesses went under when they were displaced.

Land costs.   As soon as it was understood that land was being assembled for a renewal project, speculators (to say nothing of government officials who were privy to the decision) found ways to acquire the land first and sell it at inflated prices to the government or to a developer. Alternatively, developers would make inordinate amounts of money on land they assembled for a project. In New York City, urban-renewal project densities have been substantially lower than surrounding areas. Thus, public funds were used to buy lower densities than the market had supported (aided by conventional zoning laws and slum landlords). The urban economist Wilbur Thompson notes that slum housing, through overcrowding, gets higher rents per square foot than any other housing, so its price is always the highest. (Recently, luxury condominiums, when built as high-rises, have become more profitable than retail space. Are such buildings the slums of tomorrow? It is not improbable: the slums of today were the middle-class housing of 1900.)

Destruction of existing housing stock.   It is not easy to determine exactly when it is cheaper to tear down and replace existing housing than it is to keep the old. One can safely say, however, that government policies of urban renewal have destroyed an amazing amount of perfectly good old housing. Urban-renewal advocates support their position by expressing a desire to "revitalize" the core or insisting that the old housing is dilapidated or "outmoded." In fact, as shown in chapter 6, tax policy has actually encouraged demolition of housing once it has changed hands, which is often. Especially in the 1960s, the net effect of urban renewal was to reduce the stock of housing in US cities. In Chicago, for example, between 1960 and 1970, 138,039 units were demolished, but only 120,000 units were built. While it is usually assumed that the demolished housing was in hopelessly bad shape, by the 1970s even governments were admitting that it was socially preferable and economically cheaper to rehabilitate housing. As Table 16 shows, however, even in that decade, demolitions far outnumbered construction in the central cities. Nevertheless, the economics of rehabilitation are clear. It is cheaper at two levels. The first is the house itself, whose value is traditionally assessed for its use to the demolition company: it has an "in-place" value (in 1987 dollars) of US $17 a square foot or more, which can be built on, literally as well as figuratively. Furthermore, as Richard Ernie Reed, author of *Return to the City*, puts it, "Rehabilitation projects are heavily labor intensive, with often 75% of the dollars expended on labor costs. New construction is usually about 50% labor and 50% materials. So, money invested in rehabilitation goes directly into the local economy to provide more jobs." By the 1970s, in recognition of these economics, demolition of inner-city housing to make way for newer housing had slowed in both the US and Canada.

Substitution of more expensive housing.   Private developers are not really interested in providing housing for people of low or moderate

Table 16

Changes over a three-year period in the rental housing stock of selected US central cities, different years

	Old Units Removed		New Units Built	
City	Number	Median Gross Rent	Number	Median Gross Rent
Boston (1974–77)	6300	$141	2600	$212
Chicago (1975–78)	33700	145	4300	253
Cleveland (1976–79)	6900	124	500	185
Detroit (1974–77)	13600	109	2800	131
New York (1976–79)	92400	160	27800	258
Newark (1974–77)	7200	141	1200	213
Philadelphia (1975–78)	8900	115	3000	302
St Louis (1976–79)	7900	103	400	130
San Francisco (1975–78)	5900	82	2600	281
Washington (1974–77)	6100	126	1500	294

Source: US Bureau of the Census, *New Residential Construction in Selected Metropolitan Statistical Areas* (Washington: US Government Printing Office), selected years, 1978–83.

income, for there is not enough money in it. In the 1950s and 1960s, the practice was to tear down, say 500 (or 5,000) moderate-rent dwelling units and replace them with 250 (or 2,500) luxury apartments. Now, although we are tearing down fewer old housing units, the units being built are still overwhelmingly for the middle and upper class. What is happening in many Canadian cities is the conversion of moderately priced rental housing to high-priced rental housing: the building is conserved, but the effect is the same.

While urban renewal was an incredibly expensive way to build new housing, development at the fringes of cities, or greenfields development, has also needlessly put up the price of housing. Much of this extra cost can be traced to the deconcentration and scale of the new development (see below); however, the very fact that so much of it was new made the housing more expensive than it had to be. New housing presents a wide array of opportunities for developers and financial institutions to make money. The "market price" of housing in the suburbs is artificially raised by land deals which benefit small as well as large speculators. Mark Gottdiener has thoroughly documented this process in Suffolk County on Long Island. The area just north of Metro Toronto seems to be going through this kind of development as well. Recent studies in US cities have shown that, no matter what the level of demand, cities with higher rates of construction have more expensive housing. Basically, the more new housing we build, the more expensive housing is going to be. (It will be recalled that housing is being built more rapidly than new households are forming, so there is some element of choice here.)

Housing that is deconcentrated costs more. This has already been discussed: servicing such development with police and fire protection, utilities and roads is considerably more expensive. More significantly, perhaps, deconcentrated housing needs the car and the truck to supply it with essential needs, and this has contributed heavily to the atmospheric and soil pollution which is killing trees, animals, and us.

The costs of building housing which is segregated from other functions are high. Basic economic functions which could and should normally take place in or close to home are zoned out of residential areas, at an exorbitant cost to everyone. Housing often requires each unit to have not only its own car (usually two) but also many amenities and services which in mixed-use developments can be supplied communally: washing machines, day care, children's playgrounds, tools, and workshops. Grocery stores are seldom nearby. Despite large plots of fertile land which surround suburban houses, a specialized agribusiness and distribution system supplies them with food. (Studies have shown that even in crowded cities there is room for many people to grow their own food.) Sewage and garbage are sent miles away for processing. All this functional segregation of housing from activities which should be in or near residences is expensive. Wendell Berry sums it up beautifully:

The modern household ... has set itself increasingly aside from production and preparation of food and becomes more and more a place for the consumption of food produced and prepared elsewhere ... The modern home, even more than the government and universities, has institutionalized the divisions and fragmentations of modern life.

With its array of gadgets and machines, all powered by energies that are destructive of land or air or water, and connected to work, market, school, recreation, etc., by gasoline engines, the modern home is a veritable factory of waste and destruction. It is the mainstay of the economy of money, but within the economies of energy and nature, it is a catastrophe.

Regardless of whether it has been built on vacant land or whether it is renewal of some sort, housing is more expensive in North American cities because it is built in large-scale developments. Building big is integral to the way we build housing, whether it is suburban communities of fifty thousand or high-rise condominiums. This pattern is a part of our cultural heritage, summarized by the aphorism Bigger is Better.

There is a deep conviction that big companies can do things faster and more cheaply. The argument goes something like this: it is easier for big companies to get financing, because banks prefer to negotiate one big mortgage instead of many little ones; big companies have resources to draw on if there are delays in the approval process; they can take advantage of economies of scale in the actual construction of units – Abraham Levitt was famous in the 1940s and 1950s for assembly-line house construction which lowered the selling cost considerably. With this reasoning in mind, governments in both the US and Canada encouraged the building of developments such as Levittown, New Jersey, and Don Mills, Ontario, by big developers. These companies, many of them, actually came into being to take advantage of government policy to invest capital in large real-estate ventures.

Big development companies have made North American housing more expensive, not less, in a number of ways. First, the really big developers can monopolize land markets and thus inflate prices. This seemed to happen mostly in Canada, where the unwillingness (or, in some cases, inability) of local and provincial governments to service land with trunk sewers and other infrastructures made fringe land scarce. In such a situation, small developers and speculators are no match for big developers, who are able to use their resources to buy and hold land over time. Thus, while speculation in general has made greenfields development expensive, big corporate developers who flourished in Canada made it even more so. No US developer ever reached the scale of the Canadian giants, who were able to exercise market control in some cities. Calgary Regional Planning Commission Director Rhys Smith put it this way: "The present situation [of Calgary in 1976] is a far cry from that of ten to fifteen years ago when there were a large number of developers placing relatively small developments on the market. Lot prices in a situation of a few suppliers is largely a function of control of the market place." James Lorimer specifies the effects of this control:

In most cities ... the reason that suburban houses cost too much is because the developers have staged a successful takeover of suburban land development. A few large developers have captured an effective monopoly in the supply of new house lots in many cities. These firms took advantage of their collective market power to hold the supply of new house lots after 1971 to roughly historical levels, and in the face of this limited supply intensified demand pushed prices up enormously. Developers' profit is so substantial a portion of the prices of new suburban houses that these could be reduced by $7000 to $24,000 [1976 Canadian dollars] in most large Canadian cities if suburban land developers were restricted to a margin of 10%.

Two economists, J.R. Markusen and D.T. Scheffman, challenged Lorimer's analysis, at least with respect to Toronto. Empirically, for instance, they found in 1977 that the twenty-five biggest owners of land available for suburban development around Toronto only owned forty percent of that land. Of course, much depends on how one defines availability, when leapfrog development is so common. Markusen and Scheffman included only land that would "be serviceable with all required utilities within five years." What they failed to consider, however, was that by 1977, when they were writing, the province of Ontario had made a commitment to build a multi-billion-dollar trunk sewer north of Metro Toronto, opening up tremendous new areas for development and making it unwise to hoard land for future needs. In the US (and in Quebec, where governments were more eager for development and where infrastructure investment was more generous than elsewhere in Canada), serviced land was more plentiful, smaller developers competed with each other, and prices were lower.

There are more universally applicable reasons why large-scale housing development makes dwelling units more expensive. Big developers epitomize the trend of having our housing designed and built – down to the finest details – by others. This happens with smaller builders, as well; but it *has* to happen with large developments. Having our housing built for us is what the British architect John F.C. Turner calls heteronomous housing. Turner says that,

in a market economy, heteronomy, because of inherent bureaucracy and waste, is inflationary as soon as scarcities of those resources of which they make extravagant use are perceived, feared or created. And in any kind of economy, dependence on resources limited by scarcity or by counterproductive side effects, will create conflicts of interest between those who possess the resources and those who do not ...

There are a number of measurable consequences of heteronomy in housing. The standardization and size of developments minimize variety and fit, as already observed. Unfortunately, most oversimple observations emphasize the need for physical flexibility within dwellings or of dwellings. This has led to a great deal of investment in expensive construction systems that allow for internal rearrangements and the expansion and contraction of individual units – a mechanical view of "loose-fit."

This investment in heteronomous technologies has proved both expensive and of only marginal benefit ... Large scale systems have created the most segregated cities the world has ever known.

The life of modern buildings, whether blocks of flats or office blocks, is already notoriously short. Millions have watched the demise of the infamous

Pruitt-Igoe public housing project in St. Louis, Missouri ... This is not an isolated case of public authorities giving up on unmanageable and uneconomic housing estates. Several local authorities in Britain have found that it is easier and cheaper to demolish structures that were well-built less than 40 years ago, than to rehabilitate and modernize them ...

Not only does the relatively short life of large-scale, centrally administered modern housing accelerate the exhaustion of scarce resources, but it uses vastly more. Jean Robert has estimated that the energy used in modern building is three times that used in traditional hand-hewn stone construction – and the latter, of course, is vastly longer-lived, even with low levels of maintenance. When one adds the fact that by far the greater part of all energy used in modern building is fossil-fuel based, the implications are starkly clear.

The epitome of heteronomous housing is the residential high-rise. People do not build high-rises for themselves; only large-scale construction companies can do so. Surprisingly, these buildings are extremely expensive forms of housing in a strictly economic sense. This may seem strange, since they are the essence of concentrated development and they are cheaper to service, as I have demonstrated. Let us see why this is so.

Land cost per unit for high-rise dwellings is drastically reduced from fifty percent or more for a single-family dwelling unit to five or ten percent. The resulting cost to the buyer of the actual housing unit is less than that of a new home in the suburbs, but it is far from cheap when one considers that high-rises are often the *only* form of high-density housing which developers want to build or even which municipalities permit (this is changing). A careful look at Table 14 shows that at thirty units per acre (not all that high a density), walk-up apartments are slightly cheaper to service than high-rises. This suggests that density, not the form of building, is what makes municipal services less expensive to provide. But our obeisance to the Le Corbusier tradition of huge towers surrounded by acres of open green space has put us to sleep. Peter Spurr, a researcher for Canada Mortgage and Housing Corporation, reports that medium-density walk-up apartments are the cheapest form of housing: "At a given expenditure, housing can be provided in duplex, triplex or walk-up forms, for about 10% more people than could be provided in row houses, 20% more than in detached houses and nearly 60% more than in elevator apartments. In terms of land use, the medium densities accommodate twice the population per acre that detached houses provide, at one half the intensity of use associated with high-rise buildings. Land costs, per capita, in duplex, triplex and walk-up apartment buildings are 30% lower than in row houses, 40% lower than in single and semi-detached houses, and 55% lower than in elevator apartments."

Spurr goes on to say that operating and maintenance costs are greater in elevator apartments as well. Oscar Newman, whose work on the social costs of high-rises will be reviewed in chapter 3, reports on a study of development and maintenance costs by the Housing Development Administration of New York City, which compared three-storey, three-family homes with state-subsidized high-rise buildings, both at fifty units per acre. This similar density of different housing types is achieved by zoning laws which insist that high rises be surrounded (as Le Corbusier dictated) by broad stretches of landscaping and open space. The cost per room of the high-rise was us $30,400 and of the three-family home, $17,650 (1987 dollars). Maintenance was $512 and $345 per room respectively. Newman continues: "The savings in the maintenance costs of the three-family homes were attributed to several factors, among them the willingness and ability of homeowners to make small repairs, the absence of large common circulation areas that require cleaning and maintenance, and the absence of elevators and other complex systems such as garbage chutes which require that repair work be done by expensive experts."

Thus, aside from the actual construction and land costs, high-rises, because they are so big, are expensive to maintain. It is easier to cover up cheap construction methods in a large building, and when things go wrong, which is often, they go wrong in a big way. Co-op City is a good example. It cost $413 million to build this development for fifty-five thousand people in the mid-1960s, but hundreds of millions have been spent on it since in cost overruns, carrying charges, and construction problems. By the early 1980s it needed at least $150 million (1982 dollars) in repairs. Roberta Gratz reports that by 1986, "four hundred apartments were vacant due to major mistakes allegedly covered up by contractor payoffs to building personnel, $140 million additional state money was needed for construction repairs, $150 million was owed the state in back mortgage payments, and tenants faced a 31% increase in carrying charges over five years."

Gratz puts the economic costs of large buildings nicely:

Today one marvels at the conversions of old buildings that are now offices and residences or both. Office buildings are apartment houses, mansions are office buildings, manufacturing lofts are apartments, tenement apartments are small factories, everything from a barge to a barn is a restaurant, and even a granary has become a hotel. These buildings were not designed with flexibility in mind, but their manageable scale provided inherent adjustability and their design and quality construction provided inherent appeal. Is it possible to even imagine an alternative use for any of the sterile monsters of today that could well be the white elephants of tomorrow? The rigidity of the urban fabric now being created and the overwhelming scale of some of its highly publicized new buildings precludes even a semblance of the kind of flexibility required to weather economic ups and downs and systemic change.

The reverse of the large-scale expensiveness typified by the high-rise would be small-scale housing one finds especially in the old, larger houses of central cities in eastern North America. This type of accommodation appears to be cheaper per square foot than almost any other housing. Much inner-city housing consists of big old houses which are owner-occupied, but appreciable portions of which are rented out. The system produces cheaper housing for a number of reasons. First, the owner and tenants usually make their own repairs and share in the maintenance of the building, rather than hiring a firm to do it for them, as in bigger buildings which are not owner-occupied. Because of greater face-to-face contact between landlord and tenant, there is less chance of default on the rent, and a tenant who does default is less likely to become the target of expensive legal procedures. The vandalism and theft so prevalent in high-rises are significantly reduced because occupants take pride in their residence and because it is easier for them to keep watch on the public and semi-public environment of small-scale living quarters. There are no elevators to build and fix or to be vandalized. Word of mouth finds a tenant for the owner, rather than advertisements in the newspaper. Numerous services, then, which must be part of the national monetary system when it comes to large structures, are performed as services in kind of this "other economy," as it is called by some Canadian researchers. The housing need not be old, as Newman and Spurr have already indicated; scale is more important.

The costs of housing in the postwar city are higher for a third reason, which is more difficult to pin down. As bigger and bigger subdivisions of exclusively residential housing were built, different homes took on subtly different meanings because of their prices. A few thousand dollars would represent the difference between the salary of a junior executive and that, say, of a mid-level executive, or that of a foreman in an automobile plant. As people's salaries and families changed, their aspiration was not to add on to their old house, but to move to a new one which had been built especially for someone of their salary and price range. They were encouraged in this move by zoning laws which made it difficult to get permission to do too much to the outside of their homes in "exclusive" residential subdivisions.

Whether or not all this produced some peculiarly homogeneous social mixes is open to debate; what is clear is that it encouraged people to move as their job situation, or financial situation, changed. Real-estate agents know that their livelihood depends on people's ability to sell their houses, so the more people move, the more buying and selling of homes there is, and the greater the commissions paid to real-estate agents. And each time there is the opportunity to raise the price. Sometimes this opportunity is exploited to ridiculous extremes, but in general, mobility means that house prices go up faster. This costly mobility, then, is in part the function of vast residential subdivisions whose only form of diversity is the stylistic one of "Cape Cod" versus "Colonial," which differ in price and number of bedrooms, slightly. There is no special, non-residential attraction to keep people there and encourage them to adapt the house to new needs.

To summarize, housing is more expensive in the postwar North American city because of its newness, its deconcentration and segregated nature, and, especially, its scale. To concentrate only on the dollar cost is, of course, one-sided; among other things, the system has produced a great deal of homelessness as well. Nevertheless, we need to be aware of its outrageous economic costs.

RETAIL AND MANUFACTURING

Before turning from the economic costs of the North American city, one should reflect a moment on how much its form of development has cost business itself – costs which are usually passed on to the consumer, or to the economy as a whole. The large-scale, homogeneous projects are very expensive to build, even when worked out according to the square foot. The evidence of Spurr and Newman has already been presented with respect to residential high-rises, but the principle holds for all large-scale projects: they are built because they are profitable for the developer, not because they are cheaper. The bigger the skyscraper, reports Kirkpatrick Sale, "the more costly, less efficient, less adaptive, less safe" it is. He points to the John Hancock Life Insurance building in Boston, whose glass sheathing would pop out in the wind and land on people on the sidewalks below. It "took some six years and at least $20 million to correct, and even then the company had a 24-hour crew of guards peering through binoculars ... to see where the next window was about to come loose."

Whether the large-scale project is an office building, a shopping centre, a factory, or a planned community, argue Logan and Molotch,

extraordinary resources are needed to acquire large and expensive sites, to hire consultants, and to develop "up-front" infrastructures. Complex projects must be maneuvered through government agencies, public hearings, and environmental report procedures. At least lip service must be paid to problems of natural environment, urban architecture, and historic significance of sites. Skilled hands must be available to pull in maximum subsidies from various governments and to make local publics feel good about them. A track record of past accomplishments helps convince local authorities of the investors' ability to complete the project, and to deliver the promised financial results – especially if tax abatements or other special incentives are part of the deal.

Finally, capital brings to the property business a marketing strategy that, taking advantage of the peculiar conditions of real estate markets ... leads to the pricing of rental space at maximum rates.

In many downtowns, these large-scale, multi-million-dollar projects have led to massive wastes of money. The Tower City Project in Cleveland, which was announced as costing $279 million in 1974, and which benefitted from government infrastructure grants of close to $100 million, had an "uncertain" future fourteen years after its inception because of competition from other large (and subsidized) private developments in the downtown. The $75 million Grand Avenue project in Milwaukee, over forty percent of which was paid for by government money, opened in 1982; by 1987 its financial status was still "unclear." The Broadway Project in Louisville – for which, again, private developers received millions from the city government – has also bombed: "Original projections of a positive cash flow by 1987 have proved incorrect."

Even while private corporations were getting into trouble downtown, shopping centres on the fringes of cities were earning their developers enormous amounts of money in both the US and Canada, with the costs being borne by the consumers. The shopping centre is a good example of expensive, large-scale, segregated land use: thirty, forty, a hundred and fifty shops and stores surrounded by veritable prairies of parking. The costs to the consumers – for example, how far they have to drive – may not be obvious, but goods in shopping centres are more expensive. This is because they are run by developers who are out to make a profit, in contrast to individual shopkeepers, who handle the rent situation themselves at locations they can afford. Only high-volume, conventional chains can afford the pricey rents charged by shopping centres. The shopping centres' success at enclosing themselves and controlling the internal spatial environment enables them to charge monopolistic rents which are translated, of course, into higher prices. With their own private police forces, they can minimize security problems inherent in segregated, deconcentrated land use (see chapter 3) in much the same ways as luxury condominiums with their array of sophisticated human and electronic surveillance systems.

A longer term cost of North America's preoccupation with new, deconcentrated industrial and commercial land use is the loss of innovation. Businesses that are already going concerns can afford to locate in the fancy new places, but, says Jane Jacobs, "as for really new ideas of any kind – no matter how ultimately profitable or otherwise successful some of them might be – there is no leeway for ... chancy trial and error and experimentation in the high-overhead economy of new construction. Old ideas can sometimes use new buildings. New ideas must use old buildings."

The urban economist Wilbur Thompson echoes Jacobs in his criticism of urban renewal: "The razing of cheap manufacturing loft space serves to eliminate the small job shops and the shaky new businesses that have long been the staple of core manufacturing activity." North America's decline and the ascendance of other nations in the share of the world's manufacturing cannot be blamed solely on the demolition of old garages, but wholesale destruction of smaller buildings and construction of large-scale new ones surely cannot have helped.

Certain qualifications have been made to this theory of incubation, as it is sometimes called. The geographer Allen J. Scott says the biological metaphor is "disastrous." Yet his critique centres around the "post-incubation" period, when firms may grow in size and yet organize their location strategies to use small-scale firms for special materials and cheap, non-union labour. Jacobs' central point still stands: *new* firms need, nearby, a multitude of services and materials they cannot provide for themselves, as well as smaller, older buildings.

Another qualification could be that the new commercial and industrial parks being built on cheap land in the suburbs can sometimes offer small enterprises lower rents than downtown. Perhaps here the basis for creative new businesses can be laid. Because of these parks' spread-out form, however, they discourage the kind of interaction which is as essential to businesses as it is to social life.

In general, the large firm, whether it is a "multi-establishment" firm, to use Scott's phrase, or one monolithic implantation, is characterized by (a) lack of interest in the community's economic health,

(b) reliance more on capital than on labour, (c) absentee ownership, which goes with (a), and (d) imposition of greater disaster on the community when it closes down. Considerable research has shown that it is the smaller, homegrown firms that create most of the jobs in our economy. Thus, the physical presence of big companies makes bad economic sense to cities on many levels, even though they are usually welcomed ecstatically as the bringers of jobs. It does not seem inevitable that such companies end up housing themselves in the urban landscape in large, homogeneous structures, given the careful research of geographers like Scott. My argument is that, at present, in every city on the continent, we see hundreds of new, large-scale developments built by big corporations, and that these developments tend to exclude creative little enterprises in need of cheap rent and external services and support. New ideas need old buildings.

It is not easy to quantify the cost of innovations that were never made, inventions that were never invented, or businesses that never got started. But cheap space is essential to the incubation of new ideas, and ultimately to the vitality of the economy. North American urban development is not encouraging them: it is stamping them out.

CONCLUSIONS

Our cities do not make economic sense. No attempt has been made to add up all the costs enumerated in this chapter, but its message should be clear: we are squandering billions of dollars in North America because our built environment lacks judicious amounts of concentrated land use, small-scale land-use mix, and mixtures of old and new buildings – in short, it lacks physical diversity.

Admittedly, this flies in the face of conventional indices of economic success, which highlight how many housing units or miles of highway have been built. These indices are reflections of our fascination with growth in any form, and they do not give a true picture of economic health. In fact, economic growth in general, whether connected to cities or not, has been shown to carry "significant costs to our health and safety": it "makes our working lives unhappy (for all we might gain in quality of life as consumers, we lose as producers), fails to bring about greater equality, and actually represents a desperate and futile attempt to compensate for psychological and social deficiencies." By concentrating our attention on growth as an indicator of economic health, we have convinced ourselves that something can work economically, but not socially or ecologically. If something seems to work economically but not socially, we see it as forcing us to choose between the economic value and the social value. Further, we have somehow concluded that the economic measuring stick is the most important; if we have justified something economically, we have justified it, period. "That's the market," we say. Or, "You can't argue with dollars and sense."

This is nonsense. It is obvious that both governments and individuals always seem to come up with money for the things they really want. The truth is that the dilemma of choosing between economic and social values is a false one. If we find ourselves in such a dilemma, it signals a need to reconsider our understanding of economics and society. In fact, economic and social values interpenetrate, so that if cities work economically, they will also work socially.

In this chapter I have argued that our cities' lack of diversity has involved us in an extravagant transportation system, life-threatening levels of pollution, a needlessly large infrastructure of utilities such as water mains and trunk sewers, and significantly more expensive housing and consumer goods. In chapters 3, 4, and 5, it will be demonstrated that lack of physical diversity has also created social and political problems. However, I do not end up by pointing to physical design as the crucial connecting link in a causal chain. At this juncture, the point is to stress that the economically wasteful built environment is also socially and politically harmful, and that this is not a coincidence. Economic and social health are inextricably related, and the physical structure of our cities reflects and reinforces them. I am concentrating on the impact of the built environment because we deny that impact, or simply remain unaware of it.

CHAPTER THREE

The Social Consequences of the New North American City

THE SUBURBS

The physically reality of the new North American city influences our social life in ways we are just beginning to understand. The postwar explosion of the suburbs, for instance, was more than just a shift in housing type towards single-family units or in location towards the periphery of the city. Suburbanization was a social process as well, with social values as antecedents and social behaviour as its consequence. The debate over the suburbs is a good background to a consideration of the overall social meaning of deconcentration, segregation of land use, long blocks, and large areas of new development.

"You'll know our house because our picture window is the only one on the block without a budgie cage." Lame jokes like this were common in the fifties and sixties, as millions of North Americans moved into look-alike homes on the fringes of cities. Hundreds of armchair sociologists and feature writers have excoriated this characteristic of modern life. The aesthetic judgment of many people about the purely physical face of the suburbs was plainly negative. Malvina Reynolds' song "Little Boxes" expressed it well:

Little boxes on the hillside, little boxes made of ticky tacky,
Little boxes on the hillside, little boxes all the same.
There's a green one and a pink one and a blue one and a yellow one,
And they're all made out of ticky tacky and they all look just the same.

More intellectual but no less negative critiques of suburban culture were made by a number of eminent scholars. The criticisms, as summarized by Peter Hall, went something like this:

The new suburbia ... offers only homogeneity and conformity. Because population densities are low, the possibilities for fruitful human interaction are much reduced. Even the quality of material life, in the range of shopping goods and entertainments available, is impoverished and standardized. Because the new subdivisions are inhabited by people of the same age, education, and social background, the awareness of different life styles and possibilities is atrophied. Because social relationships are restricted to the immediate neighbourhood, there is a premium on conformity and a fear of the unusual and the unknown. Because the population is transient, without roots, moving on always to the next rung of the status ladder, the society lacks the social cement that fixes standards, and readily tends to delinquency.

David Reisman (*The Lonely Crowd*) and William H. Whyte (*The Organization Man*) were among those associated with this view.

But other intellectuals defended the suburbs. The stereotype of the bland suburban culture was subjected to intense scrutiny by a new generation of sociologists, some of whom took up residence in the communities they studied and thus seemed all the more persuasive. One of these sociologists, Herbert Gans, compared the social life of those who moved into a large US suburb, Levittown, New Jersey, with their life before the move. He found that few of the changes in their ways of life could "be traced to the suburban qualities of Levittown, and the sources that did cause change, like the house, the population mix, and the newness, [were] not distinctively suburban." The policy implications for Gans were clear. He had already concluded in 1961 that "the planner has only limited influence over social relationships. Although the site planner can create propinquity, he can only determine which houses are to be adjacent. He can thus affect visual contacts and initial social contacts among their occupants, but he cannot determine the intensity or quality of the relationships. This depends on the characteristics of the people involved." Thus, for Gans, public policy might play around with urban design, but it could not thereby solve social problems. A corollary to this was that the suburbs as a physical entity had no appreciable effects on the quality of social or cultural life, as the critics had charged.

Finding no relationship at all between the suburban environment and behaviour was a way of short-circuiting the argument that suburbs had an undesirable effect on their inhabitants. Other than arguing simply that suburban residents seemed fairly happy with their new homes, defenders of the suburbs denied that the built environment had any significance for attitudes or behaviour patterns. Gans' argument was part of a larger body of work by planners, sociologists, and political economists disillusioned by the negative results of the United States' urban-renewal and public-housing programs, which were spectacularly unsuccessful from a social perspective. Protesting almost too much, Nathan Glazer wrote in 1965, "We must root out of our thinking the assumption that the physical form of our communities has social consequences." Jane Jacobs' reasoning that physical diversity – notably absent in the suburbs – helped neighbour interaction and decreased criminal activity, for instance, was labelled by Gans as "physical determinism" and therefore a "fallacy." In any case, it was the pro-suburbanites who were arguing that people were relatively independent of their physical environment, and the anti-suburbanites who were arguing the opposite. It was not always this way, however. At the turn of the century, Ebenezer Howard and other planners were insisting that the industrial city was ruining the English working class, and that only well-planned "Garden Cities" on the metropolis' periphery could provide an environment conducive to "life-maintaining functions of its inhabitants."

Despite Glazer's and Gans' protestations, then, and despite a legacy of playing down the importance of the physical environment which stretches back among sociologists at least to Durkheim, interest in the influence of the built environment keeps resurfacing, especially in the field known as the sociology of housing. It is probably time to acknowledge that some connection does exist, that our surroundings could have desirable as well as undesirable effects, and even that we may be unaware of many of those effects. We also have to deal with the reality that we ourselves – our society, our culture – have produced this environment, so that it is a reflection of our values.

The debate over the suburbs has died, perhaps because their novelty has worn off – most of us live there now – and perhaps because their greater social and physical diversity has made it more difficult to generalize about them. Whatever the reasons, the issues raised by the controversy are not trivial. To put it in a nutshell, the question has to be asked whether the physical characteristics of the postwar urban environment, including those of the suburbs, influence our social behaviour, and if so, whether they do it in desirable or undesirable ways. At some point, too, it must be asked whether that environment reflects desirable attitudes in its users and builders towards social behaviour.

While the nature of the physical postwar environment has been fairly easy to pin down, what constitutes a desirable influence has no straight answer. The debate over the suburbs is a good example: just as millions of Americans and Canadians were achieving the dream of a single-family house far from the noise and crowds of the central city, scholars and journalists were producing streams of criticism on the vacuity and conformity of suburban life. The implication is that we have built ourselves a residential environment that we think we want, but which in fact is something we do not – or should not – want.

This implication is pursued in a fascinating book by Richard Sennett, called *The Uses of Disorder*. One of Sennett's themes is that when, as adolescents, we are forming our adult personality, our predisposition is to strive for purity of self-image. The real world constantly intrudes on this purity, argues Sennett, and we end up learning to make some sort of compromise between what we would like to be, and what we think living in society demands of us. The immense wealth of postwar North Americans enabled them to realize the adolescent striving for a pure residential environment, which shielded its occupants from the rough-and-tumble intrusions of urban diversity – the taverns and drunks, extremes of wealth, noisy public celebrations, tacky-looking second-hand stores, and industrial pollution.

North Americans bought what they wanted, namely, exclusively residential areas, but it cost them more than money, according to observers such as Sennett. The exclusionary process removed them, at least temporarily, from a sense of responsibility for drunks or for extremes of wealth, from having to make difficult choices in the politics and civic management of the central city. Suburbs, Theodore Lowi has said, represent a failure of citizenship. We have removed ourselves not only from the responsibilities of civic participation but also from the challenges of social relations by zoning poor families out of our neighbourhoods. The social and political skills of adults have declined; we have lost the ability, at a personal level, to say how we feel, to negotiate, to solve problems creatively – in short, to be publicly responsive individuals. How accurate this assessment is will be explored later. But, basically, Lowi and Sennett are suggesting that ignoring difficult civic choices has political and social costs. It seems that there are some decidedly undesirable aspects to this fulfillment of the North American dream.

By getting "what we want" we have something that we do not want. Do we really know what we want?

My answer to that question begins with an exploration of the relations between the features of the new North American city and our social and psychological behaviour. More specifically, evidence will be presented which suggests that urban areas with mixed land use, concentration of land use, short blocks, and a mixture of old and new buildings are a socially more desirable environment than what is currently being built in and around the North American city. This evidence comes in part from my study of Toronto neighbourhoods of varying physical characteristics. In the study, social desirability was measured in a number of ways: likes and dislikes of residents, friendship and neighbouring patterns, and crime.

LIKES AND DISLIKES

Using as an indicator whether or not people say they like their urban environment may sound a bit circular in light of the foregoing: if we do not know what we want, can we put stock in what we say we like? Not entirely; but that is only because our perceived desires are often in conflict with each other.

Students of urban neighbourhoods are trying to disentangle people's more basic and practical needs from their feelings about the fuzzy, overadvertised concept of the Good Neighbourhood. This is hardly a value-free enterprise, but it is a step in the right direction. Typically, researchers try to identify both "objective" and "subjective" criteria for assessment, such as convenience to jobs, shopping, recreation, and friends, as well as feelings of safety and security. In these endeavours, satisfaction with urban aesthetics is usually discounted. Here is a particularly hard-line example:

There are elaborate defenses for building the beautiful city ... The fact is, of course, that convincing ones do not exist ... Modern social scientists might ... be able to ... determine what kind of measurable social benefits arise from urban beauty, and how much, if at all, they compensate for the failure to enjoy other social benefits.

But we do not have such studies today. We do not know how much edge would be taken off Watts if Copenhagen's Tivoli Gardens or London's Green Park were near at hand. The suspicion is, not much.

Because the influence of urban beauty is considered impossible to measure in social or economic terms, it is not taken seriously. It is worth asking what the existence of a Tivoli Gardens or a Los Angeles slum implies about the community that would produce it. In fact, beauty, in cities as in nature, emerges unselfconsciously from harmony of purpose. To write about whether beauty can cause social benefits is to ignore the significance of the reciprocity between what we say we like or enjoy, and what we end up doing. Each influences the other.

The issue of what citizens like and dislike about the North American city, even to the extent that they might call it beautiful, does not, of course, revolve around trees and subway art, as the quotation suggests. But the quotation does highlight a central problem: the false dichotomy between objective and subjective evaluations of cities and neighbourhoods. I say false because so-called objective indicators of neighbourhood quality are actually chosen by social scientists for subjective reasons. These reasons vary from ease of measurement to acceptability according to conventional wisdom. In a recent study by Craig St John of evaluation of neighbourhood quality, the "objective" indicators were defined as the median income of households, the percentage of owner-occupied housing units, and the percentage of college graduates. These are economic indicators. In our culture, they tend to be considered external and therefore objective measures; in fact, we are blind to the extent to which they are embedded in our social and cultural values. The researcher in this study is merely reflecting society's preoccupation with economic goals in using economic indicators of neighbourhood quality. As the psychological and ecological costs of this preoccupation rise, it becomes more obvious how arbitrary and value-laden the choice of indicators is. In a very real sense, social scientists are trying to express the whole culture's subjective likes and dislikes through their use of "objective" indicators.

It is clear that likes and dislikes of urban citizens, and of social scientists, are essentially psychological phenomena. They are the mind's reactions to the city's excitement, crime, beauty, wealth, poverty, and noise. These phenomena are prior to social, economic, and ecological behaviour. It is not simply a question of whether something like urban diversity or civic beauty pleases our minds, but whether our minds are all that important in this context.

Once the issue is put that way, it becomes clear that if we want to understand the city, we must first understand our personal interactions with it. It is personality that makes us more than behavioural units. Not only does it filter our perceptions of the so-called objective world; it is basic to our sense of well-being and to the way we act in and on the world.

An inquiry into how individuals evaluate their urban environment, then, really leads to the broader question of how our personalities interact with the environment. The most basic dimension of our relations with our environment is simply the extent to which we are aware of it. Environments can be more or less stimulating, as will be stressed, but we can choose to be more or less interested in our environments. What people like or dislike about the city is a clue to their personal relations with it, relations which also might include the symbolic richness of their interaction, or the degree of their own indifference or alienation.

The study of the interaction between the physical environment and our personalities has spawned dozens of complex theoretical schemes. My perspective in this book is relatively simple, namely, the influence of specific physical features of the North American city on significant aspects of North Americans' individual psyches: the stimulation of intelligence, a sense of orientation, a sense of personal identity, and specific sources of satisfaction or dissatisfaction with the neighbourhood. These are admittedly non-systematic categories – they are not mutually exclusive, for instance – but they cover enough ground to give an intuitive idea of the psychological implications of physical diversity as defined in this book.

Stimulation of intelligence.   The mind is like a muscle. If you exercise the muscle, it gets stronger. If the mind is stimulated by many different kinds of surroundings, it too gets stronger. Alfred Eide Parr has explored this idea in his writings: "Just as our bodies need food and exercise to grow strong and healthy, so does our brain need an adequate sensory intake and stimulation for its optimum development. And the measure of our perceptual diet is obviously not just how much we perceive, but how many significantly different images our senses transmit to our minds – in other words, the diversity rather than the repetitive quantity of our experience." Parr cites psychologists whose experiments show that diverse environments help adults to cope better with change, and infants to attain higher levels of intelligence. There is a natural aversion to places with no potential for exercising the mind. People avoid surroundings which are monotonous, and which therefore give them no opportunity to exercise their intelligence. Jacobs has observed that even when huge apartment projects have abundant criss-crossing paths, they are empty of people because "all their scenes are essentially the same."

Sense of orientation.   The monotony of sameness has a peculiar impact on the mind in another sense. As Jacobs points out, "superficially, this monotony might be thought of as a sort of order, however dull. But aesthetically, it unfortunately carries with it a deep disorder: the disorder of conveying no direction ... This is a kind of chaos." It is instructive to notice here the link between aesthetics, so often casually dismissed in deference to "harder" social and economic indicators, and the sense of well-being on a psychological level. This is not a trivial link, however hard it may be to measure. And the chaos referred to by Jacobs is everywhere in the modern city: suburbs with look-alike streets, office districts with look-alike office buildings, and shopping centres with look-alike stores.

When everything looks similar it is hard to have a clear image of different parts of the city. The physical personality of the city and its identification by residents have been explored by Kevin Lynch in his book *The Image of the City*. Lynch defines the elements of a person's image of his or her city – landmarks, edges, nodes, paths, districts – and weighs the "imageability" of three different US cities. Although his dispassionate way of discussing feelings is disconcerting, Lynch demonstrates that people are happier when they have a clear image of the city around them than when they do not.

Sense of personal identity.   Diversity, or its absence, has particular relevance to our habitual haunts. Our own niche is far more satisfying when it has a unique personality: "That sense of security which flows from identification with a personal niche in the general milieu ... is essential for a reasonably happy existence. Such identification depends upon a certain amount of physical distinction of the nook that is mine and the trail that leads to it." This sense of individuality is not something which can be just designed into a building. It is also something which a person has to give to his or her environment, in an active way. Several architects have done much creative thinking about patterns of relations between our psyches and the physical environment; an important theme emerging from their writings is the wide differences in meaning attached to the built environment by the designer on the one hand and the user on the other. These insights came from observations where the designer and the user were often the same person, a rare occurrence in North American cities in the 1990s. These architects stress that we are building – more accurately, allowing others to build – urban environments which are unmanipulable: the users are behavioural units for whom the city is designed and they are not expected to be active creators of their own environment. In a sense, then, they are denied a means of expressing their identity.

The usual whipping-boy is the high-rise apartment, whose identical cubicles frustrate any of the occupants' attempts at individuality. Some studies of high-rise living have found little evidence among residents of significantly higher crime rates (crimes are often found to have been committed by non-residents), mental disorder, social isolation, or even complaints. Yet despite such general conclusions, one of the studies, by Wellman and Whittaker, reports that high-rise dwellers are "less satisfied with their dwelling and their neighbourhood than are low-rise residents" (see Table 17). Mehrabian reports on a study of British soldiers and their families who had been placed at random in high-rises and in single-family dwellings. Researchers found that those "in high-rises had 57% more neuroses. Furthermore, those living in the upper apartments of high-rises were more neurotic, less satisfied, and had fewer friends."

Table 17
Satisfaction with housing and neighbourhood by type of dwelling

	Low-rise dwelling (single family)	High-rise dwelling
Satisfied with housing?		
very much	73%	40%
fairly well	21	44
Satisfied with neighbourhood?		
very much	69%	50%
fairly well	28	43
	N = 488	N = 190

Source: Barry Wellman and Marilyn Whittaker, *High-Rise, Low-Rise: The Effects of High Density Living* (Toronto: Centre for Urban and Community Studies, University of Toronto, January 1974).

The identical nature of suburban housing and of high-rise "units" is not by itself the source of an unhealthy relationship between ourselves and our dwellings. It is not, in other words, just a question of a negative aesthetic evaluation pronounced from a distance. The problem is that units are not only identical but also relatively impervious to change. Residents are unable to modify or rearrange housing and its environs into an active expression of their individuality. It is one thing to move into a community knowing that its Architectural Committee will probably question your planting strawberries in your front yard; it is quite another to be a high-rise resident who could not conceive of modifying his or her unit except by what can be carried into (and out of) that unit. The authoritarian designs say "Don't tamper with me," and sooner or later external structures become internalized so that North Americans do not realize the extent to which they have given up this dimension of personal expression. This is a political as well as an architectural problem and is explored in chapter 5. It takes an iconoclast like Tom Wolfe to make it all right to be publicly enraged by modern urban architecture:

But after 1945 our plutocrats, bureaucrats, board chairmen, CEOs, commissioners, and college presidents undergo an inexplicable change. They become diffident and reticent. All at once they are willing to accept that glass of ice water in the face, that bracing slap across the mouth, that reprimand for the fat on one's bourgeois soul known as modern architecture.

And why? They can't tell you. They look up at the barefaced buildings they have bought, those great hulking structures they hate so thoroughly, and they can't figure it out themselves. It makes their heads hurt.

This is very well stated; we must be uncertain about our identity if we accept buildings we hate.

Sources of satisfaction and dissatisfaction.   When considered this way, the problem of identity seems in part to be a problem of being aware of what one instinctively feels is right in one's environment. Although millions of people live in high-rises and suburbs whose monotony is distinctly unpleasant, they are unable to pinpoint why. It is hard for us to put into words what our environment means to us – Torontonians living in physically homogeneous neighbourhoods, for instance, were likely to say that those neighbourhoods were boring to them, but could not say how.

From Ebenezer Howard on, though, there has been no shortage of words to describe the many advantages of the suburban physical environment. In real-estate advertisements and planning documents, spread-out, exclusively residential suburbs are accorded generous amounts of environmental sex appeal. It is not surprising that a major theme in studies of suburbanites is the extent to which they see themselves as refugees from the downtown dirt, noise, and crowds. Sociologists like S.D. Clark in Toronto and Herbert Gans in Levittown did find this feeling among some of the people they interviewed. However, the general impression conveyed by the most careful research is that dirt, noise, and crowds are seldom the main reason for moving. As the housing advertisements suggest, the symbolic meaning of the suburbs is more important than what people actually find when they move there. For instance, even when the air in the suburb is demonstrably dirty, residents have been known to say that they like their single-family detached homes because they provide cleaner air. It seems that people are influenced by advertisements and abstract planning principles rather than relying on their own senses.

It was with the expectation that urban residents would be unaware of how they are influenced by features of their urban environment that I began my study of nineteen areas in Toronto. I compared what different people said they liked about their neighbourhoods, which ranged from the physically diverse to the physically homogeneous, in the hope of finding indirect evidence about the influence of city design on residents' feelings about their localities. The diverse areas were chosen according to Jacobs' generators of diversity: they had a concentration of all kinds of uses (residential, commercial, recreational), mixed land uses, short blocks, and a mixture of old and new buildings. The more physically homogeneous the area, the less these features were present.

One of the first things to emerge from the residents' responses was that those in the homogeneous areas were happier with what might be called their area's cosmetics than were residents of the more diverse areas. In fact, amenities such as trees, grass, a nearby park, or something beyond ho-hum landscaping were scarcer in the physically

diverse neighbourhoods. This connection between diversity and dis-
liking an area's cosmetics did not tell the whole story, however, for it
turned out that richer people lived in the less diverse areas, while
poorer people lived in the more diverse areas. Just as Sennett has
argued, then, the wealthier people can afford to move to "desirable"
areas, where desirability is not defined by physical diversity but by
lot size and the amount of greenery. (This is also what urban beauty
seems to mean to people who think only in terms of its social benefits.)

People were asked in a general way what they liked about living in
their areas. They mentioned many things: the degree of safety for
children and adults, the kind of people, the reasonableness of rents,
the noise level, or the amount of traffic. Almost everyone said his or
her neighbourhood was "convenient," no matter how isolated the area
was. And many respondents firmly stated that the main thing they
liked was that "everyone minds their own business." When they were
prompted to list their dislikes, similar criteria emerged. In addition,
there were comments about the lack of greenery, sloppy garbage habits, boredom, and poor shopping.

It was hard to make straightforward comparisons among the different areas for a number of reasons. For instance, in areas with a
higher socio-economic status, people were apt to be more at ease with
the middle-class interviewers and to talk more. Both the total number
of criteria and the total number of positive comments were higher
in these areas. To get some idea of the balance between likes and
dislikes across all of the areas, I subtracted the total number of things
disliked from the total number of things liked, and used the difference as a general measure of how much the area was liked. The
predominance of likes over dislikes was far more pronounced in the
neighbourhoods with greater physical diversity, despite their rather
scruffy appearance. In other words, conventional urban prettiness –
lots of open space, trees, and parkland – did not go hand in hand
with overall satisfaction.

Here is a clue, then, as to why aesthetic evaluations are so often
criticized as idealistic and impractical: attractiveness is narrowly conceived as open space, trees, and grass. A vital, working urban neighbourhood may not win any prizes in an urban beauty contest, but it
provides feelings of satisfaction by means other than space, trees, and
grass. And when these amenities are present, diversity gives them a
meaning which connects them to the rest of the neighbourhood.

Although some of the likes and dislikes of the residents could be
labelled economic (rent levels, proximity to job) or social (approval
of neighbours), others related to what Parr called psychic stimulation,
such as complaints of boredom or of poor shopping, or praise for

Figure 4
Toronto child's picture of his street

the interesting shops and people. At other levels of the psyche, the actual meanings of different features of the environment were not expressed by adults in their verbal responses to questionnaires, but children's pictures proved to be eloquent witnesses to the environment's personality. The picture in Figure 4 was drawn by a 6th grader of his street in midtown Toronto. Half the street is lined with high rises, and it is one way, used as a rush hour shortcut by many drivers.

One other factor, which has social, aesthetic, and economic dimensions, was mentioned by many people in certain neighbourhoods: density. Almost everyone seemed to dislike high density. This factor has attracted attention from researchers interested more in testing the theory that high density living is unhealthy than in testing whether people actually liked living in areas of concentrated land use. The specific question of crime and density will be considered a bit later in this chapter; for the moment, it should simply be noted that at least some analysts have been very cautious about or even opposed to the idea that high-density living has pathological consequences. But there is evidence that both density and crowding are connected to people's dissatisfaction with their urban environment.* External measurements of density and individuals' personal experiences of crowding are different things, of course. Whether one feels crowded is dependent on more than just some ratio of people to space. More significantly, however, both density and crowding are two-edged swords – they intensify the good as well as the bad: "Sitting in a doctor's waiting room, taking a test in a class, waiting in line at an airport, or travelling in the New York subway are usually unpleasant experiences, but most people would agree that crowding makes them even more unpleasant. In contrast, watching a football game or play, riding on a cable car in San Francisco, spending a day at an amusement park, and attending a cocktail party are pleasant experiences and for most people are made more enjoyable when the density of people is fairly high."

Recognizing the contingent nature of density is one of the most important steps forward made in the last few years. This recognition, in turn, has led analysts to study density in connection with other features of the situation, including other physical features of the city.

The findings about Toronto areas supported the value of this perspective. Many people complained about crowding, and, as might be expected, those people tended to live in densely populated areas. However, where concentration of use was combined with mixed land use, short blocks, and a mixture of old and new buildings, this relationship between density and feelings of being crowded disappeared. Now, the North American city has many areas of relatively concentrated land use, even though its pattern has been to spread itself out. These parts of the city have residential high-rises and office buildings. They are mostly all new and they have homogeneous land uses, so the unpleasant features of high density are unrelieved. People are almost sure to feel crowded. This expectation was borne out in the Toronto study. People living in high-rises were much more critical of their area's densities than people living in other densely populated parts of the city.

---

* A distinction is sometimes made between density and crowding: density is a measure of people or dwellings per acre of land, while crowding is a measure of people per room.

To recapitulate for a moment, a number of points have emerged about the personal interactions of individuals with the physical side of their urban surroundings: (1) the importance to mental growth of a lively give and take between the psyche and a diverse environment; (2) the importance of feeling clearly oriented to the physical layout of the city; (3) the sense of well-being and identity in having one's own unique physical niche; (4) the inability of many people to put into words what it is that disturbs them about a monotonous, unmanipulable physical environment; (5) the oft-stated preference for a diverse environment, regardless of much general evidence that people "like" living in exclusively residential areas; and (6) the attractiveness of concentrated use when combined with small-scale mixed land use, short blocks, and a mix of old and new buildings.

FRIENDSHIP PATTERNS

These personal responses to the urban environment serve as the groundwork for consideration of social responses to the design of cities. In fact, it means little to speak of purely individual connections to the environment. Native people, significantly, have always recognized that if we feel close to the natural environment we feel close to each other. Chief Standing Bear speaks of the Lakota:

The Lakota was a true naturist – a lover of nature. He loved the earth and all things of the earth, the attachment growing with age. The old people came literally to love the soil and they sat or reclined on the ground with a feeling of being close to a mothering power ...

That is why the old Indian still sits upon the earth instead of propping himself up and away from its life-giving forces. For him, to sit or lie upon the ground is to be able to think more deeply and to feel more keenly; he can see more clearly into the mysteries of life and come closer in kinship to other lives about him ...

The old Lakota was wise. He knew that man's heart away from nature becomes hard; he knew that lack of respect for growing, living things soon led to the lack of respect for humans too. So he kept his youth close to its softening influence.

A number of social ecologists maintain that our mistreatment of the natural environment is merely a reflection of how we mistreat each other, that there is a symbiotic link between how we relate to each other and how we relate to our physical environment.

If there is truly such a link, then the practice of urban planning takes on considerable significance. Until the 1950s, urban planners were convinced that social life was intimately related to the quality of physical surroundings. The conviction was bolstered by the rapidity of urban growth in the last one hundred and fifty years. If cities are doubling or tripling in size, or if whole new cities are being built, city planners and builders have the opportunity to play God. (Some grand planners, such as Rexford Tugwell and Ebenezer Howard, advocated the dismantling of existing cities as well.) The nub of it is this: influential urban planners like Frank Lloyd Wright, Le Corbusier, and Patrick Geddes had distinct notions of what economic, political, and social life should be, and their plans for urban development reflected these notions (see chapter 6). Le Corbusier, for instance, says Robert Fishman, "had been raised on William Morris' critique of the anarchic individualism of modern capitalism, its destruction of all sense of communal order, and the consequent ugliness and disorder of the modern city. He ... wanted to find some architectural expression for a unified, co-operative society."

Planners such as Howard and Le Corbusier have been less concerned with personal friendships than with public relationships. Neighbourhoods have been an important focus of this concern; it is felt that designing communities of certain sizes or ones that centre around a certain kind of open space will encourage neighbours to interact with each other and, in the long run, become responsible citizens by participating in public decisions. Many sociologists, as noted above, were extremely negative about any suggestion that physical design could have a social impact, but they were more concerned with private networks of friends than with public relations. For the man or woman on the street, so to speak, this distinction is not that clear; the image of the neighbourhood becomes one where one's neighbours are also one's friends.

Jane Jacobs underlined the significance of casual public contact among neighbours in *The Death and Life of Great American Cities*. Her argument was that physical diversity made neighbour contact more likely and encouraged people to care about what went on in the neighbourhood. She was quite emphatic, however, that in the large city contact between neighbours is formal and regulated by numerous rules which are quite different from those which govern relations among personal friends.

Jacobs and a few others like her were responsible for a renaissance of sentiment for cozy downtown urban neighbourhoods (this gave Jacobs an image she resents); but these same writers, it will be recalled, were criticized by some sociologists for succumbing to the Fallacy of Physical Determinism, a sort of verbal overkill which implied an error in logic rather than a misinterpretation of reality.

Once these sociologists started conducting research into the impact of the built environment on social behaviour, they came up with no strong empirical findings one way or the other – some of them found relationships, and some did not.

In one of the most exhaustive investigations, William Michelson studied what happened to people who moved from houses to apartments and vice versa; he further subdivided his sample into whether the house or apartment was downtown or in the suburbs. He found that new residential contexts such as a suburban high-rise, for example, or a downtown house influenced activities such as organizational behaviour, mutual aid among neighbours, travel habits, and sports participation. Many other traits, though, especially friendship patterns, seemed to be little affected by a move to a new residential setting. Notice that Michelson found that more public types of activities were influenced by changes in neighbourhood.

Michelson was trying to ascertain whether people moving into a given environment – high-rises, for instance – were of a particular type; if this were the case, then one might say that behaviour in high-rises came about because of the people who chose to live there, not because of the physical design of the buildings. This "self-selection" hypothesis, however, which was also tested by Gans in Levittown, has its own logical flaw: high-rises and homogeneous suburbs will attract people by virtue of their physical design, in particular those who are unconcerned about environmental diversity and its influence on one's sense of well-being, whether or not such concern can be articulated. Michelson's concluding assessment was that "our analysis of interpersonal relations among families sampled does not provide strong support for either self-selection or environmental determinism." This pretty well sums up the panoply of findings one can find scattered throughout sociological journals and books.

Yet when the evidence is looked at carefully, the planners' concern with public relationships does seem more promising than the sociologists' tendency to focus on networks of private friends and personal satisfactions. Researchers who have specified the difference have often found that neighbouring, for example, is sensitive to physical surroundings. This makes sense, because, as Jacobs argues, casual acquaintances in the neighbourhood perform place-oriented functions, such as opening communication channels about items of local interest, and making possible assistance in cases of minor need (a ladder or a cup of sugar) or major distress (a ride to the hospital). Personal friendships, on the other hand, serve personal and idiosyncratic needs of the individual which are not necessarily related to his or her physical surroundings. If anything, it would be surprising if personal friendship patterns were influenced significantly by features of the physical environment, or linked to one's knowledge or evaluation of the neighbourhood.

It has already been noted that when sociologists set out to study the impact of the physical environment on behaviour, their concept of what constitutes the physical environment is limited. Sometimes it means the juxtaposition of neighbours' doors, sometimes the number of units in a building (high-rises vs. single-family dwellings, for example), sometimes residential density. None of these conceptualizations is trivial, but each tends to be one-dimensional. A person's interaction with his or her surroundings is a multi-dimensional experience. Other researchers often compare suburbs with rural areas or with the central city; but this procedure throws together many different – and often unknown – physical features into single categories and thereby eliminates consideration of any particular feature. Suburbs are now full of high-rises, for instance, and the central city has many exclusively residential neighbourhoods. Small towns and urban core areas in transition often have mixtures of old and new buildings, while suburbs usually do not. Different features of the built environment need to be considered, both separately and in combination, before one can speak meaningfully about its relation to human interaction.

This has been done by a few people. One study of downtown Detroit, for instance, found that the higher the density of the neighbourhood, the less contact there was between neighbours. But in neighbourhoods with high density *and* judicious amounts of public open space, contact among neighbours increased dramatically; density interacted with open space to produce very different results from the presence of density alone. Jacobs has shown how parks ("urban beauty") encourage public contact among users, but only if the parks are small and interwoven with the busy complexity of a diverse neighbourhood's daily activity.

The study of areas in Toronto took into account the distinction between personal friends and neighbours. Like the Detroit study, it probed the interaction among different physical features in affecting residents' activities.

First, people were asked to estimate the number of personal friends as well as the number of casual acquaintances they had in the neighbourhood. The residents were asked how many people they knew well enough in the vicinity to nod and say hello to, perhaps exchange a word with, but not well enough to invite into their homes for coffee or a meal. Thus, a distinction was set up immediately between people in the area with whom they had a strictly public relationship, people whom they did not acknowledge, and people who also happened to be personal friends. This distinction was especially important since many European immigrants, who were an important part of the sample, seldom invite anyone into their homes except relatives. The estimates for personal and casual relationships were added up and divided by the number of respondents to give an average for each area.

In general, while personal-friendship patterns varied independently of the physical features of an area, casual acquaintances were related to those features in a number of ways. For instance, the number of casual acquaintances among neighbours decreased in highrises and in areas of more concentrated use, but increased as land use became more mixed. Note that, unlike many studies which treat individuals as the unit of analysis, the Toronto study focused on geographical areas. These areas could then be characterized as having more or less public activity, rather than as misty socio-physical contexts for an individual's activity.

In the second step, we looked at relations among neighbours in areas with varying combinations of the four characteristics of physical diversity – mixed land use, mixed building age, short blocks and concentration of use. In areas which had more of these physical features in varying combinations, people were more likely to know their neighbours and to have some kind of regular contact with them: they had opportunity to interact with each other. It was not just that there were more adjacent doors or a larger population; it was that their daily activities – working, shopping, taking out the garbage, informal and formal day care, porch-sitting, and relaxing – all brought street users into contact with each other.

These patterns of contact existed because of physical features of diverse urban areas. The presence of both dwellings and workplaces in abundance ensures the presence of users throughout the day. Short blocks maximize the number of corners and therefore meeting places. There are places, such as the sidewalks in front of stores or houses, or courtyards of small walk-ups, for which certain individuals (storekeepers, homeowners, janitors, residents) are to some extent responsible. The street is being looked after, not defensively, but as part of a natural observation process. Jacobs called it "eyes on the street." The web of mutual recognition among habitual users of the street, who need be only a minority, is the natural outgrowth of an urge to be responsible for the territory surrounding one's place of work, one's front door, and even the parks and shopping areas one frequents. This is civic government at its most local, but perhaps most crucial, level.

Sometimes the amount of traffic, the sheer volume of street users, has been equated with "eyes on the street." It is important to distinguish, however, between the number of street users and the quality of whatever connection exists among them. There are some parts of a large city where only impersonal and generally accepted rules of behaviour hold sway, places like major shopping sections or business centres for the entire metropolis.

Nevertheless, the city contains a wide variety of public and semi-public local places lower on the prime-location hierarchy where activity could be monitored by habitual users – businessmen, residents, shoppers. Some of these places are diverse, most are not. Because we are not at present building diverse places, street-level government is suffering, even though sociologists are finding no changes in personal networks. People have no day-to-day experience of taking responsibility for local spaces. The car is an important part of this pattern. Lyn Lofland suggests that by using the auto, urbanites can arrange their movements around the city so that they "almost never [have] to enter any truly public space." This lack of experience with public space constitutes a lack in the civic education of both children and adults, and poses a problem to North America's public life (I discuss this further in chapter 5).

When Gary Hart's candidacy for the American presidency was derailed in 1988 by newspaper stories uncovering his extra-marital liaisons, there was much debate over whether a politician's conduct in private life was relevant to his or her conduct in public affairs. North Americans, many of them, firmly believe that they can and should separate their public and work lives from their personal lives. This belief is reflected in the built environment in many ways. Sometimes it is by omission of details at the micro-level. For example, front porches are an important point of contact between the public life of the street and the private dwelling (Figure 5). However, not only are they missing from new houses in suburbia but they are also being removed from remodelled, older downtown houses (Figure 6). Elsewhere, intrinsic design principles preclude casual public-private contact; for example, residents in a high rise are completely cut off from the street (Figure 7). Sometimes the separation is reflected in urban design at the macro level, as in the large-scale segregation of land uses discussed earlier, wherein people expect to live far from their workplace or even from shopping. The media, by design as well as by default, have taken the place of whatever face-to-face encounters we may have even with local politicians.

One of the functions of diverse neighbourhood design is to create a constant dialogue between our public and private lives. True personal maturation can only take place in public and social contexts, but we seem bent on separating the personal from the public.

Figure 5
Front porch, downtown Toronto. Porches help connect residents to passers-by and
activities in the street

There is little doubt that the built environment reflects this ethic
of separation, but the built environment is a powerful reinforcer as
well. Once the billions in capital funds have been invested in a physical form, the result is treated as an inevitability, rather than as the
outcome of a series of wrong-headed decisions. Furthermore, children grow up with no notion that city design could or should be any
different, and thus with no awareness that their behaviour in the city
lacks a public dimension. As Sylvia Fava reports, "My studies have
suggested that the 'suburban generation'– who are under 40 since
they were born after World War II – are often afraid of the city, do
not know how to handle themselves with strangers in dense urban
public places, seldom visit the core cities of the metropolitan area
(except for stellar attractions), and tend to regard the problems of
the poor and minorities as urban problems, that is, not their suburban concern." In this way, civic immaturity is literally built into our
culture. One obvious symptom of civic immaturity is urban crime. A
specific connection can be made between neighbour contact and
crime in urban neighbourhoods.

Figure 6
Renovated house, stripped of its front porch, downtown Toronto

CRIME

Before embarking on a discussion of urban crime, a serious misconception must be dealt with: that there is more crime and violence in

Figure 7
"Front yard" of a high-rise

cities than elsewhere. The main sources of evidence for this generalization are US statistics compiled by the Federal Bureau of Investi-
gation, and other consolidated data supplied by police forces to their
national governments. These figures are suspect for a number of
reasons. Crime statistics are almost always collected by the police,
who, in the cities, patrol the streets. They are faced with innumerable
situations in which they can choose to lay charges or not (as well as
what kind of charges to lay). Police do not patrol country backroads;
for the most part, they respond to calls. This means that the more
rural the milieu, the less chance there is for police to lay charges.
The effect on the crime "rate" is obvious. Another source of inaccuracy is that rates are usually computed by dividing the number of
crimes by the resident population. Cities are used not just by people
who live there but also by many who come simply to work or shop,
visit friends, look for a good time. Significantly, crime rates at the
very centre of the city, where few people live but where many people
go, are generally very high. Finally, a number of studies indicate that
only a very small proportion of crimes are ever reported, and we have
little way of knowing whether those proportions change across time,
across place, or across different categories. Because of these and
many other inaccuracies in crime statistics, it is perhaps not surpris-

ing that careful researchers have found rates of crime and violence as high or higher in the countryside as in the evil city, and higher in thirteenth-century London than in twentieth-century New York.

The one fact which does stand out is that the us has outstandingly high crime rates – three or four times as high as those in Canada. However, the sources of variation in crime can be discerned even across national boundaries.

Despite the dubious status of figures which brand large cities with the highest crime rates, rising crime has been at the core of concerns about the urban crisis in Canada and the us. The purpose of this section is to show that the new North American city – what we have been building since World War II – has design features which encourage rather than discourage criminal behaviour. It is impossible to prove whether these features have contributed to an overall increase in urban crime, but it does seem likely that certain kinds of built environment are especially subject to criminal behaviour.

Jane Jacobs was one of the first writers to suggest the link between street management and physical design. Her reasoning was outlined in the last section: diverse neighbourhoods nurture informal control of public behaviour, and this informal control is the main ingredient in safe streets. Her observations led to a growing number of studies on safety and environmental design.

In a study of New York City subsidized-housing projects, Oscar Newman found that the higher the apartment building, the higher the crime rate, other things, including income and family structure, being equal. His argument was that in high-rise buildings it was difficult for residents to monitor what was going on in the "neighborhood" – stairwells, elevators, basements, and lobbies – and this in turn made it difficult for informal social control to be exercised over the behaviour of people in their immediate physical surroundings. Furthermore, as buildings became higher, there were more stairwells and elevators, and bigger basements and lobbies, so that break-ins per apartment did not increase appreciably, but incidents in stairwells, elevators, basements, and lobbies did. The similarities between Newman and Jacobs are clear.

Challenges to Newman and Jacobs were not long in coming. In addition to questioning Newman's interpretation of his data, critics said that both he and Jacobs one-sidedly underestimated the importance of the social environment. Crimes, said the critics, are committed by people, especially certain kinds of people; this was borne out by the well-established literature in sociology which traced criminal behaviour to social and psychological roots, such as early family experiences and social class.

The most comprehensive and bitter of these attacks came in a review of Jacobs' book by Lewis Mumford:

Her ideal city is mainly an organization for the prevention of crime. The best way to overcome criminal violence is such a mixture of economic and social activities of every hour of the day that the streets will never be empty of pedestrians, and that each shopkeeper, each householder, compelled to find his main occupations and his recreations on the street, will serve as watchman and policeman, each knowing who is to be trusted and who is not, who is defiant of the law and who upholds it, who can be taken in for a cup of coffee and who must be kept at bay ...

In judging Mrs. Jacobs' interpretations and her planning prescriptions, I speak as a born and bred New Yorker, who in his time has walked over almost every street in Manhattan, and who has lived in every kind of neighborhood and in every type of housing ...

I must remind Mrs. Jacobs that many parts of the city she denounces because they do not conform to her peculiar standards – and therefore, she reasons, are a prey to violence – were for over the better part of a century both economically quite sound and humanly secure ... With the policeman on his beat, a woman could go home alone at any hour of the night on a purely residential street without apprehension ... As for the great parks that Mrs. Jacobs fears as an invitation to crime, and disparages as a recreation space on the strange ground that no one any longer can safely use them, she treats as a chronic ailment a state that would have seemed incredible as late as 1935 ...

What is responsible for their present emptiness is something Mrs. Jacobs disregards – the increasing pathology of the whole mode of life in the great metropolis, a pathology that is directly proportionate to its overgrowth, its purposeless materialism, its congestion, and its insensate disorder – the very conditions she vehemently upholds as marks of urban vitality.

While not all of Jacobs' detractors would have agreed with Mumford, his substantive points were frequently echoed.

These criticisms were followed by specific research which raised more doubts about the empirical links between crime and the outdoor physical environment. Public high-rise developments in Britain were studied, for example, and found not to have higher crime rates than other forms of public housing. With specific reference to eyes on the street, some researchers pointed out that more bystanders, if anything, would reduce the probability of anyone's intervening in an incident of assault or vandalism, since people are afraid to call attention to themselves.

Nevertheless, more and more research is uncovering relationships between urban design and crimes, and creating a new field called Crime

Figure 8
Public contact among street users – downtown Toronto

Prevention Through Environmental Design (CPTED). The problem
with this field is its rather lopsided concentration on one-way causation
(from environment to criminal behaviour) and the single, negative
goal of protecting ourselves against danger from the outside. CPTED
focuses on small-scale changes in architecture and bypasses the larger
issue of the linkage between social values, city form, street-level government, and urban crime. Both the environment and human behaviour have become, in CPTED research, severely limited concepts.

The critics of Jacobs and Newman as well as the CPTED researchers
have ignored the fact that crime is only a symptom, just like the built
environment. Healthy attitudes towards social relations and responsibility are reflected in lower crime rates; we cannot achieve a healthy
society by first trying to lower the statistical incidence of crime. In
this sense, the sociologists are right. But they overlook the role played
by the physical environment in expressing and then reinforcing attitudes towards civic responsibility for the street. Physically diverse
neighbourhoods make natural many different kinds of public contacts among street users (Figure 8); these contacts are an important
part of a healthy public social life; and a healthy public social life
produces fewer criminals as well as fewer chances for crime to occur.

The best way to illustrate this point is to consider vandalism. Vandalism is not a trivial example: its costs in the United States have
risen to over one billion dollars a year, which is more than the costs

of armed robbery. Vandalism serves both as a barometer which measures how well the environment is cared for, and as a sign of how safe an area is from crime. It is an action performed not just in the context of the physical environment but against the physical environment itself. Newman's figures show a particularly striking relationship between physical design and vandalism rates.

Vandalism is mostly committed by children and teenagers. If adult life is insulated from the physical environment and adults themselves are indifferent to it, children pick up the message very quickly. They are much more alive than adults to their physical environment and at the same time less able to leave it. While indifference to the environment is manifest in all groups (emptying car ashtrays in the road is one good example), children express themselves more actively, in both positive and negative ways: building forts, breaking windows, decorating walls. The unpopular Pruitt-Igoe housing project in St Louis was destroyed by children long before disillusioned authorities finished the job with nitroglycerine. On the other hand, if adults on a street relate to each other, take responsibility for what goes on, and act when necessary, then children learn to do the same. In the Cunningham Road public-housing project in Britain, once residents had been mobilized to cooperate in managing the public areas of the project themselves, they also changed their attitudes towards teenagers and vandalism: "Two years ago when teenagers were causing a disturbance or smashing things, nobody dared go out and tell them to stop. Now, residents ... seldom hesitate, partly because they know the teenagers individually, and, more importantly, because they know they can rely on their neighbours to come out and support them." Although in this case responsibility for street management was "granted from above" by the housing authority, the point remains the same. If users of an urban space have reason to interact in public, the resulting network of trust and self-confidence puts an automatic damper on disorderliness and damage to the built environment.

This point needs to be extended. Note that in Cunningham Road nothing was said about private social life between neighbours: whether or not we are dealing with vandalism, it is the public dimension of neighbour interaction which carries weight in assessing a locality's crime potential. In another British housing project of single-family cottages, a "subculture of deviance" (extremely high crime rates) reportedly coexisted with close neighbourly relations among the occupants. Neighbourly relations were measured, though, by the extent to which residents visited each others' houses – their private not their public social relations. In other words, people may have had a healthy private social life, but a very sickly public one. The impor-

tance of this public dimension, aside from physical design, is underlined by Sally Merry, who studied a New York City housing project
with particular attention to CPTED: "Architectural design clearly does
influence where crimes occur and what spaces seem dangerous ...
However, this study indicates that architectural strategies alone are
not adequate ... Residents often fail to intervene because of the fragmented social organization of the project, its pervasive anonymity
and fear, the prevalence of stranger relationships among bystanders,
and a sense of futility about calling the police."

While concentrating on public-housing projects may give us some
insights into street management, such projects already have two
strikes against them as sites for a healthy system of street-level government: they are single-use residential areas. Only physical diversity
can provide functional support for the kind of public interaction that
nurtures such a system outside the artificial milieu of public-housing
projects.

When researchers have consciously combined different specific features of physical diversity into their studies of urban crime, the relation between crime and environment has stood out clearly. The
notion that mixed land use could be a deterrent to crime because of
more round-the-clock watchfulness by users was tested in Florida by
Dennis Duffala. He found that armed robbery of convenience stores
in Tallahassee occurred more often in streets more than two blocks
from a major artery, with little traffic, few neighbouring commercial
activities, and residential use or vacant lots around them. But he went
further. He identified some convenience stores with extremely high
robbery rates – he called them the high-risk stores. Each of these
stores, it turned out, had surroundings that combined all four of the
above characteristics.

Another example of how different dimensions of the physical environment interact to affect crime and safety can be found in studies
of the scale of urban development. One of the characteristics of
diverse city neighbourhoods is the relative absence of large-scale features in the physical environment. Large apartment houses or retail
stores have a deadening effect on the casual encounters which occur
naturally in physically diverse neighbourhoods. Large-scale building
also makes it harder for land use really to be mixed except at a very
coarse level: the mixture has too many big chunks. It is not surprising
that the scale of the urban landscape has an impact on crime. For
instance, if one looks at patterns of juvenile delinquency within
income and ethnic groups, the size of the building a juvenile lives in
is the best predictor of his or her criminal record. Dennis Roncek
found that, as the size of the city block (and thus what he calls the

population potential) increases, so does crime. The only reason relationships have been found between population density and crime rates, says Roncek, is that density usually occurs in conjunction with larger blocks and larger-scale dwelling units; in fact, he found that actual density of population was associated with decreases in criminal activity, and that scale, not density, fostered anonymity and the weakening of guardianship activities. One other bit of evidence on scale came from a study of robbery, burglary, and rape in Washington, DC. It was found that a large concentration of small businesses was a crime deterrent, while large retail-store areas attracted crime. It will be recalled that small businessmen are among the staunchest supporters of street-level management, since their business depends directly on sidewalk trade.

The Toronto study tested the idea that the four generators of diversity, separately or together, could be responsible for an atmosphere less conducive to crime. Residents in a number of physically different areas were asked to give an evaluation of the safety of their neighbourhoods. Feelings that the neighbourhood was unsafe were stronger in areas where the buildings were of mixed age, where use was concentrated, and where there were high-rises. However, just as Jacobs predicted, people living in physically diverse areas, where high density was combined with mixed land use, short blocks, and both old and new buildings, were more sanguine about the area's safety.

People in our sample were also asked to report on the actual number of incidents they had heard about. Both land-use homogeneity and longer blocks were related to an increase in reported incidents. More importantly, and analogous to other findings, physical diversity had a negative relationship with reports of incidents by residents. It will be recalled that diverse areas in the study had concentrated land use, so the Toronto evidence gives us further reason for being sceptical of the conventional wisdom that high density by itself is associated with a high crime rate.

In the same study, data were collected from the police, although for reasons discussed above, those data were less reliable than assessments by residents obtained through the questionnaires. However, two kinds of police-reported crime were consistently present in neighbourhoods which lacked physical diversity – juvenile offences and "other thefts," a category which in most areas consisted of bicycle thefts and shoplifting, activities particularly common among teenagers. Interviews with residents confirmed that these offences were often committed by local youth.

In this context, it is useful to distinguish between crimes which are committed by people living in an area, and those which are committed by "foreigners." For instance, expensive residential enclaves often experience high rates of burglary, but these crimes are committed by outsiders to the neighbourhood. In low-rent districts there might be more crime of all types, yet both criminals and victims tend to be from the same area. It has also been found that, in general, youthful offenders are more likely to break the law close to their homes.

Strictly speaking, if diversity discourages crime, which it seems to do, then both locals and foreigners should be discouraged. The estimates of incidents by residents and business people certainly suggest that many types of crime are less prevalent in diverse areas. The police data on juvenile offences and other thefts, however, point to the fact that youths in particular are more likely to commit crimes in areas which are not diverse and which, as noted, also tend to be their home neighbourhoods. These areas, with their lack of diversity and their weaknesses in street management, are the physical environment which the youths have grown up with and treat as normal.

Jacobs' reasoning on this matter is both clear and highly congruent with my findings. She argues that the diverse city neighbourhood helps bring up children. Without denying the central role of the parent in teaching morality or the importance of the teacher, children's street life gives them their first contact with the public, a contact which in contemporary cities occurs relatively rarely. That is to say, it is within a few doors of their homes that children learn what kind of behaviour is expected in public places. This includes behaviour with other children.

This connection between children and the physical environment is significant, so much so that it is worthwhile to spend the whole next chapter on the subject.

The point of this chapter has been to give empirical support to the notion that the kind of urban environment we have built since World War II has significant social costs. We like it less without really knowing why. In fact, it seems to have desensitized us to our physical surroundings. It has also discouraged our contact with neighbours and made it almost impossible to contribute to and maintain a civilized public life on city streets. One of the symptoms of this absence of street-level management is an increase in crime, especially juvenile crime. The evidence is clear: areas with concentrated and mixed land use, short blocks, and a mixture of old and new buildings have more neighbour contact and less crime. The social costs of the new North American city seem to be as significant as the economic ones.

CHAPTER FOUR

Children

Look for them where they are not supposed to be. They go where things are going on – in the streets, in the alleys, in the parking courts. Here is where the deliverymen come to unload, where father washes the car on weekends, and where children have the most room for wheeling around on their own vehicles.   William H. Whyte, *The Last Landscape*

Children are no different from adults in this important respect: they want to be where the action is. This is a natural and healthy predisposition which ought to be encouraged.

Our cities discourage children from mingling with the day-to-day activities of adults. In this sense, urban form reflects a dominant cultural belief that because children are different they need to be separated from adults until they are old enough to cope with the "real world." It has not always been this way. Our culture has only conceived of children as special and vulnerable within the last two centuries.

In fact, children are different, but they are going to be adults, and learning how to relate to the city is part of the path to adulthood. That is not achieved by forcing them to stay in carefully planned urban incubators like playgrounds and backyards. Instead, the urban environment needs to take account of the differences. The idea of planning a city for children as much as for adults may seem a little odd; childhood, it is argued, is only a transitory stage. If an amenity can be provided as a separate feature of the landscape, such as a school or a playground, then it has a claim on the community's resources. But arguments that the design of our entire urban fabric should accommodate children are seldom taken seriously.

What we forget is that while childhood may be transitory, children are not. We run a risk in not planning the whole city with tomorrow's adults in mind, the risk that tomorrow's adults will not know how to relate to the city. Our own inability in this regard is pronounced enough.

Let us start by looking at some of the ways children are different. To begin with, children are less mobile than adults. This is mostly because children do not drive, and cars are an important – sometimes crucial – means by which we get around our cities. Though children have shorter legs, they usually have more energy than their elders, and they would probably go much farther afield if cars were not so dangerous to them. Thus, their mobility is doubly circumscribed by automobiles: they cannot drive, and their parents forbid them to cross the streets until they reach a certain age. After another couple of years, of course, they are able to use public transit, except that in most North American cities, transit services are terrible. Also, many consider it dangerous to ride public transportation during off-peak hours. A bicycle could vastly expand a child's horizons, but, once again, the traffic patterns of North American cities make bicycle riding a decidedly hairy experience. Even adolescents tend to be geographically isolated.

Another difference is that children are seriously engaged in play; adults play as well, but are unwilling to admit that they do, so children's play is set apart, spatially as well as psychologically. Play is central to the way children learn about life, whether it is learning how to follow the rules of a game, damming a stream, or exploring an alley.

Third, children are smaller. The scale of the city is geared to adults, so that counters, telephone booths, urinals, drinking fountains, park benches, revolving doors, and similar aspects of the city's hardware are oversized for the average child.

Finally, a child has more intense experiences than the adult. For the child, experiences are newer, while adults are "dulled by familiarity," says Colin Ward, author of The Child in the City. He also notes in adults a "measurable physical decline in sensitivity to taste, to smells, to colour and sound." Basically, children do not live as much in their heads as adults.

It can be seen by the reader that the North American postwar urban environment, with its emphasis on the car and large-scale development, is not a particularly friendly place for children. Specifically, the postwar city has three unwelcome effects on the children: (1) children have difficulty feeling part of the urban environment, and therefore of the adult community; (2) socializing opportunities for pre-school children and for teenagers are sparse, with the result that adult relationships lack trust and intimacy; (3) juvenile delinquency is encouraged.

I shall consider these effects one by one.

BELONGING TO THE ENVIRONMENT

Because children are smaller and less mobile and because they have more intense experiences, they react to the city on a more detailed and less grand scale than adults. When children draw maps of their neighbourhood or the city they include things like hiding places or junkpiles, which are fun to explore, or special items, says Colin Ward, like "a telephone connection box – a large metal object on the footpath with a fluted base. Obviously, as a feature for hiding behind or climbing on, this kind of obstruction has a value for children in their use of the street." This kind of feature is totally ignored by adults. They might put large landmarks on their maps, such as a big hotel. The hotel, in turn, is ignored by the children, who might feel, however, that the lavatory in the hotel lobby is worth noting.

Because they are smaller, children consider floors to be rather important. The texture of the floor or street is a strong component of the urban experience of a three-year-old. He tumbles and rolls, and falls, and lies, and crawls. It makes a difference to him whether all this activity is taking place on sand, concrete, linoleum, grass, or hardwood.

Children see the environment in general, and their neighbourhood in particular, as places to explore and to use. If the area has no soft spaces, with dirt or mud or foliage of any kind, the child experiences it as an unmanipulable environment (adults have other, more "sophisticated" ways of manipulating the environment, and do not feel so deprived by hard surroundings). To some extent, the suburbs were envisaged as a response to these needs of children, and yet it appears that the response was too adult, too neat, too programmed. The fact is, children prefer unprogrammed space. They are adventurous and experimental, and they love to explore and to interact with their physical environment.

In the new North American city, however, various physical features frustrate this desire for unprogrammed space. Planners and politicians have focused their attention on providing more room for children both inside and outside the home, without thinking about how much interest the space holds for them. Long blocks are boring, preprogrammed paths. Homogeneous land use such as exclusively residential areas offers no hint of adventure around the corner, either in the form of a different land use or even an older house. One student of juvenile delinquency, Roul Tunley, is convinced that it stems from a thirst for adventure. He was told by a New York City gang supervisor "that 'as far as kids are concerned, the old houses were far better than the new ones.' These findings on the nature of juvenile delinquency are not merely subjective illustrations of wishful thinking. The Gluecks, for example, in *Unravelling Juvenile Delinquency*, can report that 47.9 per cent of delinquents compared with only 9.5 per cent of non-delinquents studied by them 'express a preference for adventurous activities.'" One can, of course, draw divergent lessons from observations like these. One lesson would be that juvenile delinquents tend to be over-adventurous youngsters. But it makes just as much sense to conclude that we have under-adventurous cities.

It is important to provide children with unprogrammed space for two reasons. The first is that it gives them places where they can socialize away from the scrutiny of adults. Teenagers, especially, need somewhere to hang out, as explained in the next section. The second reason is that it meets the need of children to belong to a neighbourhood; a sense of belonging is acquired through exploration and control over some space – a vacant lot, or the sidewalk, or a sparsely travelled street.

The new North American environment, by separating land use and deconcentrating it, does not satisfy this need to belong to the community, to understand what is going on in the community, and thereby to learn appropriate adult roles. The generation gap was created, it is said, when adults started physically segregating children. They learn about the adult world in school in the company of other children, from one adult who is telling them about it. They have fewer opportunities for learning by seeing and hearing or even participating, such as giving directions to strangers or keeping an eye on the toddler next door while a parent goes out to the store. We may consider a child underprivileged when she has to work after school at her father's store, but her integration into adult society will be smoother, at least along one dimension. As Michelson and Roberts point out in an excellent article on the child in the city, "the segregation of land uses means that parents with young children are seldom able to walk with them to stores and institutions during the normal week day. Although not a form of play, in the usual sense of the word, non-residential land uses offer the chance for variety and learning to children, where they see different people carrying on different activities." They go on to describe the same thing for teenagers: "Our land use patterns also tend to separate teenagers from firsthand observation and experience with the world of work, excepting certain kinds of commercial roles ... This form of segregation is one which serves as a partial obstacle to the realistic development of adult roles among teenagers."

Jacobs describes the experience of a child whose street features a grocer, funeral parlour, and locksmith, as well as residences and offices. He sees men and women at work, talking to their customers, maybe giving one they know well some credit. What he learns is that

people must take a modicum of public responsibility for each other even if they have no ties to each other. This is a lesson nobody learns by being told. It is learned from the experience of having other *people without ties or close friendship or formal responsibility to you* take a modicum of public responsibility for you. When Mr. Lacey, the locksmith, bawls out one of my sons for running into the street, and then later reports the transgression to my husband as he passes the locksmith shop, my son gets more than an overt lesson in safety and obedience. He also gets, indirectly, the lesson that Mr. Lacey, with whom we have no ties other than street propinquity, feels responsible for him to a degree.

Thus, children learn that they too might be expected to take some responsibility for others on the street, to speak up if they see a wrong committed, and simply to be active in the public life of the street. In such a milieu, it would be harder for the child to develop a habit of slashing tires or spray-painting buildings. But, in the new North American city, these milieux are scarce; residential neighbourhoods built since 1945 do not have streets with locksmiths on them. The implications of this situation are developed further under the heading of juvenile delinquency, below.

A large part of the North American child's experience of the city involves the car, riding in it, being blocked by it, and – horribly – being hit by it. As Patricia MacKay has said, "if a child damages a car, that is vandalism, but if a car hits a child, that is an accident." Cars, and streets designed for them, are such an intrinsic component of the postwar city that they take precedence over children's needs. Children know this (Figure 10). An automobile is only available to a child when an adult agrees to be the chauffeur. Cars are a tangible expression of the fact that children cannot feel that they are part of the new North American city.

The impact of cars on children is twofold. First, they are less mobile, either because their parents forbid them free range, or because children themselves are frustrated by freeways which block pedestrian circulation or by wide traffic arteries which don't allow

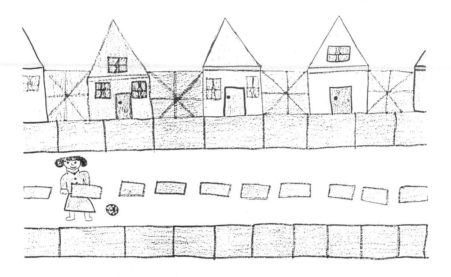

Figure 9
Suburban street, picture by ten-year-old Toronto girl

for crossing. It has been found that children are less mobile than they used to be; that is, they do not get to go as far from their homes as they used to.

Second, children are killed. Colin Ward reports that in Britain, which has fewer cars or car-oriented suburbs than North America, "800 children die and 40,000 are injured every year in traffic accidents and it is calculated that, if present trends continue, a child has a one-in-twenty chance of being involved as a pedestrian before the age of 15. In 1972, 33 casualties to children under 5 occurred every day in Britain." Accidents happen to children in part because they are as yet unequipped, it is said, to assess speed and direction. It is difficult for them to understand just how quickly a car going forty miles an hour will reach where they are standing. They also have problems understanding traffic rules. Dr Stina Sandels in Stockholm found that one can get children to learn rules by rote but they have real difficulty putting them into practice. Telling them to look left and then right, for instance, becomes an exercise in fantasy when they do not know the difference between right and left. Children are actually aware of this danger, and although they show remarkable resourcefulness in handling it, their own words show how frightening and crucial a part of their life it is. "Why do terrible car accidents kill so many innocent people?" asks an eleven-year-old in Ottawa, Canada. Petra, a girl of the same age in Germany, says "if you can afford it you shouldn't have just one car but two! I can't imagine a life without a car! You can do so many things with a car which you couldn't do without it. You save so much time that it's worth it. But I think it should be made harder to get a driving license. Otherwise people rush around the streets like crazy because they can't drive properly. I would take the driving license away from such people because they are a danger to others. Yes, I do believe we must be much stricter."

Robert Aldrich reports seeing a film about children who had to cross a freeway ramp in order to get to their elementary school. The scene is repeated in many cities: one has only a few seconds to cross because cars are not visible until they are almost on top of you. The film recorded children's reactions to this situation by zeroing in on their faces with a telescopic lens. One word sums it up: terror.

Children, then, do not and cannot feel part of the new North American urban environment. It segregates them from adults. They cannot play around with it. And, at times, it terrifies them.

SOCIALIZING

One of the many misconceptions refreshingly exposed by the architect Christopher Alexander is that while the suburbs may not be great for adolescents, at least they are a paradise for the younger child. Alexander begins by pointing to experiments with monkeys which suggested that while monkeys can do without their mothers during the first six months of life (three years in human terms), they are, if isolated from other infant monkeys, "incapable of normal social, sexual, or play relations with other monkeys in their later lives."

Although there is no identical evidence for humans, one study found that men who did not, between the ages of four and ten, have a reasonable number of friends were much more likely to suffer psychological disorders. Alexander argues that American culture is afflicted with what he calls the autonomy-withdrawal syndrome, and that this is reflected in our housing: "Autonomy and withdrawal, and the pathological belief in individual families as self-sufficient units, can be seen most vividly in the physical pattern of suburban tract development. The houses stand alone – a collection of isolated, disconnected islands. There is no communal land, and no sign of any functional connection between different houses."

Alexander's central point is that children who are three years old and under must choose their friends from their immediate neighbours, unlike their more mobile older brothers and sisters. In the seemingly ideal environment of a suburban subdivision, however, children from one and a half to four years old have few neighbours their age, because suburban density is so low that even if every house has little children, only one or two others are directly accessible. The result, says Alexander, is that "if you drive through a subdivision, watching children play, you will see that children who are old enough to have school friends do have local playgrounds of a sort. But if you look carefully, you see the smallest children squatting forlornly out-side their houses – occasionally playing with an older brother or sister and occasionally in groups of two or three, but most often alone."

Finding a playmate in such a milieu is a real challenge, especially in the absence of sidewalks. According to Alexander, these barriers to easy contact at an early age contribute to the autonomy-withdrawal syndrome, a syndrome which in most societies would be called neurotic.

The development industry in North America reflects and encourages this pathological concern for privacy both from, and for, children. One developer, quoted by Constance Perin, says that while home buyers themselves have children, he believes they do not want them to be too concentrated, and he builds accordingly: "Density is directly related, in my opinion, to the numbers of children, of all ages, that you put on the site. So that you better cut the densities when you increase the number of kids to have happy people." The image of the home as the child's private sanctuary is stressed by R. Marvyn Novick, one of the researchers in the University of Toronto's Child in the City Program:

It is evident that modern suburban housing seeks to maximize the privacy of space for children, both indoors and in backyards. It is hard to drive through a suburban subdivision without noticing in almost each (or every second) backyard a private swing, sandbox, splash pool, picnic table, or other such amenity. In contrast, what is less evident are areas such as multi-party lanes, accessible front lawns, empty lots, small equipped play areas, commercial sidewalk space for common forms of casual play and activity by children ... Good parenting and sound child development are ... associated with the amenities and space ... inside and around the home. The child can be provided with a private playground, so that he or she will not be pushed around by other children. The attempt is made to recreate, with and around the home, a microcosm of all the types of resources that historically people have moved into communities to acquire.

Thus, a wealth of personal recreational resources is supposed to make up for the stunted social life of the suburban child. This is

Figure 10
Boy with a hockey stick, Toronto suburbs

especially true for the child under three or four who must be closely
watched.

The suburbs should not be singled out for opprobrium, however.
In the new North American city large-scale developments are dominant, and high-rise buildings with relatively high densities are the
current expression of large-scale residences. These structures rob
three-year-olds of playmates by insulating each unit from the next.
Because the units are self-contained and the hallways are without any
surveillance by adults, finding playmates is difficult for high-rise children. It is a tribute to their tenacity and resourcefulness that they
do. In fact, John Farley discovered that children living in suburban
high-rises had, if anything, more friends than children living in suburban subdivisions of single-family houses. But one must remember
the bleak outlooks for friendship in the latter environment. I asked
a group of children in the suburbs of Toronto to draw pictures
of their neighbourhoods, and one child pictured himself, all alone,
in front of a row of houses. He informed me that this was an accurate
depiction: there was not a single child under fifteen on his block.
(Figure 10)

As children get older, the convenience of suburban streets for bicy-
cles, and of the high-rise's density for sheer numbers of potential
friends, makes contacts easier. If Alexander is right, however, damage
has already been done. In fact, the new North American environment
has an impact on friendship patterns of older children as well.

One reason has to do with moving. Geographers Maurice Yeates and Barry Garner show that the United States, Canada, and Australia have the "highest rates of residential mobility of eight countries for which such data is available." About nineteen percent of North Americans change residences each year. More interestingly, it is the newer cities which have the high rates of mobility, sometimes more than double the older cities of the Northeast such as Boston or New York. Jane Jacobs links this mobility to the way we have built housing: "Unlike the people who must move from a lower-middle to a middle-middle to an upper-middle suburb as their incomes and leisure activities change (or be very *outré* indeed), or the people of a little town who must move to another town or city to find different opportunities, city people need not pull up stakes for such reasons." Vance Packard provides a specific example of this process: "47.5% of [Azusa, California's] population ... was under the age of twenty. Azusa teems with children. Local informants suggested that a great many young married families settle there because they can get a three-bedroom house for $25,000 and when the family grows or the husband gets a better job they move on."

The effect of such movement* on children's friendships should not be lightly dismissed. Packard documents the devastating impact of moving every two or three years, especially as the child gets older and can talk about it. Younger children seem more resilient, but they are often deeply depressed when even one friend moves out of the neighbourhood and they are left behind. Significant psychological damage is done to children who move from neighbourhood to neighbourhood, according to many child psychologists.

As children get older and can drift further afield to find friends, the new North American city seldom provides them with likely places. One of the first places a parent forbids them to go to as they get older is the dangerous school yard or playground. This leaves them with the street, which is a throughway of some interest, but provides no focus for meeting, unless there is at least a corner store or something more interesting than houses or locked schools. Segregation of land use in the modern city makes such stores less and less common. Designing a city with meeting places for children has not been foremost in our minds. If anything, adults find congeries of young ado-

---

* Michael B. Katz has documented extremely high rates of mobility in Hamilton, Ontario in the 1850s, as well as in other cities in the Northeast, rates which approach fifty percent at times over a decade. This mobility works out to be close to the nineteen percent per year recorded in recent years in North America; and Hamilton seemed to be heir to many of the dysfunctions documented in this chapter with respect to the twentieth-century suburbs.

lescents threatening, but hanging out is just what they need at that age – being able to relate informally with members of the opposite sex as well as just being with others of the same sex.

Thus, the way we have built our cities makes it difficult for children to socialize with each other; once they have found friends, it is difficult for children to find places to meet them outside the home; finally, there is the constant threat that a friend will move away.

JUVENILE DELINQUENCY

If socializing is so difficult, if unprogrammed space is scarce, and if children have not been made to feel part of the neighbourhood, they have at least a couple of choices.

One choice is to turn inwards, to the home. In a recent study of families that had just moved, Michelson asked children what they liked about their new residential settings. Among those who had moved to single-family houses in the suburbs, the children's satisfaction was overwhelmingly expressed in terms of favourable evaluations of the dwelling unit itself; only four percent mentioned the neighbourhood as a source of satisfaction. It is almost as if suburban houses as well as high-rises have been designed for social isolation, and numerous authors have pointed this out, even though suburbs were ostensibly built as improvements on the social scene in central cities. In some cases, however, children are just basically afraid to leave their homes. A recent survey of children in New York City revealed that twenty-five percent of them felt that way.

The other choice is to turn against the neighbourhood, to attack it. This action is usually called vandalism, or juvenile delinquency. One study of a random sample of teenage boys in the American Midwest found that at least sixty percent of them had at one point deliberately damaged property. Children can break windows, burn park benches, spray paint on walls or subway cars – deface their surroundings in some way. Defacing is a good term, because it is the child who really feels defaced. The urban environment gives him (the vandal is usually male) no place to call his own and therefore robs him of a chance to define himself. Bernard Rudolfsky points to

playground furniture [which has] been set up for taming him ... He is expected to hop from rung to rung like a pet bird, or whiz along mazes that won't tax a mouse's brain ...

If the hideous toys are responsible for planting the seeds of violence in the child, architects bring them to full maturity by building what newspapers have been referring to as vandal-proof schools. Instead of trying to woo the child by subjecting him to the subtleties and charms of his art, the architect merely provokes *more* violence by challenging the child's resources as a demolition expert.

When anyone, including a child, is frustrated in the desire to be a part of the physical environment, the energy has to be channelled elsewhere, and it is often taken out on the environment itself. The destruction of the Pruitt-Igoe housing project in St Louis by its children, mentioned in the last chapter, is a good example of this principle.

Another side to the issue is highlighted by the arguments of sociologist David Popenoe. The new development, he says, which includes both high-rises and single-family-home suburbs, produces a built environment where all activities are privatized. There is no informal, adult street life, which tends to discourage juvenile mischief and also to socialize juveniles into civil public behaviour.

A fundamental problem in modern societies is a breakdown in *informal* social control mechanisms ... If juveniles are to be negatively sanctioned in public areas prior to committing crimes ... their actions must first be observed either by persons known to them or by others acting, as it were, as the agents of such persons ...

The privatized suburb ... lacks many of the elements necessary for the mechanisms of surveillance to be very effective. The inwardly focused orientation of much of suburban life means that few people are looking out their windows to survey the public scene, and few people are out walking the streets ... [so that] there will be few persons present ... who are known to the youth.

Significantly, Popenoe finds similar drawbacks to the high-rise environment.

My research in nineteen Toronto neighbourhoods lends empirical support to the above discussion. These different areas, it will be recalled, varied widely in terms of physical diversity. The following figures were also gathered for each area: (1) the average number of vandalism incidents reported by residents and business people, (2) the number of juvenile offences reported by police, and (3) the number of "other thefts" reported by police. "Other thefts" is a category in police records made up mostly of shoplifting and bicycle theft, activities which are particularly common among teenagers. The police themselves told me that they use this category as an alternative measure of illegal acts by juveniles.

Figure 11
Casual surveillance of children. A natural thing in diverse neighbourhoods.

Simple observation of the more diverse areas revealed that children
on the sidewalk and street were usually under surveillance (Figure
11). This is in direct contrast to the situation in the porchless waste-
land described by Popenoe. The results of the numerical analysis
supported his reasoning: diverse areas were significantly less likely
to experience vandalism and break-ins, judging from the number of
incidents reported by residents and businessmen. In addition, the
longer the block and the less mixed the land use, the more juvenile
crime was reported by the police. Finally, there was a relationship
between a lack of physical diversity and both juvenile offences and
"other thefts" as reported by the police (see Table 18).

The relation between long blocks and juvenile crime in particular
was strikingly illustrated by comparing two of the areas studied in
Toronto's downtown. Both Margueretta Street and the Sully-Cinder
area had large proportions of foreign-born residents, especially Italians. Most of the people were working class, and there were compa-

Table 18
Juvenile crime and physical diversity

	Juvenile offence rate*	"Other thefts" divided by total population
Less diverse areas (N = 10)	.32	.058
More diverse areas (N = 9)	.14	.016

Source: Data from E.P. Fowler, "Street Management and City Design," Social Forces 66, no. 2 (1987): 365–90.
*Number of offences by juveniles divided by juvenile population.

rable numbers of children in the two places. Both had, at one end or the other, a number of stores on a shopping street. Both had single-family or semi-detached dwellings cheek-by-jowl, at approximately the same density. The major difference between the two neighbourhoods was that Margueretta Street stretched for half a mile from Bloor Street to College Street, without a single cross street, while the Sully-Cinder area was made up of short blocks.

Talking to residents and business people in the two areas immediately suggested that the children on Margueretta Street were a real problem. They were "noisy" and "saucy." No such comments were made in Sully-Cinder. Residents and businessmen reported nearly ten times as many incidents on Margueretta Street as in the other area, and residents were four times as likely to express misgivings about the safety of the neighbourhood. In spite of Margueretta Street's family-oriented ethnic population, a long back alley that was not amenable to surveillance beckoned to anyone wanting to break into houses or to steal batteries from cars. The police spontaneously mentioned it as a trouble spot. Police data on assaults, robberies, juvenile crime, break-and-enters, and other thefts reflected residents' opinions and are shown in Table 19.

Long blocks do not of themselves create criminals, any more than mixed land use, of itself, uncreates them. But to the reader who has been following the logic of the last two chapters, it is clear that a physical design which allows street management by its users also seems to discourage criminal behaviour, by locals as much as by outsiders. In contrast, the long back alleys of Margueretta Street make management of the area by residents and shopkeepers all but impossible. Children growing up here see fewer examples of users taking responsibility for their street and respond accordingly.

Table 19
Crime rates in two Toronto neighbourhoods*

	Margueretta Street (long blocks)	Sully-Cinder Streets (short blocks)
Break and enter	.0038	.0012
Robbery	.0010	.0007
Assault	.0046	.0023
Other thefts	.0437	.0063
Juvenile offences	.6144	.0508

Source: Same as for Table 18.
*Incidents divided by population, except for juvenile offences, which were divided by juvenile population.

The urban physical environment built in the last thirty or forty years is no healthier for children than it is for adults. Although the relationship between physical diversity and juvenile crime is the most dramatic evidence of this, it is only a symptom. More profound thinking is needed about the way in which we interact with our physical surroundings. Children, sensitive as they are to their environment, are the most accurate barometers of where we have gone wrong.

The irony of the situation is that, as noted earlier, much of the new urban environment was supposedly built for children. There is at least some hypocrisy here, since ad copy acknowledges the desire of parents to be separate from their children (see Figure 12). Michelson and Roberts are close to the mark in saying that suburban housing was simply a design by white upper-middle-class men for white upper-middle-class men who wanted to feel better about leaving their wives and children each day as they went to work. Now that we have an idea of how that design and other patterns of urban development affect children's social development, their sense of belonging to the community, and patterns of juvenile delinquency, we can start to plan cities which work for children – cities with physical diversity and plenty of unprogrammed space.

The lesson of this chapter, then, seems to be, Build the city for children as well as for adults. But there is a dangerous unstated assumption in that lesson, the assumption that anyone should build *for* anyone else. One major step taken in the last few years has been a conscientious effort by planning departments across Canada and the United States to incorporate local residents and business people into discussions of plans for their areas. Indeed, where citizens have not been asked, they have often imposed themselves on the planning process. Children, in fact, have shown themselves to be perfectly com-

Figure 12
The Scarlett O'Hara Staircase, with a "parent's retreat."

petent at designing facilities for themselves. For instance, they design nursery schools which not only are different from adult-designed facilities, but better. There is an important lesson in politics embedded in all this, a rephrased conclusion to the chapter: Build the city with children as well as with adults. The issue of politics and the postwar North American city is examined next.

CHAPTER FIVE

Politics and the New Urban Environment

Politics is distasteful to many of us. We know that it deals with important matters, but getting involved or even interested seems to take a great effort. In this chapter, my aim is to show how politics is indeed built right into the patterns of our daily lives; that is, we cannot escape being political, but we can – we must – be part of an authentic politics which flows naturally from a healthy connection with each other and with the environment. I define what we currently call politics, suggest what politics ought to be, and briefly describe the functions of local government as they are at present. With this as a background, I draw a link between the suppression of authentic politics and the shape of postwar urban development. The chapter ends with a demonstration that physically diverse city neighbourhoods provide a good setting for a healthy political life.

CONVENTIONAL POLITICS

Politics is the process whereby a self-conscious community decides how its members relate to each other and to the earth. In Western society, this has come to mean one of two things. First, it means governments, elections, bureaucracies, prime ministers and presidents, and media coverage of all these phenomena. Second, it means influence and power: "playing politics" means getting people to do something they would not ordinarily do, by means of persuasion, gentle or harsh. In formal terms, these two components of politics are invested with authority by citizens. Governments, that is, have the legitimate power to maintain armed forces, to make laws, and to coerce us to obey those laws. Both the institutional side (governments, bureaucracies) and the informal side (power) are involved in managing or facilitating the economic system – the production of goods and services – and with the reproduction of ourselves and of our culture – having and housing families, educating children, looking after our communities.

The conventional meaning of politics springs from the way things are set up now, which should not necessarily be taken as normal. Within only the last hundred years we have swarmed into cities with millions of people and organized ourselves into nations with hundreds of millions of people. Rather than questioning whether this was an intelligent thing to do, we have instead organized large political systems to manage these huge cities and nations, systems which require decision making by delegated representatives and by immense bureaucracies. Enormous corporations have developed symbiotically with the public institutions. The two literally feed off of each other.

We support having our activities managed and controlled by these large-scale institutions because we think they give us things we want: a sense of economic security and even wealth; a sense of identity with a nation, a city; protection from each other; and protection from other nation states. Our daily lives have become patterns of support for these institutions, but because of their size and the division of labour among them, it is difficult to understand this.

For example, we do not normally think of buying lettuce as political. In fact, buying a lettuce at the supermarket supports a massive system of food production and distribution. This system is subsidized by public water utilities and direct grants to farmers; it has destroyed billions of tons of topsoil through the use of inorganic farming methods which also pollute our lakes and rivers and oceans; it delivers produce along thousands of miles of government-subsidized transportation networks; and it takes up massive amounts of land in our cities for warehousing and stores, with the permission of local governments.

Although most of our daily choices support big institutions in similar ways, it is almost impossible to see the connections. It is even harder to feel a connection either with these placeless, professionalized organizations or with their slick and ambitious leaders. Even the idea of becoming involved in their operation is intimidating. No wonder most of us are turned off conventional politics. Aristotle may have claimed that man is a political animal, but modern political scientists find that we are not. They report that few of us are well-informed about politics and that only a minuscule proportion of us actually participate in the system.

Once in a while, of course, we all troop to the polls. Although the vote is accorded great significance by political analysts, consider what it really is. Every few years we are asked to choose among several names on a ballot, names of people who are seeking responsibility for managing some of the community's resources. We have no say at all over who is managing other powerful organizations such as corporations, power grids, and courts of law. Despite the frequency with which elections are interpreted as victories for the left or the right, or as messages from the voters to do this or that, students of voting behaviour have demonstrated that elections have no policy content. Their main function is not to convey the voters' wishes on public policy to political leaders, but to express support for the political system. One researcher has even shown that people who vote for the losing side or who do not vote at all express more support for leaders and government after the election than before.

The winners of elections, however, do gain control over large institutions and a great deal of money, so contenders are not lacking. But the point for them is to get elected, not to solve problems. As for ourselves, the vote is a pathetic substitute for real participation in politics, which should involve taking care of each other and of the planet.

In spite of these crippling weaknesses in the representative system, most people insist that it is the only solution to governing cities and nations with millions of citizens. The wisdom of accepting such entities as the base for political institutions is seldom questioned. Consequently, the wisdom of the institutions themselves is seldom questioned, even though they have engendered an ineffective politics and a watered-down concept of citizenship.

AUTHENTIC POLITICS

An authentic politics is one that emerges clearly from our habitual social relations and economic activity. Such a politics has a direct, visceral link to our daily concerns. Everyone is involved, not as a duty imposed from the outside but as the natural consequence of the flow of community life.

The argument of this chapter is that large-scale projects, deconcentration of land use, homogeneity of land use, and unrelieved newness together have all but destroyed authentic politics and helped to create our contemporary anaemic excuse for it. In postwar urban development we have abstracted functions such as working, shopping, and recreation on a massive scale and turned the landscape into specialized places for those functions. The fragmentation of our lives and of our institutions has become expressed in the fragmentation of our spaces. Concretizing this fragmentation, making it seem real with buildings and expressways, encourages us to think that postwar urban development and the politics that goes with it are normal and natural.

By contrast, authentic politics is only possible in small-scale, diverse spaces where a variety of casual face-to-face interactions occur naturally. This suggests that politics must acknowledge its vital connection to places, places which people can relate to. This is not to say that people do not relate to a place the size of Canada or the United States. But it is to say that most of one's life concerns places which are far smaller. It seems only natural that most of our politics should do likewise.

This points to local government as an ideal focus for authentic politics. Unfortunately, many of our so-called local governments have jurisdictions covering millions of people and thousands of square miles: the governments of Cook County in Chicago, Illinois and Metropolitan Toronto in Ontario have bigger budgets and serve more people than many nation states. Nevertheless, the physical features of North America's urban landscape are intimately connected to local governments, so a brief consideration of them is needed. (There will be more on local government in chapter 6.)

LOCAL GOVERNMENT

Local governments in North America have no constitutional right to existence; they appeared in the nineteenth century as municipal corporations, created by laws passed in state and provincial legislatures. These corporations were formed to regulate and service property for the benefit of property owners, but not just for any property owners: the ones who wanted incorporation were those who saw serviced land as a way of making money. Thus, these fledgling municipalities really had no initial connection with whatever social and political life already existed in the towns and communities of nineteenth-century North America. Municipal corporations were money-making machines. To this day, in the minds of many civic officials, local government exists to service property and to protect the rights of property owners, not to be an active and significant forum on civic affairs.

Higher-level governments became more powerful as time went on, less by taking power away from local governments than by developing new functions for themselves. Nation states seemed to be especially adept at making war, and the means which they developed for extracting money from citizens in order to wage wars also proved useful for getting money to pursue domestic social and economic policies, policies which redistributed the nation's resources. One responsibility which had belonged to local governments, health and welfare, became so burdensome to localities during the Great Depression that they gladly allowed higher-level governments to take responsibility for funding programs to help the millions of homeless and unemployed created by the economic crisis. Ironically, the actual administration of these programs in the 1990s is still largely the job of local governments, especially in the US.

The main focus of local governments, however, remains the servicing and protection of property. They zone and regulate land use, for instance; they are concerned with whether or not office towers should be built to certain heights, or whether homeowners can add basement apartments to their houses. Local governments make land-use plans so that at least some land will be set aside for recreation, which they also administer; the land-use plans function to protect property owners by keeping residences separate from noisier and smellier commercial or industrial uses. Zoning and rezoning are usually done in ways that benefit developers and larger property owners, regulating the supply of land to their development needs. Local governments build streets and water mains and sewers to service houses, factories, and office buildings; they light the streets; they hire firemen to protect buildings; they hire policemen to protect people's property.

Notice that all this activity has to do with specific places. Local politics has often been called the politics of place, as contrasted with the non-place politics of bank rates, foreign policy, and unemployment insurance. Also, because of their antecedents and spheres of competence, local governments have been called growth machines: they exist to promote economic growth. The more development they encourage within their boundaries, for instance, the more property taxes they can levy and the bigger and more prestigious a city they can rule over.

All this sounds as if local governments have considerable control over what goes on within their boundaries. In fact, municipalities are relatively powerless. They are subject to the ebb and flow of increasingly large sums of international capital, and they are routinely devastated by the actions of large corporations closing factories or changing office locations. What is more, any land-use decisions by local councils in Canada can be overturned by the province. US cities have more legal autonomy, but are subordinate to powerful semi-public development corporations and are as financially tied to federal government aid programs as Canadian cities are to their provincial aid programs.

But, upon reflection, all this boils down to the domination of one administrative apparatus by other administrative apparatuses (often called the problem of local autonomy). This is the realm of what we think politics is all about – the state and its intimate connections with corporations and other big organizations. What I am calling real or authentic politics is totally absent.

THE IMPACT OF THE NEW BUILT ENVIRONMENT ON POLITICS

The very newness of the postwar urban environment has influenced the politics of its users. Since new cities, or at least very large sub-divisions, are constantly being built, lack of local political self-con-sciousness has become endemic to North American political culture. The newness and scale of this development has created local political systems without a past, and, as I have shown, social systems without a sense of place. This has implications for voting behaviour.

At the local level, electoral turnout has always been especially low, often less than half the turnout in national and state or provincial elections. Local campaigns and elections never have the breathless media coverage accorded to other levels of government. They are the lull before the lull.

There is still variation in local turnout, however, and one piece of evidence from the US from the 1960s is worth noting. In a study of votting turnout in American cities, Alford and Lee make it plain that lower turnout characterizes cities which are "younger" (that is, which reached a population of 25,000 later than other cities) and which have a mobile population. These cities are found disproportionately in the West, the South, and the Midwest, although it was shown that even within these regions, city age was positively related to turnout. Alford and Lee suggest that the newer cities have not had time to develop political self-consciousness. A political culture has not yet formed.

Turnout figures are, perhaps, rather sketchy evidence for such a conclusion. Individual accounts of politics in new communities show that it revolves around the latest development proposal or the costs of servicing new development. Such issues seldom bring citizens out to storm the barricades. Instead, small civic associations staffed by political activists fight brushfire wars with local councils and devel-opers to safeguard property values. This is what one might call rationally calculative politics. As instant communities, suburbs gen-erate little emotional attachment; all that is left is economic self-inter-est. There is little loyalty at the community level, since a person could move out at almost any time.

The governments of many of these new cities are frantically trying to cope with demands for physical services posed by phenomenal increases in population. Finding enough money to build the physical infrastructure – sewers, roads, utility lines – is such an urgent issue that social services are not even considered. Almost comically, suburban governments often decide that attracting still more residents and businesses to pay more taxes is the only way of relieving the shortage of money. The provision of sewers and roads is seen by citizens, furthermore, as mainly a technical problem, not a political one, so local politics in newer cities tends to revolve around issues which do not grab one's attention.

Herbert Gans, in a revealing comment on Levittown, remarks that Levittowners already get everything they need from the corporate economy, the national government, and local government (the job of the last is to protect the community's residential status). Middle-class Levittowners, says Gans, "have no need to participate or intervene" in local politics.

Lack of political self-consciousness, government preoccupation with technical provision of services, and self-satisfaction are only some of the reasons why no one takes part in the politics of newer communities. Another reason is that in such communities, there is nothing to get involved in. Where all the buildings are new (and this is true in many parts of downtown areas, especially in high-rises, as well as in the suburbs), nobody is starting to modify a house by adding a couple of rooms or (God forbid) making it into a storefront. If the environment is unmanipulable, arguments about how to change it do not arise, and the raw material of local politics is absent. The result is not only less interest in local politics but also a conservatism about physical surroundings.

Time does soften the edges. In the first Levittown, built on Long Island in the late 1940s, the idiosyncrasies of residents are beginning to appear, as bedrooms are added and trees and shrubs reach full maturity. In Pessac, France, Le Corbusier's intentionally homogeneous and cubist housing from the 1920s has been modified so much by its residents that the original design is almost impossible to discern. The point remains, however, that in new communities, little of this is going on.

Thus, one could say that the low voter turnout in local elections is only a symptom of how large-scale new development – whether highrises or suburban subdivisions – discourages the user from interacting with the built environment. This interaction is a significant form of political involvement, since it relates to our own personal experience.

The new development's design also discourages our interaction with each other. It was shown in chapter 3 how this occurs at the block level; but it also occurs at the city and regional levels, with important political implications. As Theodore Lowi has so accurately pointed out, the suburbs represent a failure in citizenship. Many suburbanites have no desire to participate in the larger issues of the metropolitan area. Fed up with the political and social mess of the central cities, they moved to the suburbs precisely to escape it. Once ensconced, they used exclusionary land zoning to keep out other, less well off refugees from the city who also aspired to live in the suburban ring. The same is true of high-rises, wherever they may be built. Governments have stopped building them for the poor because their design discourages neighbour contact and encourages crime, as chapter 3 showed. But high-rises are still being built for the middle and upper classes, heavily fortified with dozens of security devices and, in the ritzier buildings, security personnel.

The physical environment is not exclusively to blame for the hardness of our political hearts; but once built, it perpetuates political problems which plague cities.

The new North American development, because it dulls our awareness of our physical surroundings, even shapes what we define as political issues. Separation of land use provides a good illustration. In municipal government, zoning by-laws are used to regulate land into separate uses, not just to keep undesirable people out of our neighbourhoods. One of the classic defenses of zoning for different land uses is that some of those uses are unpleasant to be around. People do not like living next to pinball arcades. They prefer not to shop for groceries across the street from a blast furnace. Heavy industry, shopping, entertainment, and residential uses are separated from each other because it is felt they do not "mix."

Out of sight, out of mind. It is difficult to get upset about a smokestack which is belching sulphur dioxide if we put it so far away that we do not see or smell it (some people do, of course, but they are usually a minority, economically deprived and politically powerless). Environmental politics is a reflection of this problem: the average person is not confronted on a daily basis with the implications of his or her way of life. By leaving the disposal of our garbage to others – waste-management experts – we never see where it goes or how it causes problems for the environment until it is too late. When there are problems, the tendency is to give them to the next *larger* level of government instead of organizing land use that mixes small-scale garbage disposal in with businesses and residences that produce the garbage, at the block level. In such a situation, we would certainly be much more sensitive to recycling and reuse. Living next door to a steel factory (which no one does) would lead one to question whether the community needed quite so much steel. Using the back side of a used piece of paper instead of a fresh sheet would make more sense if it meant that the tree in our front yard would not be cut down.

Few important political issues are formed around how we relate to the natural environment because we have separated our land uses. While scientists warn us that the long-run implications of our behaviour are ominous, we still spend relatively little time and money on environmental problems because we have separated ourselves from the physical consequences of our way of life.

Separation of land use also has an effect on our sense of public responsibility for places we frequent. By reserving a geographical space for one function, we create places to be used. As soon as we finish the activity for which the place was designed, we leave: when we are through working or learning, we leave the workplace or the school; when we finish playing, we leave the playground, the park, or the cinema. There is no reason to care about the place as a place. It is simply the repository of a function. This makes it terribly difficult for us to feel responsible for *any* place in the city – even where we live – except in an instrumental way. Someone might spend nine hours a day in an office building, using the lights and the toilet, buying lunch, travelling on roads or subways to get there, and never be part of the community that decides where to send the sewage, how to regulate restaurant sanitation, or where to build the roads. There is a controversy typical of our culture over whether office workers pay enough to cover the services they use; no one would ever suggest, however, that the worker should have a sense of attachment or of civic responsibility for the well-being of the workplace. Owners of factories and office buildings care about the site and its immediate surroundings insofar as they contribute to profit, but the place itself has no particular meaning.

If we get involved in an issue about a place, it is likely to be where we live. Even here, however, land-use separation ensures that a minimal set of issues will arise to stir controversy. And again, when issues do arise, they revolve around what one can get from a place – peace and quiet, a home which is a valuable personal asset, pleasant neighbours – rather than what one can give to it. There is, as some political scientists have put it, a mobilization of bias against raising certain issues, issues which involve the connection between our home life and our job, our consumption habits, and our social interaction with others. That connection, of course, is we ourselves.

Treating places instrumentally as locations for separate functions also affects the way political decisions are made. Separate places have been created not just for production and reproduction, but for consumption, recreation, learning, managing, and authoritative decision making (government) as well. That is, factories and communities are separated, but so are shopping areas, parks and amusements, schools and universities, corporate offices, and government offices. Educational institutions are huge; the only knowledge we recognize is "acquired" in the classroom. Political activity outside the halls of power, especially when it is on the street, is on the fringes of legitimacy, and sometimes illegal.

The separation of functions in itself might not be so significant if the separate functions were not organized into such large-scale authorities and installations. We have not just large schools, with two and three thousand pupils, we have large school systems; not just wide streets but hundreds of miles of urban expressways. Separate, large-scale, technologically sophisticated services, and infrastructure are the products of separate, large-scale bureaucracies insulated from public input; but that infrastructure also produces insulated bureaucracies.

All kinds of autonomous local authorities are set up to "administer," free from the intrusions of politics, such services as policing, public transportation, libraries, and health services. These authorities are often so large that they cannot fit into municipal government offices, so they build their own edifices to house their administrators, which reinforces their independent decision-making authority. Although fragmentation of local government is conventionally deplored by political scientists (it certainly makes the study of local government arduous), the separation of functions is often seen as healthy for democracy: Robert Dahl argues that since élites tend to be influential in only one or two issue areas because of the functional separation, no one wields an inordinate amount of influence. In fact, the autonomy of services and agencies from politics has meant autonomy from popular control – and immovability in the face of change.

This insulation from public input is accentuated by the marriage of scale with technology. Each of the large-scale functions has, over the years, developed its own technology to go with its activity. Urban expressways are planned by transportation experts with complex computer simulations which are difficult for the average person to assess. The mathematical models, as interpreted by planners, become important political and even moral forces in expressway controversies. The same sort of process is at work with nuclear technology, educational philosophy, and health administration. Each technology has its own mystique, but real chaos is produced by the lack of communication among technologies. They are enormously fragmented into computer technology, transportation technology, construction technology, administrative technology, communications technology. One does not trespass on another technology, any more than one would trespass on private property. The property image is apt, for the system is maintained by physical separation into larger and larger clumps of land use: education centres, central business districts, recreational complexes. Each of these clumps has its collection of experts with a claim on the community's resources, a claim which is recognized as legitimate and made stronger by the facility's scale and separateness; but the validity of the claim can only be determined by experts in the field.

Now, while one may plausibly argue that the physical separation of land uses is a reflection of what is already in our minds, those ideas, once they take on the form of masses of buildings and patterns of land use, acquire a momentum of their own to persuade future generations of the naturalness and permanence of such an arrangement. In such a way does the physical environment become part of ourselves and, in particular, part of our conception of the nature of political authority.

Ursula Franklin, an eminent Canadian physicist, describes it this way:

Rarely are there public discussions about the merits or problems of adopting a particular technology. For example, Canadians have never been asked (for instance, through a bill before the House of Commons) whether they are prepared to spend their taxes to develop, manufacture, and market nuclear reactors. Yet without publicly funded research and development, industrial support and promotion, and government loans to purchasers, Canadian nuclear technology would not exist. The political systems in most of today's real world of technology are not structured to allow public debate and public input at the point of planning technological enterprises ...

The design and building of roads and the accesses to harbours and airports have always been paid for by the public. However, underneath the public agenda there is often an agenda that is very specific and sectoral ...

Public planning and ... resources have provided the infrastructures necessary for the expansion of new technologies and for the diffusion and use of the products of the new industries ... The planning processes which have fostered the development and spread of technology have provided infrastructures that we now consider as a given, normal, and unquestionable part of the real world.

In this way, says Franklin, fragmented technological planning has produced a physical infrastructure (roads, power plants, institutional buildings) whose homogeneity and immense scale take citizen compliance for granted.

This pattern of development which engenders compliance holds for private as well as public urban development. In chapter 3, it was made clear how physically diverse city neighbourhoods provided a small-scale, multi-use setting in which users could manage many of their own affairs: looking after children, keeping abreast of local developments (and organizing against undesirable ones), modifying their building, helping strangers, and keeping an eye out for people up to no good. In other words, physical diversity encourages active participation in neighbourhood management. The big new high-rises and suburban communities, large shopping malls and industrial parks encourage citizen passivity. They all need representatives and experts to keep things running: security guards, politicians and engineers to build large-scale infrastructure, elevator repairmen, corporations with enough resources to build and manage large developments, policemen, big power stations to provide energy staffed by experts, and so on. This is authoritarian architecture, but we are so used to it that we do not recognize it as such.

Some communities add to this by insisting on conformity to physical design: "In Columbia, Maryland, a Justice Department lawyer ... is waging a battle with his village's architectural committee because he planted cherry trees and strawberry plants in his front yard ... In Palos Verdes Estates a well-dressed, middle-aged woman ... silently attached a red cardboard tag to a front railing ... When the new arrival asked what it was, the woman said that a railing design around the home's front porch had not been approved by the town art jury." In high-rises, residents' potential for getting involved in the design of the physical environment is more minimal still. Even in condominiums, where individual units are owned, ownership buys control only over interior arrangements. These stacked, almost identical concrete containers are the ultimate in passive housing consumption.

It is amazing, upon reflection, how compliant we have become with respect to our housing. The newer developments in North America are built for us by the property industry, and this is an important political fact. Not just our housing, but our roads and utilities and public buildings are being built in a way that is unmanipulable by their users. They are built to be accepted, not to be fiddled with or modified in any major way. This phenomenon has occurred before. Lewis Mumford compares eighteenth- and nineteenth-century urban development with the medieval city forms which it displaced: "Instead of wiping out buildings of different styles in order to make them over wholesale in the fashionable stereotype of the passing moment, the medieval builder worked the old and the new into an ever richer pattern. The bastard aestheticism of a single uniform style, set within a rigid town plan, arbitrarily freezing the historic process at a given moment, was left for a later period, which valued uniformity more than universality, and visible power more than the invisible processes of life." Mumford shows beautifully how buildings and roads are clear reflections of a political culture. In North America, our buildings are authoritarian, both in their scale and homogeneity: they encourage political compliance.

Lack of physical diversity has been particularly hard on the political efficacy of the working class. Since working-class people can only afford certain types of housing, they are segregated into certain areas of the city, and some, like David Harvey, feel this provides a setting conducive to collective action, "well beyond that [action] required out of pure individual self-interest."

Others have argued, however, that separation of work from home has sapped the ability of Americans to make the politics of the workplace a legitimate part of the political system, and that the loser in this case is the working class. In the nineteenth century, the growth of the factory system created a dramatic separation of workplace and residence. While this separation may originally have occurred for economic or logistical reasons, politics came into it as well, following two patterns. First, when large firms started moving to the suburbs at the turn of the century, they did so, in fact, to escape from union politics in the central city. In the beginning, they built company towns so that the work force could live close to the factory. However, this mixture of land use had political repercussions: workers living under the shadow of the workplace, experiencing its pollution, and buying from the company store could connect all their discontents to the industrial capitalists, who were physically present in so many ways. The physical form of the company town thus had an important impact on political behaviour involving more focused opposition to authority, and more radical protests. The factory owners, realizing their mistake, started encouraging workers to live and shop far away from the factory, and the troublesome company towns passed from the scene. This has been a second, more recent pattern of separation of work from residence.

The separation of the workplace from the residence, the segregation of residential neighbourhoods according to class and ethnic background, and the representation of individual localities by legislators all combined to produce a politics in the United States which relies on issues surrounding the residence, while the politics of the workplace remains strictly separate, according to the political scientist Ira Katznelson. The system of city trenches, as he calls it, means that the average person experiences society's system of power in fragmented form. Since the job of legislators is to represent areas defined by where people live,* political parties gain support and politicians win elections on the basis of issues surrounding the home. Labour unions, especially in the United States and to some extent in Canada, are by now apolitical – it is not considered proper for them to get directly involved in politics. Thus, segregation of land use helps to keep our political experiences fragmented, so that it becomes difficult to understand the whole, the way it all fits together.

There are, however, two more dimensions to this connection between urban physical diversity and working-class politics.

One dimension is historical. Murray Bookchin points to the vibrant street life in working-class neighbourhoods in the nineteenth and first half of the twentieth centuries, even when their residents were being exploited in the workplace:

Left to itself, the "underground" world of the oppressed remained a breeding ground for rebels and conspirators against the prevailing authority. No less urban in character than agrarian, it also remained a school for a grassroots politics ...

The elaboration of the Industrial Revolution into a textile economy in England, a luxury goods economy in France, an electro-chemical economy in Germany (itself a second industrial revolution in the last half of the nineteenth century), and an automotive economy in America did not eliminate this "underground" communal world ...

Indeed as long as the market did not dissolve the communal dimension of industrialism, there was a richly fecund, highly diversified, cooperative, and innovative domain of social and political life to which the proletariat could retreat after working hours, a domain that retained a vital continuity with precapitalist lifeways and values. This partly municipal, partly domestic domain formed a strong countervailing force to the impact of an industrial economy and the nation state ... It would be difficult to understand not only the radical uprisings of the nineteenth century but also the twentieth ... without keeping this communal dimension of the "class struggle" clearly in mind.

Bookchin's explanation for the demise of this community life was its penetration by the postwar mass culture of consumerism, mass media, and cold war hysteria; such penetration was made possible by the incredible technical and psychological sophistication of mass marketing and the media.

---

* Only in local elections can property owners sometimes vote in places where they work but do not reside.

Without denying the significance of placeless mass culture, the changes in the physical design of working-class neighbourhoods and of the city as a whole must also be taken into account. Working-class street life was smothered by big blocks of anonymous and homogeneous housing separated from equally large workplaces (offices as well as factories) and shopping malls. Harold Chorney puts it thus:

The city and its streets were converted from a place where politics and public life were central to life, to a place where consumption and spectacle became central. Politics was pushed aside, indoors, where it has come ultimately to be reconstituted as spectacle itself, and consumed passively as television. Public space is less and less available to facilitate the social interaction, beyond the confines of the workplace itself, which is necessary for the formation of class consciousness ...

The fact that a police station and a parking garage stand on the site of the old Market Square in Winnipeg, where mass meetings of thousands of politicized urban workers once took place, is symbolic of what has transpired in urban political life in Canada.

Chorney's sweeping statement about urban political life should remind us that the changing patterns of city building affect all classes in society. The middle and upper classes, however, can use money and prestige to gain political influence in a way that transcends their physical neighbourhoods or workplaces. They are not as disadvantaged as the working class by a city which leaves no room for informal political activity in public or semi-public places. Once again, in agreement with Ursula Franklin and Murray Bookchin, Chorney stresses that these changes in the physical environment reinforce what he calls an amnesia about what political life is really about. The environment encourages us to think that our political culture is a natural and normal one.

Thus, among all the private and public activity that falls victim to this technical, large-scale, segregated development, one of the most significant is informal, spontaneous politics itself. Especially in this age of dominance by the mass media, mobilization of support for politicians is accomplished through the appeal of national leaders and through the development of issues which do not relate to specific places – the state of the economy, constitutional rights, abortion, national defense, and foreign policy. Even in the case of catastrophic local environmental damage such as that close to the Love Canal in Niagara Falls, the residents' plight was seriously addressed by the authorities only once the media had turned it into a national issue.

Special places are set aside for politics – legislatures, candidates' offices; the rest of the city seldom provides a ready context for political activity. There is, in fact, no place for politics in the suburbs: no important avenue to march down, no public square where people can gather to talk, to hear or to give political addresses (shopping centres would never allow it, of course). The design of postwar cities precludes spontaneous political expression as completely as it precludes casual social interaction. The two are closely related.

This lack of public politics is also a function of how deconcentrated the city has become, even in its core. There are fewer logical physical focuses for the great variety of activities which are the essence of city vitality. These focuses used to be paved squares, wide sidewalks, or multi-purpose public buildings. Spaces such as these have been ceded little by little to private development, where public behaviour is more strictly controlled and where any kind of political expression is discouraged because it might be identified with the owner. When public spaces are built they are not focuses of activity. Rather, they tend to be broad expanses of openness between very large public buildings. Paths criss-cross these open spaces, and they are used for travelling, but concentration of energy and life is so absent that no one would dream of using such places for political purposes. As a result, says Sennett, "the environment prompts people to think of the public domain as meaningless."

Deconcentration of urban development has had a similarly deadening influence on politics in the suburbs. Americans have built suburban houses which sit on the centre of their lots, the size of which must be as large as possible. Spreading out development accentuates the isolation of the household from the street and from neighbours; in so doing, Constance Perin argues, it leaves undeveloped our skills in negotiating disputes which naturally arise when people live next to each other. One landscape architect who "observed how poorly prepared the residents were to take over from the developers" established a firm to help people run civic associations in new developments. While the sprawl of suburban housing may have occurred as a consequence of wanting to avoid contact with neighbours, "the ready availability of physical avoidance having atrophied tactics of negotiation, mediation, and other adjudicative mechanisms, social fright is heightened ... We have been faulting suburban sprawl for everything but its implications for authentic social order, that of *self-governance*" (emphasis in original).

In fact, Perin should not point simply at "suburban sprawl," which is the object of so much criticism, but at a combination of factors. The notion of physical diversity is specifically defined here as short blocks, a concentration of use, a mixture of old and new buildings, and a mixture of land uses – a combination, in other words, which is the mirror image not only of sprawl but of wholesale construction of new communities and of large-scale, homogeneous, and segregated developments. Together, these features have produced what the sociologist David Popenoe has described as privatization of space:

The American suburb is the extreme case, but privatization is a dominant motif in most of the other ecological zones of the metropolis as well. Streets and sidewalks that once provided public pedestrian interaction and even entertainment have for the most part been abandoned to the utter privacy of the automobile; public parks have fallen into disuse and misuse; town squares have become the most ornamental appendages of commercialism. The American metropolitan apartment dweller lives behind locked doors, using public space mainly as a means of access and egress to desired private loci, not as space in which to linger and utilize for its own sake (save, perhaps for during the lunch hour at work). And where is the public space in a Houston or a Los Angeles? It does exist, but is overwhelmed by the dominance of essentially private spheres.

My argument is that physical design has been at least partially responsible for this debilitating privatization. At the humble level of the street, North Americans are frustrated in their natural tendencies towards self-management by a lack of physical diversity. There are several things that need managing on a city block. One is safety, and it has been demonstrated in chapter 3 just how important physical diversity is in helping block users keep an area safe. There is also a need for management in the bringing up of children. In chapter 4, a link was drawn between physical features of the postwar North American city and difficulties in teaching children the basics of civic responsibility.

The third management job on the block is political. It involves developing ideas about new forms of cooperation and self-help within the community. That sounds ambitious for the street level, but it is not. The only reason it may sound ambitious is that we have been brought up thinking that local politics is Mickey Mouse politics. Television and radio programs usually carry national and regional news, so we assume that that is what is important.

Decisions about our local environment are just as important, but they tend to be made by people who are not on the news and are not likely to be known to us – heads of public-works departments, or developers who build high-rises or sit on planning boards, or promulgators of tax laws. Many of these decisions have been made years before to shape the neighbourhood we now live or work in: the mix of housing and other uses, the construction technologies available at the time, or laws about setbacks from the sidewalk. Other more recent decisions control what we do to our environment, such as what we can use the sidewalk for, what kind of addition we can make to a house or store or factory, or even how loudly we can play music. These decisions have an important influence on how we feel about features of our environment. However, partly because these features are part of our everyday life, partly because they are like the air we breathe, and maybe partly because they appear so immutable (more in some areas than in others), we seldom notice them. They are not an issue, so decisions about them do not seem so important.

Still other decisions which pose obvious threats to neighbourhoods are being made all the time. A developer may have bought a parcel of land and obtained a re-zoning which allows him or her to erect a theatre, a high-rise, or an office building. Aldermen and transportation planners may have decided it is time to extend an expressway through someone's front lawn or backyard. In the case of major threats like these, everyone finds out. But the information usually comes too late, so citizens' groups are almost always fighting defensively. If an area has a good network of communications, such as in diverse areas where people are likelier to know their neighbours, people not only receive and disseminate information rapidly, but they also produce it in the form of proposals for action. This can really catch governments off guard. When a Winnipeg community organized itself into a corporation and presented a land-use plan for the area to council, the city fathers did not know whether they were coming or going.

Generally, however, we do not think of ourselves as the locus of decision making about our urban environment because it is so large-scale and monolithic. It is often argued that citizens have not willingly relinquished decision-making power: it has been taken from them. The process is subtler than that, however; it involves the way we perceive politics, which, as I have argued, is influenced by the way we have built cities that lack physical diversity.

Lack of diversity encourages the perception that politics does not take place at the local level, but only at the regional and national levels. Alternatively, local politics is considered petty, and provision of local services is considered an administrative job, not a political issue. In a political culture such as this, civic management of the affairs on one's street is almost beneath contempt; keeping kids off the street, helping strangers find their way, making neighbours realize that their parties can get a bit wild – these are jobs for fuss-budgets with nothing better to do.

Whether such a perception is the cause or result of our cities' lack of physical diversity is immaterial. But the evidence is clear that lack of physical diversity is further sapping people's ability to maintain communications networks on their blocks, making it difficult for them to take issue with what is happening there. Newness and homogeneity of many environments work together to diminish concern for anything beyond the boundaries of one's house lot. Inhabitants of the fourteenth floor retain or even nurture detachment from what goes on at the street level, let alone on the sixth floor.

Deconcentration, requiring dependence on the car, means that residents or workers seldom walk through their area; instead, they simply go from building to car and see the neighbourhood as if it were a picture, framed in the windshield. If shopping is just down the street and it seems ridiculous to take the car, the person who walks for groceries is likely to notice the condition of the sidewalk, to meet one or more of the neighbours, and generally to be aware of what the neighbourhood is. A mixture of old and new buildings makes it likelier that people may want to fix up or add to an old building, perhaps converting it to a new use if there is also a mixture of land uses. People in the neighbourhood would be sure to know about the conversion and have opinions about it.

Physical diversity as a concept also includes shorter blocks. These make the route to the store or to work more varied; a person could take one of several paths to the same destination, thereby becoming familiar with more of the neighbourhood than in an area where long blocks dictate the only route. Furthermore, if all the structures look the same, there is no urge to look around the corner and sample a new street just for the hell of it, because one knows it is going to be just the same. Variety encourages one to explore and become acquainted.

Knowing one's neighbourhood is the first step towards caring about it and wanting to protect its well-being. A diverse neighbourhood encourages this involvement. The new North American city does not.

In this chapter an important distinction has been made between two kinds of caring about a neighbourhood. One can care because one owns a house or business whose economic value is influenced by land use in the area. One can also care about a neighbourhood because it is there, because one feels part of it, because it is an extension of oneself. This may sound silly to those who are used to thinking of houses as commodities or businesses as profit machines, yet this

Figure 13
"Come on in." Picture by a child of diverse downtown neighbourhood in which she lives.

second kind of caring surfaces again and again in accounts of families that have been relocated by urban redevelopment. Marc Fried gives the example of Mr and Mrs Figella, who were forced to move from Boston's West End. They bought a house in a Boston suburb, and they were "quite satisfied with the physical arrangements but, all in all, they are dissatisfied with the move. When asked what she dislikes about her present dwelling, Mrs. Figella replied simply and pathetically: 'It's in Arlington and I want to be in the West End.' ... They have suffered from the move, and find it extremely difficult to reorganize their lives completely in adapting ... Their grief for a lost home seems to be one form of maintaining continuity on the basis of memories." Economic motives play no part in the way these people care for their neighbourhood.

Similarly, lack of caring can have little to do with money. In many downtown areas in the United States in the 1960s and 1970s, no matter how cheap the house, there were no buyers. The point is that people can define their relationship to a neighbourhood in terms of what they get from it or in terms of what they want to give to it. Children growing up in diverse neighbourhoods seem to learn this way of relating quite early (see Figure 13). When this form of thinking prevails, the market price becomes irrelevant. Thousands of

urban homesteaders in us downtown areas have recreated neighbourhoods with their own energy.

The same point can be made about politics. Someone can care
about politics because of what he or she can get from it – power,
prestige, or money. Or someone can care because he or she wants to
give energy and love to the community. In the first case we have a
politics defined by conflict and power over others; in the second case
we have an authentic politics defined by cooperation and combining
energy with others. The new North American city has been built by
and for people who want to get things from it, an attitude which is
congruent with the first kind of politics. In truth, building cities that
work involves redefining the meaning of politics, so clearly intertwined are cities and politics. This chapter is a beginning of this
redefinition.

Before we can proceed with the job, however, we need to be more
aware of the predispositions and the old ways of thinking which led
us to build such cities in the first place. We have mesmerized ourselves
into thinking that the present environment and politics are the only
reasonable alternative; until we become aware of how conditioned a
response this is, we cannot move on to the process of building human
and ecologically sane cities.

PART TWO

Exploring Why
We Built This Way:
Openings to Change

Toronto:
On April 3rd.
you get
what you deserve.

Figure 14
We get what we deserve.

CHAPTER SIX

Why Did We Do It? Explanations for the Postwar Urban Environment

It should now be clear that the North American built environment is not simply extravagant in terms of money; its unreasonable costs include disturbing and decidedly unhealthy effects on our social and political life.

Why, then, was such an environment built?

Answers to such a question can only be tentative and partial, although many of the authors I have consulted seem fairly confident of their conclusions. The real purpose in outlining even a few of them is to try to become more aware of ourselves – of attitudes and patterns of behaviour which we take for granted – and of the less-than-obvious connections between our daily life and governments, corporations, and other institutions of our society. This awareness is important as a basis on which to develop ideas about building cities that really work.

The plan of this chapter is to start with some of the more obvious explanations for the form of our urban environment, such as the economic and political ones. These explanations suggest that the public policies which helped to produce the postwar urban explosion were descended from government structures and ideologies that we tend to accept unthinkingly. From this perspective, it appears that understanding some of our cultural roots and conditioning is necessary in order to figure out why we have built the way we have.

ECONOMIC EXPLANATIONS

Much of the contemporary North American city, it has already been explained, is the product of an enormous postwar construction boom, which lasted at least until the mid-1970s and is continuing in a restrained form in the early 1990s. The roots of this construction boom lie in a continent-wide economic boom, which came out of a growth coalition made up of business and labour. A number of authors have carefully traced the postwar truce in both the United States and Canada beteween these two groups, a truce agreed upon in order to pursue economic expansion. The basic dynamic was a decision by labour to moderate its confrontational tactics of the 1930s and go along with capital's short-term ability to produce massive amounts of consumer goods. While business would still make healthy profits and wealth would not be substantially redistributed, the workers of North America would still enjoy a dramatically improved standard of living.

A central component of the growth agreement was to provide single-family homes for as many people as possible, mainly in the suburbs. In other words, just like clothing and sirloin steaks, the idea was that housing would be consumed in ever-increasing quantities. As it turned out, by the mid-1970s, over half of the us' gross national product was tied to the suburbs and suburbanization, in one way or another. However, the central city was part of the growth agreement as well. "In the period after World War II, major corporations and labor unions came together to forge new central city political coalitions. Organized around policies to maintain the city's economic growth and fiscal viability, the coalition pushed forward with costly urban renewal projects, intrametropolitan transportation, industrial parks, development corporations, zoning variances, underassessments, subsidized water and power, and so on."

The growth agreement was in fact central to the vitality of capitalism, for capital has to keep renewing itself. In order to stay in business, for instance, the developer must continue to build and sell new housing. The building boom literally created many large developers, who then wanted to keep building and selling, even when demand sagged in the 1970s. The construction and real estate industry, with its emphasis on single-family homes, has become the largest industry in both the us and Canada. It is a central focus of the economy overall. It has thus become a powerful independent force in its own right, a force which fuels further construction booms.

The dramatic increase in high-rise apartment buildings, even in an era when single-family suburban homes were becoming for many a realizable dream, is easily explained in economic terms. The burgeoning development industry found that high-rises were the most profitable form of housing, even though they also turned out to be the most inefficient to maintain, and even though most people saw them as only a step on the way to owning their own houses. High-rises were built because they were profitable.

Office concentration in the downtown also produced acres of new buildings. Profit for the development industry was the important consideration here as well, for developers were finding that conversion of land from high to exceedingly high density was very lucrative. Taking down an old office building at eight-times coverage (i.e., a building with eight times as much floor space as the land it covered) and putting up a building fifty stories high at thirty-times coverage allowed the developer to get four times as much rent from the same piece of land.

However, there had to be a market for all this office space, and there was. Firms were growing in size, as much by amalgamation as by increases in sales. Domination by offices of central-city land – making it too expensive for any other use – started after World War I, according to various economic historians, because corporations were beginning to consolidate and organize their control over industries. "They were now large enough to separate administrative functions from the production process itself, leaving plant managers to oversee the factories while corporate managers supervised the far-flung empire. Having already spurred the decentralization of many of their production plants, they could now afford to locate their administrative headquarters where it would be most 'efficient.' They chose downtown locations to be near other headquarters, near banks and law offices, and near advertising agents." After World War II this process accelerated. The result was that management and administrative offices were employing hundreds, even thousands, of workers. "Advanced" management techniques were producing firms which had only white collar workers (like developers themselves) or higher proportions of administrative personnel. In the 1970s and 1980s, increased centralization of merging corporations gave rise to very large administrative structures; even by the early 1970s, two hundred manufacturing firms controlled two-thirds of the United States' manufacturing assets, whereas in 1940 a thousand firms controlled the same amount.

The increase in white-collar employment by these expanding firms created the demand for office space. At the same time, the location of management relative to production facilities made less and less difference. Advances in technology made it possible for large corporations to direct their activities from a single point in downtown New York or Chicago without having branch offices in Atlanta, Saskatoon, or Allen's Corners. The geographer A.J. Scott has shown that large firms really need to be central with respect to the total metropolitan area if they want to keep their wages down. Although this might explain the impressive amount of new office space in the

downtown areas of large North American cities, office space in suburban locations has also been growing dramatically. Thus, the massive increases in office buildings can be seen as the result of two
economic factors: profitability of office development, and an increasing demand for office space from large corporations.

To summarize, the phenomenal amount of new building in postwar
North America – the reason why it is so hard to find a mixture of
old and new buildings – came from the labour/business truce whose
outcomes included the building of a landscape designed for consumption – the suburbs – and demand for downtown and suburban
office space combined with the profitability of high-rises; all of these
factors were evident in and reinforced by an enormous growth in the
relative importance of the development industry.

There were economic factors behind the deconcentration of the
postwar North American city, as well. As noted in chapter 1, there
were really two processes at work here, decentralization and deconcentration. Decentralization was the movement of jobs and residences
from the centre of the city to its periphery, or the building of new
housing and factories on the fringe rather than in the centre; deconcentration was the building of developments of lower and lower density – land use was becoming less intense. The residential and
industrial sprawl of postwar North America's construction boom was
the culmination of both processes.

Decentralization of residences started in the nineteenth century as
the better off sought to escape the unpleasant aspects of concentrated
industrialization. But the most dramatic decentralization occurred
after World War II, when millions of units were built in the suburbs
for the middle and working classes under the sponsorship of the
growth coalition described above, with substantial aid from governments. This boom, as noted, produced thousands of new homes and
workplaces on the periphery of metropolitan areas and in the already
decentralized sunbelt cities; a considerably smaller proportion of the
new development involved direct moves from the central city to the
suburbs.

It must be asked why the building boom expressed itself in such
a decentralized and deconcentrated form. This pattern of development ran counter to previous city building as well as to theories about
it. The old pattern was a central city with pronounced residential and
commercial densities. These densities were valued because they meant
easy access to clients or customers, support services and firms, entertainment, wide ranges of consumer goods, and generally to any type
of person or commodity desirable for carrying on a business or mak-

ing a home. This list amounts to what economists call an agglomeration economy.

The conventional economic explanations for why firms started locating or relocating in the suburbs begin with the point that downtown areas were becoming increasingly congested and that congestion costs were outweighing the advantages of economies of agglomeration. The disadvantages of the downtown were accompanied by spiralling taxes and land costs. Changes in transportation and other technology are also factored into the explanation. While for some businesses, such as brokerage houses and law firms, face-to-face contact remained essential, for many others "accessibility" was redefined to mean speed of delivery of goods and services, which could be accomplished by a variety of new technologies such as urban expressways and computer networks. Some big corporations were able to internalize many of the services and functions they had derived from the agglomeration economy, and to move where they wished.

Deconcentration accompanied decentralization. Once the decision to locate or relocate on the periphery had been made, deconcentrating technology followed – land-intensive manufacturing, cars and trucks, communications systems. Factories adopted the continuous-material-flow system which required long single-storey buildings and lots of cheap land, unavailable in the core.

These conventional economic and technological explanations for the form of urban development tell only part of the story. The politics of the workplace are an important "economic" reason for spread-out development. Long before continuous-material-flow systems were in place, even before the turn of the century, companies were moving out of the central city in order to escape its politics and unions, as described in chapter 5. There is considerable evidence that similar motives for plant movement and deindustrialization are prevalent today. Maintaining a competitive advantage and maximizing profits mean having continued political control over the worker, which in turn is helped by locating on the periphery. A.J. Scott has described a process which he calls vertical disintegration: large, unionized firms subcontract work out to smaller firms with low rates of unionization and, therefore, lower costs. Scott found this new form of deconcentrated agglomeration economy working very efficiently in Orange County south of Los Angeles. The firms which are doing the subcontracting work need not even be in the vicinity of the larger plant; many of them are overseas. The systematic way in which companies adopt these tactics makes it obvious that political and economic reasons for decentralizing are closely intertwined.

Again, there were political reasons for deconcentrating development once the move to the fringe had been made. In company towns like Pullman, "labor can easily identify the enemy – whether it be in company housing, the company store, company social services, or in the work place itself. It is no accident that some of the fiercest strikes ... occurred in company towns," says the political geographer David Harvey. Companies thus encouraged deconcentration – indeed, separation – of work and residence in the suburbs.

As significant as job sprawl was, the bulk of decentralization and deconcentration of development occurred in residential building. The first dimension of this process was land speculation. Mark Gottdiener points to the rise of agribusiness (a process intimately connected to government policy) as the reason why small farms found it impossible to sell their surplus produce; their demise freed up land on the periphery of metropolitan areas for decentralized development. Charles Sargent has shown that most of the farmers on the edges of metropolitan areas are either marginal or part-time farmers to whom speculators' prices are extremely attractive.

The speculative market encouraged leapfrog development by making available to developers land which was less costly than other undeveloped land closer to the core, but which was reasonably accessible to anyone with a car. Also, the larger developers who sprang into existence after the war and who wanted to build Levittown clones were frustrated by fragmented land markets closer to the city, so they leapfrogged out to where assembly of large tracts was a less fussy procedure.

The profits which could be earned from manipulating the supply of land at the edge of the city were surely an important factor in urban decentralization. Although many speculators lost their shirts, many others reaped awesome returns year after year simply by acquiring land and getting it rezoned (the role played by local governments in this will be described below). Homebuyers, for their part, got relatively cheaper land and absorbed the other costs of decentralization and deconcentration without understanding how it all fit together. They thought they were getting a good deal and that is why they bought.

This brings us to a consideration of the role played by individual buyers in the process. The desire to own a home inheres in North American culture, and this phenomenon will be dealt with presently as something apart from financial considerations. But North Americans are undeniably motivated by money as well. Owning a home is considered a good investment – a home always appreciates in value at least as fast as inflation, so it confers economic security. For many people, homes are commodities which can be bought and sold for a tidy profit at two- or three-year intervals. I have seen columns in the real-estate sections of newspapers urging readers not to worry, prices of downtown homes would probably not be going down. This message is clearly aimed at thousands of people looking to sell their houses and make a profit. The mentality is reflected even in the names of suburban streets (see Figure 15). North Americans seem to be in a class by themselves in this respect. J.A. Agnew compared homeowners in Leicester, England with homeowners in Dayton, Ohio; almost 73 percent of the latter said that getting a profit out of their homes was either important or very important. Only 14.4 percent of the British homeowners answered this way.

Although condominiums have become an important alternative form of "home ownership," the real desire of North Americans is to own a single-family home in the suburbs. This desire cannot be discounted as a critical source of residential deconcentration as well as decentralization; nor can it be separated from motives of personal financial gain. Those motives play a part in the homogeneity of neighbourhoods: newspapers are full of stories about irate homeowners trying to repress the creative urges of one of their less conformist neighbours, who are planting cabbages or controversial sculptures on their front lawns. The fear is that "property values will decline."

However, while the role of the individual's economic cupidity can be discerned in the encouragement of physical homogeneity, decentralization, and deconcentration, other forces have also been at work. It was argued in Part One of this book that the negative effects of postwar urbanization were tied to segregated land use and large-scale development (which are closely linked to homogeneity). Here, the most powerful shapers of the built environment were the land market and large-scale corporations.

The market system has made urban land into a commodity even though, in many senses, it is not. The economic historian Karl Polanyi calls it one of the fictitious commodities. Land is bought and sold for prices which reflect its use, and its use reflects the prices for which it is bought and sold. In other words, there is a constant circular process by which land price and land use are intertwined. In this process, development becomes concentrated and feverish over a short time, since, if one landowner sells his or her land for much money, others will be attracted to the investment possibilities of the area, and they all converge on the honey pot, to use Kevin Cox's phrase. Jane Jacobs has called this the self-destruction of diversity. In fact, as noted earlier, diversity is being destroyed by the market sys-

Figure 15
Choice Land: market mentality and the suburban home.

tem for land, for as the price goes up in the honey pot, more and more uses are excluded. This results in physical homogeneity.

The growth and movement of large corporations were another factor. Before firms moved to the suburbs, or new ones established themselves there, in both cases to escape the unions downtown, the division of labour and the growth in the size and specialization of firms had already introduced a separation of the workplace from the home within the nineteenth-century city. This separation of land uses produced homogeneous areas of the city that were devoted to manufacturing, commerce, financial and legal services, warehousing, and housing. In addition, the incentive to minimize the costs of transportation, labour, and raw input created different location priorities for different firms, which, accordingly, spread themselves out to different corners of the city. The destruction of mixed land use was started, therefore, by the growth of firms into large-scale corporations and by those corporations' production patterns.

Large corporations were able to build bigger and bigger factories, from Manchester's satanic mills in the 1830s and 1840s to Ford's immense River Rouge plant and Bethlehem Steel's Sparrows Point plant, described in chapter 1. As corporations grew bigger and more powerful, control over production became more concentrated and centralized. Both office and production facilities grew in size, eliminating the possibility of any kind of close-grained land-use mix. Since big plants have achieved dramatic short-term economies of scale, companies have had the incentive to continue building them. They are even being allowed to wipe out downtown urban neighbourhoods: a famous recent example was the Cadillac plant which General Motors built in central Detroit. A single factory of a 465-acre site eliminated fifteen hundred residences and businesses.

The growing scale of corporations has been unusually pronounced in the development industry itself, especially in Canada, where concentration of capital in the early 1970s was approaching that of the auto manufacturers. The postwar development boom produced giants like Levitt and Sons in the United States: but they looked small in comparison to Canadian companies like Cadillac Fairview and Olympia and York, with their billions of dollars' worth of assets. These huge developers have become experts at marshalling the money, land, municipal approvals, and subcontractors necessary for immense developments, not only housing but shopping malls, industrial parks, and office complexes. The only developer capable of building New York City's multi-billion-dollar Battery Park City, it seems, was Toronto's Olympia and York.

Michael Peter Smith describes the size and the determining role of large-scale developers in the United States:

In the suburbs, investment in shopping centres has had a major impact on the sprawl pattern of population movement ...

Decisions to build shopping centers in rural regions are now made increasingly at the national level by "temporary organizations" – coalitions of real estate entrepreneurs, banks, and large corporate investors, including national insurance companies and even large corporate and union pension funds. The nationalization of the investment process is nicely illustrated by a New Jersey-based development group which had developed eighty shopping centers in thirty states and was in the process of building thirty-six additional centers as of 1974.

These kinds of large scale investments no longer follow population flows but shape the pattern of population movement, so as to yield further profitable mobility.

Large-scale development – or, as Jane Jacobs calls it, cataclysmic money – destroys diversity. It is impossible for the planners and builders of these monstrous complexes to think of, let alone construct, a street with a bicycle-repair shop, a ballet school, two or three houses, a three-storey walk-up, a small public space with trees and a cafe, and a little office building with a lawyer, a chiropractor, and an insurance agent.

Instead, cataclysmic money of large corporations has produced the homogeneity and land-use segregation of the postwar city: look-alike towns of thousands of houses, complete with separate shopping malls, such as Don Mills, Ontario and Levittown, Anystate; multiple-family dwellings bunched into four, six, ten, or even twenty thirty-storey high-rises; downtown office complexes of several towers, often more than fifty stories high. These large-scale developments have created vast reaches of undifferentiated land use, even when the promoters insist they have "mixed" offices, retail stores, and sometimes dwellings. The scale simply eliminates the possibility of creating the social space of a diverse city neighbourhood.

Thus, lack of a mix of old and new buildings, deconcentration, and homogeneity of land use could all be explained by focusing on economic causes. It is obvious, however, that there were political dimensions to the development process, and it is to these political factors that I now turn.

POLITICAL EXPLANATIONS

I have dealt with economic factors separately, but in fact our economic system is inseparable from politics. If there were economic imperatives for the new North American city, then the political system made itself part of those imperatives. It did this by pursuing explicit public policies, as well as indirect ones, that not only supported capitalist city builders and individual homeowners; the political system literally created the necessary conditions for the kind of development we have. If we look deeper, we can see that our political system has a structure and ideology behind it that blend well with building booms, deconcentration, and segregated land use. I shall consider each of these layers – policy, structure, and ideology – in turn.

Public Policy

The United States, Harvey asserted in 1975, really had no "premeditated urban growth strategy," but "a strong de facto urban policy has in fact existed since the 1930s in the form of a direct byproduct of federal fiscal and monetary policies designed to prevent a return of severe depression conditions." In fact, in the US, first under President Carter's administration and then more vigorously in the early Reagan years, federal programs were directed towards helping local governments close deals with private developers to build mega-projects in city core areas. The *de facto* policies noted by Harvey were, however, important in both the US and Canada.

The first principle of these monetary policies was to use capital flow into the housing market as a way of heating up or cooling down the national economy, since housing, and the urban infrastructure supporting it, were such a large and growing component of domestic fixed-capital formation. In fact, by the 1960s, because of government policy encouraging people to go into debt to buy their own homes, residential debt was the largest single component of the financial structure of both Canada and the United States. The way that governments, especially the national governments, decided to "prevent a return to severe depression conditions," then, was to promote policies which channelled capital into home building. These policies were also a sign that government had joined the growth coalition of business and labour described earlier in this chapter.

The economic motives of governments were supplemented by political ones. In the 1940s, millions of soldiers were back in the civilian workforce and raising families. In every legislative chamber on the continent, elected representatives were falling all over themselves to get on record that they wanted returning servicemen to be able to own their own homes, even if it meant cutting back on programs to help the slums. The best way to do this was to make mortgage money readily available by guaranteeing loans so that banks would lose less money on defaults, and even by lending public money at favourable rates to big developers, for both urban renewal and suburban housing.

In general, however, government policy diverted capital flow into the housing market by minimizing the risk for large-scale investors in housing. In the US, the instrument of policy was the Federal Housing Administration (FHA); in Canada, the Central Mortgage and Housing Corporation (CMHC). In addition, mortgage payments in the US could be deducted from one's taxable income. This made it easier to own a house. Without these political decisions, as numerous authors have pointed out, the suburbs simply would not have been built, economic factors notwithstanding.

Destroying the old and putting up the new has also been favoured by national tax laws. For example, it is cheaper to tear down old buildings in the inner city than to renovate them, if land changes hands, because the owner of the property can deduct from his or her income tax each year five percent or so of the value of the buildings on the property as "depreciation." The principle is that this money can be used by owners to keep their properties in good repair. However, two things invalidate this principle: first, buildings are always gaining in value anyway; and second, if the owner is a speculator, she or he does not keep the building in very good shape, since there is no interest in retaining it over the long term. If someone has owned land and buildings for ten or twenty years, the depreciated value of the buildings approaches zero, while the actual value of the buildings may have increased. If the owner wishes to sell, he or she will have to pay capital gains tax on the difference between the present assessed value of the buildings and what they have been depreciated to. Time and again, instead of paying the tax, the owner demolishes the old but perfectly sound buildings before disposing of the property, in order to avoid paying the tax. This process has had a powerful impact on the face of North American cities, which have far more new buildings than would have been built without the depreciation allowance; in the US, the allowance has been getting steadily more permissive, through the urgings of the development industry.

Local governments are willing partners in the destruction of the old and construction of the new. The desire for increased revenues from property taxes is universal among municipal officials. Local government policy that encourages more intensive use of land under its jurisdiction has been justified by the expectation that the new use will bring in more taxes. This is as true of downtown city governments' approval of the tearing down of older and fairly dense mixed-use development to make way for high-rises as it is of suburban governments' subdivision of farmland for housing.

The other side of the coin is that more intensive development requires more intensive city services, which need to be provided and paid for even before the new tax money comes in. A number of studies have demonstrated that new development is at best a mixed blessing – the new services end up costing as much as or more than the sum of new revenues. Throughout most of North America, however, urban governments ignore such information. There is a clear political reason for this and for the prevalence of pro-growth policies in municipalities: their institutions are peopled either by developers or by aspiring developers.

Systematic research by James Lorimer and Don Gutstein in the early 1970s showed clearly that sometimes up to eighty percent of city councils and land-use advisory bodies in Canadian local government are members of the development industry. Similar figures can be inferred from analyses of US local governments. It is quite logical: the function of local government is to service and protect private property, so persons from the property industry are most likely to be interested in and knowledgeable about local government operations. It is but one step from interest and knowledge to participation.

The legacy of this boosterism is the loss of thousands of old houses and acres of farmland to high-rises and to other developments which pay higher tax rates, even though they cost more to service. The sheer number of new buildings is therefore due, in part, to the pro-growth orientation of local governments and their misplaced quest for tax revenue.

Decentralization of urban areas and deconcentrated development have also been supported by government policy. It has already been noted that the FHA and the CMHC channelled investments into suburban development, which represents much of the continent's decentralized and deconcentrated built environment. The FHA even refused to insure residential mortgages in certain parts of inner cities, a procedure which supplemented the policy of lending institutions not to commit money to those areas. This policy is known as red-lining.

Federal government policy in the US has consistently supported industrial development in the cities of the South and West, where all city building (if it can be called that) has been decentralized. Billions of dollars in defense contracts were responsible for astonishing amounts of suburban factory construction in that part of the country, followed by shopping centres and housing. (It is helpful to remember in this context that the US federal government's tax dollars have been going heavily to defense – in 1976, the proportion was fifty-four per cent.)

The northern states, when they try to stimulate growth, follow the same pattern, as Richard Hill, a sociologist from Michigan, demonstrates:

In Michigan, hi-tech entrepreneurs and state development officials are promoting a metro-Detroit suburban corridor ... Dubbed "Automation Alley" by state officials, the corridor already hosts the largest concentration of machine-vision and robotics firms in the USA.

Oakland Technology Park anchors the northwest pole of Automation Alley. Linked to Oakland University, spanning 1800 acres and housing $2 billion in research and development facilities ... Oakland Technology Park numbers among the largest and fastest growing research and development sites in the USA. The park will generate an estimated 52,000 jobs by the mid-1990s.

Oakland Technology Park is located in suburban Auburn Hills. A township until 1984, it has grown to 16,000 residents. By the mid-1990s, according to planning projections, Auburn Hills will have as many jobs downtown as the city of Detroit!

Canadian provincial governments are much more powerful *vis-à-vis* local governments than American states, but the effect of provincial policies is still to promote deconcentrated development on the fringes of cities. For example, when postwar development in Toronto spilled out over the old city's boundaries, suburban municipalities were unable to pay for all the new sewers, roads, and other services that were needed, a common problem throughout North America. To make a long story short, the province imposed a federated metropolitan government on Toronto (which had favoured annexation) and its surrounding municipalities; the new government, known as Metro Toronto, had enough fiscal solidity to finance the unprecedented growth in its physical infrastructure. The province of Ontario parachuted Frederick Gardiner, a Canadian version of Robert Moses, into the Metro chairman's position, and government policies to support urban sprawl were guaranteed. Some years later, in the 1970s, new growth in the region was spreading outside Metro Toronto's boundaries, so the provincial government obligingly scraped together several billion dollars to build trunk sewers and main highways which the suburban municipalities surrounding Metro Toronto could not possibly have afforded. Such support was crucial to the American-style sprawl which characterized the Toronto area in the 1990s.

Ontario's highway program to service suburbs looked paltry next to the vast interstate-highway programs in the US, which provided billions of dollars to build thousands of miles of expressway around, and right through, major built-up areas. This highway program, which lasted from the 1950s into the 1970s, destroyed thousands of homes and businesses in areas of high concentration (the Cross Bronx Expressway, whose construction process was described in chapter 2, was one example of this destruction). The program was critical to a policy of deconcentrated urban development which required the use of the car and truck.

Government policy was closely linked to homogeneity and segregation of land use, too. It has been stressed that homogeneity occurred because of the size of projects, which were built of necessity by big companies. Whatever economic reasons there might have been for the rise of huge corporations capable of building whole towns in just a few years, government policy certainly encouraged it. For one thing, governments in both the US and Canada found it easier to deal with large companies; it involved fewer transactions, meetings, documents, and by-laws. Larger builders ended up receiving larger amounts of money, more easily, from CMHC and the FHA. Local government reorganization in Canada favoured large developers. One example is given by Timothy Colton, the biographer of Fred Gardiner:

Metro's regulation of the expansion of the housing market, in concert with the province, elongated production lead times and gave a new advantage to firms with the capacity to hold large amounts of land in abeyance for several years. In a cruel reversal of original intentions, the new demand by Gardiner's government for developer contributions toward physical services also strongly favoured bigger companies with extensive credit resources. The result – an abrupt increase in corporate concentration – was evident by the early 1960s. Whereas no firm in the Toronto area had built as many as 100 homes a year in 1955, by 1960 6 per cent of all dwelling units in the region financed with federal mortgages were constructed by such firms. That proportion leaped to 17 per cent in 1961 and 34% the following year and reached 79% by 1970.

Tax laws encouraged big business, as well. For example, "accelerated depreciation allowances in effect grant the companies with the largest tax liabilities interest-free loans by reducing their taxable income in the earlier years. Investment tax credits allow deferral of a portion of the tax indefinitely; for the largest firms, they can approach total tax forgiveness," say Bluestone and Harrison in *The Deindustrialization of America*. This policy especially favours companies with heavy capital investments, like development companies. Large firms also benefit from being able to deduct from their taxes the interest they receive from industrial development bonds issued by state and local governments. The net effect in the US of tax loopholes favouring large companies was a tax rate of twenty-five percent for the nation's one hundred largest companies, and forty-four percent for the others. James Lorimer has shown how large developers in Canada pay virtually no income tax at all, largely because of depreciation allowances. The larger the developer, the more it benefits from these policies. This support of big business by government policy fed into the economic processes described above for big factories, office blocks, and suburban developments, and thus into homogeneous clumps of land use.

Local governments also promote large-scale homogeneous building. In the 1970s and 1980s the local governments of US cities, especially those in the Northeast and Midwest, undertook massive downtown redevelopment projects in order to "revitalize" their downtown cores. Although, as I pointed out earlier, these projects did nothing of the sort, their public and private developers thought they did – or at least expressed that opinion. It is important to see these monstrous developments as the products of active local-government lobbying for federal grants in the US (Urban Development Action Grants, for instance), and of property tax and zoning concessions by municipalities in both Canada and the US.

These projects are perfect examples of cataclysmic money destroying diversity. They often eliminate older city neighbourhoods, even whole districts, which have smaller, close-grained, mixed land use, and replace them with high-rise towers and large malls. Or, they are built close enough to such districts to ruin them with side effects such as border vacuums and speculation.

One new development in New York City is being financed entirely by the government. Hunters Point in Queens, overlooking the East River, will have 2.1 million square feet of office space, 6,385 luxury apartments, and a 350-room hotel, housed in buildings up to thirty-eight stories tall; its developers are the Port Authority of New York (Robert Moses' erstwhile fiefdom), New York City's Public Development Corporation, and New York State's Urban Development Corporation, which was described in its 1968 founding mandate as "a tool for creating housing and jobs for minority group members and the poor."

Canadian city politicians have all but manned the bulldozers in promoting megaprojects downtown. Montreal mayor Jean Drapeau was perhaps the most durable of these pro-growth office holders; he was almost singlehandedly responsible for dozens of huge projects which wiped out large sections of old downtown Montreal. Vancouver's flamboyant mayor of the late 1960s, Tom Campbell, was photographed swinging on the cable of a demolition ball. With the exception of a few "reform" councils, Toronto's city council has enthusiastically approved massive new projects over the last few years which have completely changed the face of the downtown: an immense domed stadium completely out of scale with the central city (but aggressively pushed by higher-level governments and big corporations); the Bell Canada office complex with three million square feet of office space; and the infamous Bay-Adelaide development. This last project, which may have been instrumental in the defeat of some pro-growth councillors in the 1988 civic elections in Toronto, involved giving the developer extra floors in office towers in exchange for a site for social housing which would not be available for five years. Proponents, who knew they were giving an extra sixty million dollars in profit to the developer, approved the project at three in the morning at a special meeting called once election nominations were closed and the campaign was well under way.

The homogeneous large-scale development in the suburbs – the endless industrial parks, "communities" of thirty and fifty thousand people, the shopping malls with hundreds of stores – has hardly taken place over the objections of suburban officials, who also tend to consist of past, present, and future developers. Mark Gottdiener, in his book *Planned Sprawl*, documents just how closely and eagerly politicians worked with developers to cover Suffolk County with big projects. A series of articles in the *Globe and Mail* in the fall of 1988 showed that the process in the Toronto area north of Metro was very similar. And Logan and Molotch, in *Urban Fortunes*, indicate that, although there is some variation in types of US suburbs, most of them seek out large projects and highways as a matter of course.

Both suburban and central city governments, therefore, were part of the team which has created the postwar patterns of urbanization in North America.

The desire of North Americans for single-family homes as good investments was cited above as a reason for both deconcentrated development and homogeneous residential neighbourhoods. It was also shown how FHA and CMHC policy diverted mortgage money overwhelmingly into single-family suburban housing in support of this desire. Support for homogeneous neighbourhoods and large-scale development came from another source, as well: the zoning policies of local government.

Land zoning by local governments is a way of guaranteeing the small landowner's investment in real estate, of turning it into a reasonably secure proposition by protecting it from the unpredictable whims of a completely unfettered land market. Alternatively, zoning is used by developers, who have considerable leverage in local governments, to make millions of dollars simply by persuading city and suburban councils to rezone land which the developer "happens" to have acquired at a low price. That is, zoning is often used to legitimate projects of the growth machine rather than to prevent growth.

In both cases, zoning promotes homogeneity. In the first case, zoning supports the system which treats houses as something to buy and sell rather than as something to make one's own and to grow with. In this kind of environment, homogeneous architecture and land use are an asset, not a disadvantage. Houses that are built to be passed on from one buyer to the next have to be comparable, not idiosyncratic and unique. There are more costs and hassles in making a house one's own by building additions or renovating than in moving on to a bigger "dwelling unit." While modifications to the zoning by-law are often approved, it prevents more outlandish deviations from ever being considered by property owners.

More importantly, zoning is part of a conscious government policy of segregating land use. Such segregation has been supported for years by residents who are afraid of living near industrial or commercial uses which produce unpleasant noises, smells, and traffic. Introduction of zoning encouraged an increasingly coarse land-use mix, simply because the more segregation there was, the fewer the complaints. Although the idea sounds reasonable, zoning for segregation has been woefully overused and misused. For instance, segregation of land use is also pursued as a way of excluding unwanted people – the poor, the undesirable "ethnic," the residents of halfway houses. Once again, property value considerations are foremost in people's minds. Zoning policy of this sort, aimed at protecting the homogeneity of neighbourhoods, produces even more unrelenting physical homogeneity.

I have already dealt with zoning's promotion of physical homogeneity through the legitimation of large-scale projects, by showing how local governments work with developers to promote these projects. The zoning by-law which is passed by the local council just makes the whole thing legal.

The preceding survey has connected well-known facts about government policy in postwar North America with certain specific physical results. Governments at local, regional, and national levels have all contributed to the disappearance of physical diversity in cities and to the utter lack of diversity in suburbs. Not all of these policies resulted from the whims of policy makers; they were powerfully impelled and reinforced by government structure.

Government Structure

Higher-level governments – state, provincial, federal – are big. Each collects and spends billions of dollars every year; they do not think in terms of close-grained land-use mix, of small developments of any kind; they use local governments to take care of that sort of thing. Simply because these higher-level governments are so big, their interventions into urban building tend to be on a grand scale: superhighways, domed stadiums, immense trunk sewers, mammoth office projects.

If physical diversity is to be encouraged, then, structure dictates that only local governments are likely to do it. From what we have seen, however, the policy orientations of local councillors are so consistently pro-growth that even at this level the probability for small-scale mixed and concentrated land use is pretty low. Nevertheless, there are structural factors that contribute to this orientation. That is, even if local councillors wanted to promote physical diversity (and some of them do), they would be frustrated by the whole framework of government organization.

One factor is the weakness of local governments within their own sphere. The phenomenally rapid growth in the size of

metropolitan areas, combined with an absence of adjustment to
the geographical scope of political authority within them, has
produced urban areas with hundreds of autonomous governments
and authorities. These small governments have neither the resources
nor the capability of coordinated action possessed by large developers and other corporations. The results are predictable. As
business professor William Capitman has put it, "All decisions that
cause urban crises are private decisions, and ... the most influential
private decisions, the decisive ones, are corporate." Big business, and
especially development companies, have been able to do what they
want in most cases, not only because of sympathetic government
officials but because local governments are small and control few
resources.

Central city governments tend to be larger and better organized
than suburban ones, especially in the United States. A number of
analysts claim that the fragmentation and powerlessness of suburban
governments resulted from a conscious campaign by developers and
industrialists, who wanted small, malleable municipalities independent of the hardball, more class-oriented politics of central cities. Thus,
weak and fragmented local government in the US could be traced to
economic forces. Whatever the cause, the effect has been a govern-
mental structure (or lack of structure) which makes it easier for big
companies with big building plans to carry them out.

In both Canada and the US, fragmentation of a slightly different
sort also underlies and supports deconcentrated and large-scale
development: there are scores of independent and semi-independent
agencies which make important land-use decision at the local level,
decisions over which municipal councils have little or no control.
Robert Moses, of the Port Authority of New York, is a good example:
he built Co-Op City (55,000 inhabitants), the Cross Bronx Expressway and literally *dozens* more like it, and the huge Verrazzano Bridge,
all with funds he raised on his own from the federal government,
from private developers, and from highway and bridge tolls. But
Moses was the biggest, not the only independent-authority entrepre-
neur. He had counterparts across the continent.

In the 1970s and 1980s a large number of independent development corporations emerged across North America, as instruments of
downtown building projects. As mentioned above, they were often
created under the urgings of local governments anxious to revitalize
their core areas. While their genesis and formal connections with local
governments varied, they were all powerful enough to ignore municipalities or to exercise considerable influence over them. US versions
of these corporations are described in the aptly titled *Unequal Part-*

nerships, which deals with specific examples from a dozen cities. In Canada, according to one source,

quasi-autonomous ... public development corporations have played a dominant role in ... cities such as Toronto and Vancouver for much of the past decade, and their importance will undoubtedly continue to grow across the country. Indeed, over the past few years alone, new public development corporations have been established in downtown areas in Montreal, Quebec City, Edmonton, Winnipeg, St John, and Charlottetown. In most cases, these corporations have been equipped with a substantial and strategic land base, a multimillion-dollar capital budget, or both. They have already wrought dramatic and, for the most part, positive physical and economic changes in the fabric of our cities. The corporations' implications for local governments' urban planning functions, however, are much more ominous.

The evidence I have presented contradicts this author's positive assessment of the impact of these corporations. To reiterate, by virtue of their size, they are creating for the most part a chaos of gigantic look-alike high-rises and ruining Canadian downtowns.

One good example is Harbourfront Corporation in Toronto. The governing Liberal Party, seeking re-election in 1972, gave to a Crown corporation a section of the waterfront to develop and manage as a benefit to the city of Toronto. The corporation was still subject to the city's zoning by-laws, but city council over the course of the years was extremely lax in keeping track of Harbourfront's development plans. Besides, the city was getting tourists and kudos because the corporation financed a dazzling array of cultural events and services on the site with proceeds from agreements it had made with developers. These agreements, it turned out, provided for a wall of high-rises separating the city from the lake; Harbourfront is quintessential large-scale development, with no focus.

Independent authorities are responsible for big developments not only within downtown areas but also farther out. These special agencies, of which there are thousands in North America (us cities with over 50,000 people average ninety-one governing bodies apiece) and which wield considerable control over the utilities and infrastructure necessary to development, can exist far outside the boundaries of older, compact cities. Each has a special sphere of competence – electricity distribution, sewers, transit, mosquito abatement – and often finances itself at least partially from user fees and revenue bonds. These special authorities are usually run by appointed bodies well insulated from public input; however, they do tend to be receptive to big developments that provide more user fees. The structure of independent authorities across urban North America emerged precisely because large-scale developments were able to disregard the old city boundaries and spread out over the countryside. Those authorities now serve to perpetuate the patterns of development which spawned them.

The weakness of local governments in the face of decentralized and large-scale development is also attributable to their dependent legal status. They are, in fact, corporations themselves, created by the laws of state and provincial legislatures. us cities have somewhat more autonomy than Canadian cities, while Canadian provinces are prone to give, indeed impose, more rational boundaries and sets of responsibilities on their municipalities than American states are.

When it comes to land-use decisions, the consequence of a lack of local autonomy in Canada is that big developers with large-scale projects know that they can always appeal local council decisions to the province. This happens as follows. Formally, incorporated municipalities are responsible for regulating land use; they usually have an official plan which does little more than acknowledge existing land use (with all its segregated uses) and recommend a few areas for "redevelopment," which means that planners and council know that developers are assembling land in those areas. When a large development is proposed – whether it is a new subdivision or industrial park in the suburbs or high-rises downtown – the developer almost always is seeking to build more than the official plan allows. Council must agree to rezone the land for the development to take place. As pointed out above, council usually does this. If the municipality demurs, however, and decides not to allow the proposed development, then the developer can appeal the decision to a higher body at the provincial level. The result is usually in favour of the developer, and the large-scale project is built. Smaller builders with more inventive ideas, especially ones that promote physical diversity, do not have the resources to go through such an appeal process.

In the United States, zoning appeals to state governments or to the courts are rarer. When and if they do occur, local autonomy is almost always respected. However, the autonomy of local governments is a two-edged sword; it means that large developers can manage to orchestrate the kind of project they want by exploiting different government bodies, such as planning boards and utility districts, at the local level or by giving money to political parties. Municipalities are on their own and cannot look to the state government as a defense against aggressive developers, even if they are so inclined. Although much has been made of the "no-growth" legislation which has been passed by a number of municipalities, Logan and Molotch point out that such legislation in most cases has little effect and often is passed after a spurt of development has occurred. A study which David White and I did a few years ago on a building freeze in Toronto reached similar conclusions: it came at a time when the office-space market had sagged.

In Canada, there are numerous examples in which the lack of local-government autonomy is highlighted by provincial initiatives in urban development. These initiatives invariably centre on large-scale projects which preclude any chances for the nurturing of physical diversity. In Vancouver, reports Donald Gutstein, the provincial government

announced plans [in 1980] for the redevelopment of the 200 acres on the north side of False Creek. It was to be the largest urban redevelopment in the city's history, and yet the city had no advance warning of the provincial plans, which included the 60,000-seat stadium, seven million square feet of office space (the entire downtown core contained only sixteen million square feet), and 12,000 housing units. A crown corporation, B.C. Place Ltd., was set up to develop the project, and this provincial company has forged ahead, ignoring the concerns of residents in the surrounding neighbourhoods and fighting the city every step of the way. The province also decided unilaterally to hold a major transportation exhibition – Expo 86 – on the B.C. Place lands, to celebrate the city's centennial in 1986.

Toronto has fared no better. In the summer of 1988, city council was presented with a proposal for a one billion-dollar residential community close to the downtown on sparsely used industrial land. This proposal had been worked on for the previous few months by scores of high-level civil servants, not only at the provincial but also at the city level. Unbelievably, none of the city councillors knew anything about the project; only the mayor was privy to the plans. Needless to say, the councillors were outraged at not being consulted about such a large proposal. The mayor explained the secrecy by saying it was to prevent land speculation.

There is another characteristic of local-government structure which has consequences for municipal support for the deconcentrated, homogeneous development of which big industries and development companies are so fond. Municipalities are themselves large corporations, like many of the enterprises involved in making money out of building cities. Municipal corporation boards of directors (council members) are elected by stockholders (taxpayers) to manage the affairs of the company. These affairs are concerned mainly with the servicing, regulation, and protection of private property.

Several consequences flow from this structure, which was adopted in both the US and Canada in the nineteenth century by state and provincial governments on behalf of entrepreneurs (see chapter 5). One consequence concerns the style of operation. As a corporation, it imbues both politicians and staff with the corporate mentality. Unlike other levels of government, local government is thought of as a business by the people that run it. This mentality makes them more receptive to other businesses with business goals than to individuals or organizations with social or cultural goals. Since businesses have been making short-term profit from large-scale and homogeneous development, that kind of development is received approvingly by local governments. There seems to be no obvious, up-front *business* advantage to physical diversity, which is thus ignored.

A local government which is a corporation that services property will have its own view of public policy. Especially since the 1930s, higher-level governments have taken over the functions of servicing, regulating, and even protecting individuals (it must be acknowledged that big-city police forces serve this function as well). Local governments specialize in the physical environment; they expend fewer resources and less time on the development of creative policy ideas to help the people who use places. The contemporary municipal corporation presides very comfortably over a landscape of socially isolated consumers, just making sure that property is serviced with water, gas, well-maintained streets, pretty parks, and police and fire protection. Local government is not set up to deal with the social implications of its public policy. Cities that lack diversity may have marvelous services and, at the same time, discourage contact among neighbours or any other form of community.

Finally, it was pointed out above that higher-level governments were too large to be bothered with the intricacies of allowing vital and physically diverse cities to create themselves. In fact, municipal corporations themselves are too large. Voters really have no choice but to behave as stockholders, once in a while casting a ballot in favour of some person who is given responsibility for keeping the corporation in good financial shape. This representative structure precludes a definition of citizenship which involves some responsibility for the physical environment on a daily basis; instead, the structure encourages citizens to accept large-scale shopping centres, workplaces, and residential developments which cannot be managed by individual users at the street level in the way that diverse city neighbourhoods can. The size and form of local governments produce citizens, then, who tend not to value physical diversity, especially the public and semi-public places which knit a community together.

The corporate structure of municipalities is an enduring set of rules which predispose officials and citizens alike to ignore the symbiosis between places and the social relations of those who use them. Government structure thus reinforces the economic forces and public policies which are destroying city diversity.

Ideology

This constellation of mutually reinforcing factors – the profitability of homogeneous and deconcentrated development, the public policies which supported it, the structures of government which were also consistent – surely did not spring from nowhere. At some point there had to be people making individual assessments and decisions. There had to be people desiring above all else to seek profit from industrial production and urban development. There had to be individuals in government who felt that it was right to support corporations in their production and development goals, or at least that there was nothing wrong in it. Most important, there had to be individuals willing to work for big companies, buy their products with the wages they paid, and live in the houses and urban environments they built. To anyone who doubts the role of free will in this last case, I point to the Pruitt-Igoe housing development in St Louis, where even the homeless would not live.

Thus, there had to be a set of complementary beliefs which supported the decisions that produced such inhuman and destructive patterns of urbanization. Furthermore, these had to be conscious beliefs shared by a sufficiently large number of people to take precedence and guide development.

This set of beliefs is part of our ideology. And it is clear that the ideology which underlay the urban-development process in North America is the same as the one underlying its politics. It is based on the primacy of the individual, of private property, and of what has been called interest-group liberalism.

Individualism is widely misunderstood in this context. The individualism of North America does not involve relating to anyone else. While humans are, on the one hand, inherently social beings who need others for the satisfaction of their most basic needs, North American individualism adds two perverse dimensions: an autonomy-withdrawal syndrome which stresses self-sufficiency and even isolation; and a tendency to make everyone and everything into objects.

A North American's individuality, characteristically, is defined by his or her purchases. The two major purchases are the home and the car, both promoted as symbols of self-sufficiency. The motive behind acquiring them follows the reasoning that no one has to be at the mercy of the landlord or the public-transportation system. This is an illusion, of course. The tyranny of mortgage payments, car payments, production monopolies, unmanipulable technology, and bad design is ignored. Ursula Franklin, the Canadian scientist, has shown brilliantly how each new technology, from the sewing machine to the home computer, promises us freedom from drudgery and dependence on others and ends up enslaving us.

Seeking to define our individuality by what we consume has a cruel twist in our market society. The system can only survive if all goods and services, as well as land and labour, are considered to be for sale and thus incapable of being an intrinsic part of the person. In other words, they can be what is called "alienable." (As a contrast, consider that we have certain rights under our constitutions – the right to freedom of religion, for example – which are inalienable; that is, we could not get rid of them even if we wanted to.) Practically everything, and everybody, becomes extrinsic to ourselves under such a system. Everything becomes an object, including places, and the built environment.

This strange ideology of individualism has profound consequences for *citi*zenship, the way all of us relate to cities, and thus for the way we choose to build cities. Individualism, with its illusion of self-sufficiency, rejects involvement with other people, whether at the personal or civic level, as a source of self-sufficiency. We strive for home ownership and build our suburban houses separately in the middle of treed lots. Christopher Alexander reports on a study by a psychiatrist in Vienna, whose city-planning department had devised a questionnaire to determine housing preferences. The population at large preferred apartments to single-family houses. But the psychiatrist

gave the same questionnaire to 100 neurotic patients in his clinic. He found that a much higher proportion of these patients wanted to live in one-family houses, that they wanted larger houses relative to the size of their families, that they wanted more space per person, and that more of them wanted their houses to be situated in woods and trees. In other words, they wanted the suburban dream ...

Most people who move to suburbs are not sick in any literal sense. The ... reasons people give for moving to the suburbs are ... withdrawal from stress. The withdrawal is understandable, but the suburb formed by this withdrawal undermines the formation of intimate contacts in a devastating way.

In chapter 5 it was demonstrated that this "withdrawal from stress" also undermined casual contact, street management, and community life in general. The city in our culture is thus glorified for its excitement and its money-making potential – its stress? – but not for its community.

To put it a slightly different way, North Americans are unusually anxious to avoid unwanted social contact and social conflict. In one sense, of course, as Richard Sennett admits, "the refusal to deal with, absorb, and exploit reality outside the parochial scale is ... a universal human desire, being a simple fear of the unknown." Yet Sennett's case study of an extreme situation where a community built barricades against the outside world came from a very ordinary Long Island neighbourhood. In an earlier work, Sennett points to the postwar boom as the crucial factor in enabling Americans to move to the suburbs and to form "communities of self-conscious solidarity."

Constance Perin has also noted American avoidance of social conflict and connects it specifically to urban form: "Under conditions of sprawl, social relations are framed by the structure of spaces, with distance built in to avoid social conflict. Everywhere, the size of lots and the front, back and side yard dimensions meticulously set forth in zoning ordinances translate as mechanisms for reducing the likelihood of intrusions into each homeowner's personal space." Avoidance of social conflict and of unwanted intrusions is expressed in many other ways. One does not hang one's wash out on the line, literally as well as figuratively. The renovated houses in downtown Toronto have been divested of their front porches, leaving no way for the residents to be part of the street and neighbourhood, even on warm summer evenings. New suburban development is especially revealing: two big garage doors, and a little front door off to one side (Figure 16), instead of verandahs opening on the street (Figure 17). Autonomy and withdrawal characterize our governments as well. We create little suburban jurisdictions to keep out unwanted types of people. Indeed, this is a failure of citizenship which has sprung from our ideology of autonomous individualism, a failure in which most of us have acquiesced. It goes far beyond greedy developers and their political allies in helping to explain a built environment which discourages neighbour contact and neighbourhood action.

Like individual self-sufficiency, the sanctity of private property is central to North America's political economy. The two dimensions complement each other. For Jeremy Bentham and many nineteenth-century political theorists, ownership of material property of any kind was a necessary prerequisite to individual happiness (which was the only important kind of happiness). In the tradition of John Locke, ownership of property in the form of land was the ultimate expression of individuality, and nothing should be allowed to tamper

Figure 16
Front view of suburban house, Toronto area

with it. Miles and miles of look-alike housing built by private as well as public capital make a mockery of this image, but it is nonetheless promoted tirelessly by private enterprise. Political motives are less evident in the 1990s than they were in the 1920s and earlier, when home ownership was defined in trade magazines as the surest defense against bolshevism. However, the legitimacy of the system depends on investment by the working class in the built environment. Here, then, is the ideology behind the FHA and CMHC policies of funnelling billions of dollars into suburban development, an ideology clearly compatible with the dreams of so many North Americans.

The sanctity of private property is also used by large developers and their allies against neighbourhood groups or left-wing politicians who sometimes oppose big urban projects. These projects, of course, tend to be homogeneous as well as large scale, because it is easier to make big money on that sort of development. Ironically, although developers can use the sacred cow of private property as the ground for doing what they like with their land, they also rely in many cases on governments' outright support or at least tacit agreement to inter-fere only minimally with the approval and development process. The legal zoning power of municipalities simply becomes the socially acceptable way of complying with the wishes of private and public capital, rather than a way of tempering private gain for the collective

Figure 17
Front view of downtown house, Toronto

good. The role of the political system, in North America's political ideology, is to facilitate rather than to modify the economic pressures to build large-scale, homogeneous, and deconcentrated cities, by legitimating the sanctity of private property. Enough people support this legitimizing policy for us to accept the governments which make it. It will be demonstrated in chapter 7 that withdrawing support for such a policy involves not so much voting yet another team into public office as re-examining and changing our own ideology and way of life.

Supplementing philosophies of individualism and private property is a North American philosophy of the state, which is known by its supporters as pluralism, but which Theodore Lowi has more accurately termed interest-group liberalism. Lowi has perceptively documented just how closely private enterprise and government have worked together (even in the halcyon days of *laissez-faire* in the nineteenth century), and just how illusory is the separation of economic and political spheres as portrayed by mainstream thought. The construction of the postwar urban landscape, we have seen, was a team effort between government and business.

Thus, while political philosophy exhorted North American governments not to do what the individual should be able to do for himself or to interfere with the rights of private property, it turned a blind eye to the fact that government decision making was becoming a process of negotiation with hundreds of decentralized, business-dominated agencies, both public and private: Lowi's interest-group liberalism. Jacques Léveillée found it alive and well in the politics of contemporary Montreal, even among the newly elected reform members of council whose pre-election sympathies had clearly been with the poor and the homeless. Once in power, it was important to play the interest-group game. Lorimer and Gutstein's research has shown that in Canadian cities, interest-group liberalism takes the form of planning boards and city councils whose members are mostly from the development industry. This arrangement ensures decisions which, despite the legal weaknesses of local governments, have helped to fashion the building of the postwar North American city.

An important sub-theme of the ideology of interest-group liberalism is the public corporation. Corporate legitimacy, says Karen Orren, "in the practical sense that big businessmen may expect voluntary social compliance with their decisions, has always been conditioned on the fact that people think that corporations perform a valuable social function." The legitimacy of corporate power, and the basis for North American compliance with corporate activites, stems from the nineteenth century, when government charters were being granted to corporations because they were involved in producing public goods, such as railroads, canals, and utilities. It will be recalled that municipalities, too, legitimized themselves by receiving corporate status from states and provinces. Corporations were even allowed to issue notes which were legal means of exchange and to exercise powers of eminent domain, that is, powers to interfere with the "sanctity" of private property. New York State's Urban Development Corporation has the power to override municipal zoning laws and to expropriate land, powers which delight the developers who are partners in the Corporation's projects.

As it turned out, these corporations which produced public goods and which, presumably, were agents for economic growth and well-being, were also money-making machines. Those which were not municipal corporations became more and more independent of the political and legal system while retaining many of the extraordinary powers which "private" companies did not have, such as individual officers' immunity from being sued. The fact that most North American cities were built by large corporations is therefore significant. Their legal powers and their semblance of legitimacy (which has been undermined in recent years) have given them size and prestige which are difficult to challenge. If private developers had set up a railway company in order to make it more profitable for themselves to develop the suburbs; if, furthermore, that railway company had intentionally gone into debt so that municipal governments would have to take it over, such activity would have been deemed immoral, even indictable. But such railway companies were in fact set up at the turn of the century as public corporations, established with the blessings of city governments; and they behaved in the indicated manner. Even though these corporations were used shamelessly by entrepreneurs on their boards of directors to enhance suburban property values, it somehow seemed vaguely legitimate because it was done under the aegis of a corporation.

General acceptance of the legitimacy of corporations illustrates the importance of what Orren calls the compliance structure in determining what happens politically and economically – in this case, the building of postwar cities. The implication is that there are broader cultural values which support the compliance structure – what we as North Americans are willing to put up with.

CULTURE

The construction of a homogeneous, deconcentrated urban landscape has been traced to proximate economic forces and to public policy, and thence to government structures and political ideology. Intertwined with all this have been psychological and philosophical considerations: attitudes towards growth and consumption, individualism and isolation. There are also important cultural dimensions to the question of why we build what we do, and these require examination.

First, the sacredness of home ownership is unquestioned. Certainly the important motive for home ownership is that it is the only form of secure housing in a culture where property is private and the market determines land use – non-owners have no rights, especially to permanent occupation. But the motive of making a good investment, as strong as it is, pales beside some of the more emotional sentiments connected with owning a single-family home. Outside of Iceland, only New Zealand and Australia have higher home-ownership levels than Canada and the United States, well above sixty percent. There is a distinct cultural bias against renters, who are considered to be less reliable, more transient, and unlikely to care about the neighbourhood. Home owners are seen as having attained full citizenship, while renters have not. This cultural bias, Constance Perin argues, is expressed in the conscious physical separation of renters and owners. Making it possible to rent in an area where all homes are owned "spoils" the area; apartment houses are considered to be "parasites" in such areas. Vast tracts of land on the fringes of cities are set aside exclusively for owner-occupied housing, even though, as earlier described, such developments are incredibly expensive and take good farmland out of service. The drive for home ownership is a moral as well as an economic quest.

Another characteristic of our culture which affects the physical form of cities is the apparent need to segregate family relations from the production process. Capitalism is often held responsible for the separation of home and work. But as with home ownership, the urge for separation goes beyond the economic dimension; it has acquired the stature of a moral imperative. This cultural trait, which has been traced well back into the nineteenth century, idealizes both home and work. The home is the source of the nation's moral strength, a sanctuary, both sacred and blessed. Dolores Hayden has called this set of ideals "the home as haven," a haven from the world of work and busy city streets. Work, on the other hand, is also critically important to fulfilling ourselves as responsible citizens. Separating the two activities, says Constance Perin, maintains their purity and seems to be as prevalent a value among doctors with consulting rooms in their houses as among assembly-line workers living in Levittown or Don Mills. In Houston, according to one study, complaints by one owner against another in residential areas revolved mostly around violations of rules against using the home as a workplace.

Thus, both deconcentration and land-use segregation are expressions of some basic features of the North American personality. While these features can be traced to characteristics of the market system and capitalism, they seem to have a cultural vitality and momentum of their own. Two other cultural traits are worth considering very briefly. One is what may be called the primacy of business, the other the ascendancy of the mass media.

The businessman has an extremely high status in North America. Changes in government or government policy find news reporters breathlessly asking the investment "community" how it will respond: will it bless us with more money or curse us with less? The high-rise office buildings in the downtown cores of our cities represent more than just a profitable use of land. One can be amused by the way banks compete with each other for ownership of the highest office tower in the city. But the office tower has replaced the cathedral as the central edifice of our culture, manifesting our worship of business as well as of technology. "The supremely sacred central precinct," known as the central business district in North America, is, according to David Harvey, little different from the ceremonial centres of ancient cities. The air is so rarefied there that even restaurants have a hard time surviving. As Harvey puts it, who wants to eat in church, anyway? Thus, large-scale, segregated mega-projects in downtown areas grow out of our culture's worship of business, in a pattern which mirrors the centrality of the cathedrals and temples of older cultures.

Finally, there is the role of the mass media and communications technology in building the postwar city. We believe unquestioningly in the value of such technology, and, in a very real sense, urbanization and mass communication technology belong together, as long as one understands that communication means television and urbanization means large-scale, homogeneous, deconcentrated development. The television has become so universal a part of the North American home that the census no longer considers it worthwhile to collect data on it.

Television's primary cultural function is to promote product consumption as a universal goal. The North American city is a city built for maximum consumption, as Paul and Percival Goodman have so devastatingly shown. Everyone has his or her own washing machine, house, can opener. No need to go to the neighbours to watch TV; we have our own. Even our children have their own. Living in the isolated cubicles of high-rise apartments (even if they are condominiums) or in single-family homes in the suburbs maximizes "independence" from neighbours.

The means by which this illusion of independence through consumption is created, the means by which the people are made aware of products like electric can openers, are the mass media. The phenomenal level of consumption by North Americans has been achieved in part by the use of the mass media to promote consumption, in ways which are as sophisticated as they are unrelenting. The physical appearance of our cities owes much to media-stimulated desires for "independent" living with all its accoutrements – single-family dwellings, cars, and appliances.

The mass media have also helped to increase social and political isolation. We experience our society's culture, politics, and social life through the tube, whether it is a sitcom about family life or a political debate. The range of images one receives is incredibly broad in one sense, but it is largely managed by advertisers of products who finance the stations; and there is only the illusion of communication because there is no feedback from the viewer. Direct personal experiences with politicians, with music and dance, even with one's neighbours, have been replaced by campaign messages and debates, television spectaculars, sitcoms, and movies on cable. Earlier, I mentioned Murray Bookchin's observation that even though workers and the poor were always pushed into their own ghettoes, they still had a vibrant street life and, therefore, a political life on the basis of which they could challenge decisions made by big government and corporations; that disappeared, Bookchin shows, with the advent of television, which lured the working class off the public squares and streets into individual homes.

We have all been similarly lured. The mass media lead us to experience life vicariously. We no longer consider it important to build city streets where we meet each other, shop, gossip, and discuss issues. All our needs are taken care of in our insulated dwelling units, separated from our place of work, deconcentrated into self-sufficient mini-estates.

PLANNERS

Outlining the economic, political, and cultural underpinnings of the physical form of the postwar North American city has cast a light on several overlapping sets of actors: the business and corporate community, governments, homeowners, the working man, and ourselves. There is a special set of actors I wish to deal with last, actors whose role is as paradoxical as it is significant in influencing urban form. These are the planners.

The paradox is that although they are widely blamed for many of the excrescences of the postwar city, they are politically powerless and sometimes barely accepted as legitimate parts of the policy-making process. Especially in the US, urban planners are considered to be socialist intruders on the rights of private property, and to some extent they are.

Murray Bookchin argues that the significance of planners lies in the fact that they exist at all. Their existence shows our market society's distrust that spontaneous economic and social activity can express itself in a beautiful city, let alone a habitable or efficient one.

Planners themselves play many roles within the profession. They may be staff people, hired by cities (often only because the charter or the province requires it) to advise elected politicians on the merits of particular projects and, periodically, to prepare official land-use plans for the whole municipality. Such plans tend to be affirmations of how land is already used in the city coupled with suggestions on where new development might be "advisable." These suggestions rely heavily on what planners already know about where developers are assembling land, because the two groups are in frequent and close contact with each other. (In Vancouver, recently, a large project was being reviewed by planners *hired by the developer*, under agreement with the city.)

Depending on the planner's own personality and on the politics of the city, the planner may be simply rubber-stamping projects sent his or her way for comments, or making perceptible changes in the design of developments – especially if there is no direction from the politicians on city council. Many planners are consciously grooming themselves for employment with the development industry; private developers find it very useful to have on staff someone who is familiar with a city's approval process. Some planners even become developers themselves. More usually, they become consultants to private companies, or they may stick to the academic route and teach planning at university. Still others are ambitious within the planning department itself, seeking to become they city's commissioner of planning. Many have important ideals which they are trying to realize by working with citizens' groups, writing reports, and developing new policy alternatives. Planners are often idealists whose visions, perforce, are tempered by the realities of the system; in other words, the outcome of negotiations over the design of a particular project is usually a subtle blend of planners' ideals (which reflect commonly held social values) and immediate practical demands to expedite the development process. In fact, many planning departments are called Departments of Planning and Development.

These planning ideals, which get variously translated into physical development by planners in all the roles just described, have been vividly expressed by a small but remarkably influential group of architects and city planners who have written about the ideas behind their designs. Significantly, these visionaries all had clear, though sometimes idiosyncratic, conceptions of the kind of society that would be congruent with their physical plans. In other words, they felt that if we are going to build cities that work, we must have a clear idea of a society that works.

Let me start with two writers whose ideas are strongly reflected in the deconcentration and homogeneity, the segregation and scale of the new North American city.

Frank Lloyd Wright (1867–1959) was an architect with very definite ideas about city planning. He deplored the fact that city dwellers had to rent their residences, that they were enslaved by landlords and speculators. His solution was for everyone to own his or her own bit of land; Wright calculated that if everyone in the US owned one acre, the entire population would fit neatly into an area the size of Texas. The resulting pattern of development, one-acre farmlets which Wright proposed calling Broadacre City, would produce so many independent and self-sufficient Americans that national and regional governments would simply wither away, retaining only a few functions such as regulation of natural resources. "No politician as such could make a living in Broadacre City," he wrote. His planning for the sturdy, self-sufficient individual included the clearly political and economic precept, "A human being from the time he is born is entitled to a piece of ground with which he can identify himself by use of it."

Although Wright's Broadacre City was scorned by many critics of the 1930s, its extravagant use of land foretells the suburban sprawl of postwar development, the main difference being that the big lots are never used for agriculture. Wright's prophetic ideas, therefore, were remarkably congruent with North American building patterns. And Wright's politics and his planning were intertwined; he called Broadacre City "the plastic form of a genuine democracy."

Another architect with strong ideas about city planning was Le Corbusier, who moved to Paris from his native Switzerland when he was thirty-one. In fact, for him, architecture and planning were indivisible. In his words, "The urban planner is nothing but an architect. The former organizes architectural spaces, he fixes the place and the purpose of built containers, he links all these things in time and space by a traffic network. And the latter, the architect, concerned, for example, with a simple dwelling, also erects containers, also creates spaces. At the creative level, the architect and the planner are one."

Le Corbusier advocated tearing down large central sections of old cities and replacing them with high-rise towers surrounded by large amounts of green space. High density would be achieved by tall buildings rather than covering every square foot of space. None of his own master plans was ever executed, for the simple reason that almost no one had the money and the totalitarian authority necessary to realize them. Nevertheless, his ideas were immensely influential, especially his images of groups of high-rise slabs, which were built in profusion on both sides of the Atlantic from the 1950s to the 1970s.

As with Wright, Le Corbusier's planning and politics were closely related. One of his early books, *Urbanisme*, contained a picture of Louis XIV supervising the building of Les Invalides, with this caption: "Homage to a great town planner – This despot conceived immense projects and realized them. Over all the country his noble works still fill us with admiration. He was capable of saying, 'We wish it,' or 'Such is our pleasure.'" Le Corbusier was unable to find the latter-day despot needed for his plans. He came to believe in a hierarchical syndicalism close to Italian fascism of the 1930s and dedicated a later work, *La ville radieuse (The Radiant City)*, to Authority.

Having visited Italy in 1934, he wrote, "The present spectacle in Italy, the state of her spiritual powers, announces the imminent dawn of the modern spirit. Her shining purity and force illumine the paths which had been obscured by the cowardly and the profiteers."

Politics itself "had no role in the running of the Radiant City ... a city for the Machine Age could never emerge from discussion and compromise: that was the path to chaos," writes planning historian Robert Fishman of Le Corbusier's ideas.

How many of the ideas and themes of this chapter are reflected in the writings of these two men! Physically, the plans of Wright and Le Corbusier were prototypes (almost seventy years old) of two of the most important features of the North American city – the sprawling suburbs and the downtown office towers.

Although no Broadacre City or *ville radieuse* was ever built, the impact of the ideas of these Master Builders, as architect and writer Peter Blake calls them, was tremendous.

The fact is that virtually no modern building constructed today would look the way it does if it had not been for the work of ... these ... men ... Le Corbusier ... and Wright, in their very different personalities and cultural origins, represent ... great traditions of the western world: Le Corbusier is the heir to the classic tradition of the Mediterranean ... Wright was the eternal anarchist, the defender of absolute freedom, the heir to the ideal of the America of the Revolution.

What personal traits shaped these men and what their traditions and ideals did to shape their work goes far beyond architecture; for to them architecture is simply the language they used to express their ideals of a better world ... [They] have been attacked, reviled, ignored – until years later their fellow men suddenly began to understand what [they] had tried to say against the din of professional noisemakers.

That understanding, it seems, emerged after World War II, when there was an unprecedented opportunity to apply the large-scale concepts of Wright and Le Corbusier, in the ravaged downtowns of war-torn Europe and the farmlands surrounding car-crazy North American cities. These applications, however, brought with them the anti-politics of Wright (embodied in the suburban failure of citizenship) and the authoritarianism of Le Corbusier (embodied in the compliance structure of large corporations and their high-tech buildings). Politics and urban design were symbiotically linked.

Another visionary whose ideas were woven in to the urban fabric of the twentieth century was Ebenezer Howard. Howard was not a famous architect; he was a stenographer. Yet his perseverance and

energy in pursuit of his ideals made him easily as influential as
Wright or Le Corbusier, though not so well known. Howard's planning and politics contrast sharply with those of Wright and Le Corbusier. He envisioned Garden Cities, self-governing satellite towns
with "densities like inner London's." Peter Hall writes:

The Victorian slum city, to be sure, was in many ways an horrific place; but
it offered economic and social opportunities, lights, and crowds. The late-
Victorian countryside, not too often seen in a sentimental glow, was in fact
equally unprepossessing: though it promised fresh air and nature, it was
racked by agricultural depression and it offered neither sufficient work and
wages, nor adequate social life. But it was possible to square the circle, by
combining the best of town and country in a new kind of settlement, Town-
Country.

To achieve this, a group of people – necessarily, including several with
commercial competence and creditability – should establish a limited divi-
dend company, borrowing money to establish a garden city in the countryside, far enough from the city to ensure that the land was bought at rock-
bottom, depressed-agricultural, land values. They should get agreement from
leading industrialists to move their factories there; their workers would move
too, and would build their own houses. The garden city would have a fixed
limit – Howard suggested 32,000 people, living on 1,000 acres of land ... It
would be surrounded by a much larger area of permanent green belt.

Howard's idea, outlined first in 1898, was that a constellation of these
satellite cities could be connected by rapid transit, so they would all
be easily accessible to each other. The heart of Howard's plan, says
Hall, was not physical, but social and political. "The key was that the
citizens would own the land in perpetuity," after they paid off the
money they borrowed at the start. The central idea was to have local
management and self-government. Howard's revolutionary plan was
not widely adopted. Nevertheless, the physical image of the Garden
City remained a powerful one for many city dwellers, as well as for
developers. Howard's political and social visions have been ignored.

The postwar North American city has been characterized by vac-
uous physical imitations of Garden Cities and by the forms and ideologies of Wright and Le Corbusier. The clashing ideals of Broadacre
City and Radiant City are expressed in both the physical design and
politics of our cities. While in the 1950s the new development proceeded in an authoritarian fashion, in the 1960s citizens' groups and
other organizations appeared in opposition to the massive urban-
renewal projects and expressways, and sometimes even to suburban
developments. In the middle of all this were planners, who were more

and more likely to have received training in the social sciences as well as the more traditional fields of architecture and engineering. These planners reflected the politics of the time: there was no single answer to the problems of urban development, but tentative hypotheses could be arrived at by rigorous attention to scientific methods and systematic analysis of demographic and land-use data.

By the 1970s most left-wing analysts could claim, with some reason, that the new and broader scientific approach of the planning profession was still basically in the position of legitimizing current urban development. Furthermore, that development was still unrelentingly large in scale and homogeneous, and more in service to profits than to people. Nevertheless, for others, planning had become the Planning Process, by which conflicting views of the public interest could confront each other on equal terms in the field of democratic politics. This conception of the planner's role was a reflection of the popularity of ideas put forth at the time by American political scientists such as Robert Dahl. In Dahl's view, conflicting views about public policy, held by a multitude of organized interests, got resolved by skillful politicians who were competing with each other for the right to make authoritative decisions; this competition for support (through elections) ensured the politicians' sensitivity to the needs and desires of all citizens. This was pluralism.

An interesting actor who emerged from this era was the advocate planner, the professional who decided that governments and developers had too much of a monopoly on expertise. The advocate planner went to work for citizens' groups to present a professional, scientific, alternative view. Paul Davidoff, one proponent of advocate planning, put it this way: "As a critic of opposition plans [the advocate planner] would be performing a task similar to the legal technique of cross-examination. While painful to the planner whose bias is exposed (and no planner can be entirely free of bias) the net effect of confrontation between advocates of alternative plans would be more careful and precise research."

Nothing could express more clearly the dilemma we are in. We have an urban environment that is costing us billions, indeed, killing us with its pollution, cutting us off from meaningful contact with neighbours and destroying authentic politics, preventing our children from developing a sense of responsibility, turning our public spaces into fearsome battle zones where no one dares to venture, and yet we look everywhere but to ourselves for solutions. Instead, we put our faith in technology, or in the outcome of a process which pits two competing technologies against each other. Ursula Franklin stresses that technology need not be this way; she contrasts what she calls prescriptive technologies, which demand compliance from their users, with holistic technologies, when "the doer is in control of the work process." We have allowed ourselves to be overwhelmed by prescriptive technologies, and they are ruining us and the planet. The significance of the Garden City concept has been reversed from its original intention of local self-reliance to the practice of planning whole communities right from the start.

As democratic as the pluralist notion of competing technologies sounds, we have allowed profoundly authoritarian structures to dominate our lives. We get an occasional choice among politicians who all promise vaguely to fix everything up for us. We are bombarded by advertisements which treat us like morons. Market power and property are accumulating in the hands of a few hierarchically controlled corporations. We are dependent on such corporations and on huge distribution systems for necessities like food, jobs, energy, clothing, and shelter. We rationalize it all by clinging to the belief that we are free because we can choose between technologies, soaps, and politicians. This is the kind of freedom we can all do without.

Visionaries like Wright, Le Corbusier, and Howard have done us the service of showing that a new city form implies new kinds of economics, politics, and culture: for Wright, it means a John Wayne self-sufficiency; for Le Corbusier, a mechanized authoritarianism; and for Howard, a network of municipal cooperatives. I have argued that our own unfriendly urban development is the product not only of big governments and corporations but of a compliant social structure as well. People who plan our cities for us are simply the most transparent symbols of a system and culture where responsibility for the built environment has passed from the hands of the individual citizen — with awful results, as Ebenezer Howard saw so clearly. An attempt is made in the next two chapters to show how responsibility can pass back.

CHAPTER SEVEN

Basic Assumptions

The purpose of this chapter and the next is to suggest what we, individually and in small groups, can do to promote a saner built environment. Some concrete examples of what some people have done will be given in chapter 8. However, these people's behaviour presupposes a significant shift in values. They have questioned and found unsatisfactory some basic aspects of our value system; they have also realized how those aspects inform choices we make in everyday life, and that the choices have produced the built environment we have. For now, I want to explain the nature of the old values which are being questioned and how they can be transcended, especially in the case of cities.

As a brief preliminary example of the link between basic values and the shape of cities, consider the value we place on economic growth. The postwar building boom, which produced most of the current urban landscape, is perhaps the most tangible expression of that value; but in fact, our entire natural environment is being threatened by the pursuit of economic growth which has dominated Western culture, and therefore city building, over the last two centuries. Thus, anyone thinking about designing better cities must be conscious of how the uncritical pursuit of growth as a value has produced our present, unworkable built environment.

Growth, or at least development of some kind, is intrinsic to every living organism. But in the West we have acquired a peculiar fascination with indiscriminate material growth. We worship the gross national product (GNP), which is gross indeed: included within it are the costs of "health" (i.e., sickness) care, litigation, and automobile accidents. Doctors, lawyers, and body shops are entitled to an income, but should that income be considered a positive product of the nation? If it is included in the GNP, we should be cautious about rejoicing over growth in the GNP. Our worship of growth leads to glorification of increased production and more products. But it is questionable whether the economy is growing just because General Mills came out with a new chocolate-covered cereal or because Americans bought more television sets last year. The awesome but predictable consequence for a culture which worships growth so indiscriminately and insanely is self-destruction. The signs are clearer and clearer: the ozone layer is disappearing; huge, previously healthy forests are dying before our very eyes; thousands of species of animals are being wiped out; water has to be treated before it is potable. The causal links have been drawn again and again by scientists between these ecological signs and the "products" of our advanced economy such as pesticides, hamburger wrappers, and automobiles.

Thus, growth may not be inherently bad, but the kind of growth we have been experiencing certainly is. Our postwar cities, with their large-scale developments, segregated land use, and deconcentration, express this ideology of growth historically, politically and economically. Histories of cities, with a few exceptions, tend to be written as the history of their physical and demographic growth. The politics of cities are concerned mainly with the planning, approval, and servicing of large new developments. Our economy, with its multinational corporations and its flows of placeless, international capital, ends up being expressed physically by the huge office complexes, the shopping centres, the industrial parks, and the vast stretches of suburban housing which make up what has been called by Melvin Webber our non-place urban realm. Hence, cities are the most massive physical example of our growth economy, sustaining perhaps the most serious consequences. Solving the problems posed by lack of physical diversity is thus part of solving the larger problem of environmental destruction. But how do we start?

Finding conventional explanations for the form of postwar urban growth unsatisfactory, I have suggested that the design elements of the North American city could be traced to cultural habits and beliefs such as this worship of consumption and material growth. Acknowledging this fact is actually a source of strength, because spreading awareness that we harbour outmoded or dysfunctional beliefs on an individual level is the surest path to changing those beliefs and their consequences. Most people are willing to admit that beliefs have consequences, but it is worth stressing that the beliefs with the most powerful consequences are the ones we are least aware of, the ones we use as working assumptions. Two or three of these assumptions and their relationship to city building are now considered.

SEPARATION FROM NATURE

The first belief concerns our conception of the nature of physical reality. The sixteenth and seventeenth centuries saw a revolution in science which centred around the ideas of men such as Galileo Galilei, Isaac Newton, René Descartes, and Francis Bacon. The ideology of the scientific revolution was that valuable and powerful new truths could be achieved by a new method – the scientific method – of studying the natural world. This world was made up of little balls of matter, each separate from the next and, indeed, separate from us. The activity of these little balls, furthermore, was seen as conforming to discoverable laws which could be expressed mathematically as a series of cause-and-effect relationships. Nature transformed into a bunch of little balls loses its beauty in our eyes; it becomes dehumanized and disenchanted, divested of spirits and of spirit.

Seeing nature this way signalled a profound shift from medieval conceptions about it. Roger Jones, the physicist, illustrates this shift in terms of our view of space.

The sensing of human character and life in so-called inanimate objects by many primitive and even pre-Renaissance people should not be viewed as some kind of magical network of relationships existing within space as we know it today. Rather, it is part of the actual experience of space for these peoples. Suppose I, as a medieval man, diagnose myself as mercurial and I symbolize this through a *felt* connection to the planet Mercury or the element quicksilver in the earth's crust. Within the framework of my medieval mind, I do not picture all of this to myself as some mysterious influence of the planet Mercury acting at a distance across the vast reaches of empty space or as some chemical spell that quicksilver casts over my personality regardless of its distance and separation from me in the earth. These are not relationships *in* space to me; they *are* space. It is the sum of all the felt organic connections between my inner and outer worlds that I experience as space itself. Space is the synthesis of all my feelings of relatedness, connectivity, orientation. (Emphasis in original)

The new view of the natural world as something separate from us, from our perceptions, was not accepted without resistance, but it gradually became dominant in the eighteenth century and after, so dominant that we in the twentieth century find it completely unremarkable. Yet it is hard to overestimate the enormous impact of perceiving ourselves as separate from nature. This perception left us in something of a predicament: we are insecure about being provided for by the natural world. Not being totally sure that our survival is guaranteed by nature's abundance, by the planet which spawned us, we view scarcity as a threat; we feel incomplete and needful. This sense of need is quickly transformed into fear, desires, goals, conflict, and especially into feelings of separateness from each other.

While raw emotions such as these have been around for millennia – some would say ever since we started worshipping a male deity in the sky – there seemed to be a growing tendency in the seventeenth and eighteenth centuries to view these emotions as an inherent and dominant part of the human condition. This tendency was most evident in the writings of thinkers we still look up to as the source of our political and economic institutions. These thinkers participated in a self-conscious and concentrated effort to apply the Galilean, Cartesian, and Newtonian methods to the study of humans and of society, and in so doing to deduce or infer principles of politics and economics. The effort produced a politics and an economics whose premises and rules underlie the way we have built the North American urban landscape.

For example, the dismal view of Thomas Hobbes became our way of perceiving politics. He argued that humans are naturally separate material entities, each seeking endlessly to gratify insatiable desires and to extend power over others. The only solution to such madness (which Hobbes claims can only occur in unbridled form in a hypothetical state of nature) is to impose an exterior authority – the state, or Leviathan – which we all agree to obey in order to protect ourselves from each other's savagery. Today, we rely on the legal system and the police to protect us from assaults and burglary, as well as to make us contribute taxes to pay for public services. We have to be forced to be civilized, let alone community-minded. We are, in short, plugged into a compliance structure which tells us what to do because we are too scared or too greedy to do it ourselves. The postwar North American city as described in chapters 5 and 6 is a physical expression of this political immaturity.

We have dismal economics as well. Always viewing scarcity as a threat, even as we consume more and more per capita, we have used Newtonian physics to exploit nature to meet the needs which we are afraid a dehumanized nature may not be able to satisfy without being prompted. The desire for increasing amounts of material goods underlay the incredible growth of industry and industrial technology in the last three centuries. It also spurred an unprecedented exploitation of non-renewable resources, which provided the means for explosive economic growth. (As an indication of how our attitude towards extracting natural resources has changed, consider the practice of fifteenth-century miners of praying each morning to Mother

Earth before taking out the ore.) Now it has become clear that our short-lived dependence on cheap fossil fuels not only made possible wasteful urban sprawl; it has also exhausted their supply and irretrievably polluted the planet's air and water. Thus, there are strong links between the feeling of being separate from nature, exploitation of natural resources, the shape of our cities, and the environmental mess we find ourselves in today.

We have even created an economics of scarcity, whereby the scarcer something is, the higher its price, whether it is gold, wheat, or the right downtown location. Our whole market system depends on making people feel as if something is valuable because it is scarce. Hence we have cities with millions of new homes being constructed and thousands of homeless; we throw away wheat while millions are starving to death in the city core. This surely is a form of madness.

Our illusion of scarcity has created a preoccupation with progress, the syndrome referred to at the start of the chapter. It was only in the seventeenth and eighteenth centuries that the idea arose that life, at least for humans, was not cyclical. Our harmonious connection with the ebb and flow of nature was replaced by a belief that we are on a path of progress, what we call growth. We are always "ahead" of what has gone before. While worship of linear growth characterized city building before the postwar era, it has been responsible for an unprecedented orgy of destruction ("urban renewal") as well as construction since the 1940s, and thus for the absence of a healthy mix of old and new buildings in our cities.

Since there is a link between our concept of physical reality and our current problems, it makes sense to ask whether there are concepts of physical reality other than the one inherited from the scientific revolution. Without delving too deeply into newer trends in science, we find that it is exploring much broader conceptions of reality from those of Newton, Descartes, and Bacon. For example, the search by physicists for the smallest, most basic units of matter has uncovered scores of so-called "elementary particles," whose lifespan is a few milliseconds or less. These particles do not follow Newtonian laws of movement; the physicist can only compute probabilities that they are in any particular place at a particular time. The nearer we get to pinning down the (admittedly tiny) mass of these particles, the less certain we are about where they actually are. Intriguingly, they are not causally independent of each other – they can only be defined in terms of their relationship to other particles. Their realities interpenetrate each other. This is a far cry from a view of physical reality as a set of separate, hard little balls of matter whose movements can be precisely mapped out by mathematical equations.

These little balls of matter, on close inspection, disappear into a realm of probabilities and relationships. Those relationships are not of the form of "A causes B"; but rather, they are organic and interdependent networks.

The organic interdependence of the built environment, or at least of a built environment that works, has been underscored by a number of writers. Christopher Alexander, in *The Timeless Way of Building*, points out that the elements of a church, for example, are meaningless except in relationship to other parts of the church: "In a gothic cathedral, the nave is *flanked by* aisles which run parallel to it. The transept is at *right angles* to the nave and aisles; the ambulatory is *wrapped around* the outside of the apse" (emphasis in the original). Alexander applies the same reasoning to urban regions, where subway stops and office buildings, front yards and manhole covers are meaningless except insofar as they relate to other tall buildings, houses, streets, and so on. To put it the other way around, try imagining a manhole cover in the middle of a corn field. There, it has no meaning. It only makes sense on a street, defined by its relation to other features of the physical environment.

Yet, as Jane Jacobs has pointed out, we insist on planning and building cities as if their elements were independent globs which can be plunked down anywhere in a city to do their thing. She is most eloquent in her discussion of parks, which are often treated as an unalloyed benefit, wherever they are placed. Jacobs shows convincingly that parks which are successful, parks which are popular and attractive, are perceived that way because they weave into the fabric of a surrounding diverse neighbourhood. No matter how well designed the park is, if it is placed in a dead neighbourhood, it will be a dead park. In fact, it can be a deadly park, dangerous to venture into.

Echoing Jacobs, the landscape architect Anne Whiston Spirn traces the growing environmental problems of our cities to our habit of treating buildings and developments as isolated installations instead of as parts of the urban ecosystem – its air, water, and earth.

Thus, whether we choose to perceive it or not, the elements of our cities, just like the elementary particles, have realities which interpenetrate each other, which literally define each other. The sooner we start moving in harmony with this physical reality, the sooner we shall have cities that work.

Modern physics has also come to some conclusions about our own relationship to nature which go against the relationship defined in the seventeenth century. In positing our separation from nature, we were able to assume that we could observe it, make inferences about it, impute cause-and-effect relationships to it, predict it, all without having any effect on our object of study, whether it was a planet, a tulip, or even a fellow human being.

Throughout the nineteenth century, physicists were trying to figure out the nature of light: some were convinced that it was composed of particles, while others insisted that it was a wave. One experimental procedure would verify the first theory while another, with equal authority, would verify the second. The way the experiment was set up, in other words, determined what the scientists would find. By the twentieth century it had become obvious that light could be both waves and particles, and that it was the observer's choice as to which was "reality." Thus, the scientist's way of asking the question determined the answer. The experimenter could not separate himself or herself from what was being studied.

"The way we have been asking the question" has been a function of our sense of separation from nature. Assuming ourselves to be objective observers of the natural environment, and manipulating the cause-and-effect relationships we could predict, we built machines and cities and went to the moon. But we were very poor at exploring the implications of how we related to our environment, whether that environment was nature or the cities we had built ourselves. Now we are discovering that our technologies are destroying nature along with ourselves, who are an integral part of nature. Our experimental and manipulative posture towards nature and towards each other clouded our awareness of the world as a network of mutual relations, and of the intimate links between our consciousness and the world we perceive. In particular, we have been blind to the effects of our behaviour on the environment and equally blind to the effects of our environment on ourselves. The built environment affects us in ways we are just beginning to understand, even as it is a reflection of our values. Being conscious of our symbiosis with the environment, whether natural or built, is a crucial first step in solving the "problems" we have with it. The gift of the physicists who studied the nature of light was to help us be conscious of this symbiosis. We cannot be objective observers.

ECONOMIC INSTITUTIONS

The scientific revolution and its belief that we are separate from nature was more than just a revolution in consciousness; it spawned institutions which expressed and reinforced this separation. A couple of these institutions and their underlying values have already been sketched – Leviathan, or the state, and the market system. There are clear connections between these modern institutions and the construction of cities which do not work.

It must be stressed that institutions are basically beliefs. They are neither buildings nor money. They are roles which people play each day, patterns of behaviour such as going to an office, writing reports, pushing buttons, asking certain questions, responding to others, coming home again. For these roles to be played, we must *believe* they are necessary. That is, when we really look closely, institutions are patterns of beliefs about behaviour. The belief produces the activity. From this perspective, it can be seen that our economic institutions, for example, are a set of beliefs which underlie the way we build cities. These institutions are regularized patterns of behaviour which go beyond the basic attitudes already mentioned – belief in exploitation of natural resources, in scarcity, and in continuous progress.

One of the keystones of our economic system is the web of rules and regulations surrounding the sanctity of private property. This was referred to in chapter 6 as an important underlying value of North American culture with specific connections to urban form. Here I wish to explore the concept of property further. Building cities that work requires us to look very closely into the meaning of property as a sacred right. This right has, of course, become circumscribed by public agencies, but the myth and its basic legal protection persist. Property is not only important as a passive right, a form of security against scarcity; in a capitalist system, it becomes an aggressive power. For Karl Marx in the nineteenth century, it was the basic source of all political power and authority. Even today this is not an unreasonable position to adopt.

But our culture's concept of land ownership, however potent a force it may be in our belief system, is narrow. We have been transfixed by John Locke's image of a person who, by putting work into the land, makes it truly his or her own. This image still forms the powerful moral foundation of our views on the sanctity of private property. By examining our ideas about property, we shall see how those ideas might be expanded, or even transformed.

There are at least two directions for expansion. One has been well explored, namely, the extension from individual to social ownership. This distinction takes no notice of how ownership is expressed, only of the fact that it may be held individually or collectively. Many proposals for change revolve around this distinction – land banking, cooperative ownership of housing, and government-owned enterprises. Collective ownership, especially when it is cooperative, can remove some of the more vexing problems of urban growth by private development; but the fact that ownership is collective does not remove problems associated with the concept of ownership itself. As a citizen, I am often affronted by the anomaly of a sign saying "Private – Keep Out" on public lands, especially public lands which have been developed out of scale, or in some sense at cross purposes, with a healthy cityscape, such as a military installation or an educational institution. The Keep Out sign excludes me from something I "own" along with everyone else. This situation raises the question of what ownership, individual *or* collective, really means.

Here is a second direction for expansion of the concept of ownership, from exclusiveness to inclusiveness. Native people in North America believed that the land was theirs, but only to use and to respect, not to have an exclusive right to. The thought of having exclusive privileges to a plot of land did not make sense to them. Nevertheless, the land was "theirs."

The Western concept of legal ownership of land emerged with the globalization of markets, described by Karl Polanyi in *The Great Transformation*. As the economic institution of market behaviour (i.e., beliefs about how one should behave) spread to become the dominant ethic of economic activity in the West, land was transformed from the place where one worked and lived and played – the place, in other words, which was woven in with one's personal identity – into a factor of production in the manufacturing sector and into a location from which to extract profitable rents in the real-estate sector.

Under this new, exploitative attitude towards land, ownership had to mean a set of exclusive rights to the land, rights which enabled the owner to build a factory or to graze sheep or to rent stores and "dwelling units." These rights extended, more importantly, to selling the land to someone else, who would be buying these rights to that particular place. These rights pertained to one human's (the owner's) relationship to other humans (non-owners); no one was thinking about rights pertaining to the owner's relationship to land, or to the planet. Land became a commodity, although a fictitious commodity according to Polanyi, since it could not be produced for a market the way tomatoes and cars could. But because it was bought and sold, a set of laws had to be derived to define transfer of ownership and therefore to define ownership.

Exclusive ownership distances the owner from the land in the same way Cartesian reality distances the human from nature. For one thing, when land is designated as something for us to use, we do not think of it as part of ourselves, as the earth upon which we depend for our existence. Rather, it is a tool to further our own aims. In addition, landowners are under no compulsion to take care of land in general. For instance, zoning laws can tell us if we can build a house or a factory on a piece of land, but only recently have we started passing laws about the use of pesticides or about what we can legally dump into sewers. That is, we might take care of a piece of land as long as we own it, but because we do not "own" the rest of the planet, sending our toxic garbage elsewhere causes us no concern. We think of land in pieces, not as a whole. In this way the market system combined with the Newtonian world view to legitimize making a mess of the planet, through this view of property. We are just beginning to understand the costs of such idiocy.

Exclusive ownership guaranteeing the marketability of land has had a peculiar effect on our social concept of space, and thus on patterns of North American urban development. This applies whether land is thought of as a factor of production or as a commodity in the real-estate market. Dividing the planet's surface into a grid of marketable spaces not only prevented us from thinking about the earth (or the city) as a whole; it divided people because it defined spaces where people may not go, a function of ownership's exclusivity. Where many people have a right to a space, they must negotiate the way their activities interpenetrate. This process of negotiation has been pre-empted by the law (that is, laws about private property) in the case of exclusive ownership.

Exclusive ownership is simply an additional way of separating ourselves from each other. As noted in chapter 6, the most pathetic expression of this is the suburbs, whose little "exclusive" lots extend for miles; everyone wants to own a piece of land, no matter how small. We even obey rules which hold that the (marketable) value of land changes if a different kind of person, which is to say, a black person, owns it.

It might seem that personal ownership of land would encourage rugged individualism and personal expression in the owner. Ironically, it does not. Ownership tied to marketability produces a standardizing effect. The owner is not as likely to invest his or her true spirit into the land since that could lower its exchange value, or the exchange value of the properties next door. Even John Locke would be perplexed. The owner is more likely to think in terms of "improving" his or her property in a conventionally accepted manner, to appeal to a reasonable range of possible (future) buyers. I noted in chapter 5 how zoning laws support and reflect this behaviour. In this way, the law and the market together help to produce impersonal space to maximize exchange value.

Impersonal land parcels which have been turned into commodities can be grouped together and monopolized by those who are more skillful in using the legal and market systems. Hence, the impersonality of land, like the impersonality of capital, is the very factor which permits it to be agglomerated. Large-scale development companies and their developments are a direct result of this process of agglomeration.

Deindustrialization is another result of our impersonal attachment to land. If the factory is not making money – if the factory is not making *enough* money – the firm sells the property and moves its operations elsewhere. The philosophy of North American land development is to make money from land sales or to make money from production on the land. The landscape reflects this philosophy. Huge, closed factories. And high-rises: these are profitable for the developer but not, as I have shown, for anyone else. They sprout in the suburbs, whose land values of themselves do not justify such concentrated development. The search for real-estate profits does justify it, however, wherever municipal governments can be persuaded to approve it.

Thus, beliefs about ownership, and consequently about exclusiveness and marketability of land, form a basic institutional framework which has ensured the physical form of the North American city. It may sound extreme to propose changing our beliefs about private property, but the reader is reminded of how narrow and time-bound our beliefs can be, as well as of how strong the links are between our ideas about physical reality and our ideas about property. In particular, our beliefs and laws concerning private property in the form of land are a modern Western aberration in the history of mankind. And, once again, they are threatening to destroy the planet. Perhaps it is time for a change.

A variety of urban homesteaders, squatters, housing cooperatives, and cohousing experiments are demonstrating that their communities are working physically, socially, economically, and ecologically, in part because they have let go of the belief in exclusive ownership and private property in the conventional sense. We shall meet this motley group in the next chapter.

The modern Western economic system as an institution has other unpleasant features which have been ably pointed out by E.F. Schumacher. His basic point is that while economics masquerades as an objective science, it is in fact the most subjective of disciplines since it deals with what men value. Modern Western economics, based on the meta-economic value of materialism, has but one criterion by which to judge anything. "The judgement of economics is an extremely *fragmentary* judgement; out of the large number of aspects which in real life have to be seen and judged together before a decision can be taken, economics supplies only one – whether a thing

Table 20
Contrasting economic values

Concept	Western values	Buddhist values
Work	– a necessary evil for the worker – to the employer, a cost, which is to be minimized – wages are compensation for sacrifice of leisure and comfort – mechanization encouraged – highest value is productivity	– a chance to use and develop the worker's faculties – an overcoming of ego by joining in a common task – bringing forth goods and services – nourishes and enlivens the higher man
Goods and consumption	– the more material consumed, the better – maximize production	– the more we are liberated from desire for material goods, the better – maximize well-being, minimize consumption
Natural resources	– choice of material or energy source based on immediate cost – cost related to effort of extracting them, never to replace them	– renewable resources used in preference to non-renewable, regardless of cost – every Buddhist plants a tree every few years and looks after it

Source: Extracted from E.F. Schumacher, *Small is Beautiful: Economics as if People Mattered* (London: Abacus 1973), chapter 4.

yields a money profit *to those who undertake it* or not" (emphasis in original). Schumacher asks us to notice that the judgment does not include whether money profit accrues to society as a whole, simply whether it accrues to those who undertake the project in question.

To give an idea of the narrowness of our beliefs about economics, Schumacher juxtaposes assumptions of Western materialist economics with those of what might be called a Buddhist economics (see Table 20).

Without going into detail, it can be seen from Table 20 that a cityscape based on Buddhist economics would not have the North American features of large-scale development and deconcentrated land use. What is not so obvious is that we think the North American urban form is inevitable because we are unaware that our own specific and limited set of economic beliefs have produced that form.

I would add one further dimension to the baneful set of beliefs that comprise our economic institutions: the idea that money can solve most of our problems. We have been taught that money is there

Figure 18
Scrap metal mural. This firm is deep in the industrial district of Toronto and does
not depend on passers-by for its business, yet the owner chose to pay a skilled artist to
paint the exterior wall of the yard, simply to add something special to the
neighbourhood.

for us to earn and to spend, in order to consume. This attitude leads
to the view that we give only to get – the exchange philosophy of the
market. We give money to someone and get something in return for
it. Western economics recognizes only this form of behaviour. It does
not, it cannot include in its paradigms people who work because they
love their work or people who give because it makes them feel good;
money has nothing to do with this behaviour. The city has many
examples of people who decorate buildings for reasons completely
beyond the ken of someone with a money mentality (Figure 18). Furthermore, in the context of cities, we have seen that huge sums of
money have done tremendous damage rather than good. This is a
product of thinking about money itself as the answer rather than
about what can, and must, be done by people.

As more people reject the assumptions of Western economics, the
face of our cities can change. Some examples of what is happening
will be given later. But first we must recognize that the translation of
changes in economic attitudes into a new urban form will involve
some kind of political activity. Our political institutions represent a
third set of dysfunctional beliefs which get in the way of intelligent
urban development.

POLITICAL INSTITUTIONS

The fundamental changes in economic attitudes I have been discussing imply similar changes in assumptions about the nature of politics. Chapter 5 suggested some notions of politics which departed considerably from the usual idea of what politics is. I would like to take these notions a bit further.

For example, it was argued that although many writers define politics in terms of influence and power, there was a need to redefine politics in terms of cooperation and energy. It has been noted that there are at least two basically different concepts of power. One concept sees it as a relationship, especially a relationship of control, whereby one actor is making someone or a group of people do something they would otherwise not do. From this perspective, it is pointless to speak of power as an attribute, for it only has meaning when it comes up against something else. Power is seen as a relationship between two or more people or two or more groups of people. This concept of power fits into a political system in which different groups are locked in a competitive struggle to ensure that their interests become legitimate public policy. The struggle is usually for control over scarce resources, or, more bluntly, over money and land.

The other concept of power defines it as a creative force. Power to do what? Power is thought of as an ability to get things done, as an energy to create, to inspire others, to do for oneself. The distinction between the two kinds of power is put thus by Marilyn French: "*Power* and *control* are often used synonymously ...

[T]here are different sorts of power: there is power-to, which refers to ability, capacity, and connotes a kind of freedom, and there is power-over, which refers to domination. Both forms are highly esteemed in our society.

Power-to is considered a personal attribute, based on innate ability and development through self-discipline. But in fact, power-to is achieved not by individuals but by communities or networks supporting individuals."

These concepts of power are related to our treatment of urban land and to the role of government. We have pointed out that in our culture, much of our activity is controlled by the market system, which defines power in terms of property.* This is power of the first kind: people who own land in North America can do what they like

---

* Robert Dahl would disagree. He feels that power is a function not only of wealth and property but of expertise, charisma, control over jobs, and other things. In fact, all of these, except for real (not television-fabricated) charisma, are direct or indirect functions of property ownership.

with it, and this is considered a legitimate form of power as control. One can control others' access to property, exploit natural resources without replacing them, or build whatever one likes (although in certain North American suburbs this last freedom may be limited to the colour of the wood trim on one's house). The right to control is protected by government laws and police power, institutions which make up Hobbes' Leviathan, the State.

Mark Gottdiener has argued that, in fact, "the principal function of the local state is its role as the socially legitimated guardian of property expropriation. As such, its fundamental purpose is social control." Expropriation is an extreme-sounding word, but it fits with our notion that property involves active exclusion of, and control over, non-owners. Local government regulation and protection of property sustain this conception.

The development industry and local government, which teamed up to build our homogeneous, large-scale urban landscape, are expressions of property as power-over, or the ability to tell other people what to do. Other ideas about power are associated with other kinds of built environment. For example, people who think of power as a creative force which should be shared with others tend to see the built environment as an extension of themselves rather than as an objective commodity, and no more amenable to market exchange than their noses, or their love. As we start sensing the built environment as an expression of our values (good as well as bad), it becomes easier to see the role played by our beliefs and our daily actions in producing that environment. From this realization, power as the ability to do, as well as the choice not to do, emerges.

Another central element in our political belief system is the primacy of the nation-state. There is no need to document the official propaganda, media imagery, and enculturation which perpetuate this belief. But there is a need to understand the nation as a set of beliefs like any other, a relatively new set of beliefs which have had a far-reaching and exceedingly destructive impact on humankind. The nation-state came into being a mere hundred and fifty to two hundred years ago. It became the dominant form of political organization somewhere between the middle and the end of the nineteenth century. Even in terms of human history, it is a remarkably recent phenomenon.

Since the growth of the nation-state, we have experienced the two most extensive and bloody wars in all of history. We have lived through a cold war sustained by the presence of weapons which could wipe out every vestige of life on earth. Religion and oil have proved to be deadly when combined with national interests.

In short, the nation-state is a war machine. National government powers to tax and legislate have always grown during wartime. After the wars, those powers remained. C. Northcote Parkinson's wickedly incisive little book, *Parkinson's Law*, was based on his observation that the British Admiralty – the civil service supporting the ships, men at sea, and dockyard workers – grew inexorably at a little over five and a half percent per year during *and after* World War I. No matter how few ships and seamen the bureaucracy had to look after, it continued to grow throughout the 1920s and 1930s. The income tax, introduced in many nation-states to help support "the war effort," remained in place to support burgeoning government bureaucracies.

Unfortunately, the nation-state has become the important institution in domestic politics as well as in foreign affairs. Domestic issues are always defined at the national level by media networks organized at the same level. The pre-eminence of national affairs is taken for granted. Even though electoral politics in both the United States and Canada are widely perceived as a technique of submerging and mystifying the really important issues of the day, they are the subject of millions of dollars' worth of coverage by radio, TV, and newspapers. Local affairs are the least featured, the last covered, items on the news. Rookie reporters always start out on the city beat and get "promoted" to national coverage. The really top reporters get assigned to foreign desks. All this is important because we ourselves have given the media the power to define what we call The News. (Did it ever seem odd to you that newscasts last for a set length of time? Are there not some days when there is "more" or "less" news?)

Economically, especially because of national currencies and trade laws, nation-states have reified a national economy when in fact the economy's true energy is provided by cities and their supporting regions. Jane Jacobs has pointed this out in her book *Cities and the Wealth of Nations*. Cities and their regions within a nation differ much more from each other than cities and regions across national boundaries. The result, she says, is economic stagnation because of uniform national policies which are built into the structure of the system. For example, a single national currency precludes the possibility of having one currency which supports imports in an import-dependent region, and creating another currency which supports exports in a different region with export industries. Having a single currency means that, when its value fluctuates *vis-à-vis* other currencies, one region is always helped while another one is always hurt. Needless to say, this provides endless fodder for political debates over economic policy.

To the extent that we give the nation-state hegemony over economic and political affairs, cities and city governments are given a background role in solving our problems. It was demonstrated in chapters 5 and 6 that in federal systems like the United States and Canada, local governments must defer to provincial and state governments as well as to national governments, all of which, because they are larger, are considered to have more power to solve economic, social, and ecological problems. But their power is power-over, control over other agencies. It is at the local level that we must collect garbage and start recycling, or shape our land use in a way which prevents a boom or bust economy. Solving the problems generated by poor urban design requires that we shed our unquestioning belief in the primacy of the nation-state and its government, with their emphasis on power-over.

I have already outlined the destructive impact of national policies on the physical form of cities. Instead of blaming national governments, however, we should think about how our belief in their importance supports the political and economic power of these governments. They are only important because we believe them to be important. They, with the media's support, do discourage us from taking responsibility for our own lives. Because they are so huge, most of us consider ourselves powerless next to them. But we are only powerless to the extent that we are unaware of how much our daily choices support large national governments. People can make alternative choices about where and how they live, and these choices have great potential in helping to build cities that work, in part because they tend to make nation-states irrelevant.

Finally, our notion of politics is intimately related to conflict. Paradoxically, although North Americans tend to avoid conflict situations in their personal public life, and although they seek refuge from the social issues of the central city, it is widely accepted that political life – even all social and personal life – is permeated with conflict. Most of us would go further: we nod sagely when someone remarks that conflict is creative, that it produces desirable changes, that it is healthy as well as inevitable. One psychologist puts it like this: "Conflict, per se, is not harmful. In fact, its absence suggests people who are frightened (to challenge a superior), resentful, or bereft of their rational faculties (as the total agreement among cult members demonstrates)." Thus, "reality" is full of conflicts. A long list of social theorists from everywhere on the political spectrum affirm this ageless kernel of human wisdom, from Karl Marx and his theory of class conflict to right-wing entrepreneurs salivating over their next corporate takeover. A majority of political scientists would say that politics always involves conflict. E.E. Schattschneider puts it most unequivocally: "The crucial problem in politics is the management of conflict. No regime could endure which did not cope with this problem. All politics, all leadership and all organization involves the management of conflict."

It is time to blow the whistle. Politics may involve conflict now, and it may have involved conflict in the past, but, just as with the Newtonian view of reality, conflict need not be our reality. In fact, if current assessments of Canadian and American political processes and public policy are any indication, we need a new way of looking at politics as well as reality. As long as we are questioning, indeed, denying the full accuracy of Newtonian reality, we might as well question the inevitability of human conflict.

The basis of the argument for the inevitability of conflict lies in assumptions about human nature, assumptions we have lived with at least since the time of Hobbes. Not only are humans considered to be conflict-oriented; this characteristic is seen as unchangeable: "You cannot change human nature."

This is an untenable position. First, human nature does change. If the human has evolved to what humankind is today (though sometimes it is questionable to me how far we have come), then future evolution is not only possible; in one way or another it is inevitable. To the degree that we are thinking, choosing beings, we have a chance and a responsibility to shape our present lives and therefore our future; whatever we may say, we act on this principle every day by going to school, saving money, having children, and making and breaking relationships.

Second, conflict is not an ineluctable characteristic of human nature. The "life is a struggle" hypothesis (or opinion) has a sordid intellectual history. Unsubstantiated assertions about humankind's aggression, competitiveness, and conflict-oriented behaviour date back to Thomas Hobbes' description of the state of nature – that is, where humans would be without the state's authority to keep the peace. In the state of nature, a purely hypothetical concoction of Hobbes which he derived from some of the new scientific thinking of that time, humans would be continuously involved in a war of all against all, because of their innate aggressiveness, an aggressiveness, it must be stressed, that is simply assumed by Hobbes. This assumption was echoed by many writers throughout the eighteenth and nineteenth centuries.

Charles Darwin's thesis – that the better adapted a species is to its environment, the more likely it is to survive – was transformed by Herbert Spencer and others into the doctrine of survival of the fittest (Spencer's phrase). For anyone who wished to see life as a struggle, the survival process was interpreted as a struggle for survival, in competition with the environment, including other species. Apologists for the new industrial order of the nineteenth century who, like Spencer, wished to find a scientific rationale for unrestrained free enterprise and for withdrawal of any spending on social services, used Darwin's theory as support for their construction of reality. Ironically, in the same era, Karl Marx was finding comfort in Darwin as well. He was arguing that conflict between classes was inevitable, and that this conflict was the source of social change. Marx even wanted Darwin to write an introduction to one of his books.

We see what we choose to see. Numerous ethologists and biologists, including Darwin himself, have pointed out that the basic theme in nature is cooperation. Animals survive through cooperative behaviour. Not surprisingly, so do humans. "The restriction of differential survival to mean simply conflict," writes Patrick Bateson, "is an obvious abuse of Darwin's thinking." George Gaylord Simpson summarizes the point this way:

Struggle is sometimes involved, but it usually is not, and where it is, it may even work against, rather than toward natural selection. Advantage in differential reproduction is usually a peaceful process in which the concept of struggle is really irrelevant. It more often involves such things as better integration into the ecological situation, maintenance of a balance of nature, more efficient utilization of available food, better care of the young, elimination of intra-group discords (struggles) that might hamper reproduction, exploitation of environmental possibilities that are not the objects of competition or are less effectively exploited by others.

If we choose to see conflict, that is what we shall see. If we choose to see (and participate in) cooperation, that is what we shall see. We create our own realities, just as the physicists do. When humans choose to cooperate with nature, they find nature extremely cooperative. Michael J. Roads, a livestock owner in Australia, was losing his herd because wallabies were grazing his meadows. He tried poison, but felt cowardly doing that. He tried shooting the wallabies one by one, and hiring locals to help him. No result. Coming face to face unexpectedly one night with a wallaby, he became unnerved. He lowered his gun and decided then and there to try another way. The next day he went near a group of trees in the centre of the paddock and shouted, "I don't know if you wallabies can hear me, but I am offering an agreement with you by which we each meet our own needs. I am asking you to stop eating our pasture, and in exchange for this I will see to it that nobody shoots you again. However, because I realize I must share this land with you, I will allow you to graze around the outside of the paddock. Please don't take more than twenty yards." He continued his story: "Within only a few weeks the pasture was thickening so rapidly that I was able to introduce an extra ten cows and calves. It continued to improve." The wallabies kept to their bargain as long as Roads was there. When someone else took over the pasture and started shooting them again, the pasture quickly reverted to its former state.

The argument about inevitability of conflict is often supported by two other pseudo-empirical arguments. One is that conflict is desirable; without conflict, it is said, we are all lifeless, without spark. I used to feel that way, too. Now it has become clearer to me the extent to which we have been brainwashed about this point of view. There is no hard evidence, only opinions, such as that conflict's "absence *suggests* people who are frightened ... resentful ... or bereft of their rational faculties" (emphasis added). Well, one can suggest what one wishes. J. Krishnamurti's response is especially appropriate. A questioner challenged him with, "If we have no conflict we will go to sleep." Krishnamurti answered, "Are you speaking from experience, or have you merely an idea about it? We are imagining what it would be like to have no conflict and we are preventing the experiencing of whatever that state is in which all conflict has ceased." Krishnamurti does not deny that we experience conflict, but he does question the assumption that it is desirable.

The other argument supporting the inevitability of conflict revolves around the assumption that life is a zero-sum game; that whatever you "win" the other fellow loses, and vice versa. Our attitude towards money is typical. In the discussion of our assumptions about economics it was pointed out that we only give money to someone else to get something in return for it. That is, there is a finite amount of money which I can keep or spend; but if I spend it I do not have it any more. Now, we make this a central precept of our lives: if we have a shoe shop and someone else opens another one next door, we think we shall only get half the number of customers; if we discourage crime in this housing project, it will pop up elsewhere; if I spend time painting the house, then I shall not have it to play with my daughter; if the Third World keeps growing in population, there will not be enough food for the planet; if we let too many people into our country, there will not be enough jobs to go around (because there is a finite number of jobs).

Once again, this is a belief about reality, a way in which we choose to see things. There are other ways of looking at the world. In Louisville, when shoe stores started opening up next to each other, they attracted more shoppers who came for comparison shopping, and business boomed for everyone. In chapter 3, it was shown how proper design did not just reduce the incidence of crime: it reduced the attraction to young people of the possibility of criminal behaviour. I learned how to paint the house in company with my daughter. As long as the Third World does not adopt the West's chemical fertilizers and pesticides, it will be able to feed itself better than the West, whose fertilizers have almost destroyed the land's ability to produce. Finally, it could be pointed out that a great many of us are immigrants to Canada and to the United States and we have always created jobs with our skills and imagination, not taken existing ones. Why should this change?

In short, life is not a zero-sum game except to those who want to see it that way. The best example is love. The more you give, the more there is.

CHAPTER EIGHT

Our Cities, Our Selves

This is the most fearful part of my task, for what I have described at great length here is a big problem, and it is the overwhelming tendency of our time to assume that a big problem calls for a big solution. I do not believe in the efficacy of big solutions. I believe that they not only tend to prolong and complicate the problems they are meant to solve, but that they cause new problems. On the other hand, if the solution is small, obvious, simple, and cheap, then it may quickly and permanently solve the immediate problem and many others as well.   Wendell Berry

We have come a long way from city building, it seems. Yet the problem with the design of urban spaces outlined earlier in this book can be traced to basic beliefs about physical reality and to untested and dangerous assumptions about economics and politics. These beliefs are powerful in part because they have become expressed in the physical shape of the metropolis. They are powerful because so many of us hold them. And they are powerful because we are unaware that we hold them.

On the other hand, *we* are powerful because we are able to change our beliefs. There are many things we can do. But before any action is taken, we have to wake up. We have to be aware of our beliefs, aware of our experiences, and aware of our daily choices. Or, as Mark Satin has put it, since our own consciousness has created a prison, it is our own consciousness which will free us.

This book has questioned some of our assumptions about the way the world works. The next step is to develop our awareness to the point where action springs from a deeply felt, personal sense of purpose, rather than from an impersonal, vague sense of obligation.

There are a number of reasons why waking up is difficult. In an aptly titled book, *City of Dreams*, Harold Chorney traces the development of urban numbness and anonymity in the nineteenth-century city, long before postwar North American city building. Georg Simmel, the German sociologist, was one of the first writers to describe passive withdrawal by urbanites "from an often hostile and overwhelming world." Chorney's argument is that the metropolitan environment's function has been to stimulate material consumption by individuals and to discourage public, face-to-face contact, which is the necessary condition for effective collective action (there are many modern examples of ineffective collective action). The increase in the impersonality and abstract quality of daily experience – which is directly tied to modern urban architecture – has, in a very real sense, put us to sleep.

This chapter starts, then, with awareness. The idea is to show how awareness at the individual level leads to changes in individual behaviour and how consciousness of community leads to changes in how we relate to others. These changes in individual and group activity will create more civilized cities and a more enlightened level of existence on this planet.

At the individual level, the politics of building cities that work starts with noticing the city around us. The idea of this book was to contribute to a heightened consciousness of the physical shape of cities, but reading a book is no substitute for direct experience. It is only by first being aware, truly aware, of the physical city that we can have healthy city politics and, in turn, healthy cities. We might think this awareness would take concentration, but what it really takes is a sort of relaxation, when we let names for things and labels for experiences fall away. Then, in the space created, we start to be conscious of doorknobs, plants in the cracks, sounds of people, sounds of machines, different smells, the massiveness of buildings, the feel of spaces *between* buildings. Try walking a street you normally drive along and see what you experience. If you take public transit, walk along the transit route. I like to notice things like special front yards. In addition, in the past few years, I have become especially sensitive to the number of dead or dying trees along city streets. Without exaggeration, we make the city more our own by expanding our awareness of it in this way. It is the first step in developing an authentic politics as defined in chapter 5: the process of a self-conscious community deciding how its members relate to the earth and to each other.

An important way of relating to the earth is noticing the way we use space. The city is essentially a place. But our habits and laws about property have overridden our awareness of places. Notice how, despite the importance of exclusive private property, many of the

Figure 19
Street performer, Queen Street, Toronto

most exciting parts of the city are available spaces to which people
give temporary meaning with their activities. Families make a corner
of a city park their own environment for the afternoon; a shopkeeper
makes his or her goods part of the sidewalk; street performers can
create an instant stage for passers-by (Figure 19) by choosing a spot
where pedestrians accumulate; a political organization uses a main
avenue for a parade (it usually needs a police permit).

Even in the semi-private sphere, relaxation of customs surrounding
formal legal ownership produces urban vitality. For instance, when
some people move into an unfurnished apartment or flat, they do a
minimum of work to personalize it – it is just rented, they say. Others,
especially where renting for long periods is common and where ownership in the Western legal sense is considered to be out of the question, spend hundreds of dollars and hours of their spare time fixing
up places.

Once we start looking for exceptions to legal ownership, examples
appear everywhere. A certain Mrs Ivy in Berkeley, California owned
and lived on a private lot which extended from one street through
the centre of the block to another. Over the course of thirty or more
years, she transformed the lot into a lively, semi-public place by slowly
turning her existing garages and back porches into infill apartments,
here and there adding a building. Residents are free to use the spaces

left over as they wish. A path winds through the lot. Although it is private, the design gives non-residents "permission" to use the path. This permission to be included imposes a certain urban civility. Not only would it be difficult to misbehave; it is likely that the stranger would come across a poetry reading, a barbecue in progress, someone gardening, or someone just sitting. Mrs Ivy has produced not a private space, not a public space, but an urban space which has transcended conventional ideas about property.

Noticing here and there that space can be used in this way is an important step in changing our own attitude and behaviour towards ownership: the narrow view of property which helped produce the postwar North American city is far from the only view.

Being aware includes noticing how distant-sounding phrases, such as transportation policy or social services, are translated into our everyday experience. For example, it may be easy to see that a transportation decision results in having one's house torn down because it is in the path of an expressway; it is harder to be aware that trees are dying on our street because policies to widen streets have encouraged greater use of cars, whose exhaust kills the trees. It is a longer chain of connection, but it is still there.

The consequences of our own actions are often similarly obscure, because of the way we have separated land uses in the North American city. We buy sprayed produce from agribusiness farms we never see, whose pesticides come from factories we never see. Thus, as noted earlier, a trip to the supermarket has the consequence of encouraging a whole system of agriculture and product distribution.

Because such consequences are always there, however, it is instructive to become more aware of the impact of daily – of hourly – choices we make. We are often unconscious of our own habits (Figure 20). Take one day, for instance, to consider how much garbage you generate, not just the plastic bags you throw away with your own hands, or the number of times you flush the toilet, but the exhaust from the vehicles you ride in, and the smoke and industrial waste from factories that make the products you use. Notice what the packaging is like on the products you buy, as well as how many chemical additives they contain, assuming these are even listed on the label.

This expanding awareness can be applied to longer-term choices. Many such choices are only made in a personal context. We seldom think whether our desire for a bigger house or a new car has social or ecological ramifications. In chapter 2, however, it was seen that the most important decision we make about energy consumption is where we live; if we decide to live in spread-out suburbs, we shall be

Figure 20
It's hard to be aware of our daily habits ...
"Bizarro" cartoon by Don Piraro reproduced by permission of Chronicle Features

responsible, directly and indirectly, for three, four, even ten times as much energy consumption. Considering our jobs, how many chances a day do we have to improve the quality of someone else's life, to improve the quality of the environment? Is our job contributing to the spoiling of the planet?

At this point, it is simply important to be aware of the nature of these choices; being aware of how our actions connect to global problems is an important first step in raising our political consciousness and in solving those problems. Harold Chorney makes it clear that becoming aware of the narrowness of our perceptions, of waking up, is frustrated constantly by our daily experience of the modern urban environment, which we have grown up accepting as normal (see chapter 3). We think it is normal to walk around like zombies in a shopping centre, relating only to consumer products and not to each other. We think huge high-rises and sprawling suburbs are normal because we have experienced little else. We are victims, says Chorney, of a sort of collective amnesia. In such a state, authentic politics seems remote.

Thus, if we want to change, the first challenge is to commit ourselves to this daily process of staying awake. As Duane Elgin puts it in his book *Voluntary Simplicity*, "unless we are conscious of our passage through daily life, we tend to run on automatic. When we run on automatic we act in habitual and preprogrammed ways and our behaviour can hardly be considered voluntary. Thus, our capacity to act voluntarily – freely, choicefully, intentionally, deliberately – is inextricably bound up with our capacity to be consciously attentive to ourselves as we move through life."

Thus, somewhere along the line, awareness leads to voluntary action, although before that it more likely leads to selective non-action. For example, if we know that each time we eat at a burger chain we are contributing to the destruction of the Amazon rain forest, because the chain buys beef from Brazilians who are wiping out the jungle in order to raise cattle, then we might choose not to eat those hamburgers.

Another area of non-action could be in conventional politics. Disgust with the posturing and hypocrisy of elected politicians of large-scale politics has led to a significant decline in support for North American political institutions. The decline shows up in public-opinion surveys, but it is also obvious in low turnout at the polls, lack of attachment to political parties as important symbols, and indifference to and ignorance of political affairs. Conventional analysts often put this down to "failings" on the part of citizens, but the judgmental nature of such analysis is obvious. I suggest that it is our institutions which are at fault. (It is we, of course, who have created and supported our institutions.) Considering the time and money spent on making people into enthusiastic boosters of the national state, it is at least mildly puzzling to see so much negativity towards government and lack of interest in its affairs. It is simply too big and too far removed. We express this by staying away from the polls; or if we vote, we do little else in the political arena, which is dominated by political professionals with dubious motives. The empirical evidence of this phenomenon is now considerable. (See chapter 5.)

Our first positive actions might spring, say, from awareness of our personal contribution to the garbage problem in big cities: we start thinking about changing our habits. This approach is now becoming widespread. Composting kitchen waste, recycling bottles, using our own permanent shopping bags, and buying foods sold in bulk instead of in expensive packaging – small choices, but ones which make us constantly aware of our connection to the environment, and make a difference not only in our own garbage production but in others', who notice our behaviour and are ready to change. I am becoming impatient, however, with the idea that once such incremental changes are undertaken, one has satisfactorily discharged one's responsibility to the environment. The function of doing something about our garbage is to expand our awareness of other patterns of behaviour which support the North American urban form and its ecological excrescences.

Without following some kind of guidebook, enormously positive contributions to the quality of the environment can be made in millions of small ways. One expression of this is found in front yards, or on many high-rise balconies. I am constantly delighted by the imagination and energy poured into little plots at the front of houses in downtown Toronto. Walking along a residential street, one can see hand-carved wooden balconies, miniature waterwheels, glorious combinations of flowers, madonnas surrounded by lights and roses, carefully tiled front walks, or a veritable explosion of potted flowers covering every square inch of space, all presided over by an array of chairs and benches on the front porch (Figures 21, 22, 23). Throughout most of the good weather, from April or May to October, these chairs are occupied by the front yards' creators and their families, who make themselves part of the street life. What they have also done, though perhaps unconsciously, is make the passer-by feel part of the street too, because the front yards and their families are facing the street, not the house. Creating a beautiful front yard and sitting on the porch are not done just for passers-by; but the way it is done includes them.

Aside from making the street more civil, the individual members of this front-yard culture also influence each other. One can easily spot how one person on the street had an idea – about the design of a fence, a new kind of tree or statue, or a particularly exuberant display of wildflowers – which has been picked up by others. Friendly front yards are thus remarkably infectious, a good example of what one person can do. Similar processes have been observed on high-rise balconies and window sills: potted plants and flowers transform blank walls into colourful parts of the city.

Gardeners also are starting to make a considerable contribution to the health of cities by planting wilderness gardens and by not using herbicides, fertilizers, or pesticides. One writer on such gardens reported that "home gardens receive more pesticides per acre than any other kind of land. According to a 1980 report by Cornell University, about one-half of all money spent annually for insecticides is

Figure 21
Man with his rose garden

Figure 22
Carved wooden porch, downtown Toronto

Figure 23
Front yard and its creators, downtown Toronto

dedicated to home lawns, golf courses and other non-farm uses."
Traditional gardeners are starting to be converted by their more
adventurous neighbours, by the process of influence described above.
It is important to see this as more than just a change in gardening
habits. It is a social process involving communication among neighbours with the idea of making the whole community a healthier place
to live. The fact that the process is highly informal adds to its significance.

Our personal choices about housing and jobs can be positive
actions which affect urban form in good ways. Developers of suburbs
tell us we are buying into communities, but this is an illusion created
for marketing purposes. A friend of mine, who recently moved into
one of these so-called communities, was dismayed to find that his
house not only had no front porch; the house front was so completely
dominated by the garage door and the front door that there was not
even a front window. Residents in his neighbourhood have no way of
relating to the street. Design like this (and it is ubiquitous) makes
street-level management difficult if not impossible. No wonder working local communities in North America are hard to find. People may
still pay taxes to local governments, but the notion of a block, or a
neighbourhood, or the city as a political community in the 1990s
seems laughably out of date. The reason for this is traceable to our

attitudes. We consider the city to be simply a lot of real estate. Few have a personal stake in the city except to make profits from it. We continue to buy houses like my friend's because our consciousness is not tuned in to the civic importance of relating to neighbours. The crunch comes when we simply refuse to choose housing which does not relate to the street. Better yet, we design our own housing that does.

Our personal decision about where to live is extremely important. Most of us are spending a quarter or a third of our income on our living space, which translates into hundreds of dollars a month in support of a particular physical form. We can support something like Mrs Ivy's garden apartments or we can support mass-produced homogeneous housing in undiverse neighbourhoods. During the seventies and eighties, thousands of people who could afford to live in the suburbs rejected them and moved back downtown in North American cities. Although many did it because it was fashionable, and although considerable displacement of low-income families resulted from this movement, the point is that there was something about the downtown street which attracted people.

These urban homesteaders, as they have sometimes been called, along with many working-class and lower-class families, have contributed to downtown-neighbourhood street life in our cities. As more residents invest their time and energy (not just money) into old downtown houses, as more people treat their streets and neighbourhoods as extensions of their personalities, then portions of the city can become more than just real estate. Nevertheless, the popularity of this pattern has activated the market side of our personality. As soon as there is a buck to be made from the sale or exchange of such properties, there will be a test of this attitude towards the use of urban land. The interesting thing is the level on which such a confrontation will take place: not at the national level, or even at the level of city government, but within the hearts of the urban homesteaders themselves. Do they want to treat the property as something to exchange and earn money from, or is it a part of their personality, along with the street and neighbourhood? The place of individual choice is clear.

Personal decisions about jobs are important to the shape of our cities. Most of us assume that if we live in a big city, we shall not have a job close to our home. We do not even consider the possibility of going home for lunch. This would not be "normal." A huge number of us travel ten, twenty, thirty miles and more to work, because we think we have to. Work and home are split in our minds, so they are split in the city: keeping our decisions about workplace and living space almost totally separate (I know many couples who work in different cities) supports segregated land uses which sprawl out over the countryside.

There are times when we need to ask ourselves why we, in our heart of hearts, are doing the job we are. This question relates to Schumacher's discussion of the nature of work. Some of us have begun to operate according to different rules. Stewart Scriver and his wife Pat Roy were teachers in the Toronto public-school system. Neither was totally satisfied with that career. After some casting about, they opened a second-hand clothing store in a tiny brick structure which had housed a Chinese laundry just off the east side of Spadina Avenue in downtown Toronto. Spadina had been the street for jobbers for years. A few blocks down Spadina is a bustling Chinatown, and one block west is Kensington Market, a European-style, open-air market which attracts thousands of pedestrian shoppers. These shoppers are a diverse lot, ranging from curious tourists to recent arrivals from the Azores, punks, teenagers, and WASP professionals from north Toronto. Pat and Stewart's store, while it was definitely in a retail backwater, was halfway between Kensington Market and the University of Toronto, further north.

The store, called Courage My Love, featured second-hand clothing and a hodgepodge of articles from the thirties, forties, and fifties. The prices were low – not junk-store low, but very reasonable – and the merchandise was always interesting, for Stewart and Pat enjoyed the challenge of finding bargains at flea markets, or from stores with 1950s merchandise that were closing up in some small rural town. It is worth noting that numerous other second-hand clothing stores started opening in Toronto, but Courage My Love continued to prosper. The reasons were many: Stewart and Pat worked extremely hard to make sure all the clothing was clean and ironed (sometimes dyed); the prices were so reasonable that dealers in the store often outnumbered regular shoppers off the street; they both cherished their vast and growing knowledge of unorthodox, bizarre, out-of-the-way sources of merchandise; they were friendly and generous to their customers (for many years they held a post-Christmas sale with lavish amounts of home-cooked food and drink). They never stood still. In the last few years their buying trips have extended to the Far East and their store has become even more eclectic.

There is another part to the story. The couple, with their growing family, have kept their residence within a few steps of their store. As they became more successful, they bought a much bigger store in Kensington Market. The new store was only a five-minute walk from their old house, which had been half a block from the old store. But a five-minute walk was too far, and Pat and Stewart bought a house in Kensington, a few hundred feet from the new place of business; in this respect they are similar to some other Kensington Market merchants who live above or near their stores. The continuing success of their store, combined with some shrewd investments in real estate in the area surrounding the new store, has resulted in their reviving what was essentially a backwater on the southern fringe of the market. In addition to being responsible for encouraging specific people to move into the neighbourhood, Courage My Love seems to have spawned no fewer than five other second-hand clothing stores on the same block. A few other businesses have also appeared, in among residential uses.

Pat and Stewart have unquestionably knitted into the community. They babysat children other than their own – they fed and sheltered one such child for a few years; they eat in neighbourhood restaurants; their own children work in the store. They are acquainted with everyone.

A degree of physical revitalization and the success of several businesses in the area, then, seem to revolve around two people operating by a different set of rules. Stewart and Pat did not have to overthrow the government or rearrange the structures of the national economy in order to make a good living for themselves and provide opportunities for others. They certainly did not conduct market research to see if people would be interested in their type of store, because there was nothing like it in 1974 in Toronto. Significantly, they did not seek to maximize profits for their own sake or to accumulate property, and yet they became extremely successful. Stewart and Pat's power came from their enjoyment of what they were doing and the labour they infused into the land, not so much to make a profit but to participate fully in what lay around them. Their economic success is, in fact, only a by-product of the much more profound success they have made of their lives.

The multi-dimensional character of what the proprietors of Courage My Love are doing is important to understand. So is their independence from big organizations, especially government. Another good example of this multi-dimensional independence is chronicled by Eleanor Magid, an art teacher whose child was out of school for six weeks in New York City during the teachers' strikes in the late 1960s. "The mothers were meeting because it was very difficult for them. We lived in a poor area and many of them worked. We had no access to day care. It was like a war-torn area. There were children wandering around by themselves because the mothers couldn't stay home ... The mothers who had enough space and had something to offer opened their homes for the children in a community effort." Magid had a studio with "an etching press, bookbinding facilities, printmaking supplies, woodcut tools, ink rollers, and so on," which she offered; with the help of two or three other mothers, she helped the school children to marble paper, bind books and number the pages, make pictures, and write "stories that included almost the entire school curriculum."

At the same time, Magid's own campus was closed by a strike, so she told her students they could come and use her studio as well, which they did.

There would be ten to fifteen little kids and as many college kids, plus three or four mothers. Other people would drop by. The English teacher came and taught the little kids and the big kids. Lois, a painter, and Louise, a sculptor who lived upstairs, joined the group. A friend from Paris came with new etching techniques ...

Some of the mothers didn't have very constructive feelings about themselves, either because they were on welfare or had dead-end jobs, or were struggling alone to raise their children. Certainly, they had never made a print before. But the college students and the little kids pulled them in. The college crowd would say, "Come on!" and then the daughter or the son would say, "Yeah, come on, Mom!" I would have to say that the most striking look of wonder and pleasure came from those mothers.

When the strikes were over, the workshop kept going on weekends. Some fathers started coming as well. Since the work produced healthy appetites, people started bringing the fixings for stews, which bubbled all day while they were working. "In the evening, we would have the meal. It was startling to me: there were no hierarchies, no stars or kings. It was the best kind of family."

Magid described how all this was a strain on her family life, and presently the workshop was given a loft by the local urban-development office. As their independence from government ended, so did the project's success. "All kinds of squabbling started over money and responsibilities. Everything became bureaucratic. I became the official coordinator, and had to write fund-raising proposals and arrange for community art shows."

This woman obviously had something going at the group level, which provided a wonderful learning experience on many different levels for everyone involved. No one was in charge. Individuals were each contributing unselfconsciously to the process. When people are aware that something good is going on, they act spontaneously; no orders need be given. When a formal outside authority enters the scene, the whole chemistry breaks down.

This brings me to what happens when our individual awareness and activity moves us to reach out to others and to pursue our purpose at the group level. The example above has a familiar ring to some of us who have tried to extend our energy into some kind of organized group activity. Often we end up exhausting ourselves with the process of organizing and forgetting about our original purpose. Meanwhile, society's large-scale institutions, with built-in guarantees of funding and manpower, seem overwhelmingly dominant. These attitudes towards organization, which stem from traditional ways of looking at politics, need to be examined.

Imagine for a moment how our interdependence on each other is mediated by large organizations. A male worker at Chrysler, whose job is temporarily saved by a government loan to the company, has his well-being put at stake when the national government has trade talks with Japan, when the nationwide unemployment plan is under review in Congress or Parliament, or when Chrysler decides to close the plant because labour is cheaper and more manipulable in south Texas or Brazil. The worker lives in housing which he probably could not afford without a mortgage guarantee from the us Federal Housing Administration or the Canada Mortgage and Housing Corporation; the housing, furthermore, was mass-produced by a large developer who got tax concessions from national governments and whose project was enthusiastically approved by a local council seeking more property tax revenue. In fact, services to the new subdivision cost more than the local council anticipated, so the taxes on the worker's home have more than doubled in the last eight years. The size of the Chrysler plant and the housing project and their distance from each other make it necessary for him to commute by car along highways built with taxes on his income and on the gasoline he buys. If he lives in the United States, he probably uses an urban expressway built with federal tax money and planned by state departments of public works. The price of gas, set by national and international forces beyond his control, is taking a larger and larger proportion of his salary, but there is no alternative way of getting to work, or, for that matter, of getting to the nearest grocery store two miles away. The store is part of a nationwide chain which has not been doing that well lately, so this store might be closed soon. All of us are embedded in a similar physical and economic urban trap, seemingly under the control of large organizations.

It bears repeating that one major barrier to gaining some sense of control over our lives is our belief that these large organizations are still legitimate structures of decision making, and that by participating in at least some of them we can bring about change. Once again, however, their size and their hierarchical structure discourage participation, or exclude it. It is also unlikely that we are going to rise up and overthrow the system; we are only dimly aware of what to overthrow. Anyway, seeking to overthrow something like the tangled web of multinationals, regulatory and quasi-independent agencies, and central-government structures gives the whole mess more reality, more solidity, than it really has. Furthermore, it implies the need to replace it with something else, which is the last thing we want to do.

In fact, it is worth pointing out the self-destructiveness inherent in these large-scale organizations which seem at present to be so invincible. Some of them are not making money at all but are trying to keep themselves afloat by investing in businesses which are still solvent. The one exception, ironically, seems to be the giant real-estate developer, whose financial viability is assured as long as we accept the legitimacy of the market for land and its concomitant, the sanctity of private property.

But large-scale organizations are, in general, inefficient entities. Jane Jacobs has remarked that the huge new textile plants of Manchester in the 1840s were thought to be the wave of the future, since they were so efficient, which is to say that much work was accomplished in return for a small amount of energy. The size of these mechanized leviathans precluded their adaptation when other economies started making cheap fabric as well. Manchester stagnated while Birmingham, with numerous "inefficient" small-scale enterprises that were considered positively medieval in the 1840s, continued to flourish and grow.

Short-term efficiency achieved through economies of scale produced a similar situation in the United States in the twentieth century. Immense steel plants like Bethlehem's Sparrows Point dragged the industry into decline while its managers refused to adopt technological innovations, thus allowing Japanese and other steelmakers to manufacture better quality, cheaper steel. Meanwhile, mini-plants in the United States were producing cheaper and better steel as well, claiming a larger and larger share of the market.

It is a message our culture continues to ignore: achieving short-term economic efficiency by means of large-scale organizations produces long-term economic stagnation presided over by large-scale organizations. And the truth is that we are allowing ourselves to be dominated by such organizations.

Governments are justifiably held up as stereotypes of inefficiency, and one wearies of all the stories. One example, however, should be given. In the late 1980s, before the military build-up in the summer of 1990, a quarter to one-third of the United States' military budget was being spent on protection of the country's access to natural resources on foreign soil. Now, the United States was getting about six percent of its oil from the Persian Gulf. According to Amory Lovins, the military force to protect that source of oil was costing eighteen times what the oil cost, bringing the total cost of the oil to US $495 a barrel, a price clearly not reflected at the fuel pumps. Nation-states are inherently inefficient economic units partly because they are war machines, but also because they are so big.

Organizations which behave this way are like cancerous cells, out of control with no feedback mechanism to help them adjust to reality. If they run their course, they kill their host and die with it. This is as true of the United States government as it is of large industrial plants which become obsolete and kill their host cities. The Chrysler worker, the drywaller, the artist, the dentist – we are all in a position to start constructing an alternative to this situation. Part of our task is to be more aware personally and to take individual action as described above. The other part is to extend our awareness of how we connect with others outside of these large-scale organizations. As the example of the art teacher's workshop implies, building cities that work requires a different approach to organization. We need to look at new (as well as long-forgotten) ways we can cooperate with each other and how those ways relate to city design.

There has been a flood of literature in recent years about how people are grouping themselves for cooperative participation without being caught in the misconceptions of traditional organization. While these groups of people may be found in the country as well as the city, the urban groups are usually linked in a symbiotic way with what we have been calling physical diversity in design.

Most assessments of the impact of urban community groups on the city have been negative. Saul Alinsky, whose innovative style of community organizing will be examined below, puts it harshly:

The American urban scene is virtually cluttered with so-called community organizations. They present a grotesque vista. The overwhelming majority can best be described as stillborn corpses identified with a letterhead; then there are a substantial number who occasionally huddle in lifeless meetings dealing with lifeless issues and present the modern approximation of group zombies. They travel by many names, such as health and welfare councils, neighbourhood councils, Mobilization for Whosis, Operation Whatsis, or Task Force Wheresis. Their annual meetings are always concerned with "New

Horizons in Community Organizations" since, not knowing what to do with the present horizons, prudence would suggest their looking to new horizons.

In spite of some optimistic analyses, the current consensus among academics is that community organizations can do little to confront the problems of the postwar North American city. Their negative attitude stems partly from the context in which they frame the problem, which for them is the trend toward a global restructuring of capital: capital has become increasingly concentrated and decreasingly tied to any particular city *or nation*, which leaves localities powerless to affect their own future.

Alinsky's approach to organizing, however, was remarkably successful in influencing large-scale governments and corporations. Although I disagree with some of Alinsky's views, such as his belief in the inevitability of conflict, it is clear that he saw accurately through the fiction that representative democracy was rule by the people. In fact, Alinsky argued as I did in chapter 5 that, by supporting a representative system, we give away our power, and our responsibility, to elected officials. His solution was to build organizations whose primary purpose was to illustrate to people, especially poorer people, that they have the power to create their own services, jobs, and neighbourhoods.

The strategy of Alinsky organizers was to go from door to door and ask people in the neighbourhood what their concerns were. (Alinsky insisted that his organizers be invited into a neighbourhood; they never initiated contact.) The organizer would then suggest calling a meeting, chaired and run by local residents, to discuss these concerns. Then he or she would urge the residents to take direct action, rather than asking a representative (an alderman, a member of the state or provincial legislature) for help. Direct action usually involved identifying one person who had the most power in the situation, such as the owner of a company polluting the environment or the head of a housing authority, and confronting that person as an equal to request that something be done. Negotiating directly with business people and bureaucrats in this way, Alinsky groups in Toronto and elsewhere achieved remarkable results.

Two problems emerged, however. One was that when people got what they wanted, they were scared by their own effectiveness. They backed off. They would no longer participate in their group because they suddenly realized the extent to which they did have responsibility for their own situations: they could no longer blame anyone else.

The other problem was that despite their avowal to keep clear of big institutions, many Alinsky groups succumbed to them, becoming part of the social-service bureaucracy and therefore subordinate to money and authority from "above." The groups which persisted were groups with their own goal or activity which existed independently of government or any other organization.

There is an important kernel of truth here. Change comes about not by confronting existing institutions but by acting personally, independently, and locally. The growth of the national state, it will be recalled, did not occur because national governments took away powers from lower-level governments; national governments created new functions for themselves. Once functions had been assumed by national governments, those functions gradually became encrusted with bureaucracy. This encrustation proceeded at an inexorable rate, regardless of external demands made on the agency. This is known as Parkinson's Law, outlined in the very funny little book by C. Northcote Parkinson, referred to above. We do need to laugh at ourselves. But the time has come for us to create a process for getting things done which is non-bureaucratic. Alinsky's organizations are one example of this process.

When community organizations are effective, which is seldom, it is because they spend a minimum of energy on organizational maintenance and a maximum on creative action. The more organized and routinized our activity, the more things grind to a halt. The art teacher's print workshop is a good lesson in that respect. Its own force, its own energy, kept it going until it became organized for the sake of interacting with government.

The physical environment is important to community organization. Alinsky's groups were most successful in diverse downtown working-class neighbourhoods, where there was sufficient concentration of use not only to get people together but also to make the problem reasonably clear: pollution of residential areas by factories, the need for daycare and decent housing, unemployment, and crime. When people live in spread-out suburbs like the worker from Chrysler, definition of the problem is much more difficult, and the lack of casual public encounters makes local organization less spontaneous.

The first part of this book makes it clear that we have deconcentrated and segregated our urban space, and that this is a reflection of how we separate our lives into neat little packages of activity – work, play, shopping, family life. Urban places like diverse city neighbourhoods permit humans to be at one with themselves again, making prints while the stew bubbles on the stove, looking after children while minding the store, visiting with neighbours while fixing up a house.

Postwar North American development has destroyed many diverse neighbourhoods, but new ones are being built by people who are aware of the symbiosis between urban design and social action. The new types of group which are the most promising harbingers of change are both creations and creators of multi-functional urban places. The dynamic between these groups and their places denies the relevance of the old concepts of exclusive private property, individual material affluence, power as control, the primacy of the nation-state, and conflictual politics. These groups are also doing ecologically sensible things. They are living illustrations of how the politics, economics, ecology, and organization of cities that work all fit together.

I want to close with a few examples.

The South Bronx in New York City is the postwar city at its nadir. It has hundreds of abandoned, burned-out tenements and vacant lots. Its inhabitants tend to be jobless, addicted to drugs and ill housed, if housed at all. The Institute for Local Self-Reliance (ILSR) has been working in the South Bronx to help its inhabitants make use of locally available resources – land, buildings, skills, materials – to start rebuilding their lives and their communities. About the only resources these people have, other than their own amazing energy and fertile imaginations, are vacant lots and piles of garbage. Putting these two things together, they started to compost kitchen garbage, which produced one thousand cubic yards of compost a month, and then used it to garden in the vacant lots. Community garden groups were formed to grow produce.

This sounds very specialized. But in the course of organizing themselves to grow food, the people also organized a project to generate their own power, and established numerous self-help housing cooperatives. These housing cooperatives were formed to rehabilitate abandoned tenements. The rehabilitation process employed dozens of local workers, whose "pay" was a home which they had fixed up with their own labour. One can only imagine the kind of investment these people have in the health of their local community. The point is that the compost project generated activity in other spheres than gardening. When people are given the chance, they cooperate as humans, not as home buyers, workers, or gardeners. Significantly, when New York City's blackout occurred in 1977 and there was widespread looting and vandalism, neighbourhoods with community gardens experienced very little lawlessness. It all fits together:

composting, gardening, housing, ecologically sensible development, street safety. It cannot be planned from above; but people will do it naturally if they are given the space and the opportunity.

In fact, the South Bronx, destroyed through the cooperative efforts of Robert Moses, developers, absentee landlords, and various levels of government, has been the scene of some remarkable rebirths. While the ILSR project started with gardening and ended up with housing, in other parts of the area redevelopment started with housing and ended up with gardening. Roberta Brandes Gratz, in her book *The Living City*, describes the achievements of a group called Banana Kelly, which slowly but surely reclaimed several blocks of the devastated South Bronx – for housing, for community life, for vegetable gardening. Once again, the principle of sweat equity, or the substitution of labour for capital by residents working on their own dwellings, turned dozens of derelict buildings and vacant lots into solid, working-class neighbourhoods. The residents of these neighbourhoods developed self-confident political consciousness, a healthy community life, considerable experience in a number of building trades, and a significant source of food grown right on the block. The gardening was not just a frill; it was a crucial part of the whole enterprise. The physical design of these reclaimed neighbourhoods, built almost literally from the ground up by their residents, included short blocks, small-scale mixture of land use, a healthy mixture of renovated, newer, and older buildings, and reasonable concentration of use.

In another part of New York City, on Manhattan, Dolores Hayden has pointed to a similar process.

In contrast to those government programs that pushed the worlds of "home" and "work" farther apart, some new programs have attempted to see housing as a source of jobs and as a strategy for environmental conservation ...

At 519 East 11th Street (in New York City) ... also known as The Solar Tenement, the urban homesteading approach to the problems of inner city housing was developed by ... architects and community organizers concerned with the abandonment of 30,000 units of deteriorated housing every year by landlords in New York City. They determined to ... create a model of cooperative home ownership by tenants whose labor on the rehabilitation of a tenement would be their only capital investment. The project involved training local male residents in construction skills, as well as experimenting with new technologies to create demonstrations of solar and wind energy. In the neighborhood, the residents of 519 also developed a community garden called El Sol Brilliante on five vacant lots.

Since Hayden wrote, more community gardens have sprung up in the neighbourhood.

In Cheyenne, Wyoming, fifteen delinquent youths built three sixteen-by-twenty-foot solar greenhouses to provide food for a group home for the handicapped; the labour was undertaken by the youths as an alternative to going to jail.

The success of the small greenhouses led to a larger ... three-stage, three-growing climate, 500-square-foot greenhouse [which] produced its first harvest in May of 1978 ... The project attracted about eighty gardeners ranging in age from ten to ninety-two, including retirees and the handicapped.

[In] the Cheyenne system ... cultivation proceeds collectively. The greenhouse's paid staff select plantings, make up work schedules, and assign participants to jobs. Harvesting is more remarkable: " ... individuals simply take what they need ... [and] there have been no problems with this system of distribution. It seems that people get to know each other through working side-by-side in the structure and develop strong bonds of mutual understanding and respect."

Yields are constantly increasing ... [and] a third section of the greenhouse is used for commercial production of plants to generate income. Environmental education is also essential to the experience: "A visitor at the greenhouse may be greeted by a retired school teacher, a little girl, or a weather-beaten old cowboy. Any of them will gladly conduct a tour and explain how everything works. A visitor will see a cross-section of the community – young and old, rich and poor – working side-by-side. Some are there to socialize, some to learn, while others need the food."

Consider the many levels on which the Cheyenne project has worked: from a modification of the prison-incarceration system, to provision of year-round fresh produce for handicapped and other residents of a northern city, to education about growing vegetables, to an invaluable process of social interaction among different members of the community, to a remarkable saving of energy required to transport fresh produce to Cheyenne during nine months of the year.

One more good example is cohousing, which has emerged in Denmark and other European countries over the last twenty years. Cohousing reflects an awareness that the conventional model of city living is undesirable and clearly applies the idea that development has to work on all dimensions – social, economic, political, and ecological. These small housing projects are designed by residents themselves from the start, although they usually have the help of architects and builders (some of them have done the finishing work themselves).

Their average size is about twenty-five households, with or without children. The development is compact, though buildings are seldom more than two stories. The housing units are modest, with a minimum of large appliances; in contrast, there is always a generously proportioned community hall, with many facilities and functions. Here, member families will often eat together three or more times a week (rotating responsibility for meal preparation), send their children to a cooperatively run daycare centre, use workshops with a wide range of tools and machines, watch a large television with other residents, teach classes, hold meetings, use the laundry facilities, or simply pass the time. Significantly, in almost all of these cohousing projects, energy conservation is an important goal; in addition to saving energy through the sharing of facilities and appliances, many of them use solar, wind, and other alternative energy sources.

Anyone who doubts that a group of people can actually do a competent job of designing their own living (or working) space should consult the writings and experience of Christopher Alexander. This architect and urban planner shows persuasively that we all have the ability to conceptualize and design spaces that really work for us. Alexander's experiments throw into relief our conditioned idea that the built environment must be designed and constructed for us. It took considerable prodding by Alexander to convince people that they really knew what felt right. His point is that we can all recognize when a place is alive; when it has, as he calls it, the Quality without a Name. He has worked intensively with different groups for periods of a week or more, starting in empty fields and putting stakes in the ground, simply to design buildings. Each group has ended up shaping a building or buildings which have been truly successful, alive, and in harmony with their users (who, in some cases, were both designers and builders).

Kathryn McCamant and Charles Durrett, who wrote a book about Denmark's cohousing, report that not only are these communities working economically and environmentally but they are a tremendous social success: there is privacy without isolation, cooperation without feelings of dependence, intimate friendships without nosiness, and rare levels of community spirit. McCamant and Durrett are now working with twenty-seven groups in the US to help them start their own cohousing communities.

These projects have clearly been undertaken by people who have become aware. They have become aware of the destructive impact of postwar urban-development practices on their personal lives – some of them, as in the South Bronx, with painful immediacy, others by observing thoughtfully the alienation and physical waste they see around them.

The examples also show that in order to build cities that work we need to let go of narrow preconceptions about "the way things are." Economics need not be a world of global markets, vast sums of mobile capital, trade deficits, high interest rates, and profit taking; it can be a world of cooperative service to others, especially to those in our communities. Social life need not be limited to some fragmented relationships at work and others inside the home; it can be a web of public, semi-public, and intimate interactions that relate harmoniously to spaces we frequent. Politics need not be anonymous politicians trying to sound friendly on the television; it can be a group of neighbours deciding that something needs to be done and then doing it.

Breaking the rules of the old system is what these projects are all about, and they work beautifully. In many cases, the projects are the product of urban space which has fallen outside the rules of the marketplace, vacant lots which the market doesn't want. Here sprout the seedlings of the new order, literally as well as figuratively.

They are not offered as blueprints. We do not need blueprints for how to build cities. Building cities that work has to be a process, not an endpoint, because cities which work ecologically as well as socially are an organic phenomenon, incapable of being planned by rules or conceptualized by generalities. As soon as we posit an endpoint, we restrict ourselves. Furthermore, to characterize these examples as advances in urban food production, or housing, or employment is to miss their point. They are all those things, because in them daily life is meaningfully integrated so that it involves the many different facets of who we humans are. Just as our postwar cities reflect the way we have fragmented ourselves, our time, our energy, and our spaces, these new projects are exciting and alive because they express our unity, both within ourselves and with each other.

In the end, there is a glorious simplicity to it all: no one else can do it for us. In our minds, and with our hands, we ourselves must be the builders of cities that work.

Appendix

Each area was rated on a scale with a maximum of six. Scores were based on mix of building age, shortness of block length, concentration of use, and land-use mix.

AREA 1. Niagara Street and Walnut Avenue from King Street to   *Scores*
Richmond Street (6.3 acres)

49 out of 55 buildings built before 1946	5
Average block length: 279 feet	6
Users: 250 residents, 290 workers, 136 other; 76 people per acre	2
Primary land uses: residential and manufacturing	6

AREA 2. Wellesley and Maitland Streets from Church Street to
Jarvis Street; Alexander Street from Church to Mutual Street
(11.3 acres)

53 out of 58 buildings built before 1946	5
Average block length: 521 feet	5
Users: 1,135 residents, 446 workers, 675 other; 142 people per acre	3
Primary land uses: office, retail, residential, educational	6

AREA 3. Margueretta Street between Bloor and College Streets
(22.3 acres)

All houses built before 1946	1
Average block length: 1,870 feet	1
Users: 1,325 residents, 34 workers, 52 other; 61 people per acre	2
Primary land uses: residential, one or two retail stores	2

AREA 4. Gulliver Road from Keele Street to Hurdman Street;   *Scores*
Hurdman Street, Paramount Court, and Comay Road
    All buildings built since 1946   1
    Average block length: 714 feet   4
    Users: 1,100 residents; 44 people per acre   1
    Primary land uses: residential   1

AREA 5. Balliol and Merton Streets between Pailton Crescent and
Yonge Street; Pailton Crescent and Yonge Street between Balliol
and Merton Streets (6.1 acres)
    22 out of 57 buildings built before 1946   4
    Average block length: 1,414 feet   1
    Users: 1,225 residents; 1,736 workers, 975 other; 430 people per
    acre   6
    Primary land uses: residential and commercial, but not close-
    grained or side-by-side   4

AREA 6. Veery Place and Ternhill Crescent – Don Mills (11.3 acres)
    All buildings built since 1946   1
    Average block length: 1,055 feet (Ternhill forms a loop)   3
    Users: 425 residents; 42 people per acre   1
    Primary land uses: residential   1

AREA 7. Oakwood and Robina Avenues from Glenhurst Avenue to
St Clair Avenue (5.5 acres)
    48 out of 50 buildings built before 1946 (this area includes one
    large high-rise)   3
    Average block length: 564 feet   5
    Users: 490 residents, 37 workers, 81 others; 97 people per acre   3
    Primary land uses: residential, a little commercial and retail
    along St Clair Avenue   3

AREA 8. St Jamestown (11.0 acres)
    2 out of 6 buildings built before 1946   2
    Average block length: 908 feet   3
    Users: 4,010 residents, 55 workers, 45 others; 416 people per
    acre   6
    Primary land uses: residential, a few retail stores used lightly by
    non-residents   2

AREA 9. Rusholme and Dovercourt Roads from Bloor Street to   *Scores*
Hepbourne Street (9.0 acres)

 21 out of 24 buildings built before 1946 (the other three are
large high-rises)   3
 Average block length: 555 feet   5
 Users: 1,570 residents, 52 workers, 460 other; 193 people per
acre   3
 Primary land uses: residential, some commercial and retail along
Bloor Street   4

AREA 10. Dufferin Street, Bristol Avenue, and Bartlett Street, from
Davenport Road to Geary Avenue (23.1 acres)

 118 out of 130 buildings built before 1946   3
 Average block length: 756 feet   4
 Users: 755 residents, 571 workers, 200 other; 51 people per acre   2
 Primary land uses: residential, industrial, some retail   5

AREA 11. Adelaide and Front Streets from Ontario Street to
Sherbourne Street (9.1 acres)

 29 out of 32 buildings built before 1946   3
 Average block length: 318 feet   6
 Users: 612 workers, 468 other; 58 people per acre   2
 Primary land uses: industrial, warehousing   1

AREA 12. Thorncliffe Park Drive from Milepost Point to #65
Thorncliffe Park Drive (5 acres)

 All buildings built since 1946   1
 Average block length: 1,503 feet   1
 Users: 1,480 residents; 296 people per acre   4
 Primary land uses: residential   1

AREA 13. Spadina Avenue, Huron Street, and Ross Street from
Cecil Street to College Street (12.8 acres)

 76 out of 78 buildings built before 1946   2
 Average block length: 396 feet   6
 Users: 768 residents, 200 workers, 338 others; 78 people per
acre   2
 Primary land uses: retail, wholesale, residential   6

AREA 14. Spadina Road, Madison Avenue, and Huron Street from   *Scores*
Dupont Street to Bernard Avenue (7.4 acres)
 27 out of 29 buildings built before 1946   2
 Average block length: 726 feet   3
 Users: 405 residents, 7 workers; 55 people per acre   2
 Primary land uses: residential, retail (facing, but not within area)   3

AREA 15. Montrose Avenue and Crawford Street from Cinder
Avenue to College Street; College Street from Montrose Avenue to
Crawford Street; Cinder Avenue; Sully Crescent (4.1 acres)
 33 out of 35 buildings built before 1946   3
 Average block length: 448 feet   6
 Users: 235 residents, 62 workers, 238 other; 83 people per acre   2
 Primary land uses: residential, retail, offices   4

AREA 16. Rosedale Road between Park Road and Cluny Avenue;
Cluny Avenue; Cluny Drive between Rosedale Road and Cluny
Avenue; Avondale Road between Park Road and Rosedale Road
(7.4 acres)
 22 out of 24 buildings built before 1946   3
 Average block length: 542 feet   5
 Users: 150 residents; 20 people per acre   1
 Primary land uses: residential   1

AREA 17. Cosburn and Gowan Avenues between Donlands Avenue
and Pape Avenue (17.0 acres)
 65 out of 77 buildings built before 1946   4
 Average block length: 1,214 feet   2
 Users: 1,665 residents, 314 workers, 150 other; 114 people per
 acre   3
 Primary land uses: residential, retail   3

AREA 18. Golden Avenue, Silver Avenue, Morrow Avenue; Dundas
Street between Morrow Avenue and Golden Avenue (6.3 acres)
 All buildings built before 1946   1
 Average block length: 509 feet   5
 Users: 400 residents, 94 workers, 115 other; 79 people per acre   2
 Primary land uses: residential, retail, industrial   6

AREA 19. Barber Greene Road from Southill Drive to Wren Court; *Scores*
Prince Arthur Place; Foxden Road, Embla Street, and Wren Court
— Don Mills (22.7 acres)

All buildings built after 1946	1
Average block length: 662 feet	4
Users: 200 residents, 502 workers, 38 other; 23 people per acre	1
Primary land uses: residential, industrial, and commercial, but the last two uses completely separated by Barber Green Road	3

Table A-1
The areas and their scores on diversity — The Toronto Study

	Mix in building age	Average block length	Concen-tration of use	Mix in land use	Composite score on diversity
1 Niagara Street	5	6	2	6	360
2 Maitland Street	5	5	3	6	450
3 Margueretta Street	1	1	2	2	4
4 Gulliver Road	1	4	1	1	4
5 Merton Street	4	1	6	4	96
6 Don Mills (Veery)	1	3	1	1	3
7 Robina Avenue	3	5	3	3	135
8 St Jamestown	2	3	6	2	72
9 Dovercourt Ave.	3	5	3	4	180
10 Bristol Ave.	3	4	2	5	120
11 Ontario Street	3	6	2	1	36
12 Thorncliffe Park	1	1	4	1	4
13 Spadina Avenue	2	6	2	6	144
14 Madison Avenue	2	3	2	3	36
15 Sully/Cinder Crescent	3	6	2	4	144
16 Rosedale	3	5	1	1	15
17 Gowan Avenue	4	2	3	3	72
18 Golden Avenue	1	5	2	6	60
19 Don Mills (Foxden)	1	4	1	3	12

Notes

CHAPTER ONE

Page 3
– *Man-Made America* is by Boris Pushkarev and Christopher Tunnard.
– The Canadian study is by Peter Spurr, *Land and Urban Development*.
– The US figures are from US Bureau of the Census, *Statistical Abstract*, 705.

Page 4
– On downtown office projects, see Collier, *Contemporary Cathedrals*, Conway, "The Case Against Urban Dinosaurs"; Ley, *A Social Geography*, 42–4.
– On Moses and Co-Op City see Caro, *The Power Broker*.
– Robert Collier describes St Jamestown, and Herbert Lottman treats French urban-planning laws in *How Cities are Saved*, 145 ff.
– Gans, *The Levittowners*, and Jackson, *Crabgrass Frontier*, have good and not-so-good things to say about Levittowns.

Page 5
– For Don Mills, see Sewell, "Don Mills," 28–38.
– Lorimer, *The Developers*, compares Canadian and American suburban developers.
– Checkoway, "Large Builders," 29.
– On railroad sidings in Chicago's suburbs, see Schwartz, "The Evolution of Suburbs," 22.

Page 6
– On Bethlehem Steel, see Reutter, "The Rise and Decline of Big Steel," 71 *passim*.
– The deconcentration process started early in the nineteenth century, according to Jackson, *Crabgrass Frontier*, 307 ff.

– On greater space needed for workplaces in general, see Niedercorn and Hearle, "Recent Land Use Trends," 105–9; and Gruen, *The Heart of Our Cities.*

– The Don Mills figures are from Sewell, "Don Mills."

– New York City and the continuous-material-flow process are described in Hoover and Vernon, *Anatomy of a Metropolis*, 27; and Vernon, *Metropolis 1985.*

– Scott, *Metropolis*, 211. The point about de-integration is also Scott's.

Page 7

– New York's office-space figures are from Hoover and Vernon, 296, note 15.

– Toronto's outer-core office-space statistics are from Code, *Controlling the Physical Growth of the Downtown Core.*

– Vancouver information is from *The Core Employment Study*, prepared for the Vancouver Planning Department by the IBI Group, February 1982.

– On the move to the suburbs, see Marsh and Kaplan, "The Lure of the Suburbs," 37–58; and Jackson, *Crabgrass Frontier*, chapter 16.

– The quotation from Hoover and Vernon is in *Anatomy*, 127; their figures on zonal density, 130.

Page 8

– Jackson's quotation is in *Crabgrass Frontier*, 7.

– Canadian figures and quotations are from Pearson, "The History of Canadian Settlement," 65.

– Montreal figures are from Marsan, *Montréal en évolution*, 326.

Page 9

– Lorimer, *The Developers*, documents profit taking by charging more for suburban land.

– The changing population of Los Angeles is from Jackson, *Crabgrass Frontier*, 303.

– Hoover and Vernon, *Anatomy*, 126.

– Economic Council of Canada, "The Challenge of Rapid Urban Growth," 66; and on parking space see *Newsweek*, 18 January 1971.

Page 10

– The report on Gruen is from Jacobs, *Death and Life*, 350–1.

– Los Angeles' use of downtown land is from Hébert, *Highways to Nowhere*, 66.

Page 11

– On streetcar suburbs, see Jackson, 118–24.

– The ideas about the inevitable similarities of architecture from the same era are from Jacobs, *Death and Life*, 225.

Page 13
– See chapter 3 on the heterogeneity of suburbs.

Page 16
– Niagara Street area as a slum, see Mann, *The Underside of Toronto*, 33–64.

Page 25
– Goldberg and Mercer, *The Myth of the North American City.*

CHAPTER TWO

Page 30
– Municipal spending on transportation worldwide was drawn from Brown and Jacobson, *The Future of Urbanization*, 39–40.
– For descriptions of life and land use in the medieval city, see Mumford, *The City in History*, 284; and Holenberg and Lees, *The Making of Modern Europe*, 33–4.
– The Mumford quotation is from *The City in History*, 323.
– The mobility of merchants is treated in Bellan, *The Evolving City*, 45.

Page 31
– On the explosions of scale in eighteenth- and nineteenth-century cities, see Mumford, *The City in History*, chapter 16.
– Katznelson, *City Trenches*, describes the separating of work from home; as does Jackson, *Crabgrass Frontier*, 24–30, 319, and *passim*.
– Whether transportation technology pushed suburbanization or vice versa is discussed in Walker, "A Theory of Suburbanization," 389; and in contradictory ways by Jackson, *Crabgrass Frontier*, 41–2, 91–2.
– The phrase streetcar suburbs comes from Warner, *Streetcar Suburbs.*
– On the development of land as a commodity, see Polanyi, *The Great Transformation*, chapter 15.
– The way the land market separates land use is explained in Ley, *A Social Geography*, 27–9.

Page 33
– The phenomenon of Western cities' annexation of surrounding territory is described in Lowry, "The Dismal Future of Central Cities," 174. The pattern is not quite so clear in Canada, but it is there; see Higgins, *Local and Urban Politics*, chapter 5.

Page 34
– Jackson's quotation is from *Crabgrass Frontier*, 149. On Drapeau's annexation politics, see Sancton, *Governing the Island of Montreal*, 146–7 *passim*.

Page 35
– Displacement of residences by commercial and other job uses in the core is analyzed by Ley, *A Social Geography*, 31.
– Information on street maintenance of single cities was given to me by the following helpful individuals: Ed Gilmour in San Jose; Chip Wood in San Diego; Paul Sachs in San Francisco and the Bay area; and M. Faysal Thameen in Baltimore.

Page 37
– It should be noted that states in the US also vary in the total package of responsibilities they require municipalities to take on; so cities vary in how much of a fiscal burden their property and other taxes are placed under. See Ladd and Yinger, *America's Ailing Cities*, chapter 8.

Page 38
– In Canada, I was given much help by T.J. Corrigan in London, Ontario; Colin Kerr and Doug Farquar in Hamilton; Terry McDonough in Toronto; Trevor Price in Windsor.
– Charles Fitzsimmons and Dave Roberts of the Canadian Urban Transit Association were generous with their time in discussing Canadian transit data with me.

Page 39
– Goldberg and Mercer, *The Myth of the North American City*, 176.
– The more recent figures were calculated from the transit sources listed in Tables 5 and 8.

Page 40
– Newman and Kenworthy, *Cities and Automobile Dependence*.

Page 41
– Michelson, *Environmental Choice*, 203–4.
– The Toronto study is reported in Fowler, "Street Management and City Design," 365–89.

Page 42
– Los Angeles and Indianapolis: Hébert, *Highways to Nowhere*, 66.
– On the land needed to park a car and on government policies which only consider private benefits, see Stern, "The Use of Urban Roads," 135–72. Stern also discusses government valuation of land. The transportation survey is US Department of Transportation, *Urban Data Supplement of 1974*.

Page 43
– Quotation from Stern, "The Use of Urban Roads," 152. I have converted
  Stern's original figures into 1987 dollars for comparison purposes.

Page 44
– Stern, "The Use of Urban Roads," 152.
– Toronto figures calculated from City of Toronto Planning Board, *Technical Report*, Appendix II; Boston's from Boston Redevelopment Authority,
  Transportation Facts. These figures are old, and therefore will be conservative in that they underestimate the amount of land currently devoted to
  streets and parking. Newman and Kenworthy show that Boston trebled
  its parking spaces per office worker between 1960 and 1980. I use their
  figures on the proportion of people biking or riding to work in Phoenix
  and Boston.
– The probability figures are from Ingram, "The Interaction of Transportation," 330.

Page 45
– On some early expressway controversies in the US, see Lupo, Colcord,
  and Fowler, *Rites of Way*; for Canada, see Leo's excellent work, *The Politics
  of Urban Development*.
– Caro, *The Power Broker*, chapters 37–8; quotation 886–7.

Page 46
– The story of the slaying is from the *New York Times*, quoted in Jacobs,
  Death and Life, 260.
– Noise externalities are reported on in Finsterbusch, *Understanding Social
  Impacts*, 215.
– Border vacuums are covered in Jacobs, *Death and Life*, chapter 14.
– The figure on highway deaths is from Lyman, "Rethinking Our Trans-
  portation Future," 38.

Page 47
– Most of the facts on cars and oil consumption come from Renner,
  Rethinking the Role, 9–16, 28.
– Newman and Kenworthy's figures on use density differ from mine
  because I used central-city use densities and they used metropolitan-area
  use densities.
– The comparative gas use in Houston and Chicago is from Brown and
  Jacobson, *The Future of Urbanization*, 18.
– The information about Toronto can be seen from an examination of the
  Canadian census.

Page 48
– Renner, *Rethinking the Role*, 36, for quotation and figures on crop losses.

Page 49
– Forest die-off is treated by French, *Clearing the Air*, 19–22.
– Quotation from Renner, *Rethinking the Role*, 36–7.
– The thirty percent figure is from David Suzuki's CBC program, "A Matter of Time," 14 July 1989.
– The personal cost of running a car in the city is reported on by Casey Mahood, "Car Owners' Costs Driven Up 12% in Metro," *Toronto Star*, 2 August 1990, A26.

Page 50
– Newman and Kenworthy, *Cities and Automobile Dependence*, 83, 85; they cite Neilson Associates, *Net Community Benefits*.

Page 51
– Nowlan and Stewart, "The Effect of Downtown Population Growth."

Page 52
– Bahl and McGuire, "Urban Sprawl," 247–66.

Page 53
– The BTU figures are reported from a US Government study reported by Lawrence Solomon, "Suburbs are Big Energy Consumers," Toronto *Globe and Mail*, 14 August 1980, T7.

Page 54
– For a good review of the literature on the crumbling infrastructure in the US, see Kaplan, "Infrastructure Policy," 371–88.
– A series of studies has been made of the state of individual cities' infrastructure by the Urban Institute; the first one is Grossman, *The Future of New York City's Capital Plant*.

Page 55
– The Canadian figure from 1975 is in Spurr, *Land and Urban Development*, 25. The US figures come from US Bureau of the Census, *Statistical Abstract*, 45, 705. For more recent figures in Canada, see *Canadian Economic Observer*.

Page 56
– On nineteenth-century Paris, see Mumford, *The City in History*, 387–8.

– On Le Corbusier, see Fishman, *Urban Utopias*, 206.
– The neat comparison between Le Corbusier's drawings and contemporary buildings is made by Robert Goodman, *After the Planners*, 60–1.
– On destruction of businesses by early urban renewal, see Zimmer, "The Small Businessman and Relocation," 384. The value of long years of face-to-face relations is also documented in Alperovitz and Faux, *Rebuilding America: A Blueprint for the New Economy*, 144. See also the conservative Anderson, "The Federal Bulldozer," 497.
– Inflated land prices in the US are described in Caro, *The Power Broker*, 980–1, 1006. In Canada, see Lorimer, *A Citizen's Guide*, 102.
– Inordinate amounts of money: see Proudfoot, "Private Gains and Public Losses," 203–26; Walker, "A Theory of Suburbanization," 402–3; Cox, "Capitalism and Conflict," 443.

Page 57
– On slum housing, see Thompson, *A Preface to Urban Economics*, 296.
– Chicago demolitions are given in Berry, "Short-Term Housing Cycles," 170–1.
– On the net effect of urban renewal, see the various articles in Squires (ed.), *Unequal Partnerships*.
– For housing demolitions in Montreal, see Wolfe and Jay, "The Revolving Door," 205–6.
– Reed, *Return to the City*, 114–15.

Page 58
– On the "usual practice" in the 1960s, see Gans, "The Failure of Urban Renewal," 539
– On why new housing is so expensive, see Lorimer, *The Developers*, chapter 5; Gottdiener, *Planned Sprawl*, chapters 5 and 6.
– Toronto's northern suburbs are treated by Jock Ferguson, "Land is Money North of Metro," and "Behind the Boom: The Story of York Region," Toronto *Globe and Mail*, 26 October and 3 November 1988.
– On rates of construction and housing costs, see Appelbaum and Gilderbloom, "Housing Supply and Regulation," 1–18.

Page 59
– On the lower costs of communally supplied services, see Hayden, *Redesigning the American Dream*, chapters 4, 7 and 8; also McCamant and Durrett, *Cohousing*.
– On land for gardening in cities, see Stokes, *Helping ourselves*, 85.
– Berry, *The Unsettling of America*, 51–2.

Page 60
– On the advantages of large companies, see Bettison, *The Politics of Canadian Urban Development*, 66, 85; Checkoway, "Large Builders"; and Thompson, *A Preface to Urban Economics*, 302–7.
– On the creation of companies by government policy, see Checkoway, "Large Builders," 32; and Lorimer, *The Developers*, 16–24. Canadian stinginess on infrastructure, relative to the us, was reported to me by Shoukry Roweis, in private conversation.
– Both Smith and Lorimer are quoted from Lorimer, *The Developers*, 127.

Page 61
– Markusen and Scheffman, *Speculation and Monopoly*, 62.
– Information on Montreal's infrastructure policy and cheaper houses is reported in Lorimer, *The Developers*, 86, 110–18. See also Walker, "A Theory of Suburbanization," 403, 421, note 143.
– Turner, *Housing By People*, 41–7.

Page 62
– Spurr, *Land and Urban Development*, 429.

Page 63
– Newman, *Community of Interest*, 117–20, quoted from 118–19.
– The figures on Co-op City and the quotation are from Gratz, *The Living City*, 95.

Page 64
– Gratz, *The Living City*, 151.
– Krohn, Fleming, and Manzer, *The Other Economy*.

Page 65
– On homogeneous housing, peculiar social mixes, and encouragement of mobility, see Jacobs, *The Death and Life*, 139; Checkoway, "Large Builders"; and Packard, *A Nation of Strangers*.
– For a defense of the social heterogeneity on the suburbs, see Gans, *The Levittowners*.
– Sale, *Human Scale*, 95.

Page 66
– The quotation is from Logan and Molotch, *Urban Fortunes*, 239–40. See also their comments on Columbia, Maryland, 237–8.
– The examples from different downtown areas come from the following articles in Squires (ed.), *Unequal Partnerships*; Keating, Krumholz, and Metzger, "Cleveland: Post-Populist Public-Private Partnerships," 131;

Norman, "Congenial Milwaukee: A Segregated City," 194; and Cummings, Koebel, and Whitt, "Redevelopment in Downtown Louisville," 211. On the economics of shopping centres, see Logan and Molotch, *Urban Fortunes*, 238; and Lorimer, *The Developers*, chapter 10.

Page 67
– Jacobs, *Death and Life*, 188. Thompson, *A Preface to Urban Economics*, 308.
– Scott, *Metropolis*, 206–15, 208.
– On the interaction essential to business, see Alperovitz and Faux, *Rebuilding America*, 144.
– Scott, *Metropolis*, 211.

Page 68
– See Alperovitz and Faux, *Rebuilding America*, 144–6, for the cost of large firms.
– Sale, *Human Scale*, 317, presents persuasive empirical evidence that smaller firms use capital more efficiently than larger firms. Smaller firms also create more jobs; see Gratz, *The Living City*, 147–8.
– The quotation is from Kohn, *No Contest*, 71; he is referring to Wachtel, *The Poverty of Affluence*.

CHAPTER THREE

Page 70
– The social antecedents for the postwar city must be considered as well as the consequences, but that task will be taken up in Chapters 5 and 6. The works of Constance Perin and Mark Gottdiener are especially important in this regard.
– Malvina Reynolds' song copyright 1962 Schroder Music Co.

Page 71
– Peter Hall quoted from "The Urban Culture," 166.
– There was, of course, a tremendous outpouring of books on the suburbs. Two of the most famous critiques were Reisman et al., *The Lonely Crowd*; and Whyte, *The Organization Man*. Three well-known defenders were Berger, *Working Class Suburb*; Clark, *The Suburban Society*; and Gans, *The Levittowners*.
– The quotations are from Gans, *The Levittowners*, 288; and Gans, *People and Plans*, 160.
– Other than Gans, it is useful to turn to the books of William Michelson for summaries of much of the literature, especially that reporting on suburbanites' satisfaction with their new homes: see *Man and His Urban Environment*; and *Environmental Choice*.

Page 72
- Glazer – who, it should be noted, co-authored *The Lonely Crowd* – was propounding his views in "Slum Dwellings do not Make a Slum," 57–9.
- Gans's review of Jacobs was called "The Fallacy of Physical Determinism" and may be found in *People and Plans*.
- Howard is quoted in Mumford, *The City in History*, 515–16.
- The legacy leading back to Durkheim was traced by Dunlap and Catton, Jr, "What Environmental Sociologists Have in Common." See also Pipkin, LaGory, and Blau (eds.), *Remaking the City*.
- On the proportions of North Americans in suburbs, see Jackson, *Crabgrass Frontier*, 283–4.
- In addition to Berger and Clark, the works of Leo Schnore should be consulted for evidence of how the suburbs were becoming more heterogeneous in terms of land use: see "The Social and Economic Characteristics" and *The Urban Scene*. On suburban hetereogeneity in Canada, see Dansereau, "Les transformations."

Page 73
- Sennett, *The Uses of Disorder*.
- Lowi's point is made in *The End of Liberalism*, 267.
- Barry Checkoway has argued that the suburbs were built for us, not provided as something we demanded: see "Large Builders," 43–4.
- On the interplay between unselfconscious and conscious decisions about building, see Alexander, *Notes on the Synthesis of Form*; and Studer, "Prospects."

Page 74
- The Toronto study is reported on in Fowler, "Street Management."
- The work by researchers on subjective reactions to "objective" environments is voluminous. Here are a couple of references which would lead the interested reader further: Blau and Pipkin, "Introductory Remarks"; Michelson, "The Reconciliation"; St John, "Racial Differences"; and Francescato, Weidemann, and Anderson, "Residential Satisfaction."
- The quotation is from Burchard, "Design and Urban Beauty," 234–5.

Page 75
- The study on neighbourhood evaluation is St John's "Racial Differences."
- For an enlightened discussion of how a particular form of economics is central to our value system, see Schumacher, *Small is Beautiful*.
- One theoretical scheme on environment-personality interaction is presented by Jeffrey, *Crime Prevention*. Another is in Alexander, *The Timeless*

Way of Building. See also Gottdiener, "Urban Semiotics," 101–14; and Rapoport, *The Meaning of the Built Environment*.

Page 76
– Alfred Eide Parr wrote extensively on the relationship between the mind and the physical environment during the 1960s; these words come from "City and Psyche," 73.
– See also Parr, "Environmental Design and Psychology," 15–18.
– A similar point is made by Wohlwill, "The Physical Environment."
– Jacobs' quote on projects is from *Death and Life*, 186.
– Jacobs' words on chaos can be found in *Death and Life*, 223.

Page 77
– Lynch, *The Image of the City*.
– The words on identification with a personal niche are from Parr, "Environmental Design and Psychology," 18.
– The architects include Rapoport, *The Meaning of the Built Environment*; Lerup, *Building the Unfinished*; and Alexander, *The Timeless Way of Building*.
– On the anonymity of high-rises, much has been written. One eloquent example is Bookchin, *The Limits of the City*, 83–4.
– Studies finding few differences between high-rise residents and residents of other housing types include Michelson, "The Reconciliation of 'Objective' and 'Subjective Data'"; Wellman and Whittaker, "High-Rise, Low-Rise"; and the Social Planning Council of Metropolitan Toronto, *Families in High Rise Apartments*, 35, 103–4.
– The quote and figures on high-rises vs. low-rises are from the study by Wellman and Whittaker, "High-Rise, Low-Rise."
– Another extremely comprehensive study of people who moved both to and from high-rises (to take into account "self-selection" of high-rise residents) is Michelson's *Environmental Choice*.
– The figures on neuroses come from Mehrabian, *Public Places*, 119. See also Michelson, *Man and His Urban Environment*, 161–2.

Page 78
– On suburban strawberries, see Perin, *Everything In its Place*, 107.
– Tom Wolfe, *From Bauhaus to Our House*, 10.

Page 79
– Clark, *The Suburban Society*, 62 ff.; Gans, *The Levittowners*, 33, 236.
– Evidence that dirt, noise, and crowds are not so important comes from Michelson, *Environmental Choice*, 114–20.
– One other study which investigated what residents liked about land-use mix and age of buildings (but not mixtures of old and new buildings)

was Lansing and Marans, "Evaluation of Neighbourhood Quality," 195–9.
- Residents who thought they had cleaner air are referred to in Rapoport, *The Meaning of the Built Environment*, 32.
- The Toronto study is "Street Management and City Design."
- Gender has also been pointed to as an important variable determining attitudes towards the urban environment. See Shlay and DiGregorio, "Same City, Different Worlds"; and Hayden, *Redesigning the American Dream*.

Page 82
- Those unconvinced of the pathological effects of high-density living include Wellman and Whittaker, "High-Rise, Low-Rise"; Mitchell, "Some Social Implications of High Density Housing"; and Freedman, *Crowding and Behaviour*.
- Evidence that people do not like high density, in general, can be found all over; one specific example is Rodgers, *Density, Crowding and Satisfaction*. Rodgers and others, however, stress the multi-dimensionality of the experience of being crowded: Rodgers, *Residential Satisfaction*; Roncek, "Density and Crime"; Stokols, "On the Distinction"; and Stokols, "The Experience of Crowding."
- The quote is from Freedman, *Crowding and Behaviour*, 93.
- Specific empirical studies on the contingent nature of density can be found in Harries, *Crime and the Environment*; and Michelson and Roberts, "Children."

Page 83
- Chief Standing Bear's words may be found in McLuhan, *Touch the Earth*, 6.
- The foremost writer on social ecology is Murray Bookchin. His *magnum opus* on this topic is *The Ecology of Freedom*.

Page 84
- Fishman, *Urban Utopias*, 179, for the connection between William Morris and Le Corbusier.
- Jacobs, *Death and Life*, chapter 3.

Page 85
- Michelson's research is reported on in his book, *Environmental Choice*.
- In her research on social networks in Montreal, Andrée Fortin took pains to include casual acquaintances in the research design, but her summary of findings did not mention any significant patterns of acquaintance networks; see Fortin, "Du voisinage à la communauté?"

– Quotation from Michelson, *Environmental Choice*, 249. For another full-scale study of social relations among residents of towns, suburbs, and cities, see Fischer, *To Dwell Among Friends*. Fischer does take account of relations with neighbours, but they are all private relations; he is not interested in the public dimension of people's interactions (see 36–7). Another well-known study of the link between neighbourhood connections and personal networks which, again, finds no relationship is Hunter, *Symbolic Communities*.

Page 86

– Michelson's *Man and His Urban Environment* bears out this generalization about the sociologist's concept of the physical environment. Michelson himself developed a more sophisticated framework. One interesting exception to sociologists' thinking about the physical environment is feminist writing on housing and cities. See Hayden, *Redesigning the American Dream*; and Werkele, "Canadian Women's Housing Cooperatives."
– Fischer, *To Dwell Among Friends*, is an example of someone comparing suburbs with the central city.
– The Detroit study is reported by Fox, Fox, and Marans, "Residential Density."

Page 87

– Misty contexts are created by many sociologists who include neighbourhood characteristics ("urban," or "high-rise") as attributes of individuals whom they are interviewing. This is a dubious practice, since it plays around with the assumption necessary for statistical analysis that each respondent's answers are independent from the next respondent's answers; it also involves grouping by the dependent variable. See my article, "Street Management," and Blalock, *Casual Inferences*, chapter 4.
– The discussion on this page and the next relies heavily on Jacobs.
– An example of research which starts out considering simply the volume of street users is Hunter and Baumer, "Street Traffic." To give them credit, they find that people have to be "socially integrated" before volume of street users becomes significant.

Page 88

– Greenbie, *Spaces*, made me aware of what Greenbie calls the distemic nature of some places, which are "those parts of the city which are actively shared by people with diverse cultural values and [where] codes of conduct must be readily intelligible to all" (112).
– Lofland's point about public space is in *World of Strangers*, 136.
– One of the most interesting discussions of American separation of public and private life and its expression in the urban landscape can be found

in Perin, *Everything in its Place*. See also Popenoe, *Private Pleasure*, chapter 7.
- On the dialogue between public and private, see Lerup, *Building the Unfinished*, 109–10.

Page 89
- On the way in which the built environment becomes built into our expectations, and on how we are unaware of its influence, see Nelson's extraordinary little pamphlet, *The Illusions of Urban Man*.
- Hayden has a wonderful discussion of the separation of public from private life and how it is part of the separation of women and children from the urban experience, in *Redesigning the American Dream*, 210–12. See also Popenoe, "Suburbanization."
- Fava is quoted from "Reston, Virginia," 145.

Page 91
- See Tilly, *An Urban World*, for the careful research on rates of crime and violence in the countryside as opposed to the city.
- The discretionary police decision whether or not to lay charges has been widely researched. An excellent Canadian study of this is Ericson, *Reproducing Order*. On us crime, see Currie, *Confronting Crime*. Other studies include Mawby, *Policing the City*; and Lundeman (ed.), *Police Behaviour*. Many of these works claim that police discretion is not all that extensive; Ericson's discussion shows, however, that it is easy to fool oneself with statistics.
- For different perspectives on what to put in the denominator of crime figures (instead of resident population) see Harries, "Alternative Denominators"; see also Farley and Hansel, "The Ecological Context of Urban Crime."
- Finally, for a discussion of the vast differences between reported crime and unreported crime, see Sewell, *Police*; and Hood and Sparks, *Key Issues in Criminology*.

Page 92
- The rates for thirteenth-century London can be found in Tuan, *Landscapes of Fear*, 131–4.
- Newman, *Defensible Space*. For a critique of Newman's book, see Samuel Kaplan's review in the *New York Times Book Review*.

Page 93
- Mumford, "Home Remedies for Urban Cancer," 190–2.
- British studies casting doubt on Newman's thesis can be found in Harries, *Crime and the Environment*. For evidence from Britain supporting

Newman, see Coleman, *Utopia on Trial*. See also Booth, "The Built Environment."

- For research on the inactive bystander, see Sadalla, "Population Size"; and Latané and Darley, *The Unresponsive Bystander*.

Page 94

- CPTED originated with Jeffery, *Crime Prevention*. Jeffery is not one to ignore the larger-scale issues.
- A good example of overemphasis on architectural versus human concerns in CPTED research is *Designing Against Vandalism* (no author listed).
- The figures on vandalism come from Castelman, "Crime Free."
- Although the cost of crime should be obvious, there are those who have put a dollar figure on it, including the costs of public and private protection, victimization, and the "distribution of justice." See Gray (ed.), *The Costs of Crime*.

Page 95

- See Rapoport, *The Meaning of the Built Environment*, 171–2, for evidence on crime as a barometer of the neighbourhood; Castelman also points this out.
- For insightful remarks on what children learn from adults about the environment, see Michelson and Roberts, "Children." Colin Ward has much to say on this topic as well; see *The Child in the City*. Ward makes the point about Pruitt-Igoe, p. 73.
- Popenoe has hypothesized that juvenile delinquency is higher in the suburbs because the physical design discourages informal social control; see "Suburbanization."
- The Cunningham Road quote is from Blaber, "The Cunningham Road Scheme," 38.
- Different examples of community networks of trust as crime deterrents are described in Curtis (ed.), *Policies to Prevent Crime*.
- The "deviant subculture" is found in Bottoms and Xanthos, "Housing Policy and Crime."

Page 96

- Quotation from Merry, "Defensible Space Undefended," 419.
- Duffala, "Convenience Stores."
- Juvenile delinquency and building size are related in Leroy, "Some Socio-Political Consequences."

Page 97

- Roncek's research is reported in "Dangerous Places."
- For the study of Washington, see Rhodes and Conly, "Crime and Mobility."

Page 98
– There has been much research on the criminal's "trip to work"; a good deal of it is summarized in Harries, *Crime and the Environment*.
– On the child's contact with the public in contemporary cities, see Michelson and Roberts, "Children"; Lofland, *World of Strangers*, 76–7; and Sennett, *The Fall of Public Man*, 91–8.

CHAPTER FOUR

Page 99
– Quotation by Whyte, *The Last Landscape*, 296.
– For a historical look at childhood, see Aries, *Centuries of Childhood*; and Summerville, *The Rise and Fall of Childhood*.

Page 100
– Ward, *The Child in the City*, 22.
– See also Tuan, *Topophilia*, 12, 96.

Page 101
– The telephone box with the fluted base is described in Ward, *The Child in the City*, 28.
– On the unmanipulable environment and the child's desire for unprogrammed space, see Alexander, "The City as a Mechanism," especially 425; Lynch (ed.), *Growing Up in Cities*, 13; Michelson and Roberts, "Children," 457; Whyte, *The Last Landscape*.

Page 102
– I found out about Roul Tunley and juvenile delinquency from Parr, "City and Psyche," 76. It is his words that are quoted.
– For a wonderful photo essay on children's activities in city spaces, see Wagenvoord, *Hangin' Out*.
– Quotes from Michelson and Roberts, "Children and the Urban Physical Environment," 453, 461.

Page 103
– Jacobs' example of the locksmith is in *Death and Life*, 82; emphasis in the original.
– For more on what the child learns from street life, see Nicholson, "How Not to Cheat Children."
– Patricia MacKay, quoted in Michelson, Levine, and Michelson (eds.), *The Child in the City*, 21; MacKay is quoting from "Fair Play for Children," National Playing Fields Association, England.

Page 104
– Ward (121) is the source of reports on the lower mobility of children.
– See Ward, *The Child in the City*, 118, for the quotation on deaths and injuries.
– Sandels' report is *The Skandia Report II*; Ward, *The Child in the City*, 123.

Page 105
– The child's question from Ottawa is from Spencer, *Questions Kids Ask*, 45; Petra is quoted in Lepman, *How Children See Our World*, 45.
– The film is described by Robert Aldrich, Professor of Preventive Medicine and Pediatrics, University of Colorado, in Michelson, Levine, and Michelson (eds.), *The Child in the City*, 96. Aldrich points out that the areas where most children are hurt by cars have very specific design characteristics (e.g., low-cost housing development across a busy street from a recreational facility).
– Alexander, "The City as a Mechanism," 413, 418, and 420.

Page 106
– Perin, *Everything in Its Place*, 121.
– R. Marvyn Novick is quoted in Michelson, Levine, and Michelson (eds.), *The Child in the City*.

Page 107
– On the friendships of children in high-rises, see Michelson and Roberts, "Children," 447–8; Jephcott, *Homes in High Flats*; and Farley, *Effects of Residential Settings*.

Page 108
– The mobility figures come from Yeates and Garner, *The North American City*, 269.
– Jacobs is quoted from *Death and Life*, 139.
– Packard, *A Nation of Strangers*, 214.
– Katz, *The People of Hamilton*, 119.
– Packard treats children's friendships in chapter 18.
– Psychological damage to children is documented in Killinger, *The Loneliness of Children*, chapter 8.
– Jacobs is one writer who documents the "dangerous" school yard; see *Death and Life*, 79.

Page 109
– The four percent figure is reported in Michelson, *Environmental Choice*, 284.

– Among the "numerous authors" are Alexander, "City as a Mechanism";
Peter Kong-ming New, "Comments," in Michelson, Levine, Michelson
(eds.), *The Child in the City*; and Hayden, *Redesigning the American
Dream*.
– The New York survey was reported on by Lash and Sigal, *State of the
Child: New York City*.
– The sixty percent figure is reported in Hood and Sparks, *Key Issues in
Criminology*.
– The Rudofsky quote is in *Streets for People*, 328.

Page 110
– On the destruction of Pruitt-Igoe, see Ward, *The Child in the City*, 73.
– Popenoe, "Suburbanization," 125, 129–30.
– For the Toronto research by the author, see "Street Management"; and
"Diversity and Healthy Cities."

Page 113
– Michelson and Roberts, "Children," 452; Hayden, in *Redesigning the
American Dream*, shares their view.
– I acknowledge there is reason for considerable scepticism about the
amount of real decision-making power citizens have been granted in the
planning process; see chapter 5; see also Feldman (ed.), *Politics and Government*, 61–86.

Page 114
– For nursery planning, see Pfluger and Zota, "A Room Planned for Children." See also De Bono, *How Children Solve Problems*.

CHAPTER FIVE

Page 115
– My understanding of how real politics connects to daily life comes mostly
from Bookchin, *Urbanization*, chapter 3; on our self-consciousness as a
community, see Wood, *Mind and Politics*. Bookchin also inspired my conceptualization of citizenship.

Page 116
– On the link between our buying habits and networks of production and
distribution, see Seymour and Girardet, *Blueprint for a Green Planet*; also
Will et al., *Shopping for a Better World*.
– Walsh, *Staying Alive*, makes clear our personal responsibility for the state
of the world.

Page 117
— Burnham, *The Current Crisis in American Politics*, discusses the meaning-lessness of the vote.
— On support for the system as a function of the vote and description of the empirical research, see Ginsberg, *The Consequences of Consent*, chapter 5.
— North Americans' interest in politics is described in Dahl, *Who Governs?*, 225; Berelson et al., *Voting*; Milbrath, *Political Participation*; Mishler, *Political Participation in Canada*.
— An excellent critical discussion of Dahl's point of view can be found in Ricci, *Community Power and Democratic Theory*, 125–204.
— On the inability of elections to provide a mandate, see Harold Clarke et al., *Absent Mandate*, chapters 6 and 7.

Page 118
— Kaplan, *Urban Political Systems* has a discussion of the distinctiveness of local politics, 211 ff.; see also Gottdiener, *The Decline of Urban Politics*, chapter 6, where he argues that the essential nature of what he calls the local state is concern with social control; and Lorimer, *A Citizen's Guide*.
— On the incorporation of municipalities as growth machines, see Taylor, "Urban Autonomy in Canada," 419; Gottdiener, *The Decline of Urban Politics*, 30–3; and Logan and Molotch, *Urban Fortunes*, 44–5 and *passim*.
— The growth of higher-level governments by the invention of new functions is elucidated in Riker, *Federalism*.

Page 119
— The takeover of social services by higher-level governments is described for the US in Harrigan, *Political Change in the Metropolis*, 115–16; for Canada, in Dupré, *Intergovernmental Finance in Ontario*, 15–19; and Terry Copp, "Montreal's Municipal Government." On present-day social-service administration, see Wharf, "Social Services"; and Sancton, *Municipal Government*, 1–3. Sancton compares Canada to the US and Britain.
— On the powerlessness of local governments, see Gottdiener, *The Decline of Urban Politics*, and the many sources he cites; see also Clarke and Kirby, "In Search of the Corpse."
— Examples of the vulnerability of municipalities to the flow of international capital abound in Bluestone and Harrison, *The Deindustrialization of America*; see also Muszynski, *Deindustrialization*.
— Legal autonomy of local government is covered in numerous books; see Harrigan, *Political Change in the Metropolis*; and Higgins, *Local and Urban Politics in Canada*.

Page 120
- Alford and Lee, "Voting Turnout in American Cities," 796–813.
- On issues and structures in suburban politics, see Kaplan, *The Regional City*; Clark, *The Suburban Society*; Gottdiener, *Planned Sprawl*; Perin, *Everything in its Place*, especially Appendix 4; Harrigan, *Political Change in the Metropolis*, 171 ff.; Gans, *The Levittowners*.

Page 121
- Gans' quotation is from *The Levittowners*, 359.
- Pessac's evolution is described in Boudon, *Lived-in Architecture*.

Page 122
- Lowi's remark on the suburbs is in *The End of Liberalism*, 267.
- On how segregation of land use and scale distance us from the effects of daily decisions, see Sale, *Human Scale*, part 3; for the view that people seem to have become concerned with environmental issues remote from their everyday experience, see Schrecker, "Resisting Environmental Regulation," 177–8.

Page 123
- The controversy over whether office workers are paying their share can be found in Collin, "Le partage fiscal banlieue-ville centrale," 109–31; Thompson, *A Preface to Urban Economics*, 283–6.
- On mobilization of bias, see Bachrach and Baratz, "Decisions and Nondecisions: An Analytical Framework."

Page 124
- On autonomous local authorities, see DelGuidice and Zacks, "The 101 Governments of Metropolitan Toronto"; Harrigan, *Political Change in the Metropolis*, 143–6; and Plunkett and Betts, *The Management of Canadian Urban Government*, 120–1.
- Dahl's point on the limited power of élites is in *Who Governs?* A perfect counter-example is Robert Moses, whom we met in chapter 2; see Caro, *The Power Broker*.
- On transportation models and muddles, see Alan Lupo et al., *Rites of Way*, chapters 12 and 13.
- On the mystique and fragmentation of technique, see Ellul, *The Technological Society*.

Page 125
- Ursula Franklin, *The Real World of Technology*, 68, 69, 75–6.

Page 126
– Suburban examples of architectural conformity are from Perin, *Everything in its Place*, 107. Perin is quoting from the *New York Times*, 25 August 1975, 1.

Page 127
– Mumford is quoted in Miller (ed.), *The Lewis Mumford Reader*, 124. Another insightful book on the politics of the built environment is Goodman, *After the Planners*.
– Harvey, "The Urban Process under Capitalism," 118; his words are from "Labour, Capital and Class Struggle," 292. See also Turner, *Housing by People*, ch. 8.
– Working-class communities in postwar North America and their inability to spawn political organizations are considered in Bailey, Jr., *Radicals in Urban Politics*, chapter 8; Bookchin, *Urbanization*, chapters 7 and 8; Logan and Molotch, *Urban Fortunes*, 135–9.
– The separation of home and workplace is treated in Harvey, "The Urban Process under Capitalism," 104; and Walker, "A Theory of Suburbanization," 385.
– Allen J. Scott has mapped residential patterns of workers in the Los Angeles area and shown some fascinating relationships between occupation and residence clustering; however, the clustering does not seem to bear any relationship to political (especially union) activity: see *Metropolis*.
– The trials and tribulations of company towns are described in Harvey, "Labour, Capital and Class Struggle," 283.
– Factory owners fleeing central-city politics are quoted in Gordon, "Capitalist Development," 49.
– Katznelson, *City Trenches*.

Page 128
– On apolitical unions in Canada and the US, see Horowitz, *Canadian Labour in Politics*, chapter 1, 239–41, 259.
– Bookchin is quoted from *Urbanization*, 212–15.

Page 129
– Chorney's words are from "Amnesia, Integration, and Repression," 557. See also Chorney, *City of Dreams*, chapter 10, especially 167–70.

Page 130
– I am indebted to John Sewell for the point about lack of public politics in the suburbs.

– Sennett, *The Fall of Public Man*, 12.
– Perin's points and quotation are from *Everything in Its Place*, 105–6.

Page 131
– Popenoe is quoted from *Private Pleasure*, 117.
– Several authors have argued that the main task of local government is the exercise of social control, with respect both to property and to our everyday life. See Gottdiener, *The Decline of Urban Politics*, 195; and Katnelson, *City Trenches*, 110.
– The remarkable impact of tax laws on the physical environment is covered in chapter 6. See especially Smith, *City, State, and Market*, chapter 2.

Page 132
– On Winnipeg, see Axworthy and Kuroptawa, "An Experiment in Community Renewal."

Page 133
– On short blocks, see Jacobs, *Death and Life*, 178–81.

Page 134
– For an extended discussion of the "use value" (as opposed to the exchange value) of the neighbourhood, see Logan and Molotch, *Urban Fortunes*, chapter 2. But seeing the neighbourhood as something we are getting "use" out of is not going far enough. For examples of how people give to their neighbourhoods, see Stokes, *Helping Ourselves*; and chapter 8 of this book. Fried's article is "Grieving for a Lost Home," 371.

Page 135
– Satin's *New Age Politics* was a pioneering effort in defining a more authentic politics along the lines sketched here.

CHAPTER SIX

Page 140
– The growth coalition between business and labour is described in Wolfe, *America's Impasse*; Przeworski and Wallerstein, "The Structure of Class Conflict"; Bluestone and Harrison, *Deindustrialization*, 133–9; and Brodie and Jenson, *Crisis, Challenge and Change*, chapters 8 and 9.
– On the proportion of the economy tied to the suburbs, see Ashton, "The Political Economy of Suburban Development," note 18.
– The quotation is from Friedland, "Class Power and Social Control," 459.
– On the self-renewal of capitalism, see Cox, "Capitalism and Conflict Around the Communal Living Space," 442.

– Chapter 2 gives figures on continuous building by the development industry; see also Berry, *The Human Consequences of Urbanization*; and Gottdiener, *The Social Production of Urban Space*, 245.
– The development industry as a central force in the economy is treated in Gottdiener, 242, 245; Harvey, "The Political Economy of Urbanization"; Lorimer, *The Developers*; and Caulfield, *The Tiny Perfect Mayor*.
– See the references in chapter 2 on high-rise inefficiency; as to their being a stepping stone, see Michelson, *Environmental Choice*.
– On high-rise profitability, see Lorimer, *The Developers*, chapter 6; Spurr, *Land and Urban Development*, 428; Newman, *Community of Interest*, 112–13.

Page 141
– Growth in firm size and administrative functions is documented in Bluestone and Harrison, *Deindustrialization*, chapter 3; Gordon, "Capitalist Development," 48–52.
– Office domination is treated by Chandler, *Strategy and Structure*; and Edwards, "Corporate Stability and the Risks of Corporate Failure."
– The quotation is from Gordon, "Capitalist Development," 51–2.
– Higher proportions of management are graphed in Lowi, *The End of Liberalism*, 24–9.
– On corporate centralization, see Feagin and Smith, "Overview," 14–15.
– Bluestone and Harrison, *Deindustrialization*, elucidate the ability of corporations to separate office activity from production, 115–26.
– Scott's argument is developed in *Metropolis*, chapter 7.

Page 142
– Nineteenth-century residential patterns are covered in Jackson, *The Crabgrass Frontier*; and Walker, "A Theory of Suburbanization," 395–6.
– For an interesting alternative distinction between deconcentration and decentralization, see Hudson and Plum, "Deconcentration."
– The fact that urban sprawl was the result of new development rather than movement from the centre to the periphery is stressed in many places; for a summary of the literature, see Gottdiener, *The Social Production of Urban Space*, especially 240 and 250.

Page 143
– For summaries of the conventional explanations for job decentralization, see Hoover and Vernon, *Anatomy of a Metropolis*, 27; Yeates and Garner, *The North American City*, 352–9; Richardson, "The Contribution of Urban Economics," 220; and Logan and Molotch, *Urban Fortunes*, 184.

– Internalizing functions by big firms is addressed in Walker, "A Theory of Suburbanization," 399.
– The movement by companies at the turn of the century for political reasons is treated by Ashton, "The Political Economy of Suburban Development"; Gordon, "Capitalist Development," 48–50; and Walker, "A Theory of Suburbanization," 400–1; contemporary versions of the same process are described by Ley, *A Social Geography of the City*, 213–15; Bluestone and Harrison, *Deindustrialization*, 164–70; Scott, *Metropolis*, 153–7, 180, and *passim*.

Page 144
– Harvey is quoted from "The Political Economy of Urbanization," 283.
– Gottdiener's point on agribusiness is from *The Social Production of Urban Space*, 231–6.
– Sargent's article is "Land Speculation and Urban Morphology," 270–3, 276, and 282. See also Gottdiener, *The Social Production of Urban Space*, 246–7; Gottdiener, *Planned Sprawl*; Lorimer, *A Citizen's Guide*; and Lorimer, *The Developers*. All of these authors analyze the role of the speculator in the urban land market.
– Roweis and Scott point out that road building, particularly the interstate-highway system, made land so much more available in the us that land hoarding by speculators did not drive up the price of land the way it did in Canada. See "The Urban Land Question," 126.

Page 145
– Most of my information on North American attitudes towards home ownership comes from Perin, *Everything in Its Place*, 129 ff.; and Agnew, "Homeownership and the Capitalist Social Order," 470–3.
– For a view that lends less weight to the role of consumer preferences than I do, see Roweis and Scott, "The Urban Land Question," 134. As this chapter progresses, it will be seen that my position is not all that far removed from theirs.
– Michael Polanyi's fascinating book is *The Great Transformation*. See chapter 6 of Polanyi, and Logan and Molotch, *Urban Fortunes*, chapter 2.
– Kevin Cox describes the honey pot in "Capitalism and Conflict," 441.
– Jacobs, *Death and Life*, chapter 13.

Page 146
– On land-use separation in the nineteenth-century city, see Walker, "A Theory of Suburbanization," 385–8; and Katznelson, *City Trenches*, 46–50.
– Centralization and concentration of control by large corporations is outlined in Bluestone and Harrison, *Deindustrialization*, 119.

Page 147
– Economies of scale are discussed by Bluestone and Harrison, as well as by Reich, "The Next American Frontier."
– The Detroit Cadillac factory case is chronicled in Jones and Bachelor, *The Sustaining Hand*.
– The growth of the development industry in the US is explained in Gottdiener, *The Social Production of Urban Space*, 183–94, 244–6; and Checkoway, "Large Builders." Canadian experience is covered in Lorimer, *The Developers*; and Caulfield, *The Tiny Perfect Mayor*, 53–4.
– Battery Park City's history is in Fainstein and Fainstein, "New York City," 69–70.
– Smith's quotation is from *The City and Social Theory*, 240.
– For Jacobs on cataclysmic money see *Death and Life*, chapter 16. See also Keith, *Politics and the Housing Crisis*, 120; and Castells, *The Urban Question*, 155–6.

Page 148
– Harvey is quoted in "The Political Economy of Urbanization," 137.

Page 149
– Squires (ed.), *Unequal Partnerships*, has a whole series of articles describing US urban megaprojects. See also Smith, *City, State, and Market*.
– Housing as fiscal policy is discussed in Lorimer, *The Developers*, and Harvey, "The Political Economy of Urbanization," 120–2.
– The relative size of residential debt is documented in Harvey, 136, and Lorimer, chapter 11. See also Gottdiener, *Social Production*, 183 ff.
– The enthusiasm of legislators is recorded in Keith, *Politics and the Housing Crisis*, 58–9; Checkoway, "Large Builders," 22, 30; and Bettison, *Canadian Urban Development*, 82, 94.
– The judgment that suburban development required federal policies to succeed is made by authors on all points of the political spectrum; see Bettison, *Canadian Urban Development*; Checkoway, "Large Builders"; Smith, *City, State, and Market*, 11–2; Gottdiener, *Social Production*; and Clawson, *Suburban Land Conversion in the United States*.

Page 150
– Explanations of the logic of the depreciation allowance can be found in Lorimer, *A Citizen's Guide*, 71–3; see also Lorimer, *The Developers*, 64–6. On depreciation allowances in the US, see Feagin and Smith, "Overview," 18; and Swanstrom, *The Crisis of Growth Politics*, 28. Also see Lottman, *How Cities Are Saved*, 14, for a comparison with European policies suggesting that it does not have to be this way.

- Mixed blessings of new development are documented in Logan and Molotch, *Urban Fortunes*, 86–8; Smith, *The City and Social Theory*, 243–5; Kentridge and Oliphant, "High-Rise versus No-Rise"; and Elizabeth and Philip Pacey, "The Cost of Development."
- The research by Lorimer is reported in *A Citizen's Guide*, chapters 7 and 8; Gutstein's is in *Vancouver, Ltd.* Although I am not aware of specific research similar to Lorimer's and Gutstein's in the US, see Logan and Molotch, *Urban Fortunes*, 66–8; and Gottdiener, *Planned Sprawl*, chapters 5 and 7.

Page 151
- On US federal government mortgage policy, see Checkoway, "Large Builders," 33; Harvey, "The Political Economy of Urbanization"; Smith, *The City and Social Theory*, 240. On similar Canadian policies, see Bettison, *The Politics of Canadian Urban Development*; and Higgins, *Local and Urban Politics in Canada*, 106–8.
- National policy sending development to the Sunbelt is documented in many places; see Smith, *The City and Social Theory*, 248; and Gottdiener, *Social Production*, 257–8.
- The figures on defense spending are from Gottdiener, 257.
- Richard Hill's description of Oakland Park is in "Industrial Restructuring," 17–18.

Page 152
- Metro Toronto's origins are described in Kaplan, *Urban Political Systems*, chapter 2.
- For a biography of Gardiner, see Colton, *Big Daddy*.
- In the US, $26 billion was spent for 42,500 miles of highway; see Jackson, *Crabgrass Frontier*, 249–50.
- On the favouring of larger companies by the FHA and the CMHC, see Checkoway, "Large Builders," 32–3; and Lorimer, *A Citizen's Guide*, 90; and Lorimer, *The Developers*, 17–18.

Page 153
- Colton, *Big Daddy*, 163.
- Bluestone and Harrison are quoted in *Deindustrialization*, 127; see also Lorimer, *A Citizen's Guide*, 51–6; Lorimer, *The Developers*, 64–6, and Logan and Molotch, *Urban Fortunes*, 166–78.
- The figures on income tax paid in the US are from Bluestone and Harrison, 128.
- The development consortiums of private developers and local governments in different US cities are well described in Squires (ed.), *Unequal Partnerships*.

Page 154
– Hunters Point is reported in *The Village Voice*, 21 August 1990, 15. The mandate for the NYS Public Development Corporation is quoted in Logan and Molotch, *Urban Fortunes*, 171.
– On Montreal's Drapeau, see Joyal, *Action Montréal*, 51–3; Lanken, "Montreal: At the New Crossroads," 11–12.
– Vancouver's mayor is pictured in Lorimer, *A Citizen's Guide*, 95.
– For Toronto, see Layton, "Toronto at the Turning Point?", 8; Taylor, "City Council in Last Minute Fight Over $500 Million Development," *Globe and Mail*, 22 October 1988, A15.

Page 155
– Gottdiener, *Planned Sprawl*, 100–3.
– Logan and Molotch, *Urban Fortunes*, 187–92.
– On zoning in the US, see *Urban Fortunes*, 154–62; and Perin, *Everything In Its Place*, 147–50.
– For an excellent empirical demonstration on the "distributive" dimension to zoning (i.e., how land developers use it to make money) see Proudfoot, "Private Gains and Public Losses." See also Gottdiener, *Planned Sprawl*, chapters 4 and 5.

Page 156
– On legitimation of large-scale projects, see Logan and Molotch, *Urban Fortunes*, 154–9.
– Montreal reformers' frustration with higher-level governments is described in Tindal and Nobes Tindal, *Local Government in Canada*, 237.

Page 157
– On the number of governments at the local level in the US, see Goodman, *The Dynamics of Urban Government and Politics*, 237–8; and Harrigan, *Political Change in the Metropolis*, 195–217.
– The quotation on corporate decisions is from Capitman, *Panic in the Boardroom*, 226.
– Almost every text on local government stresses its weakness. For an especially strong view, see Peterson, *City Limits*.
– For a list of independent authorities in seventy-two US standard metropolitan statistical areas, see Goodman, *The Dynamics of Urban Government*, 240–7.
– The standard reference on Moses is Caro, *The Power Broker*.
– Squires (ed.), *Unequal Partnerships*, has already been cited.

Page 158
– The quotation is from Kiernan, "Land-Use Planning," 77–8.

– On Harbourfront, see Kemble, *The Canadian City*, 10–12.
– Canadian independent boards and commissions are discussed in Plunkett and Betts, *The Management of Canadian Urban Government*, 120–1. See also DelGuidice and Zacks, "The 101 Governments of Metropolitan Toronto."

Page 159
– On local government autonomy in the us, see Goodman, *The Dynamics of Urban Government*, 68–76; and Gottdiener, *The Decline of Urban Politics*, 46–8. In Canada, see Higgins, *Local and Urban Politics in Canada*, 74–101. Two recent treatments are Wolman and Goldsmith, "Local Autonomy as a Meaningful Analytic Concept"; and Magnusson, "The Political Insignificance of the Municipality."
– On the role of provincial governments reviewing municipal land-use decisions, see Higgins, *Local and Urban Politics in Canada*, 84–5.
– For a current issue, see Reid, "Foes Gear for Battle Over Rail Lands," *Toronto Star*, 4 September 1990, A6; the developer spokesperson was "extremely confident" that the Ontario Municipal Board (omb) would overturn a ruling by Toronto city council to stop a development, if only temporarily. Over the years, I have attended numerous omb hearings and the spokesperson's confidence was justified. The one exception was during the late 1960s and early 1970s, when J.A. Kennedy was chair of the omb and smaller landowners tended to be favoured over larger developers. See also Lorimer, *A Citizen's Guide*, chapter 6.
– On us zoning appeals, see Perin, *Everything in Its Place*, 185.
– On alternative strategies by developers in that country, see Gottdiener, *Planned Sprawl*, chapters 4 and 6.

Page 160
– Logan and Molotch, *Urban Fortunes*, 159–62; Logan and Molotch also highlight another dimension of local governments' lack of autonomy, their helplessness in the face of fiscal policies of higher-level governments which encourage big developers, 174–8.
– Fowler and White, "Big City Downtowns."
– Gutstein is quoted from "Vancouver," 214.
– The Toronto development is described in Taylor, "Not Told of Housing Project, Councillors Miffed at Mayor," *Globe and Mail*, 14 July 1988, A12.
– On municipal government as a corporation, see Anderson, "Nonpartisan Urban Politics in Canadian Cities"; Lorimer, *A Citizen's Guide*, chapter 1; Gottdiener, *Planned Sprawl*, 82–7; Gottdiener, *The Decline of Urban Politics*, 30–1; and Goodman, *The Dynamics of Urban Government*, 68–74.

Page 161
- The business mentality is stressed in Lorimer, *A Citizen's Guide*; Anderson, "Nonpartisan Urban Politics"; and Markusen, "Class and Urban Social Expenditure," 104. See also Ley, *A Social Geography of the City*, 299–304.
- On the instrumentality of local-government services, see Kaplan, *Reform, Planning, and City Politics*, 62.
- On citizenship and local governments, see chapter 5 of this book; and Bookchin, *Urbanization*.

Page 162
- Hall gives a good description of Pruitt-Igoe in *Cities of Tomorrow*, 235–8.
- Some Canadians might protest that this analysis lumps Canadians and Americans together indiscriminately; see for example, Goldberg and Mercer, *The Myth of the North American City*, chapter 2. While acknowledging that there is a difference, I would argue that my analysis still applies to Canada.
- On the basic needs of humans, see Bookchin, *The Limits of the City*, 77; Fromm, *The Sane Society*, 33–41; and Sorokin, "The Power of Creative Unselfish Love."

Page 163
- Franklin, *The Real World of Technology*, chapter 5.
- On alienable versus inalienable rights as they relate to changing concepts of property, see MacPherson, *The Rise and Fall of Economic Justice*, 82.
- On rejection of involvement with other people, see Bookchin, *The Limits of the City*, 76–88.
- Alexander's quotation comes from "The City as a Mechanism," 419.

Page 164
- Sennett, *The Fall of Public Man*, 310–11, contains his words on reality; his case study of Long Island is on 301 ff. Communities of solidarity are treated in *The Uses of Disorder*, 44–9.
- On glorifying the city for money, see Arkes, *The Philosopher and the City*, 3.
- Perin's quotation is from *Everything in Its Place*, 86.
- Autonomy and withdrawal of suburban governments is dealt with in many places; see Walker, "A Theory of Suburbanization," 397; and Ley, *A Social Geography of the City*, 308. Ley makes it clear that, in spite of greater government fragmentation in the US than in Canada, Canada's suburban governments are just as anxious to keep out undesirables.
- On private property, see Macpherson, *The Rise and Fall of Economic Justice*, 76–85; also Locke, *Second Treatise on Government*, 329.

Page 165
- For home ownership as a bastion against bolshevism, see Holdsworth, "House and Home in Vancouver," 192–4; Spragge, "A Confluence of Interests," 260–1; and Hayden, *Redesigning the American Dream*, 32–3.
- On zoning as a legitimization of capital's wishes rather than a collective good, see Lorimer, *A Citizen's Guide*, 9; Perin, *Everything in Its Place*, 148–53; see also Goodman, *After the Planners*, 147–57. Goodman quotes from a 1953 court case: "The real object, however, of promoting the general welfare by zoning ordinances is to protect the private use and enjoyment of property and to promote the welfare of the individual property owner" (151).

Page 166
- Lowi, *The End of Liberalism*.
- For Canadian examples of corporate welfare, see Clement, *The Canadian Corporate Elite*, 62–6, 263–5, and 349–53.
- For examples of mainstream political science which suggest that more politically developed countries have learned to separate political from economic spheres, see Huntington, *Political Order in Changing Societies*; and Almond, "Introduction." For application to urban politics, see Dahl, *Who Governs?*, *passim*, but especially chapters 6 and 24. Domhoff highlights Dahl's blind spots in *Who Rules America Now?*, chapter 6; see also Smith, *City, State and Market*.

Page 167
- Léveillée, "Pouvoir local et politiques publiques à Montréal," 37–63. Orren, "Corporate Power and the Slums," 49.
- Orren lists powers of corporations, 50. See also Gottdiener, *The Decline of Urban Politics*, 30–1.

Page 168
- On railway companies and developers, see Orren, "Corporate Power"; Armstrong and Nelles, *The Revenge of the Methodist Bicycle Company*, and Hall, *Cities of Tomorrow*, 61–6.
- On the North American quest for a single-family home, see Perin, *Everything in Its Place*, chapter 2.
- The figures on home ownership are from Agnew, "Homeownership and the Capitalist Social Order," 462.
- On bias against renters, see Perin, chapter 2; and Agnew, 467.

Page 169
- On separation of home and work, see Katznelson, *City Trenches*. For a

criticism of Katznelson, see Gottdiener, *The Decline of Urban Politics*, 246.
- The home as sanctuary is described by Perin, *Everything in Its Place*, 48; and Hayden, *Redesigning the American Dream*, 67–9, 74–82. Perin's argument about purity is on 116, as is the evidence from Houston.
- Competition among banks is noted by Collier, *Contemporary Cathedrals*. And see Ley, *A Social Geography of the City*, 43–4.

Page 170
- Harvey, *Social Justice and the City*, 280–1.
- Paul and Percival Goodman, *Communitas*, chapter 5. See also Harvey, *Social Justice and the City*, 271; and Walker, "A Theory of Suburbanization," 408–9.
- Illich argues that the education system also teaches us to be good consumers: see *Deschooling Society*, 86.
- On social isolation and the media, see Sennett, *The Fall of Public Man*, 283–5.

Page 171
- Bookchin's point is in *Urbanization*, 212–24.
- Jacobs, for instance, blames the planners: see *Death and Life*, chapter 1.
- Bookchin, *The Limits of the City*, 100–1.

Page 172
- On the role of planners in urban politics, there is a considerable literature. See, as examples, Gottdiener, *Planned Sprawl*, chapters 5 and 6; Smith, *The City and Social Theory*, 254–63; Harrigan, *Political Change*, 273–84; Clavel, *The Progressive City*. Clavel is especially interested in how progressive planners work with progressive city politicians. One of his examples is Norman Krumholz of Cleveland, who not only had progressive ideas but was an accomplished political tactician; see Swanstrom, *The Crisis of Growth Politics*, for more on Krumholz.
- For Canada, see the set of essays entitled "Planning and the Realities of Development," in Artibise and Stelter, *The Usable Urban Past*. Especially useful from this collection is Moore, "Zoning and Planning: The Toronto Experience, 1904–1970."
- See also Lorimer, *A Citizen's Guide*, 163–74.
- The other sources of my generalizations about the roles of planners are from my own experiences and conversations with planners and city politicians. See also Hodge, *Planning Canadian Communities*.
- On Metro Toronto planners who expedite the development process, see Colton, *Big Daddy*, 153–4.

Page 173
– On Frank Lloyd Wright, see Fishman, *Urban Utopias in the 20th Century*,
104, 124–7; Wright on politicians is from Wright, *Broadacre City*, 25. See
also Wright, *The Living City*, 28. The quotation on the right to a piece of
ground is from Hurst, *I Came to the City*, 299. Other material on Wright
can be found in Hall, *Cities of Tomorrow*, 285–90; and Blake, *The Master
Builders*.
– Le Corbusier's quotation is in Choay, *L'urbanisme*, 240–1.
– The influence of Le Corbusier (despite the fact that many of his designs
were never built) is detailed in Blake, *The Master Builders*, and Hall, *Cities
of Tomorrow*, 213–23. The Louis XIV caption is from Hall, 207.

Page 174
– Le Corbusier on Italy is in Fishman, *Urban Utopias*, 240. Fishman's words
are on page 239.
– Blake, *The Master Builders*, xiv.

Page 175
– The material on Howard is from Hall, *Cities of Tomorrow*, 88–97; the quotation is gleaned from 91–3.
– On the relative influence of Howard, see Fishman, *Urban Utopias*, as well
as Hall, *Cities of Tomorrow*. For negative assessments of Howard's legacy,
see Jacobs, *Death and Life*, 18–20; and Middleton, *Man Made the Town*, 76.

Page 176
– On planners' growing interest in sociology, see Gans, *People and Plans*;
and Alonso, "Cities and City Planners," 580–95.
– The planning process is described in Schubert, *The Public Interest*; Meyer-
son and Banfield, *Politics, Planning and the Public Interest*; Davidoff,
"Advocacy and Pluralism in Planning," quote from 603; and Alonso, "Cit-
ies and City Planners," 582–3. An insightful critique of advocacy plan-
ning is in Lefebvre, *La production de l'espace*, 420–1.
– On pluralism and its critics, see Dahl, *Who Governs?*; and David Ricci,
Community Power and Democratic Theory.

Page 177
– Franklin, *The Real World of Technology*, chapter 1, 116.

CHAPTER SEVEN

Page 178
– Satin has made many of the points in this chapter in *New Age Politics*.

– There are many critiques of the GNP as a measure, and of its political uses. See Daly and Cobb, *For the Common Good*, chapter 3; Wachtel, *The Poverty of Affluence*, 87–9; Henderson, *The Politics of the Solar Age*, 27–37; and Leipert, "From Gross to Adjusted National Product," 132–40.

Page 179
– Webber, "The Urban Place and the Nonplace Urban Realm."
– On becoming aware of our dysfunctional beliefs, see Walsh, *Staying Alive*.

Page 180
– Most of my ideas about the changing nature of physical reality have come from Capra, *The Tao and Physics*; and Capra, *The Turning Point*.
– An excellent work by an historian of science on disenchantment and the scientific revolution is Berman, *The Reenchantment of the World*.
– Jones, *Physics as Metaphor*, 60.
– On resistance to the scientific revolution, see Bonelli and Shea (eds.), *Reason, Experiment, and Mysticism*.

Page 181
– The male deity is treated in Spretnak, *The Spiritual Dimension of Green Politics*. Separation of humans from nature, she writes, started several millennia before Christ. For the more conventional view, see Gay, *The Enlightenment: An Interpretation*, 160 ff.
– On Hobbes, see Gay, 179 ff; and Barber, *Strong Democracy*, 29, 50.
– In addition to Capra, *The Turning Point*, one of the best books on cyclical nature as the victim of male-dominated exploitation is Merchant, *The Death of Nature: Women, Ecology, and the Scientific Revolution*; on medieval mining, see 27–41.

Page 182
– Capra has been my main source of information about quantum physics; see also Talbot, *Beyond the Quantum*.

Page 183
– Alexander, *The Timeless Way of Building*, 86.
– Jacobs, *Death and Life*, chapter 5.
– Spirn, *The Granite Garden*, 230, 246, 272.

Page 184
– On light experiments, see Talbot, *Beyond the Quantum*, chapter 1.

Page 185
- A superb contemporary explanation of Marx's link between effective property and political power can be found in Dahrendorf, *Class and Class Conflict*, chapter 1.
- On Locke and our morals, see Bell, *The Cultural Contradictions of Capitalism*, 77; see also Macpherson, *The Political Theory of Possessive Individualism*, chapter 5. Macpherson makes it clear that the meaning of property has changed dramatically since the seventeenth century: see his essay "Human Rights as Property Rights," in *The Rise and Fall of Economic Justice*, 76–85.

Page 186
- On native peoples' view of property and especially the anomaly of land "ownership" see McLuhan, *Touch the Earth*.
- Polanyi, *The Great Transformation*; see especially chapter 6.
- For Marx, the beginning of capitalism was the separation of the labourer from the land; see McNally, *Political Economy and the Rise of Capitalism*, 258.
- For the distinction between the real-estate sector and other sectors as they relate to urban development, see Gottdiener, *The Social Production of Urban Space*, 185–93. Gottdiener's book deals in general with the relationship between our socio-political organization and the physical form of the urban landscape; so does Smith, *City, State and Market*. See also Logan and Molotch, *Urban Fortunes*, especially chapter 1.

Page 188
- A devastating look at deindustrialization in the United States can be found in Bluestone and Harrison, *Deindustrialization*.
- Schumacher, *Small is Beautiful*, 35. Early economists readily admitted the value-laden nature of economics in general and of prices in particular. David Hume remarked that the basis of economics lay in the "passions" (see Gay, *The Enlightenment*, 355); Adam Smith argued that prices of commodities depend not so much on an invisible hand as on "custom" (see McNally, *Political Economy*, 217–18). See also Smith, *City, State and Market*, chapter 1 and *passim*.

Page 189
- The table is a kind of summary of chapter 4 of Schumacher's *Small is Beautiful*.

Page 190
- On how money does harm, see Jacobs' chapter on cataclysmic money in *Death and Life*.

– Satin has a more comprehensive discussion of what a new economics would look like in *New Age Politics*, 132–52.

Page 191
– For examples of mainstream political science textbooks which treat power as a relationship of control, see Deutsch, *Politics and Government*, 26; or Dahl, *Modern Political Analysis*, 17.
– For a truly alternative political-science text, see Wolfe and McCoy, *Political Analysis: An Unorthodox Approach*, which discusses power as a creative force (16 ff.).
– For an extended discussion of alternative concepts of power, see Satin, *New Age Politics*, 118 ff.
– French's thoughts on power are from *Beyond Power: Of Women, Men, and Morals*, 505.
– For an explicit link between quantum physics and a new politics, see Morgan, *The Anatomy of Freedom*, 291–6.
– Dahl, *Who Governs?*, 226–8.

Page 192
– Gottdiener, *The Decline of Urban Politics*, 195.
– See Satin, *New Age Politics*, 30–2, on the artificiality of national sentiment.

Page 193
– C. Northcote Parkinson, *Parkinson's Law*.
– On the vacuity of electoral politics, see chapter 5 of this book and Clarke et al., *Absent Mandate: The Politics of Discontent in Canada*; Burnheim, *Is Democracy Possible?*, 96 105; and the writings of Walter Dean Burnham, especially *Critical Elections and the Mainsprings of American Electoral Politics*.
– Jacobs, *Cities and the Wealth of Nations: Principles of Economic Life*. See also Smith, *City, State, and Market*, chapter 2.

Page 194
– The psychologist is Kohn, *No Contest: The Case Against Competition*, 156.
– Schattschneider's views on conflict are in *The Semi-Sovereign People*, 71.

Page 195
– Hobbes' ideas about concocting a hypothetical "pure" state came from Galileo. See Verdon, "On the Laws of Physical and Human Nature," 653–63.

– On the "natural aggressiveness" of mankind, see Hobbes, *Leviathan*, chapters 11 and 13; Hobbes writes, "if one plant, sow, build, or possess a convenient seat, others may probably be expected to come prepared with forces united, to dispossess, and deprive him, not only of the fruit of his labour, but also of his life, or liberty" (99). Why? On other writers, see Gay, *The Enlightenment*, especially 338 ff.

– Kohn, *No Contest*, elucidates Spencer's connections to Darwin. See also Bowler, *Evolution: The History of and Idea*.

Page 196

– On Marx's attraction to Darwin's theories as an underpinning for the inevitability of class struggle, see Himmelfarb, *Darwin and the Darwinian Revolution*, 421.

– Bateson is quoted in Kohn, *No Contest*, 201, note 27.

– The quotation from Simpson is on page 21 of Kohn, *No Contest*.

– The story about the wallabies is in *Talking with Nature*, 26–30.

Page 197

– The "opinion" is from Kohn, *No Contest*, 156.

– Krishnamurti, *Commentaries on Living, First Series*, 173.

– The Louisville example comes from Jacobs, *Death and Life*, 161.

Page 198

– The most eloquent statement (there are many) of Western farming's destruction of the land is by Fukuoka, *The One Straw Revolution*; see also Schumacher, *Small is Beautiful*, especially 87 ff., and Berry, *The Unsettling of America*, chapter 9.

CHAPTER EIGHT

Page 199

– Berry, *The Unsettling of America*, 218–19.

– Eloquent statements on the importance of being aware of our beliefs include Walsh, *Staying Alive*; and Elgin, *Voluntary Simplicity*.

– Satin's point is from *New Age Politics*, 19, 73, and *passim*.

– Chorney, *City of Dreams*, 162; also chapters 9 and 10.

Page 200

– Believe it or not, there are excellent books on becoming more sensitive to the physical environment, including how-to books. For example, Leff, *Playful Perception: Choosing How to Experience Your World*. See also the marvelous Clay, *Close-Up: How to Read the American City*; Hough, *Out of*

Place: Restoring Identity to the Regional Landscape; and Hiss, *The Experience of Place*.

— See Chorney, *City of Dreams*, on how politics is connected to daily perceptions of city dwellers, 166–83, and chapter 11.
— My wife, Shelly, was the first person to point out spaces between buildings to me, perhaps twenty years ago; recently, I ran across Gehl's insightful book, *Life Between Buildings: Using Public Space*.

Page 201
— I learned about Mrs Ivy from Lerup, *Building the Unfinished*, 88–96 and 102–6. Lerup's book influenced me a great deal in the writing of this chapter.

Page 203
— Chorney, *City of Dreams*, 178–81.

Page 204
— Elgin, *Voluntary Simplicity*, 161.
— Examples of guidebooks for ecologically responsible individual behaviour include the excellent *The Canadian Green Consumer Guide*, prepared by Pollution Probe in consultation with Warner Troyer and Glenys Moss; another good one is Johnson, *Green Future*.

Page 207
— Home garden contributions to pollution are documented in Johnson, *Green Future*, 181; the quotation is from Hoepfner, "Vernacular Landscaping."

Page 208
— On profit making and the city, see Long, *The Unwalled City*, 184–5.
— For an intriguing analysis of the attraction of a vibrant street culture to gentrifiers, see Caulfield, "'Gentrification' and Desire." Caulfield also discusses the role of the market in gentrification.
— On not expecting to be home for lunch, see Nelson, *The Illusions of Urban Man*, 33. Nelson's ideas are very similar to the ones presented in this chapter.

Page 210
— Eleanor Magid's story, "Healing the Split," is in Burch (ed.), *Mothers Talking: Sharing the Secret*, 228, 229, and 230.

Page 212
– Smith, *City, State, and Market*, shows persuasively the way workers get locked into dependence on benefits packages of big companies, packages held in place by government tax policy; see chapter 2.

Page 213
– The story of Manchester and Birmingham is told in Jacobs, *The Economy of Cities*, 86–96.
– The analysis of the US steel industry is in Reutter, "The Rise and Decline of Big Steel."
– Among the books documenting the inherent inefficiency of large-scale organizations are Parkinson, *Parkinson's Law*; Lowi, *The End of Liberalism*, 22–31; Reich, *The Second American Frontier*, especially chapter 8; Bluestone and Harrison, *Deindustrialization*; Krohn et al., *The Other Economy*; and Schumacher, *Small is Beautiful*.

Page 214
– The example of US oil is from Amory Lovins, "Energy and Security," 14–15.

Page 215
– Alinsky, "Citizen Participation," 217.
– Other negative views may be found in Logan and Molotch, *Urban Fortunes*, 134–46; and Fainstein, "Local Mobilization and Economic Discontent."
– On Alinsky and community organizing, see Alinsky, *Rules for Radicals*; Finks, *The Radical Vision of Saul Alinsky*; and Keating, *The Power to Make It Happen*. Keating organized Alinsky-style in Toronto and experienced people's backing off their own success: *The Power to Make It Happen*, 57.

Page 216
– On creating new functions in the federal system, see Riker, *Federalism*.
– On creative action and organizational maintenance, see Keating, *The Power to Make It Happen*, 99.
– Castells, *The City and the Grassroots*, 70 and *passim.*, stresses the role of space in spawning urban social movements. He also documents the multi-dimensional character of many of these movements.

Page 217
– The example from the Bronx is in McRobie, *Small is Possible*, 159–61.
– On vandalism during the blackout, see Stokes, *Helping Ourselves*, 81. Stokes gives other examples of the multi-dimensionality of self-help on 70, 118–19.

Page 218
- Gratz, *The Living City*, 101–20.
- Hayden, *Redesigning the American Dream*, 156–9.
- The El Sol Brilliante Garden is further described in Francis et al., *Community Open Spaces*, 84–97.

Page 219
- The Cheyenne project is described by Hayden, *Redesigning the American Dream*, 190–1.
- McCamant and Durrett, *Cohousing: A Contemporary Approach to Housing Ourselves*.

Page 220
- Alexander, *The Timeless Way of Building*; Alexander et al., *The Oregon Experiment*, especially chapter 2; and Alexander et al., *The Production of Houses*. See also Rudofsky, *Architecture Without Architects*.

Bibliography

Agnew, J.A. "Homeownership and the Capitalist Social Order." In *Urbanization and Urban Planning in Capitalist Society*. Edited by Michael Dear and Allen J. Scott. London: Methuen, 1981.

Alexander, Christopher. "The City as a Mechanism for Sustaining Human Contact." In *People and Buildings*. Edited by Robert Gutman. New York: Basic Books, 1972.

– *The Timeless Way of Building*. New York: Oxford University Press, 1979.

– *Notes on the Synthesis of Form*. Cambridge: Harvard University Press, 1964.

Alexander, Christopher, with Howard Davis, Julio Martinez, and Don Corner. *The Production of Houses*. New York: Oxford University Press, 1985.

Alexander, Christopher, Murray Silverstein, Shlomo Angel, Sara Ishikawa, and Denny Abrams. *The Oregon Experiment*. New York: Oxford University Press, 1975.

Alford, Robert, and Eugene Lee. "Voting Turnout in American Cities." *American Political Science Review* 62, no. 3 (1968): 796–813.

Alinsky, Saul D. "Citizen Participation and Community Organization in Planning and Urban Renewal." In *Strategies of Community Organization: A Book of Readings*. Edited by Fred M. Cox, John Erlich, Jack Rothman, and John E. Tropman. Itasca, Ill.: Peacock Publishers, 1970.

– *Rules for Radicals*. New York: Random House, 1971.

Almond, Gabriel. "Introduction." In *The Politics of Developing Countries*. Edited by Gabriel Almond and James Coleman. Princeton: Princeton University Press, 1960.

Alonso, William. "Cities and City Planners." In *Taming Megalopolis, Volume 1: What Is and What Could Be*. Edited by H. Wentworth Eldridge. New York: Doubleday, 1967.

Alperovitz, Gar, and Jeff Faux. *Rebuilding America: A Blueprint for the New Economy*. New York: Pantheon Books, 1984.

Anderson, James D. "Non-partisan Urban Politics in Canadian Cities." In *Emerging Party Politics in Urban Canada*. Edited by Jack K. Masson and James D. Anderson. Toronto: McClelland and Stewart, 1972.

Anderson, Martin. "The Federal Bulldozer." In *Urban Renewal: The Record and the Controversy*. Edited by James Q. Wilson. Cambridge, Mass.: MIT Press, 1966.

Appelbaum, Richard P., and John Gilderbloom. "Housing Supply and Regulation: A Study of the Rental Housing Market." *Journal of Applied Behavioural Science* 19, no. 1 (1983): 1–18.

Arendt, Hannah. *The Human Condition*. Chicago: University of Chicago Press, 1958.

Aries, Philip. *Centuries of Childhood*. New York: Vintage, 1965.

Arkes, Hadley. *The Philosopher and the City: The Moral Dimensions of Urban Politics*. Princeton: Princeton University Press, 1981.

Armstrong, Christopher, and H.V. Nelles. *The Revenge of the Methodist Bicycle Company*. Toronto: Peter Martin, 1977.

Ashton, Patrick J. "The Political Economy of Suburban Development." In *Marxism and the Metropolis: New Perspectives in Urban Political Economy*. Edited by William K. Tabb and Larry Sawers. New York: Oxford University Press, 1978.

Axworthy, Lloyd, and Ralph Kuroptawa. "An Experiment in Community Renewal." Paper presented to the Canadian Political Science Association, Winnipeg, 1970.

Bachrach, Peter, and Morton S. Baratz. "Decisions and Non-decisions: An Analytical Framework." *American Political Science Review* 57, no. 3 (1963): 632–42.

Bahl, Roy W., and J. Michael McGuire. "Urban Sprawl: Policies for Containment and Cost Recoupment." In *Local Service Pricing Policies and Their Effect on Urban Spatial Structure*. Edited by Paul Downing. Vancouver: University of British Columbia Press, 1977.

Bailey, Robert, Jr. *Radicals in Urban Politics: The Alinsky Approach*. Chicago: University of Chicago Press, 1974.

Barber, Benjamin. *Strong Democracy: Participatory Politics for a New Age*. Berkeley, Calif.: University of California Press, 1984.

Bell, Daniel. *The Cultural Contradictions of Capitalism*. New York: Basic Books, 1978.

Bellan, Ruban. *The Evolving City*. Toronto: Copp Clark, 1971.

Berelson, Bernard, Paul Lazarsfeld, and William J. McPhee. *Voting*. Chicago: University of Chicago Press, 1954.

Berger, Bennett. *Working Class Suburb: A Study of Auto Workers in Suburbia*. Berkeley, Calif.: University of California Press, 1960.

Berman, Morris. *The Reenchantment of the World*. New York: Bantam, 1984.

Berry, Brian J.L. *The Human Consequences of Urbanization*. New York: St. Martin's Press, 1973.
– "Short-Term Housing Cycles in a Dualistic Metropolis." In *The Social Economy of Cities*. Edited by Gary Gappert and Harold M. Rose. Beverly Hills, Calif., Sage Publications, 1975.
Berry, Wendell. *The Unsettling of America: Culture and Agriculture*. San Francisco: Sierra Club Books, 1977.
Bettison, David G. *The Politics of Canadian Urban Development*. Edmonton: University of Alberta Press, 1975.
Blaber, Ann. "The Cunningham Road Scheme." In *Designing Against Vandalism*. Edited by the Design Council. New York: Van Nostrand Reinhold, 1980.
Blake, Peter. *The Master Builders: Le Corbusier, Mies van der Rohe, Frank Lloyd Wright*. New York: W.W. Norton, 1960, 1976.
Blalock, Hubert M., Jr. *Causal Inferences in Nonexperimental Research*. Chapel Hill, North Carolina: University of North Carolina Press, 1961, 1964.
Blau, Judith R., and John S. Pipkin. "Introductory Remarks on Form, Meaning, and Practice." In *Remaking the City: Social Science Perspectives on Urban Design*. Edited by John S. Pipkin, Mark E. LaGory, and Judith R. Blau. Albany, NY: State University of New York Press, 1983.
Bluestone, Barry, and Bennett Harrison. *The Deindustrialization of America*. New York: Basic Books, 1982.
Bonelli, M.L., and William Shea, eds. *Reason, Experiment, and Mysticism in the Scientific Revolution*. New York: Science History Publications, 1975.
Bookchin, Murray. *The Ecology of Freedom: The Emergence and Dissolution of Hierarchy*. Palo Alto, Calif.: Cheshire Books, 1982.
– *The Limits of the City*. New York: Harper Colophon, 1974.
– *Urbanization and the Decline of Citizenship*. San Francisco: Sierra Club Books, 1987.
Booth, Alan. "The Built Environment as a Crime Deterrent: A Reexamination of Defensible Space." *Criminology* 18, no. 3 (1981): 557–70.
Boston Redevelopment Authority. *Transportation Facts for the Boston Region*. 2d ed. Boston: Boston Redevelopment Authority, 1968.
Bottoms, A.E., and Polii Xanthos. "Housing Policy and Crime in the British Public Sector." In *Environmental Criminology*. Edited by Paul J. Brantingham and Patricia L. Brantingham. Beverly Hills, Calif.: Sage Publications, 1981.
Boudon, Philippe. *Lived-in Architecture: Le Corbusier's Pessac Revisited*. Cambridge, Mass.: MIT Press, 1972.
Bowler, Peter J. *Evolution: The History of an Idea*. Berkeley, Calif.: University of California Press, 1984.
Brantingham, Paul J., and Patricia L. Brantingham, eds. *Environmental Criminology*. Beverly Hills, Calif.: Sage Publications, 1981.

Brodie, Janine, and Jane Jenson. *Crisis, Challenge and Change: Party and Class in Canada*. Toronto: Methuen, 1980.

Brown, Lester R., and Jodi L. Jacobson. *The Future of Urbanization: Facing the Ecological and Economic Constraints*. Washington, DC: Worldwatch Institute, May 1987.

Burch, Frances Wells, ed. *Mothers Talking: Sharing the Secret*. New York: St Martin's Press, 1986.

Burchard, John. "Design and Urban Beauty in the Central City." In *The Metropolitan Enigma*. Edited by James Q. Wilson. New York: Doubleday, 1968.

Burnham, Walter Dean. *Critical Elections and the Mainsprings of American Electoral Politics*. New York: W.W. Norton, 1970.

– *The Current Crisis in American Politics*. New York: Oxford University Press, 1982.

Burnheim, John. *Is Democracy Possible?* Berkeley: University of California Press, 1985.

Canadian Economic Observer: Historical Statistical Supplement, 1988–89. Ottawa: Ministry of Supply and Services, 1990.

Capitman, William. *Panic in the Boardroom*. New York: Doubleday, 1973.

Capra, Fritjof. *The Tao of Physics*. New York: Fontana Collins, 1976.

– *The Turning Point: Science, Society, and the Rising Culture*. New York: Simon and Schuster, 1982.

Caro, Robert. *The Power Broker: Robert Moses and the Fall of New York City*. New York: Alfred Knopf, 1974.

Castells, Manuel. *The City and the Grassroots: A Cross-Cultural Theory of Urban Social Movements*. Berkeley: University of California Press, 1983.

– *The Urban Question: A Marxist Approach*. Cambridge, Mass.: MIT Press, 1977.

Castelman, Michael. "Crime Free." *Social Policy* 14, no. 4 (1984): 5–14.

Caulfield, Jon. "'Gentrification' and Desire." *Canadian Review of Sociology and Anthropology* 26, no. 4 (1989): 617–32.

– *The Tiny Perfect Mayor*. Toronto: Lorimer, 1974.

Chandler, Alfred D. *Strategy and Structure*. Cambridge, Mass.: MIT Press, 1962.

Checkoway, Barry. "Large Builders, Federal Housing Programmes, and Postwar Suburbanization." *International Journal of Urban and Regional Research* 4, no. 1 (1980): 21–45.

Choay, François, ed. *L'urbanisme: utopies et réalités*. Paris: Éditions du Seuil, 1965.

Chorney, Harold. "Amnesia, Integration, and Repression: The Roots of Canadian Urban Political Culture." In *Urbanization and Urban Planning in Capitalist Society*. Edited by Michael Dear and Allen J. Scott. London: Methuen, 1981.

– *City of Dreams: Social Theory and The Urban Experience*. Toronto: Nelson Canada, 1990.

– "The Decline of Neighbourhood and the Rise of Social Services." *City Magazine* 6, no. 3 (1984): 24–7.

City of Toronto Planning Board. *Technical Report of the Core Area Task Force.* Toronto: City of Toronto Planning Board, September 1974.

Clark, S.D. *The Suburban Society.* Toronto: University of Toronto Press, 1966.

Clarke, Harold D., Jane Jenson, Lawrence LeDuc, and Jon H. Pammett. *Absent Mandate: The Politics of Discontent in Canada.* Toronto: Gage Educational Publishing, 1984.

Clarke, Susan E., and Andrew Kirby. "In Search of the Corpse: The Mysterious Case of Local Politics." *Urban Affairs Quarterly* 25, no. 3 (1990): 389–412.

Clavel, Pierre. *The Progressive City: Planning and Participation, 1969–84.* New Brunswick, NJ: Rutgers University Press, 1986.

Clawson, M. *Suburban Land Conversion in the United States.* Baltimore: Johns Hopkins University Press, 1971.

Clay, Grady. *Close-Up: How to Read the American City.* Chicago: University of Chicago Press, 1980.

Clement, Wallace. *The Canadian Corporate Elite: An Analysis of Economic Power.* Ottawa: Carleton University Press, 1975.

Code, William. *Controlling the Physical Growth of the Downtown Core.* Toronto: The Industry and Labour Advisory Committee, 1975.

Coleman, Alice. *Utopia on Trial: Vision and Reality in Planned Housing.* London: Hilary Shipman, 1985.

Collier, Robert. *Contemporary Cathedrals: Large-Scale Development in Canadian Cities.* Montreal: Harvest House, 1974.

Collin, Jean-Pierre. "Le partage fiscal banlieue-ville centrale: les Montréalais subventionnent-ils les banlieusards?" *Revue canadienne de science politique* 17, no. 1 (1984): 109–31.

Colton, Timothy. *Big Daddy: Frederick G. Gardiner and the Building of Metropolitan Toronto.* Toronto: University of Toronto Press, 1980.

Conway, William G. "The Case Against Urban Dinosaurs." *Saturday Review,* 14 May 1977.

Copp, Terry. "Montreal's Municipal Government and the Crisis of the 1930s." In *The Usable Urban Past: Planning and Politics in the Modern Canadian City.* Edited by Alan F.J. Artibise and Gilbert A. Stelter. Ottawa: Carleton University Press, 1979.

Cox, Kevin. "Capitalism and Conflict Around the Communal Living Space." In *Urbanization and Urban Planning in Capitalist Society.* Edited by Michael Dear and Allen J. Scott. London: Methuen, 1981.

Cummings, Scott, C. Theodore Koebel, and J. Allen Whitt. "Redevelopment in Downtown Louisville: Public Investments, Private Profits, and Shared Risks." In *Unequal Partnerships: The Political Economy of Urban Redevelopment in Postwar America*. Edited by Gregory D. Squires. New Brunswick, NJ: Rutgers University Press, 1989.

Currie, Elliot. *Confronting Crime: An American Challenge*. New York: Pantheon, 1985.

Curtis, Lynn, ed. *Policies to Prevent Crime: Neighborhood, Family, and Employment Strategies*. The Annals of the American Academy of Political and Social Science. Beverly Hills, Calif.: Sage Publications, 1987.

Dahl, Robert. *Modern Political Analysis*. 2d ed. Englewood Cliffs, NJ: Prentice-Hall, 1970.

– *Who Governs? Democracy and Power in an American City*. New Haven: Yale University Press, 1961.

Dahrendorf, Ralf. *Class and Class Conflict in Post-Industrial Society*. Stanford, Calif.: Stanford University Press, 1959.

Daly, Herman E., and John B. Cobb. *For the Common Good: Redirecting the Economy Toward Community, the Environment and a Sustainable Future*. Boston: Beacon Press, 1989.

Dansereau, Francine. "Les transformations de l'habitat et des quartiers centraux: singularités et contrastes des villes canadiennes." *Cahiers de recherche sociologique* 6, no. 2 (1988): 97–103.

Davidoff, Paul. "Advocacy and Pluralism in Planning." In *Taming Megalopolis, Volume I: What Is and What Could Be*. Edited by H. Wentworth Eldridge. New York: Doubleday, 1967.

De Bono, Edward. *How Children Solve Problems*. London: Penguin, 1972.

Dear, Michael, and Allen J. Scott, eds. *Urbanization and Urban Planning in Capitalist Society*. London: Methuen, 1981.

DelGuidice, Dominic, and Stephen M. Zacks. "The 101 Governments of Metropolitan Toronto." In *Politics and Government of Urban Canada*. 4th ed. Edited by Lionel D. Feldman. Toronto: Methuen, 1981.

Deutsch, Karl. *Politics and Government: How People Decide Their Fate*. Boston: Houghton Mifflin, 1980.

Domhoff, G. William. *Who Rules America Now? A View for the '80s*. Englewood Cliffs, NJ: Prentice-Hall, 1983.

Downing, Paul, ed. *Local Service Pricing Policies and Their Effect on Urban Spatial Structure*. Vancouver: University of British Columbia Press, 1977.

Duffala, Dennis. "Convenience Stores, Armed Robbery, and Physical Environment Features." *American Behavioral Scientist* 20, no. 3 (1976): 227–46.

Dunlap, R.E., and W.R. Catton, Jr. "What Environmental Sociologists Have in Common (Whether Concerned with 'Built' or 'Natural' Environments)." *Sociological Inquiry* 53, no. 2 (1983): 289–313.

Dupré, Stefan. *Intergovernmental Finance in Ontario: A Provincial – Local Perspective*. Toronto: The Ontario Committee on Taxation, n.d.

Economic Council of Canada. "The Challenge of Rapid Urban Growth." In *Urban Problems: A Canadian Reader*. Edited by Ralph Krueger and R. Charles Bryfogle. New York: Holt, Rinehart and Winston, 1971.

Eldridge, H. Wentworth, ed. *Taming Megalopolis, Volume I: What Is and What Could Be*. New York: Doubleday, 1967.

Elgin, Duane. *Voluntary Simplicity: Toward a Way of Life That is Outwardly Simple, Inwardly Rich*. New York: William Morrow, 1981.

Ellul, Jacques. *The Technological Society*. New York: Alfred Knopf, 1964.

Ericson, Richard V. *Reproducing Order: A Study of Police Patrol Work*. Toronto: University of Toronto Press, 1982.

Fainstein, Susan. "Local Mobilization and Economic Discontent." In *The Capitalist City: Global Restructuring and Community Politics*. Edited by Michael Peter Smith and Joe R. Feagin. Oxford: Basil Blackwell, 1987.

Fainstein, Susan, and Norman Fainstein. "New York City: The Manhattan Business District, 1945–1988." In *Unequal Partnerships: The Political Economy of Urban Redevelopment in Postwar America*. Edited by Gregory D. Squires. New Brunswick, NJ: Rutgers University Press, 1989.

Farley, John E., and Mark Hansel. "The Ecological Context of Urban Crime: Further Exploration." *Urban Affairs Quarterly* 17, no. 1 (1981): 37–54.

Farley, John E. *Effects of Residential Settings, Parental Lifestyles and Demographic Characteristics on Children's Activity Patterns*. PHD diss., Department of Sociology, University of Michigan, 1977.

Fava, Sylvia. "Reston, Virginia, at Age 20." In *Housing and Neighborhoods: Theoretical and Empirical Contributons*. Edited by Willem Van Vliet --, Harvey Choldin, William Michelson, and David Popenoe. New York: Greenwood Press, 1987.

Feagin, Joe R., and Michael Peter Smith. "Overview." In *The Capitalist City: Global Restructuring and Community Politics*. Edited by Michael Peter Smith and Joe R. Feagin. Oxford: Basil Blackwell, 1987.

Feldman, Lionel D., ed. *Politics and Government of Urban Canada*. 4th ed. Toronto: Methuen, 1981.

Finks, P. David. *The Radical Vision of Saul Alinsky*. Ramsey, NJ: Paulist Press, 1984.

Finsterbusch, Kurt. *Understanding Social Impacts: Assessing the Effects of Public Projects*. Beverly Hills, Calif.: Sage Publications, 1980.

Fischer, Claude. *To Dwell Among Friends: Personal Networks in Town and City*. Chicago: University of Chicago Press, 1982.

Fishman, Robert. *Urban Utopias in the Twentieth Century*. New York: Basic Books, 1977.

Fortin, Andrée. "Du voisinage à la communauté?" *Cahiers de recherche sociologique* 6, no. 2 (1988): 147–59.

Fowler, E.P. "Diversity and Healthy Cities." *Urban Forum/Colloque urbain* 2, no. 4 (1977): 18–27.

– "Street Management and City Design." *Social Forces* 66, no. 2 (1987): 365–89.

Fowler, E.P., and David White. "Big City Downtowns: The Nonimpact of Zoning." In *The Determinants of Public Policy*. Edited by Thomas Dye and Virginia Gray. Lexington, Mass.: D.C. Heath, 1980.

Fox, Bonnie J., John Fox, and Robert Marans. "Residential Density and Neighbor Interaction." *Sociological Quarterly* 21, no. 3 (1980): 349–59.

Francescato, Guido, Sue Weidemann, and James R. Anderson. "Residential Satisfaction: Its Uses and Limitations in Housing Research." In *Housing and Neighborhoods: Theoretical and Empirical Contributions*. Edited by Willem Van Vliet --, Harvey Choldin, William Michelson, and David Popenoe. New York: Greenwood Press, 1987.

Francis, Mark, Lisa Cashdan, and Lynn Paxson. *Community Open Spaces: Greening Neighborhoods Through Community Action and Land Conservation.* Washington, DC: Island Press, 1984.

Franklin, Ursula. *The Real World of Technology*. Toronto: CBC Enterprises, 1990.

Freedman, Jonathan. *Crowding and Behaviour: The Psychology of High Density Living*. New York: The Viking Press, 1975.

French, Hilary. *Clearing the Air: A Global Agenda*. Washington: Worldwatch Institute, January 1990.

French, Marilyn. *Beyond Power: Of Women, Men, and Morals*. New York: Ballantine, 1985.

Fried, Marc. "Grieving for a Lost Home: Psychological Costs of Relocation." In *Urban Renewal: The Record and the Controversy*. Edited by James Q. Wilson. Cambridge, Mass.: MIT Press, 1966.

Friedland, R. "Class Power and Social Control: The War on Poverty." *Politics and Society* 5, no. 4 (1976): 459–90.

Fromm, Erich. *The Sane Society*. New York: Holt, Rinehart and Winston, 1955.

Fukuoka, Masanobu. *The One Straw Revolution*. Emmaus, Pa.: Rodale Press, 1978.

Gans, Herbert. "The Failure of Urban Renewal." In *Urban Renewal: The Record and the Controversy*. Edited by James Q. Wilson. Cambridge, Mass.: MIT Press, 1966.

– *The Levittowners*. New York: Pantheon, 1967.

– *People and Plans*. New York: Basic Books, 1968.

Gappert, Gary, and Harold M. Rose, eds. *The Social Economy of Cities*. Beverly Hills, Calif.: Sage Publications, 1975.

Gay, Peter. *The Enlightenment: An Interpretation*. New York: Alfred Knopf, 1969.

Gehl, Jan. *Life Between Buildings: Using Public Space*. New York: Van Nostrand Reinhold, 1987.

Ginsberg, Benjamin. *The Consequences of Consent: Elections, Citizen Control, and Popular Acquiescence*. Reading, Mass.: Addison-Wesley, 1982.

Glazer, Nathan. "Slum Dwellings do not Make a Slum." *New York Times Magazine*, December 1965.

Goldberg, Michael A., and John Mercer. *The Myth of the North American City: Continentalism Challenged*. Vancouver: University of British Columbia Press, 1986.

Goodman, Jay S. *The Dynamics of Urban Government and Politics*. New York: Macmillan, 1975.

Goodman, Paul, and Percival Goodman. *Communitas: Means of Livelihood and Ways of Life*. New York: Vintage, 1960.

Goodman, Robert. *After the Planners*. New York: Simon and Schuster, 1971.

Gordon, David. "Capitalist Development and the History of American Cities." In *Marxism and the Metropolis: New Perspectives in Urban Political Economy*. Edited by William K. Tabb and Larry Sawers. New York: Oxford University Press, 1978.

Gottdiener, Mark. *The Decline of Urban Politics: Political Theory and the Crisis of the Local State*. Beverly Hills, Calif.: Sage Publications, 1987.

– *Planned Sprawl: Private and Public Interests in Suburbia*. Beverly Hills, Calif.: Sage Publications, 1977.

– *The Social Production of Urban Space*. Austin, Texas: University of Texas Press, 1985.

– "Urban Semiotics." In *Remaking the City: Social Science Perspectives on Urban Design*. Edited by John S. Pipkin, Mark E. LaGory, and Judith R. Blau. Albany, NY: State University of New York Press, 1983.

Gratz, Roberta Brandes. *The Living City*. New York: Simon and Schuster, 1989.

Gray, Charles M., ed. *The Costs of Crime*. Beverly Hills, Calif.: Sage Publications, 1979.

Greenbie, Barrie. *Spaces: Dimensions of the Human Landscape*. New Haven: Yale University Press, 1981.

Grossman, David A. *The Future of New York City's Capital Plant*. Washington, DC: The Urban Institute, 1979.

Gruen, Victor. *The Heart of Our Cities*. New York: Simon and Schuster, 1964.

Gutman, Robert, ed. *People and Buildings*. New York: Basic Books, 1972.

Gutstein, Donald. "Vancouver." In *City Politics in Canada*. Edited by Warren Magnusson and Andrew Sancton. Toronto: University of Toronto Press, 1983.

Gutstein, Donald. *Vancouver, Ltd*. Toronto: Lorimer, 1975.

Hall, Peter. *Cities of Tomorrow*. New York: Basil Blackwell, 1987.

– "The Urban Culture and the Suburban Culture." In *I Came to the City*. Edited by Michael E. Eliot Hurst. Boston: Little, Brown, 1975.

Harries, Keith D. "Alternative Denominators in Conventional Crime Rates." In *Environmental Criminology*. Edited by Paul J. Brantingham and Patricia L. Brantingham. Beverly Hills, Calif.: Sage Publications, 1981.

– *Crime and the Environment*. Springfield, Ill.: Charles C. Thomas, 1980.

Harrigan, John J. *Political Change in the Metropolis*. Boston: Little, Brown, 1976.

Harvey, David. "Labour, Capital and Class Struggle Around the Built Environment in Advanced Capitalist Societies." *Politics and Society* 6, no. 3 (1977): 265–95.

– "The Political Economy of Urbanization in Advanced Capitalist Societies: The Case of the United States." In *The Social Economy of Cities*. Edited by Gary Gappert and Harold M. Rose. Beverly Hills, Calif.: Sage Publications, 1975.

– *Social Justice and the City*. London: Edward Arnold, 1973.

– "The Urban Process under Capitalism: A Framework for Analysis." In *Urbanization and Urban Planning in Capitalist Society*. Edited by Michael Dear and Allen J. Scott. London: Methuen, 1981.

Hayden, Dolores. *Redesigning the American Dream: The Future of Housing, Work, and Family Life*. New York: W.W. Norton, 1984.

Hébert, Richard. *Highways to Nowhere*. Indianapolis: Bobbs-Merrill, 1972.

Henderson, Hazel. *The Politics of the Solar Age: Alternatives to Economics*. New York: Doubleday, 1981.

Higgins, Donald J.H. *Local and Urban Politics in Canada*. Toronto: Gage Educational Publishing 1986.

Hill, Richard. "Industrial Restructuring, State Intervention, and Uneven Development in the United States and Japan." In *A Tiger by the Tail: Urban Policy and Economic Restructuring in Comparative Perspective*. Albany, NY: Lewis Mumford Center for Comparative Urban and Regional Research at the State University, 1989.

Himmelfarb, Gertrude. *Darwin and the Darwinian Revolution*. New York: W.W. Norton, 1968.

Hiss, Tony. *The Experience of Place*. New York: Alfred Knopf, 1990.

Hobbes, Thomas. *Leviathan*. New York: Collier, 1962. [Originally published in 1651.]

Hodge, Gerald. *Planning Canadian Communities*. Scarborough, Ont.: Nelson Canada, 1989.

Hoepfner, Eva. "Vernacular Landscaping." *Harrowsmith* 9, no. 6 (June/July 1984): 54–67.

Holdsworth, Deryck W. "House and Home in Vancouver: Images of West Coast Urbanism, 1886–1929." In *The Canadian City: Essays in Urban and*

Social History. Edited by Gilbert A. Stelter and Alan F. J. Artibise. Ottawa: Carleton University Press, 1984.

Holenberg, Paul, and Lynn Hollen Lees. *The Making of Modern Europe, 1000–1950*. Cambridge, Mass: Harvard University Press, 1985.

Hood, Roger, and Richard Sparks. *Key Issues in Criminology*. New York: McGraw-Hill, 1970.

Hoover, Edgar M., and Raymond Vernon. *Anatomy of a Metropolis*. New York: Doubleday, 1959.

Horowitz, Gad. *Canadian Labour in Politics*. Toronto: University of Toronto Press, 1968.

Hough, Michael. *Out of Place: Restoring Identity to the Regional Landscape*. New Haven: Yale University Press, 1990.

Hudson, Ray, and Viggo Plum. *Deconcentration or Decentralization? Local Government and the Possibilities for Local Control of Local Economies*. Vancouver: University of British Columbia, School of Community and Regional Planning, 1984.

Hunter, Albert. *Symbolic Communities*. Chicago: University of Chicago Press, 1974.

Hunter, Albert, and Terry Baumer. "Street Traffic, Social Integration, and Fear of Crime." *Sociological Inquiry* 52, no. 2 (1982): 123–31.

Huntington, Samuel. *Political Order in Changing Societies*. New Haven: Yale University Press, 1968.

IBI Group. *The Core Employment Study*. Prepared for Vancouver Planning Dept. Vancouver: IBI Group, February 1982.

Illich, Ivan. *Deschooling Society*. New York: Harper and Row, 1972.

Ingram, Gregory K. "The Interaction of Transportation and Urban Land Use." In *The Prospective City: Economic, Population, Energy, and Environmental Developments*. Edited by Arthur P. Solomon. Cambridge, Mass.: MIT Press, 1980.

Jackson, Kenneth T. *Crabgrass Frontier: The Suburbanization of the United States*. New York: Oxford University Press, 1985.

Jacobs, Jane. *Cities and the Wealth of Nations: Principles of Economic Life*. New York: Random House, 1984.

– *The Death and Life of Great American Cities*. New York: Random House, 1961.

– *The Economy of Cities*. New York: Random House, 1969.

Jeffery, C. Ray. *Crime Prevention Through Environmental Design*. 2d ed. Beverly Hills, Calif.: Sage Publications, 1977.

Jephcott, Pearl. *Homes in High Flats*. Edinburgh: Oliver and Boyd, 1971.

Johnson, Lorraine. *Green Future: How to Make a World of Difference*. Harmondsworth, Middlesex: Penguin Books, 1990.

Jones, Brian, and Lynn Bachelor. *The Sustaining Hand: Community Leadership and Corporate Power*. Lawrence, Kans.: Kansas University Press, 1986.

Jones, Roger. *Physics as Metaphor*. New York: New American Library, 1983.

Joyal, Serge. *Action Montréal*. Montréal: Les éditions de l'homme, 1978.

Kaplan, Harold. *Reform, Planning and City Politics*. Toronto: University of Toronto Press, 1982.

– *The Regional City: Planning and Politics in Metropolitan Areas*. Toronto: CBC, 1965.

– *Urban Political Systems: A Functional Analysis of Metropolitan Toronto*. New York: Columbia University Press, 1967.

Kaplan, Marshall. "Infrastructure Policy: Repetitive Studies, Uneven Response, Next Steps." *Urban Affairs Quarterly* 25, no. 3 (1990): 371–88.

Kaplan, Samuel. "Design will not solve society's ills." Review of *Defensible Space*, by Oscar Newman. *New York Times Book Review*. 29 April 1973: 16–17.

Katz, Michael B. *The People of Hamilton, Canada West*. Cambridge, Mass.: Harvard University Press, 1975.

Katznelson, Ira. *City Trenches: Urban Politics and the Patterning of Class in the United States*. Chicago: University of Chicago Press, 1981.

Keating, Dennis, Norman Krumholz, and John Metzger. "Cleveland: Post-Populist Public-Private Partnerships." In *Unequal Partnerships: The Political Economy of Urban Redevelopment in Postwar America*. Edited by Gregory D. Squires. New Brunswick, NJ: Rutgers University Press, 1989.

Keating, Donald. *The Power to Make It Happen*. Toronto: Greentree Publishing, 1975.

Keith, N.S. *Politics and the Housing Crisis*. New York: Universe Books, 1973.

Kemble, Roger. *The Canadian City: St. John's to Victoria*. Montreal: Harvest House, 1989.

Kentridge, Leon, and Peter Oliphant. "High-Rise versus No-Rise: The Municipal Cost-Benefit Equation." In *The City: Attacking Modern Myths*. Edited by Alan Powell. Toronto: McClelland and Stewart, 1972.

Kiernan, Matthew J. "Land-Use Planning." In *Urban Policy Issues: Canadian Perspectives*. Edited by Richard A. Loreto and Trevor Price. Toronto: McClelland and Stewart, 1990.

Killinger, John. *The Loneliness of Children*. New York: The Vanguard Press, 1980.

Kohn, Alfie. *No Contest: The Case Against Competition*. Boston: Houghton Mifflin, 1986.

Krishnamurti, J. *Commentaries on Living*. 1st ser. Wheaton, Ill.: The Theosophical Publishing House, 1967.

Krohn, Roger, Berkeley Fleming, and Marilyn Manzer. *The Other Economy: The Internal Logic of Local Rental Housing*. Toronto: Peter Martin, 1977.

Krueger, Ralph, and R. Charles Bryfogle, eds. *Urban Problems: A Canadian Reader*. New York: Holt, Rinehart and Winston, 1971.

Ladd, Helen F., and John Yinger. *America's Ailing Cities: Fiscal Health and the Design of Urban Policy*. Baltimore: Johns Hopkins University Press, 1989.

Lanken, Dane. "Montreal: At the New Crossroads." In *Grassroots, Greystones, and Glass Towers: Montreal Urban Issues and Architecture*. Edited by Bryan Demchinsky. Montreal: Véhicule Press, 1989.

Lansing, John, and Robert Marans. "Evaluation of Neighbourhood Quality." *Journal of the American Institute of Planners* 35, no. 4 (1969): 195–9.

Lash, Trude W., and Heidi Sigal. *State of the Child: New York City*. New York: New York Foundation for Child Development, 1976.

Latané, Bibb, and John Darley, *The Unresponsive Bystander: Why Doesn't He Help?* New York: Appleton Century Crofts, 1970.

Layton, Jack. "Toronto at the Turning Point." *City Magazine* 10, no. 3 (1988): 8–9.

Lefebvre, Henri. *La production de l'espace*. Paris: Éditions Anthropos, 1974.

Leff, Herbert L. *Playful Perception: Choosing How to Experience Your World*. Burlington, Vermont: Waterfront Books, 1984.

Leipert, Christian. "From Gross to Adjusted National Product." In *The Living Economy: A New Economics in the Making*. Edited by Paul Elkins. London: Routledge & Kegan Paul, 1986.

Leo, Christopher. *The Politics of Urban Development: Canadian Urban Expressway Disputes*. Toronto: Institute of Public Administration, 1977.

Lepman, Jella. *How Children See Our World*. New York: Avon, 1971, 1975.

Leroy, Harcel. "Some Socio-Political Consequences of High Population Density and Crowding." Paper presented to the Canadian Political Science Association, Université Laval, 1976.

Lerup, Lars. *Building the Unfinished: Architecture and Human Action*. Beverly Hills, Calif.: Sage Publications, 1977.

Léveillée, Jacques. "Pouvoir local et politiques publiques à Montréal: renouveau dans les modalités d'exercise du pouvoir urbain." *Cahiers de recherche sociologique* 6, no. 2 (1988): 37–63.

Lewis, Eugene, and Frank Anechiarico. *Urban America: Politics and Policy*. 2nd ed. New York: Holt, Rinehart, and Winston, 1981.

Ley, David. *A Social Geography of the City*. New York: Harper and Row, 1983.

Lineberry, Robert L., and Ira Sharkansky. *Urban Politics and Public Policy*. 3d ed. New York: Harper and Row, 1978.

Lipset, Seymour Martin. *Political Man: The Social Bases of Politics*. New York: Doubleday, 1961.

Locke, John. *Second Treatise on Government*. Edited by Peter Laslett. New York: Cambridge University Press, 1963. [Originally published in 1698.]

Lofland, Lyn. *A World of Strangers: Order and Action in Urban Public Space*. New York: Basic Books, 1973.

Logan, John R., and Harvey L. Molotch, *Urban Fortunes: The Political Economy of Place*. Berkeley, Calif.: University of California Press, 1987.

Long, Norton. *The Unwalled City*. New York: W.W. Norton, 1972.

Lorimer, James. *A Citizen's Guide to City Politics*. Toronto: James Lewis and Samuel, 1972.

– *The Developers*. Toronto: Lorimer, 1978.

Lottman, Herbert. *How Cities Are Saved*. New York: Universe Books, 1976.

Lovins, Amory. "Energy and Security." *In Context* no. 19 (Autumn 1988): 14–19.

Lowi, Theodore J. *The End of Liberalism: The Second Republic of the United States*. 2d ed. New York: W.W. Norton, 1979.

Lowry, Ira. "The Dismal Future of Central Cities." In *The Prospective City: Economic, Population, Energy, and Environmental Developments*. Edited by Solomon. Cambridge, Mass.: MIT Press, 1980.

Lundeman, Richard J., ed. *Police Behaviour: A Sociological Perspective*. New York: Oxford University Press, 1980.

Lupo, Alan, Frank Colcord, and E.P. Fowler. *Rites of Way: The Politics of Transportation in Boston and the US City*. Boston: Little, Brown, 1971.

Lyman, Francesca. "Rethinking our Transportation Future." *E: The Environmental Magazine* 1 no. 5 (1990): 38.

Lynch, Kevin. *Growing Up in Cities*. Cambridge, Mass.: MIT Press, 1977.

– *The Image of the City*. Cambridge, Mass.: MIT Press, 1960.

Macpherson, C.B. *The Rise and Fall of Economic Justice and Other Essays*. New York: Oxford University Press, 1987.

– *The Political Theory of Possessive Individualism*. New York: Oxford University Press, 1962.

Magid, Eleanor. "Healing the Split." In *Mothers Talking: Sharing the Secret*. Edited by Frances Wells Burch. New York: St Martin's Press, 1986.

Magnusson, Warren. "The Political Insignificance of the Municipality." *City Magazine* 11, no. 2 (1990): 23–8.

Mann, W.E., ed. *The Underside of Toronto*. Toronto: McClelland and Stewart, 1970.

Markusen, Ann. "Class and Urban Social Expenditure: A Marxist Theory of Metropolitan Government." In *Marxism and the Metropolis: New Perspectives in Urban Political Economy*. Edited by William K. Tabb and Larry Sawers. New York: Oxford University Press, 1978.

Markusen, J.R., and D.T. Scheffman. *Speculation and Monopoly in Urban Development: Analytical Foundations with Evidence for Toronto*. Toronto: Ontario Economic Council, 1977.

Marsan, Jean-Claude. *Montréal en évolution*. Montréal: Fides, 1974.

Marsh, Margaret S., and Samuel Kaplan. "The Lure of the Suburbs." In *Suburbia: The American Dream and Dilemma*. Edited by Philip Dolce. New York: Doubleday, 1976.

Mawby, R.I. *Policing the City*. Farnborough: Teakfield/Lexington, 1979.

McCamant, Kathryn, and Charles Durrett. *Cohousing: A Contemporary Approach to Housing Ourselves*. Berkeley, Calif.: Ten Speed Press, 1988.

McLuhan, T.C. *Touch the Earth: A Self-Portrait of Indian Existence.* New York: Simon and Schuster, 1971.

McNally, David. *Political Economy and the Rise of Capitalism: A Reinterpretation.* Berkeley: University of California Press, 1988.

McRobie, George. *Small is Possible.* London: Abacus, 1981.

Mehrabian, Albert. *Public Places and Private Spaces.* New York: Basic Books, 1976.

Merchant, Carolyn. *The Death of Nature: Women, Ecology, and the Scientific Revolution.* San Francisco: Harper and Row, 1980.

Merry, Sally. "Defensible Space Undefended: Social Factors in Crime Control Through Environmental Design." *Urban Affairs Quarterly* 16, no. 4 (1981): 397–421.

Meyerson, Martin, and Edward Banfield. *Politics, Planning, and the Public Interest.* Glencoe, Ill.: The Free Press, 1955.

Michelson, William. *Environmental Choice, Human Behavior, and Residential Satisfaction.* New York: Oxford University Press, 1977.

– *Man and His Urban Environment.* 2d ed. Boston: Addison Wesley, 1976.

– "The Reconciliation of 'Subjective' and 'Objective' Data on Physical Environment in the Community: The Case of Social Contact in High Rise Apartments." In *The Community: Approaches and Applications.* Edited by Marcia Pelly Effrat. New York: Free Press, 1974.

Michelson, William, and Ellis Roberts, "Children and the Urban Physical Environment." In *The Child in the City: Changes and Challenges.* Edited by William Michelson, Saul Levine, Anna-Rose Spinas, and colleagues. Toronto: University of Toronto Press, 1979.

Michelson, William, Saul Levine, and Ellen Michelson, eds. *The Child in the City: Today and Tomorrow.* Toronto: University of Toronto Press, 1979.

Middleton, Michael. *Man Made the Town.* London: The Bodley Head, 1987.

Milbrath, Lester, and M.L. Goel. *Political Participation in America.* Chicago: Rand McNally, 1977.

Miller, Donald, ed. *The Lewis Mumford Reader.* New York: Pantheon, 1986.

Mishler, William. *Political Participation in Canada.* Toronto: Macmillan of Canada, 1979.

Mitchell, Robert Edward. "Some Social Implications of High Density Housing." *American Sociological Review* 36, no. 1 (1971): 18–29.

Morgan, Robin. *The Anatomy of Freedom: Feminism, Physics, and Global Politics.* New York: Doubleday Anchor, 1982.

Mumford, Lewis. *The City in History.* New York: Harcourt, Brace and World, 1961.

– "Home Remedies for Urban Cancer." In *The Lewis Mumford Reader.* Edited by Donald Miller. New York: Pantheon, 1986.

Muszynski, Leon. *The Deindustrialization of Metropolitan Toronto: A Study of Plant Closures, Layoffs and Unemployment.* Toronto: Social Planning Council of Metropolitan Toronto, 1985.

Neilson Associates. *Net Community Benefits of Urban Consolidation.* Prepared for the City of Melbourne. Melbourne: Neilson Associates, November 1987.

Nelson, Ruben F.W. *The Illusions of Urban Man.* Ottawa, Ont.: Square One Management, 1979.

Newman, Oscar. *Community of Interest.* New York: Anchor Press, Doubleday, 1980.

– *Defensible Space.* New York: Macmillan, 1973.

Newman, Peter, and Jeffrey Kenworthy. *Cities and Automobile Dependence.* Brookfield, Vt.: Gower Publishing, 1989.

Nicholson, Simon. "How Not to Cheat Children – the Theory of Loose Parts." Unpublished paper presented to University of Wisconsin at Milwaukee, Conference on Children and the Urban Environment, October 1976.

Niedercorn, John, and Edward F.R. Hearle. "Recent Land Use Trends in Forty-Eight Large American Cities." *Land Economics* 40, no. 1 (1964): 105–9.

Norman, Jack. "Congenial Milwaukee: A Segregated City." In *Unequal Partnerships: The Political Economy of Urban Redevelopment in Postwar America.* Edited by Gregory D. Squires. New Brunswick, NJ: Rutgers University Press, 1989.

Nowlan, David, and Greg Stewart. *The Effect of Downtown Population Growth on Commuting Trips.* Toronto: Program in Planning, University of Toronto, January 1990.

Orren, Karen. "Corporate Power and the Slums: Is Big Business a Paper Tiger?" In *Theoretical Perspectives on Urban Politics.* By Willis D. Hawley, et al. Englewood Cliffs, NJ: Prentice-Hall, 1976.

Pacey, Elizabeth, and Philip Pacey. "The Cost of Development." *City Magazine* 1, no. 4 (1975): 30–6.

Packard, Vance. *A Nation of Strangers.* New York: David McKay Co., Inc., 1972.

Parkinson, C. Northcote. *Parkinson's Law.* Boston: Houghton Mifflin, 1957.

Parr, Alfred Eide. "City and Psyche." *The Yale Review* 55, no. 1 (1965): 71–85.

– "Environmental Design and Psychology." *Landscape* 14, no. 1 (1964): 15–18.

Pearson, Norman. "The History of Canadian Settlement." In *Urban Problems: A Canadian Reader.* Edited by Ralph Krueger and R. Charles Bryfogle. New York: Holt, Rinehart and Winston, 1971.

Perin, Constance. *Everything in Its Place: Social Order and Land Use in America.* Princeton, NJ: Princeton University Press, 1977.

Peterson, Paul E. *City Limits*. Chicago: University of Chicago Press, 1981.

Pfluger W., and Jessie M. Zota. "A Room Planned for Children." *Design for Children*. Vancouver: Urban Design Center, 1974.

Pipkin, John S., Mark E. LaGory, and Judith R. Blau, eds. *Remaking the City: Social Science Perspectives on Urban Design*. Albany, NY: State University of New York Press, 1983.

Plunkett, T.J., and George M. Betts. *The Management of Canadian Urban Government*. Kingston, Ont.: The Institute of Local Government, 1978.

Polanyi, Karl. *The Great Transformation: The Political and Economic Origins of Our Time*. Boston: Beacon Press, 1957.

Pollution Probe, in consultation with Warner Troyer and Glenys Moss. *The Canadian Green Consumer Guide*. Toronto: McClelland and Stewart, 1989.

Popenoe, David. *Private Pleasure, Public Plight: American Metropolitan Community Life in Comparative Perspective*. New Brunswick, NJ: Transaction Press, 1985.

– "Suburbanization, Privatization and Juvenile Delinquency: Some Possible Relationships." In *Housing and Neighborhoods: Theoretical and Empirical Contributions*. Edited by Willem van Vliet --, Harvey Choldin, William Michelson, and David Popenoe. New York: Greenwood Press, 1987.

Proudfoot, Stuart. "Private Gains and Public Losses: The Distributive Impact of Urban Zoning." *Policy Sciences* 11, no. 2 (1979): 203–26.

Przeworski, Adam, and Michael Wallerstein. "The Structure of Class Conflict in Democratic Capitalist Societies." *American Political Science Review* 76, no. 2 (1982): 215–38.

Pushkarev, Boris, and Christopher Tunnard. *Man-Made America*. New Haven: Yale University Press, 1963.

Rapoport, Amos. *The Meaning of the Built Environment*. Beverly Hills, Calif.: Sage Publications, 1982.

Reed, Richard Ernie. *Return to the City*. New York: Doubleday, 1979.

Reich, Robert B. *The Second American Frontier*. New York: Times Books, 1983.

– "The Next American Frontier." *Atlantic Monthly* 251, no. 3 (March 1983): 43–56.

Reisman, David, Reuel Denney, and Nathan Glazer. *The Lonely Crowd: A Study of the Changing American Character*. New Haven, Connecticut: Yale University Press, 1950.

Renner, Michael. *Rethinking the Role of the Automobile*. Washington: Worldwatch Institute, June 1988.

Reutter, Mark. "The Rise and Decline of Big Steel." *The Wilson Quarterly* 12, no. 4 (1988): 46–85.

Reynolds, Malvina. *Little Boxes*. Song copyright 1962, Schroder Music Co.

Rhodes, William M., and Catherine Conly. "Crime and Mobility: An Empirical Study." In *Environmental Criminology*. Edited by Paul J. Brantingham and Patricia L. Brantingham. Beverly Hills, Calif.: Sage Publications, 1981.

Ricci, David. *Community Power and Democratic Theory*. New York: Random House, 1971.

Richardson, Harry W. "The Contribution of Urban Economics to City Planning and Spatial Structure." In *Remaking the City: Social Science Perspectives on Urban Design*. Edited by John S. Pipkin, Mark E. LaGory, and Judith R. Blau. Albany, NY: State University of New York Press, 1983.

Riker, William. *Federalism*. Boston: Little, Brown, 1964.

Roads, Michael. *Talking with Nature*. Tiburon, California: H.J. Kramer, Inc., 1987.

Rodgers, Willard. *Density, Crowding, and Satisfaction with the Residential Environment*. Ann Arbor: Institute for Social Research, 1979.

– *Residential Satisfaction in Relationship to Size of Place*. Ann Arbor: Institute for Social Research, 1979.

Roncek, Dennis. "Dangerous Places: Crime and Residential Environment." *Social Forces* 60, no. 1 (1981): 74–96.

– "Density and Crime: A Methodological Critique." *American Behavioral Scientist* 18, no. 6 (1975): 843–60.

Roweis, Shoukry T., and Allen J. Scott. "The Urban Land Question." In *Urbanization and Urban Planning in Capitalist Societies*. Edited by Michael Dear and Allen J. Scott. London: Methuen, 1981.

Rudofsky, Bernard. *Architecture Without Architects: A Short Introduction to Non-Pedigreed Architecture*. New York: Doubleday, 1969.

– *Streets for People*. New York: Doubleday, 1969.

Sadalla, Edward. "Population Size, Structural Differentiation, and Human Behavior." *Environment and Behavior* 10, no. 2 (1978): 271–91.

Sale, Kirkpatrick. *Human Scale*. New York: Coward, McCann, and Geoghegan, 1980.

Sancton, Andrew. *Governing the Island of Montreal: Language Differences and Metropolitan Politics*. Berkeley: University of California Press, 1985.

– *Municipal Government and Social Services: A Case Study of London, Ontario*. London: Department of Political Science, University of Western Ontario, 1986.

Sandels, Dr. Stina. *The Skandia Report II: Why are Children Injured in Traffic: Can We Prevent Accidents in Traffic?*. Stockholm: Skandia Insurance Co. Ltd., 1974.

Sargent, Charles. "Land Speculation and Urban Morphology." In *Remaking the City: Social Science Perspectives on Urban Design*. Edited by John S. Pipkin, Mark E. LaGory, and Judith R. Blau. Albany, NY: State University Press of New York, 1983.

Satin, Mark. *New Age Politics: Healing Self and Society*. West Vancouver, BC: Whitecap Books, 1978.

Schattschneider, E.E. *The Semi-Sovereign People: A Realist's View of Democracy in the United States*. New York: Holt, Rinehart and Winston, 1960.

Schnore, Leo. "The Social and Economic Characteristics of American Suburbs." *The Sociological Quarterly* 4, no. 2 (1963): 122–34.
– *The Urban Scene*. Glencoe, Ill.: The Free Press, 1965.
Schrecker, Ted. "Resisting Environmental Regulation: The Cryptic Pattern of Business-Government Relations." In *Managing Leviathan: Environmental Politics and the Administrative State*. Edited by Robert Paehlke and Douglas Torgerson. Peterborough, Ont.: The Broadview Press, 1990.
Schubert, Glendon. *The Public Interest*. Glencoe, Ill.: The Free Press, 1960.
Schumacher, E.F. *Small is Beautiful*. London: Abacus, 1973.
Schwartz, Joel. "The Evolution of Suburbs." In *Suburbia: The American Dream and Dilemma*. Edited by Philip Dolce. New York: Doubleday, 1976.
Scott, Allen J. *Metropolis: From the Division of Labor to Urban Form*. Los Angeles: University of California Press, 1988.
Sennett, Richard. *The Fall of Public Man: The Social Psychology of Capitalism*. New York: Random House, 1977.
– *The Uses of Disorder: Personal Identity and City Life*. New York: Random House, 1970.
Sewell, John. "Don Mills: E.P. Taylor and Canada's First Corporate Suburb." *City Magazine* 2, no. 6 (1977): 28–38.
– *Police: Urban Policing in Canada*. Toronto: Lorimer, 1985.
Seymour, John, and Herbert Girardet. *Blueprint for a Green Planet*. New York: Prentice Hall, 1987.
Shlay, Anne B., and Denise A. DiGregorio. "Same City, Different Worlds: Examining Gender and Work-Based Differences in Perceptions of Neighbourhood Desirability." *Urban Affairs Quarterly* 21, no. 2 (1985): 66–86.
Smith, Michael Peter. *City, State, and Market: The Political Economy of Urban Society* London: Blackwell, 1988.
– *The City and Social Theory*. New York: St Martin's Press, 1979.
Smith, Michael Peter, and Joe R. Feagin, eds. *The Capitalist City: Global Restructuring and Community Politics*. Oxford: Basil Blackwell, 1987.
Social Planning Council of Metropolitan Toronto. *Families in High Rise Apartments*. Toronto: Social Planning Council of Metropolitan Toronto, May 1973.
Solomon, Arthur P., ed. *The Prospective City: Economic, Population, Energy and Environmental Developments*. Cambridge, Mass.: MIT Press, 1980.
Sorokin, Pitrim. "The Power of Creative Unselfish Love." In *New Knowledge in Human Values*. Edited by Abraham Maslow. New York: Harper and Row, 1959.
Spencer, Douglas Barry. *Questions Kids Ask: For Those Who Care to Listen*. Toronto: Simon and Pierre Publishing Co., Ltd., 1975.
Spirn, Anne Whiston. *The Granite Garden: Urban Nature and Human Design*. New York: Basic Books, 1984.

Spragge, Shirley. "A Confluence of Interests: Housing Reform in Toronto, 1900–1920." In *The Usable Urban Past: Planning and Politics in the Modern Canadian City.* Edited by Alan F.J. Artibise and Gilbert A Stelter. Toronto: Macmillan of Canada, 1979.

Spretnak, Charlene. *The Spiritual Dimension of Green Politics.* Santa Fe: Bear and Company, 1986.

Spurr, Peter. *Land and Urban Development.* Toronto: Lorimer, 1976.

Squires, Gregory D., ed. *Unequal Partnerships: The Political Economy of Urban Redevelopment in Postwar America.* New Brunswick, NJ: Rutgers University Press, 1989.

St John, Craig. "Racial Differences in Neighborhood Evaluation Standards." *Urban Affairs Quarterly* 22, no. 3 (1987): 377–98.

Stern, Martin O. "The Use of Urban Roads and Their Effects on Spatial Structure of Cities." In *Local Service Pricing Policies and Their Effect on Urban Spatial Structure.* Edited by Paul Downing. Vancouver: University of British Columbia Press, 1977.

Stokes, Bruce. *Helping Ourselves: Local Solutions to Global Problems.* New York: W.W. Norton, 1981.

Stokols, Daniel. "The Experience of Crowding in Primary and Secondary Environments." *Environment and Behaviour* 8, no. 1 (1976): 49–86.

– "On the Distinction between Density and Crowding: Some Implications for Future Research." *Psychological Review* 79, no. 2 (1972): 257–77.

Studer, Raymond G. "Prospects for Realizing Congruent Housing Environments." In *Housing and Neighborhoods: Theoretical and Empirical Contributions.* Edited by Willem van Vliet --, Harvey Choldin, William Michelson, and David Popenoe. New York: Greenwood Press, 1987.

Summerville, John. *The Rise and Fall of Childhood.* Beverly Hills, Calif.: Sage Publications, 1981.

Swanstrom, Todd. *The Crisis of Growth Politics: Cleveland, Kucinich, and the Challenge of Urban Populism.* Philadelphia: Temple University Press, 1985.

Tabb, William K., and Larry Sawers, eds. *Marxism and the Metropolis: New Perspectives in Urban Political Economy.* New York: Oxford University Press, 1978.

Talbot, Michael. *Beyond the Quantum.* New York: Bantam, 1988.

Taylor, John H. "Urban Autonomy in Canada: Its Evolution and Decline." In *The Canadian City: Essays in Urban and Social History.* Edited by Gilbert A. Stelter and Alan F.J. Artibise. Ottawa: Carleton University Press, 1984.

Thompson, Wilbur. *A Preface to Urban Economics.* Baltimore, Md.: Johns Hopkins Press, 1965.

Tilly, Charles. *An Urban World.* Boston: Little, Brown, 1974.

Tindal, C.R., and S. Nobes Tindal. *Local Government in Canada.* 3d ed. Toronto: McGraw Hill Ryerson, 1990.

Tuan, Yi-Fu. *Landscapes of Fear*. Minneapolis, Minn.: University of Minnesota Press, 1979.

– *Topophilia*. Englewood Cliffs, NJ: Prentice-Hall, 1974.

Turner, John F.C. *Housing By People: Towards Autonomy in Building Environments*. London: Marion Boyars, 1976.

US Bureau of the Census. *Statistical Abstract of the United States, 1989*. Washington, DC: Department of Commerce, 1989.

US Department of Transportation. *Urban Data Supplement of 1974*. Washington: US Department of Transportation, 1976.

Van Vliet --, Willem, Harvey Choldin, William Michelson, and David Popenoe. *Housing and Neighborhoods: Theoretical and Empirical Contributions*. New York: Greenwood Press, 1987.

Verdon, Michael. "On the Laws of Physical and Human Nature: Hobbes' Physical and Social Cosmologies." *Journal of the History of Ideas* 43, no. 4 (1982): 653–63.

Vernon, Raymond. *Metropolis 1985*. Cambridge, Mass.: Harvard University Press, 1960.

Wachtel, Paul L. *The Poverty of Affluence: A Psychological Portrait of the American Way of Life*. Philadelphia: New Society Publishers, 1989.

Wagenvoord, James. *Hangin' Out: City Kids, City Games*. Philadelphia: Lippincott, 1974.

Walker, Richard A. "A Theory of Suburbanization: Capitalism and the Construction of Urban Space in the United States." In *Urbanization and Urban Planning in Capitalist Societies*. Edited by Michael Dear and Allen J. Scott. London: Methuen, 1981.

Walsh, Roger. *Staying Alive*. Boulder, Colo.: Shambhala Publications, 1984.

Ward, Colin. *The Child in the City*. London: The Architectural Press, 1978.

Warner, Sam Bass, Jr. *Streetcar Suburbs*. Cambridge, Mass.: Harvard University Press, 1962.

Webber, Melvin. "The Urban Place and the Nonplace Urban Realm." In *Explorations into Urban Structure*. Edited by Melvin Webber. Philadelphia: University of Pennsylvania Press, 1964.

Wellman, Barry, and Marilyn Whittaker. *High-Rise, Low-Rise: The Effects of High Density Living*. Toronto: Centre for Urban and Community Studies, University of Toronto, January 1974.

Werkele, Gerda R. "Canadian Women's Housing Cooperatives: Case Studies in Physical and Social Innovation." In *Life Spaces: Gender, Household, Employment*. Edited by Caroline Andrew and Beth Moore Milroy. Vancouver: University of British Columbia Press, 1988.

Wharf, Brian. "Social Services." In *Urban Policy Issues: Canadian Perspectives*. Edited by Richard Loreto and Trevor Price. Toronto: McClelland and Stewart, 1990.

Whyte, William H. *The Last Landscape*. New York: Doubleday, 1970.

– *The Organization Man*. New York: Doubleday, 1957.

Will, Rosalyn, Alice Tepper Martin, Benjamin Corson, and Jonathan Schorsch. *Shopping for a Better World*. New York: Council on Economic Priorities, 1989.

Wilson, James Q., ed. *Urban Renewal: The Record and the Controversy*. Cambridge, Mass.: MIT Press, 1966.

Wohlwill, Joachim. "The Physical Environment: A Problem for a Psychology of Stimulation." In *People and Buildings*. Edited by Robert Gutman. New York: Basic Books, 1972.

Wolfe, Alan. *America's Impasse*. Boston: South End Press, 1980.

Wolfe, Alan, and Charles A. McCoy. *Political Analysis: An Unorthodox Approach*. New York: Thomas Crowell, 1972.

Wolfe, Jeanne, and William Jay. "The Revolving Door: Third Sector Organizations and the Homeless." In *Housing the Homeless and the Poor: New Partnerships among the Private, Public, and Third Sectors*. Edited by George Fallis and Alex Murray. Toronto: University of Toronto Press, 1990.

Wolfe, Tom. *From Bauhaus to Our House*. New York: Washington Square Press, 1981.

Wolman, Harold, and Michael Goldsmith. "Local Autonomy as a Meaningful Analytic Concept: Comparing Local Government in the United States and the United Kingdom." *Urban Affairs Quarterly* 26, no. 1 (1990): 3–25.

Wood, Ellen Meiksins. *Mind and Politics: An Approach to the Meaning of Liberal and Socialist Individualism*. Berkeley, Calif.: University of California Press, 1972.

Wright, Frank Lloyd. *Broadacre City: Book Six of An Autobiography*. Spring Green, Wisc., 1943.

– *The Living City*. New York: New American Library, 1970.

Yeates, Maurice, and Barry Garner. *The North American City*. 3d ed. New York: Harper and Row, 1980.

Zimmer, Basil. "The Small Businessman and Relocation." In *Urban Renewal: The Record and the Controversy*. Edited by James Q. Wilson. Cambridge, Mass.: MIT Press, 1966.

Index

Acquaintances: affected by physical design, 87. *See also* Contact; Friendship; Neighbours; Public Contact

Administration: separated from production, 141

Administrative personnel: in large corporations, 141

Agglomeration economy: deconcentrated, 143; and high density, 143

Aggressiveness: assumed by Hobbes, 195

Agnew, J.A.: on home ownership, 145

Aldrich, Robert: on children and cars, 105

Alexander, Christopher: on autonomy-withdrawal syndrome, 105–6; on buildings as relationships, 183; on single-family houses and neurotic patients, 163; *The Timeless Way of Building*, 183; on toddlers' need for friends, 105–6; on user-designed Spaces, 220

Alford, Robert, and Eugene Lee: on turnout in US local elections, 120

Alinsky, Saul: and community organizing, 214–16

Alinsky groups: and concentration of land use, 216; as non-bureaucratic, 216; problems with, 215–16; in Toronto, 215. *See also* Citizens' groups; Collective action; Community organizations

Amnesia: collective, and urban life, 204; political, reinforced by built environment, 129. *See also* Awareness; Normal

Annexation: by cities to ensure tax base, 33–4; by Montreal, of Pointe-aux-Trembles, 34

Anti-politics: of Frank Lloyd Wright, 174

Architecture: large-scale, and citizen passivity, 126; modern, hated by many, 78; and planning, as indivisible, 173

Assumptions, basic: underlying postwar city building, 179–98

Atlanta: downtown land devoted to cars, 42

Atlantic Village: large-scale residential development, 4

Auburn Hills, MI: location of Oakland Technology Park, 151

Authoritarian design: of buildings, as problem of politics, 78

Authoritarianism: of Le Corbusier, 174

Authorities. *See* Independent local authorities

Authority: need for, and postwar city buildings, 181; outside, as destructive to local initiative, 211; quest for, by Le Corbusier, 173

Autonomy: of independent local authorities, counter to popular control, 124

Autonomy-withdrawal: of governments, 164; syndrome, and suburbs, 105; syndrome, and North American individualism, 162–3. *See also* Withdrawal

Awareness: of beliefs which are dysfunctional, 179; of city around us, 200–5; of costs of individual choices, 50; of daily choices supporting national government, 194; of environment, 75; of garbage as a problem, 204–5; lack of, giving strength to unexamined assumptions, 199; of link between daily experiences and government; of places, 200–2; as prerequisite for change, 220; as problem, 204–5; of public street life, 89; of our symbiosis with built environment, 184; and voluntary action, 204; of why we built the way we did, 138; of why one likes a neighbourhood, 79. *See also* Amnesia; Choices, Daily; Normal

Azusa, California: mobility and children in, 108

Bacon, Francis: and scientific revolution, 180

Bahl, Roy W., and J. Michael McGuire: on costs of leapfrog development, 52, 54

Baltimore: as special case in road-building, 35

Banana Kelly: self-help group in South Bronx, 218

Bateson, Patrick: on abuse of Darwin's thinking, 196

Battery Park City, New York City: built by Olympia and York, 147

Bay-Adelaide Centre, Toronto: large-scale project, 154

Beauty, urban: taken seriously, 74; as more than trees and grass, 80

Beliefs: in legitimacy of large corporations, 212–13; underlying postwar city building, 179–98

Bentham, Jeremy: on property ownership, 164

Berry, Wendell: on costs of segregated housing, 59; on small solutions, 199

Bethlehem Steel: Sparrows Point Plant, 6, 146

Birmingham, Eng.: and small-scale efficiency, 213

Blake, Peter: on Frank Lloyd Wright and Le Corbusier, 174

Block length: in Margueretta Street area, 19. *See also* Long blocks; Short blocks

Bluestone, Barry, and Bennett Harrison: *The Deindustrialization of America*, 153; on tax laws favouring large corporations, 153

Bolshevism: home ownership as defense against, 164

Bookchin, Murray: on planners, 171; on the local politics of the working class, 128; on television and the decline in workers' social life, 170–1

Boosterism: and loss of old buildings, 151. *See also* Progress; Pro-growth policies

Border vacuum: as economic cost of expressways, 46

Boredom: and juvenile delinquency, 102

Boston: downtown land devoted to cars, 44; mode of travel to work, 44; West End, urban renewal in, 134

Break-ins: in Ontario Street area, 23; in Spadina Avenue area, 24

Bristol Avenue: area of Toronto study, 225

Broadacre City, 172–3; never built, 174; its politics, 173; and urban sprawl, prototype, 173

Broadway project: costly office project, Louisville, 66

Bronx, New York City. *See* South Bronx

Brookline, MA: voting against annexation, 34

Builders, large: in various US cities, 5. *See also* Construction industry; Developers; Development corporations; Development industry

Building boom: expression of pro-growth values, 178; and homogeneity, 10–11; developers, large, created by, 140. *See also* Construction boom

Building freeze: in Toronto, 160

Buildings: new, their short life span, 61–2; political culture reflected in, 127. *See also* Old buildings; Mix of old and new buildings

Built environment. *See* Environment, built

Bureaucracies: large-scale, related to large-scale infrastructure, 124

Bureaucracy: government functions encrusted with, 216; inexorable growth of, 193, 216

Business: costs to, of postwar city building, 65–8; growth coalition with labour, 140; losses from Cross Bronx Expressway, 46; primacy of in North American Culture, 169–70

Businessman: high status of in North American Culture, 169

Cadillac Fairview, 147

Calgary: land monopoly in suburbs of, 60

Campbell, Tom, 154

Canada Mortgage and Housing Corporation (CMHC): developers, large, favoured by, 152; mortgage guarantees from, 212; political ideology behind policies, 165. *See also* Central Mortgage and Housing Corporation

Capitalism: global restructuring of, and community organizations, 215; need for growth, 140

Capitman, Willima: on corporate decisions as most decisive, 157

Caro, Robert, 45

Cars: as cause of air pollution, 47–9; and children, harmful to, 103–5, mobility impeded by, 103–4; cost to individual, 49; and detachment from local environment, 133; as killers, 46, 104; and public spaces, 88. *See also* Traffic; Transportation technology; Urban transportation

Carter, Jimmy: policies toward central city, 148

Cataclysmic money: and destruction of diversity, 147–8, 154, 190

Central city: decline in population, 11; government, relative power of, 157; importance to growth of GNP, 140; variations in census definition, 34. *See also* Downtown

Central Mortgage and Housing Corporation: tool of housing policy in Canada, 149. *See also* Canada Mortgage and Housing Corporation

Chicago: density and gasoline consumption, 47; housing loss, due to urban renewal, 57; industrial sites on fringes of city, 5; not a local government, 118

Chief Standing Bear: on being close to the earth, 83

Child in the City Program, 106

Children: afraid to leave homes, 109; in Azusa, California, 108; and cars, frightened by, 104–5, killed by, 104; as competent planners, 113–4; differences from adults, 100; in diverse areas, under surveillance in, 111; in Don Mills area, 20; experiences, intensity of, 100; home as sanctuary for, 106; and learning from adults' behaviour, 95, in Margueretta Street area, 18, 19; meeting places for, scarce in postwar city, 108; and mobility, less than adults', 100, lessened by the car, 103–4; and mixed land use, their need for, 102; and physical environment, more connected to, 95; and postwar city building, 99–114; their pictures, as responses to environment, 81; and play, seriousness of for, 100; privacy from, as principle of postwar city building, 106, 113; and scale of city, 100, 101; separated because different, 99; in suburbs, home-oriented not neighbourhood-oriented, 109, social life, 105–9, toddlers, no playmates for, 105–6; taking responsibility for street, 103; traffic rules, confused by, 104; unprogrammed space, need for, 101; and urban planning, 99

Choices, daily: awareness of, 199–205; important role of, 204–5; as political, 116; as supporting national governments, 194. *See also* Daily lives; Daily actions

Choices, personal: about housing and jobs, important for city, 207–8

Chorney, Harold: and amnesia in modern urban environment, 203–4; *City of Dreams*, 199–200; on political amnesia, 129; and urban space for politics, lack of, 129; on urban withdrawal syndrome, 199–200

Church Street: in Maitland Street area, 17, 18

Cities: Canadian, interest-group liberalism in, 167, vs US, 25; large, considered normal, 116, prerequisite to big government, 116; physical form of, supported by personal choices, 208; and politics, intertwined, 135; and regions, as source of economic energy, 193. *See also* City

Citizens' groups: 214–16; and advocate planners, 176; fighting defensively, 132. *See also* Alinsky groups; Collective action; Community organizations

Citizenship: suburbs as failure of, 73; weak sense of, in suburbs, 122

City: awareness of, as physical place, 200–5; built for consumption, 170; politicians in, support for postwar city building, 4, 154; trenches, as politics of workplace separate from residence, 127

Clark, S.D.: on evaluation of suburbs, Toronto, 79

Cleveland: Tower City in, costly office project, 66

CMHC. *See* Canada Mortgage and Housing Corporation

Cohousing: alternative model for housing, 219–20

Collective action: and need for face-to-face contact, 290; by working class, and segregated housing, 127. *See also* Alinsky groups; Citizens' groups; Community organizations

Colton, Timothy, 152

Columbia, MD: conformity to physical design in, 126

Communication: face-to-face, of urban gardeners, 207; replaced by mass media, 170. *See also* Face-to-face contact; Mass media.

Community: as illusion in suburbs, 207

Community organizations: limited impact of, 214–15; and physical environment, 216–17; in St Jamestown area, 22. *See also* Alinsky groups; Citizen groups; Collective action

Community organizing: and Saul Alinsky, 214–16

Company towns: as politically confrontational, 144

Competitiveness: of humans, assumed, 195–6

Compliance: political, integral to physical infrastructure, 125; and postwar urban development, engendered by, 126; structure, and legitimacy of corporations, 167–8

Concentration of use: and community organizing, 216; and crime, 97; and friendship patterns, 87; and homogeneity of land use, 11; and vitality, urban, 13. *See also* Diversity, physical; Density; Decentralization; Deconcentration

Condominiums: as alternative from of home ownership, 145; unmanipulability of, as environment, 126

Conflict: as a choice, 196; as creative, 194; and Darwin's thinking, peripheral to, 196; as desirable, 197; as not inevitable, 195–8; and politics, essential part of, 194–8; as reality, 194; social, avoidance of in North America, 164; and zero-sum games, 197–8

Conformity: to physical design, in suburbs, 126

Congestion: as reason for decentralization, 143

Construction boom: postwar, and newness of North American city, 139–42. *See also* Building boom

Construction industry: as largest industry, 140. *See also* Builders, large; Development corporations; Development industry

Construction, new: promoted by local governments, 150

Consumer goods: production of as goal of labour-business truce, 140

Consumption: of energy and suburban living, 202–3; as function of city, 170; as means to independence, 170; and self-sufficiency, 163

Continuous-material-flow: manufacturing process, factor in deconcentration, 6

Convenience: as reason for liking neighbourhood, 80; and St Jamestown, 22

Cook County, Chicago: not a "local" government, 118

Co-Op City: costly high-rises, example of, 63; homogeneity due to scale, 11; large-scale residential development, 4; and Moses, Robert, 157

Cooperation: as a choice, 196; as principle in nature, 196

Cooperatives: housing, 217–18

Corporate mentality: in local government, 161

Corporations: administrative personnel, growing proportions of, 141; government, big, symbiosis with, 116; influenced by Alinsky groups, 215, as destructive to local economies, 119, in development industry, 147, and large-scale development, 146–7, and segregated land use, 146, and tax laws, favoured by, 153; legitimacy of, history, 167; as local governments, 118; as market for office space, 141; postwar city, builders of, 167–8; municipal, as money-making machines, 118, 119; as municipalities, 160–2; more powers than ordinary businesses, 167. *See also* Developers; Development corporations; Development industry; Large companies; Large firms

Costs: economic, of postwar city building, 29–69; of high-rises, excessive, 62–4; of housing, large-scale, 59–64, postwar, 55–65; of services, municipal, due to postwar city building, 29–54; social, of postwar city building, 70–98

Courage My Love, 24, 209–10

Cox, Kevin: and the honey pot, 145–6

Crime: and built environment, influenced by, 92–8; due to Cross Bronx Expressway, 46; and large-scale development, 96–7; in Ontario Street area, 22; and outsiders to neighbourhood, committed by, 98; and postwar city building, 90–8; Prevention through Environmental Design (CPTED), its limitations, 93–4, qualified by Merry, 96; rates, in cities vs countryside, 90–2, countryside, higher in, 92, as function of residents vs users, 91, in high-rises, 92, inaccuracy, sources of, 91; in St Jamestown area, 22; as symptom, 94; and urban crisis, 92. *See also* Juvenile crime; Juvenile delinquency

Crop losses: due to pollution by cars, 49

Cross Bronx Expressway: damage caused by construction of, 45–6; independent local authority, built by, 157; interstate-highway system, part of, 152

Crowding: as both positive and negative, 82; sense of, mitigated by physical diversity, 82

Culture: North American, and form of postwar city building, 168–71

Cunningham Road: housing project, self-management in, and drop in vandalism, 95

Currency: single national, harm of, 193

Dahl, Robert: on pluralism and planning, 176; on power, sources of, 191n; on separation of functions as healthy for democracy, 124

Daily actions: and built environment, 192. *See also* Choices

Daily experience: link with public policies, 202

Daily lives: as determinant of city's destiny, 14; and support for large institutions, 116. *See also* Choices

Darwin, Charles: on adaptation to environment, 195–6; and Karl Marx, 196; on nature as cooperative, 196

Davidoff, Paul: on advocate planning, 176

Dayton, Ohio: home ownership in, 145

Debt: residential, largest item in debt structure, 149

Decentralization: and deconcentration, distinct from, 142; economic explanations for, 142–5; and government policy, 151–2, *see also* Policies, public; and home ownership, 144–5; and postwar city building, feature of, 6; residential, economic explanations for, 144, as effect of growth coalition, 142; and vertical disintegration, 6, 143. *See also* Concentration of use; Deconcentration; Density; Diversity, physical

Decisions: about local environment, 131–2; political, affected by segregated land use, 123–4

Deconcentration (of land use): and Buddhist economics, 189; and cars, 9–10; and children, cut off from adults because of, 102; and costs of water and sewage, 50–1; as expression of North American culture, 169; and decentralization, distinct from, 142; and detachment from local environment, 133; economic explanations for, 142–5; and government policy, 151–2, *see also* Policies, public; and home ownership, 144–5; and independent local authorities, 157; industrial and continuous-material-flow, 6; and interstate-highway program, 152; political explanations for, 144; and postwar city building, 6–10; and public spaces for politics, 130; residential, economic explanations for, 144–5; resistance to change, 9; and technology, 6, 143. *See also* Density; Decentralization; Concentration of use; Diversity, physical

Defense contracts: in Sunbelt, and growth of suburbs, 151

Deindustrialization: and impersonal land, 188

Democracy: separation of functions healthy for, 124. *See also* Representative system

Denmark: cohousing in, 219

Density: and car use, world-wide, 40; of children, kept low, 106; contingent nature of, 82; and crime, 97; and crowding, distinction between, 82; evaluations by residents, 81–2; feelings of, in St Jamestown area, 21; and gasoline consumption, 47; gradient, compared, 9–10, defined, 9; high, with tall buildings and Le Corbusier's designs, 173, why traditionally valued, 142; low, deprives toddlers of friends, 106; and neighbour contact, 86; as both positive and negative, 82; residential, and costs of city services, 50; and spending, on sewage and sanitation, 49–52, on urban transportation, 35–41; of suburban housing, 7–8. *See also* Concentration of use; Decentralization; Deconcentration; Diversity, physical

Depreciation allowance: and destruction of old buildings, 150

Descartes, René: central to scientific revolution, 180

Detachment: from local environment, and lack of physical diversity, 133

Detroit: density and neighbour contact, 86; neighbourhood in, destroyed by General Motors, 147

Developers: bigger in Canada than US, 60; financial viability of, 213; large, created by building boom, 140, as independent force, 140, 147, and local governments in US, 159, paying no income tax in Canada, 153, *see also* Builders, Cadillac Fairview, Levitt, Olympia and York; and planners, in contact with, 171, employers of, 172. *See also* Construction industry; Corporations; Development corporations; Development industry

Development. *See* New development; Large-scale development; Residential development

Development corporations: semi-public builders of large-scale projects, 157–9. *See also* Builders, large; Construction industry; Developers; Large companies; Large firms

Development industry: and building booms, 140; large-scale corporations in, 147; and local government bodies, 150; and profit from high-rise offices, 141; and property as power-over, 192. *See also* Builders, large; Construction industry; Developers; Development corporations

Direct action: tactic of Alinsky groups, 215

Disintegration, vertical: and deconcentration of firms, 143; of large firms, factor in decentralization, 6

Distribution system: in cooperative greenhouse, 219; and daily choices, supported by, 116; and land-use separation, 202

Diversity, physical: and block-level communication, 133; and block-level management, 131, 132–3, *see also* Government, street-level; and children, as healthy for, 98; and community organizations, 216–17; and cooperative participation, 214; and corporate mentality, unappealing to, 161; and crime, as discouragement to, 92–8; and crowding, mitigates sense of, 82; defined, 13; in Don Mills area, 20; evaluations of, by residents, 80; and eyes on the street, 87–8; and government policy, 148–56, *see also* Policies, public; and intelligence, stimulant to, 76; and juvenile crime, deterrent to, 97–8, 111; and large-scale development, destroyed by, 147–8; and local government, discouraged by size and form of, 161, unaided by weakness of, 156–60; of Maitland Street area, 17; of Margueretta Street area, 19; of Niagara Street area, 15; of Ontario Street area, 22; and personal identity, sense of, 77; and political efficacy of working class, 127; and political ideology, 162–8; and privatization of space, 130–1; and public contact, 87; in reclaimed neighbourhoods, 218; self-destruction of, 145–6; and street-level government, 87–8; and street life, healthy, 94; and urban vitality, determinant of, 13. *See also* Concentration of use; Density; Land-use: mix; Mix of old and new buildings; Short blocks; Urban design

Diversity, social: of Don Mills area, 20; of Maitland Street area, 17; of Margueretta Street area, 19; of St Jamestown area, 21; of Spadina Avenue area, 24

Don Mills, Ontario: built by large corporations, 148; deconcentration of its industrial development, 6; large-scale residential project, 5; the Toronto study, area of, 20–1

Dovercourt Road: area of the Toronto study, 225

Downtown: land, devoted to roads and parking, various cities, 42, 44; as location for corporate headquarters, 141. *See also* Central cities

Drapeau, Jean: and annexation of Pointe-aux-Trembles, 34; promoter of large-scale projects, 154

Duffala, Dennis: on physical diversity and robberies, 96

Economic Council of Canada: on space taken up by cars, 9–10

Economic explanations: for postwar city building, 139–48

Economic growth: of city: from fear of Scarcity, 181; and labour-business growth coalition, 140; value of, dubious, 68, 178–9; valued in our culture, 178. *See also* Growth; Growth coalition; Progress; Pro-growth policies

Economic indicators: as "objective" criteria of evaluation, 75

Economic institutions: of North America, and postwar city building, 184–90

Economic motives: for caring about neighbourhood, 133

Economics: beliefs about, expressed in postwar city, 199; Buddhist, and urban development, 189; profit as criterion of, 188–9; of scarcity, underlying postwar city, 181; as a subjective discipline, 188–9. *See also* National economy; Other economy

Economic stagnation: and large-scale organizations, 213

Economies of scale: in housing, 60; and large factories, 147; in large-scale development, 5; and short-term efficiency, 213

Ecosystem: urban, 183

Efficiency: short-term, and economies of scale, 213

Elections: local, turnout in, 120, in new cities, 120; no policy content, 117; as support for political system. *See also* Participation, political

Elementary particles: offering new view of reality, 182

Elgin, Duane: *Voluntary Simplicity*, 204

El Sol Brillante: community garden, 218
Energy: conservation, and cohousing, 220; consumption of, and suburban living, 202–3; in new buildings, excessive use of, 62
England: vs US, attitudes toward home ownership, 145
Evaluation: of city, beauty as more than trees and grass, 80, positive when clear image of, 77, subjectivity of "objective" criteria, 75; of neighbourhoods, in child's picture, 81, and their density, 81–2, differing, sources of, 79–82, misperceptions of, 79, objective and subjective, 74–5, in Toronto study, 79–83; see also Likes and dislikes; of urban Environment, role of personality, 75
Environment, built: and consumption, stimulator of, 200; and daily actions, outcome of, 192; Howard's views on impact of, 72; interdependence of its effects, 183; and identity of user and of designer, 77; land market, shaped by, 145; its multi-dimensionality, 86; objectified by ideology of individuality, 163; perpetuation of past by, 159; social life, impact on, 71–2, 83–9; street life discouraged by, 88–9; unmanipulability of, and interest in local politics, 121; user-designed, 220. See also Density; Diversity, physical; Environment, local; Environment, physical
Environment, local: decisions about, 131–2
Environment, natural: front yards, as helping, 205; and separation of land use, ignored because of, 122
Environment, physical: belonging to, discouraged in children, by postwar city, 101–5; and community organizing, 216–17; a multi-dimensional experience, 86; and psyche, influence on, 75–83; and social relations, views of social ecologists, 83; sociologists' conceptualization of, 85; and teenagers, 95
Environmental problems: of cities, and interdependence of their elements, 183
Everyday experience: non-obvious link with public policies, 202. See also Daily lives
Exchange philosophy: giving to get, 190
Exclusion: of others, by moving to suburbs, 73
Expenditures, capital and operating: for urban transportation, US and Canada, 32–3; See also Spending
Expressways: destruction caused by, 45–6; as products of authoritarian technology, 124
Eyes on the street: and physical diversity, 87; and safety, no guarantee of, 93; and street users, volume of, 87–8. See also Surveillance

Face-to-face contact: and cheaper housing costs, element of, 64; in downtown businesses, important to, 143; of urban gardeners, 207. See also Communication; Public contact
Factories: large-scale, and destruction of housing, 147. See also Industrial development; Industrial parks; Industrial sites; Industry
False Creek: large-scale project, Vancouver, 160
Farley, John: on children's friendships in high-rises, 107
Fava, Sylvia: on the suburban generation, 89
Federal Housing Administration (FHA): housing policies in US, tool of, 149; and large developers, favouring, 152; mortgage guarantees from, 212; political ideology behind policies of, 165; and red-lining, 151. See also Canada Mortgage and Housing Corporation
Financial gain: personal, as motive for home ownership, 145. See also Profit; Security
Fiscal policies: used to divert capital to housing, 148–9. See also Policies, public
Fishman, Robert: on Le Corbusier's politics, 174; on Le Corbusier's search for order, 84
Floors: important to children, 121
Ford, Henry: River Rouge plant of, 6

Forests: destruction of, 47–8

Fort Worth: road space needed, 10

Fossil fuels: exploitation of, and urban sprawl, 182. *See also* Gasoline; Oil

Foxden Road: in Don Mills area, 227

Fragmentation: of lives, concretized in built environment, 117–18; of local government, 124; of technologies, and built environment, 124–5. *See also* land-use: mix; land-use segregation; separation

Franklin, Ursula: on authoritarian design of infrastructure, 125; on technology, enslavement by, 163; on technologies, prescriptive vs holistic, 176–7

Freedom: taken by technology, 163

Free enterprise: and doctrine of survival of the fittest, 196

French, Marilyn: on definitions of power, 191

Fried, Marc: on emotional attachment to neighbourhood, 134

Friendship: children's, in high-rises and suburbs, 107, and mobility, 108; patterns of, and postwar city building, 83–90, personal, and built environment, 84–7, and physical environment, 87; in Don Mills area, 20, in Maitland Street area, 17, in Margueretta Street area, 18, vs public, 84–7, in St Jamestown area, 22. *See also* Acquaintances, casual; Public contact; Neighbours

Galileo: central to scientific revolution, 180

Gans, Herbert: and Jacobs, critique of, 72; on physical environment, 71; on self-selection hypothesis, 85; and suburbs, defender of, 71, evaluations of, 79, political participation in, 121

Garbage: awareness of, 202

Garden Cities: as healthy environments, 72; envisioned by Howard, 175; and physical image, its legacy, 175; their politics, 175. *See also* Howard, Ebenezer

Gardening: urban, as social process, 207

Gardens: and pesticide use, 205–6; community, in New York City, 218–19, and in South Bronx, 217; less vandalism in areas with, 217–18

Gardiner, Frederick: and Metro Toronto's infrastructure, 152; policies favouring large builders, 152–3

Gasoline: use as fuel, as cause of death in us, 47. *See also* Fossil fuels; Oil

General Motors: destruction of Detroit neighbourhood, 147

Geographical areas: as units of analysis for Toronto study, 87

Glazer, Nathan: on social life and physical form of cities, 72

Global restructuring: of capital, and community organizations, 215

Goldberg, Michael, and John Mercer: on how Canadian and us cities differ, 25, with respect to urban transit, 39

Golden Avenue: area of Toronto study, 226

Goodman, Paul and Percival: on city built for consumption, 170

Gottdiener, Mark: on land speculation, 58, 144; on local state's function of social control, 192; *Planned Sprawl*, 155; on politicians and developers, in suburbs, 154–5

Government, local: autonomy of, exploited by large developers, us, 159, as source of weakness, us, 157; large builders favoured by, 152–3; of central cities, vs suburban governments, 157; corporate mentality in, 161; and corporations, weak *vis-à-vis*, 119, 157; description of, 118–20; and development corporations, 157–8; and development industry, 150, staffed by, 167; fragmentation of, 124; and higher-level governments, link with large-scale development, 159–60, subordinate to, 118–20, 159–60, 193; and land-use regulation, 119; and homogeneity, promoted by, 60, 153; as not local, 118; and old buildings, destruction of, 150; participation, discouraged by, 161; and physical vs social services, 161; pro-growth policies of, 150–1, 153–5, in Montreal, New York City, Toronto, Vancouver, 154; and property, as power-over, 192, as regulator of, 118, 160–2, services and protects, 119; social services given up by, 118–19; structure, as corporations, 118, 160–2; technical matters, concerned with, 121; weakness of, and physical diversity, 156–60. *See also* Independent local authorities; Local state; Municipalities; Spending by cities

Government, metropolitan: of Toronto, created to build infrastructure, 152

Governments: in Broadacre City, withering away of, 172; and business, as ally, 166; dependence on, and failure of community organizations, 211; their expenditures, 32–3, *see also* spending by cities; higher-level, creating own functions, 118, 216, and large-scale development, promoters of, 60, 156, 159, 160, *see also* Governments, provincial; independence from, as key to success, 210; and large companies, favouring, 152–3; national, inefficiency of, 213–14, supported by daily choices, 194, *see also* nation-states; provincial, as builder of suburban infrastructure, Toronto, 152, *see also* Governments, higher-level; structure, and postwar city building, 156–62; suburban, and pro-growth policies, 154–5, *see also* Politics, local, in new cities. *See also* Policies, public; Political institutions; Political systems; Politics

Gowan Avenue: area of Toronto study, 226

Grand Avenue, Milwaukee, 66

Gratz, Roberta Brandes: on costly inflexibility of high-rises, 63; on costs of Co-Op City, 63; *The Living City*, 218; on self-help in South Bronx, 218

Great Depression: forcing local governments to give up social services, 119

Greenfields development: costs of, 58

Greenhouse: cooperative, 219

Greenhouse gases: produced by car emissions, 49. *See also* Gas; Oil; Pollution

Gross National Product (GNP): negative components, 178; tied to suburbs, 140

Growth coalition: business-labour, 140; central to capitalism, 140; and governments, joined by, 149; and suburbanization, 142. *See also* Truce

Gruen, Victor: on space devoted to car, 10

Gulliver Road: area of Toronto study, 224

Gutstein, Donald: on False Creek, Vancouver, 160; on interest-group liberalism, 167; on local government in Canada, ties to developers, 150

Hall, Peter: on Howard, Ebenezer, 175; on suburbs, 70–1

Hamilton, Ont.: mobility rates in, in 1850s, 108

Harbourfront Corporation, 158

Harlem, New York City: product of building boom, 11

Hart, Gary: private vs public life, 88

Harvey, David: on business district as sacred precinct, 169–70; on strikes in company towns, 144; on urban policies of US government, 148, 149; on working class, segregation of, and political action, 127

Haussman, Baron: destruction of downtown Paris, 56

Hayden, Dolores: on home as haven from work, 169; on the solar tenement, 218

Hierarchies: absent from, in successful community organizations, 211

High-rises: and children, social contacts of, 107; crime rates in, 92–3; and costs as form of development, 62–3; evaluations of, by residents, 77; fortification, need for, 122; as identity-denying, 77; and Le Corbusier, 173; maintenance costs of, 63; in Maitland Street area, 17; and middle class, built for, 122; neuroses in, 77; office towers, costs of, 65–6; and privatized activities, 110, *see also* Privatization; high profits associated with, 140; in St Jamestown area, 21; their unmanipulability, 78, 126

Highways: spending on, by governments, US and Canada, 32–3. *See also* Transportation

Hill, Richard: on urban growth policies in Michigan, 151

Hobbes, Thomas: on authority, need for, 181; on human nature, assumptions about, 195; Leviathan, the right to control, 192

Home: as commodity, 145; as sanctuary, 169

Homebuyers: role in decentralization and deconcentration, 144–5

Home ownership: defence against bolshevism, 165; Economic motives for, 144–5; and individualism, 163; level, in Canada and US vs in other countries, 168; sacredness of, in North American culture, 168–9

Homesteaders, urban: caring for neighbourhood, 135; role of personal choice in, 208

Homogeneity, physical: and detachment from local environment, 133; and government policies, 152, favouring large firms, 153; and housing as a commodity, 145; and postwar city building, feature of, 10–13; and technology and architecture of era, 11. See also Land-use: homogeneity; Land-use: mix; Land-use segregation

Honey pot: and self-destruction of diversity, 145–6. See also Land market

Hoover, Edgar M., and Raymond Vernon: on deconcentration's resistance to change, 8

Housing: cohousing as successful experiment, 219–20; as commodity, and physical homogeneity, 145; cheaper in "other economy," 64; costs greater with deconcentration of, 59, when heteronomous, 61–2, due to large developers, 60–4, in moving, 64–5, when new, 55, 58, when segregated, 59, when postwar, 55–65; destruction of, by expressways, 45, by urban renewal, 57–8; detached, and deconcentration, 8, 55, 145, in Levittowns, 4, see also Single-family homes; in Greenfields development, 58–9; heteronomous, defined, 61, see also Housing, political implications; household formation vs units built, 55; large-scale, costs greater, 59–64; new, US and Canada, 3, 55; personal choices for, importance for city, 207; and fiscal policy, 149; and investors, minimizing risk for, 149; political implications when built for us, 216, see also Housing, heteronomous; projects, French size limits, 4; rehabilitation, as cheaper than urban renewal, 57; segregation of, and duplication of goods and services, 59, evidence of, 55; self-help, in cooperatives, in South Bronx, 217–18; policies, for servicemen returning in 1940s, 149; unmanipulability, political implications of, 216, in suburbs, 78. See also High-rises

Houston: density and gasoline consumption, 47; home as workplace in, 169; public space, lack of, 131

Howard, Ebenezer: and built environment, impact of, 72; and city planning, ideas on, 174–5; on dismantling cities, 84; on private vs public contact, 84

Human nature: change in, as inevitable, 195

Hunters Point: New York City, large-scale development, financed by government, 154

Ideology: political, and postwar city building, 162–8

Imageability: of city, as important to user, 77

Incubation theory: that old buildings help business innovation, 67

Independence: achieved through consumption, 170. See also Self-sufficiency

Independent agencies. See Independent local authorities

Independent local authorities: as appointed bodies, 158; and deconcentration, 157; and infrastructure, large-scale, 158–9; large, housed in big buildings, 124; and large-scale development, 157; local government circumscribed by, 157; physical separation of, 124; power of, reinforced by technology, 124. See also Government, local

Indianapolis: downtown land devoted to cars, 42

Individualism: of North America, distinct, 162–4; and ownership, 163, 187; and postwar city building, 162–4

Individuality: and consumption of material goods, 162–3; as objectifying the built environment, 163

Industrial development: deconcentration of, as cause or effect of technology, 6, 143; in Sunbelt, created by US government policy, 151. *See also* Factories; Industry

Industrial parks: and business innovation, 67; homogeneity due to scale, 11

Industrial sites: on fringes of city, 5–6; large-scale, 5–6

Industry: large-scale, in sixteenth century, 30; odour, in Niagara area, 15. *See also* Factories

Inefficiency: of national governments, 213–14

Infill apartments: on Mrs Ivy, 201

Infrastructure: and compliance, 125; land prices and investment in, 61; and large bureaucracies, 124; large-scale, built by independent local authorities, 158–9; of Metro Toronto, 152–3; rebuilding of needed, 54; social services superseded by, 121

Innovation: in business, and postwar city building, 67

Insecurity: and feelings of separation from nature, 180–1

Institute for Local Self-Reliance (ILSR): work of in the South Bronx, 217

Institutions: large, supported by daily choices, 116, our dependence on, 212–13; as patterns of beliefs, 185; as providers of our needs, 116; their separation in large-scale buildings, 124. *See also* Bureaucracies; Corporations; Large organizations; Nation-states

"Integrated communities": Don Mills as example, 5; homogeneity due to scale, 11; the Levittowns as examples, 4–5. *See also* Land-use: mix

Intelligence: stimulated by physical diversity, 76

Interest-group liberalism: as political philosophy of postwar city building, 166–7. *See also* Ideology; Pluralism

Interstate-highway program: and deconcentration and decentralization, 152

Italians: in Margueretta Street and Sully-Cinder areas, 111

Italy: fascism in, admired by Le Corbusier, 174

Ivy, Mrs: creator of semi-public space, 201

Jackson, Kenneth: on density of Los Angeles, 9; on sprawl and detached housing, 8; on US suburbs, annexation of, 34

Jacobs, Jane: on border vacuums, 46; on cataclysmic money, 147–8; central thesis, 13; *Cities and the Wealth of Nations*, 193; on city vitality, determinants of, 13; on crime, critiques of, 92–3; critique by Gans, 72, by Mumford, 93; on physical diversity, definition of, 13, and public contact, 84, and safety on streets, 92, self-destruction of, 145–6; on eyes on the street, 87; on housing design and mobility, 108; on inefficiency of large organizations, 213; on interdependence of city parts, 183; *Life and Death of American Cities*, 13, 84; on the national economy, fiction of, 193; new ideas need old buildings, 67; on parks, 86, 183; on physical monotony's lack of stimulation, 76; on taking responsibility for the street, 103

Jobs: lost, as cost of urban renewal, 56; personal choices about, and urban design, 208–9; and quality of the environment, 203; and small businesses, 68

John Hancock building: expensive high-rise, 65–6

Jones, Roger: on medieval view of space, 180

Journey to work: in sixteenth century, 30; in various North American cities, 44. *See also* Separation of workplace from home

Juvenile crime: committed closer to home, 98; and long blocks, 111–12; "other thefts," as index for, 110; and physical design, sensitivity to, 97–8; and physical diversity, lack of, 111. *See also* Children; Crime; Teenagers

Juvenile delinquency: and adventure, need for, 102; and postwar city building, 109–13. *See also* Children; Crime; Teenagers

Katz, Michael B.: on mobility rates in 1850s in Hamilton, Ont., 108n
Katznelson, Ira: on politics of workplace as separate from residence, 127
Kensington Market: Toronto, and Courage My Love, 209–10; in Spadina area, 23, 24
Krishnamurti, J.: on conflict, 197

Labour: growth coalition with business, 140; replaced by capital, and vice versa, 67–8, 218. *See also* Working class
Labour unions: apolitical, tradition of, 128; avoided by vertical disintegration, 67, 143; as reason for businesses leaving central city, 127, 143
Laissez faire: myth of, 166
Land: as commodity, 31, 186; costs, and decentralization, 143, and speculators, 58; per unit for high-rises, 62–3; as factor of production, 186; impersonal, and deindustrialization, 188, and large-scale development, 187–8; prices, high due to urban renewal, 56–7, and land use, intertwined, 145; as tool, 186. *See also* Land market; Land speculation; Land use
Landlords: decried by Wright, 172
Land market: and exclusive ownership, 186; and homogeneity, product of, 145, 187; and land-use segregation, product of, 145; monopoly, and housing costs, 60–1. *See also* Honey pot; Land; Land speculation; Land use; Market
Land speculation: and deconcentration and decentralization, 144; and leapfrog development, 144. *See also* Land; Speculators
Land use: homogeneity of, boring to children, 101, defined, 11, and zoning, 155–6, *see also* Land-use: mix, Land-use segregation; and land-price intertwined, 145; and local government, major focus of, 119; mix, in Don Mills area, 20, 148, in Niagara Street area, 16, and urban vitality, 13, walking encouraged by, 41. *See also* Diversity, physical; Fragmentation; Land-use segregation
Land-use plans: and separation of activities, 119. *See also* Planning; Zoning
Land-use segregation: and awareness of daily choices, 202; and children, cut off from adult world by, 102–3, meeting places of, 108; and costs of city services, 51, 52, 53; and decision-making process, 123; and fragmentation of politics, 128; and government policies, 152–6; and insensitivity to environment, 122–3; and land market, 31, 145; and large firms, growth of, 146; and North American culture, 168–9; and dampening of political controversy, 123; and responsibility for places, 123, in sixteenth century, 30; and transportation costs, 30, 41, 44; and water and sewage costs, 50. *See also* Fragmentation; Homogeneity; Land-use: mix; Separation
Land-use separation. *See* Land-use segregation
Large companies: favoured by governments, 152. *See also* Corporations; Large firms
Large firms: costs to local community, 67–8; and downtown location, need for, 141, *see also* Face-to-face contact; move to suburbs to escape labour unions, 127. *See also* Corporations; Large companies
Large organizations: and Alinsky groups, 215; beliefs in legitimacy of, 213; daily lives embedded in, 212; and economic stagnation, 213; independence from, as key to success, 210; inefficiency of, 213; participation in, discouraged, 213. *See also* Corporations; Institutions; Nation-states
Large-scale buildings: and crime, 96–7; mixed with small, in Maitland Street area, 18; difficult reuse of, 63; in St Jamestown area, 21. *See also* Buildings; Large-scale development
Large-scale development: vs Buddhist economics, 189; and children's social contacts, 107; diversity destroyed by, 147–8; feature of postwar city building, 3–6; and impersonal land, 187–8; and independent local authorities, supported by, 157; interest in local politics discouraged by, 121; and land market, 145; and property

as power-over, 192; in the suburbs, and government approval, 154. *See also* Large-scale buildings; Large-scale projects

Large-scale projects: costs of, 66–7; and dependent local governments, 159; and higher-level governments, 159; and lack of local autonomy, Toronto, Vancouver, 160; with offices, 3–4. *See also* Large-scale buildings; Large-scale developments

Leapfrog development: costs in services, 52, 54; and land speculation, 144

Le Corbusier: and central city, destruction of, 56, 173, 174; on city planning, 173–4; and despot, the need for to realize his plans, 173; and high-rises, 173; housing project in Pessac, France, 121; and order in architecture, search for, 84; and Paris, proposals for razing the downtown of, 56; and postwar city building, influence on, 56, 173–4, 175; his politics and planning, 173–4; on private vs public contact, 84; *Urbanisme*, 173; *La ville radieuse*, 173–4

Leicester, England: home ownership in, 145

Les Invalides: large-scale project of Louis XIV, 173

Léveillée, Jacques: on interest-group liberalism in Montreal, 167

Leviathan: Hobbes' state, the right to control, 192. *See also* Power; Power-over

Levitt, Abraham: developer of large-scale projects in suburbs, 4, 5, 147; and economies of scale in Housing, 60. *See also* Developers, large

Levittown, N.Y.: its decline in physical homogeneity, 121

Levittown, N.J.: residents' political participation, 121; subject of Gans' research, 71

Levittowns: built by large corporations, 148; homogeneity due to scale, 11; large-scale development, examples of, 4–5

Liberal party, Canada: election gift of Harbourfront to Toronto, 158

Likes and dislikes: about neighbourhoods, 74–83; as psychological phenomena, 75; in St Jamestown area, 21. *See also* Evaluations

Local authorities. *See* Independent local authorities

Local autonomy: lack of, in Canada, and large-scale projects, 160; problem of, 119. *See also* Government, local, autonomy of; Governments, higher-level; Toronto; Vancouver

Local state: function of social control, 192. *See also* Government, local; Independent local authorities; Municipalities

Locke, John: on property ownership, 164; on work and property, 185

Lofland, Lyn: on cars and public space

Logan, John R. and Harvey Molotch: on costs of large-scale projects, 66; on no-growth legislation, 159–60; on suburbs seeking large-scale projects, 155; *Urban Fortunes*, 155

Long blocks: children bored by, 101; and juvenile crime, 111. *See also* Block length; Diversity, physical; Short blocks

Lorimer, James: on developers in Canada, 150, 153; and interest-group liberalism, data on, 167; on monopoly of land market, 60; research on local government, 150

Los Angeles: density increase, 9; downtown land devoted to car, 10, 42; public space, lack of, 131

Louisville, KY: and Broadway project, costly office project, 66; shoe stores in, 197

Love: excluded from economics, 190; not a zero-sum game, 198

Love Canal, Niagara Falls: mass media's role in, 129

Lovins, Amory: on costs of oil from Persian Gulf, 214

Lowi, Theodore: on interest-group liberalism, 166; on suburbs as failure in citizenship, 73, 122

Lynch, Kevin: *Image of the City*, 77; on image of the city, 76–7

McCamant, Kathryn, and Charles Durrett: on cohousing, 220

MacKay, Patricia: on cars and children, 103

Madison Avenue: area of Toronto study, 226

Magid, Eleanor: and community art workshop in New York City, 210–12

Maitland Street: area of Toronto study, 17–18, 223

Manchester, England: large-scale factories in, 213

Manhattan: the solar tenement in, 218

Man-Made America: book reflecting spirit of postwar building, 3

Margueretta Street: area of Toronto study, 18–20, 223; juvenile crime in, 111–13

Markesen, J.R., and D.T. Scheffman: on monopoly of land market in Toronto area, 61

Market: as economic institution, 186; for housing, and caring for neighbourhood, 134–5, and urban homesteaders, 208; for office space, from growing firm size, 141; and scarcity, dependence on, 182; and property as power-over, 191–2. *See also* Kensington Market; Land market

Market Square, Winnipeg: replaced by parking and police, 129

Market Street East: example of large-scale development, Philadelphia, 4

Marx, Karl: on conflict as reality, 194; and Darwin, admirer of, 196; on property as political power, 185

Mass culture: and destruction of working-class public life, 128. *See also* Culture

Mass media: and consumption, 170; and informal politics, destructive of, 129; and isolation, 170; and national vs local affairs, 193; and postwar city building, role in, 170; and public life, destructive of, 128

Meadowvale, Ont.: example of large-scale residential development, 5

Media. *See* Mass media

Melbourne: services, savings on, from building housing in central city, 50

Men: white, upper-middle class, as builders of suburbs, 103

Merchandise: quality, in St Jamestown area, 22

Merry, Sally: on Crime Prevention Through Environmental Design, 96

Merton Street: area of Toronto study, 224

Michelson, William: on built environment and behaviour, 85; on self-selection hypothesis, 85; on transportation habits of urban residents, 41

Michelson, William, and Ellis Roberts: on land-use segregation and socialization of children, 102–3; on suburbs, built by men for women, 113

Michigan: urban growth policies in, 151

Milwaukee, WI: Grand Avenue, costly office project in, 66

Mix of old and new buildings: and ideology of progress, 182; and involvement in neighbourhood, 133; and vitality, determinant of, 13. *See also* New buildings; New development; Old buildings

Mobility: of businesses, in Spadina Avenue area, 23; of children in city, 100; rates, in Hamilton, Ont. in 1850s, 108n, in postwar city, 108; residential, and children's social life, 108, in Don Mills area, 20, and housing design in suburbs, 108, and housing prices, 64–5, in Maitland Street area, 17, in Niagara Street area, 15, 16, in Spadina Avenue area, 23

Mobilization of bias: against raising certain issues, 123

Money: and conflict, source of, 211; as problem-solving device, 189–90; as zero-sum game, 197–8. *See also* Cataclysmic money; Economics; Profit

Monopoly: of land markets in Canada by big developers, 60–1

Monotony: physical, as disorienting, 76–7

Montreal: annexation of Pointe-aux-Trembles, 1983, 34; interest-group liberalism in, 167; large-scale projects in downtown of, 154

Morris, William: influence on Le Corbusier, 84

Mortgages: guaranteed for returning servicemen, 1940s, 149; payments deducted from income, US, 149. *See also* Politics, public

Moses, Robert: and Co-Op City, 4; and Cross Bronx Expressway, 45–6; as head of Port Authority of New York, 154, 157; South Bronx destroyed by, 218

Multi-dimensional: character of cities that work, 210–11, 217–21; Cheyenne Greenhouse, 219; Cohousing, 219

Mumford, Lewis: on buildings as reflection of political culture, 127; critique of Jacobs' views on crime, 93; on urban redevelopment through history, 126–7, see also Urban renewal

Municipalities: as corporations, 160–2; as large-scale, 161. See also Governments, local; Independent local authorities

National economy: fiction of, 193. See also Economy

Nation-state: as a destructive set of beliefs, 192–4; large-scale, considered normal, 116, prerequisite to big government, 116; and mass media, focus for, 193; and power-over, 194; primacy of, 192–4; as recent phenomenon, 192; as a war machine, 118. See also Governments, national

Native people: their concept of ownership, 186

Nature: blindness to our links with it, 184; as cooperative, 196; seen as separate by the scientific method, 180. See also Reality

Negotiation: art of, and exclusive ownership, 187. See also Political skills; Politics, informal; Public contact; Public life; Self-governance; Self-management; Street-level government

Neighbourhoods: evaluations of, subjective and objective, 75; knowledge of, and caring about, 133–4; reclaimed, as example of physical diversity, 218; threatened by decisions made elsewhere, 132; working-class, politics and street life in, 128

Neighbours: awareness of importance of, 208; contact with, and density, 86; and physical diversity, 87; in suburbs, avoidance of, 130. See also Acquaintances, casual; Friendship; Public contact

New buildings: economic explanations for, 139–42; energy use in construction of, 62; interest in local politics discouraged by, 121, see also Participation; and pro-growth policies of local government, 151. See also Construction, new; Mix of old and new buildings; New development; Old buildings

New cities: and physical services in, need for, 120–1; their politics, 120–1. See also Suburbs

New development: costs for services to, 150

Newman, Oscar: critiques of, 92–3; on high-rises, costs of, 63, crime rates in, 92

Newman, Peter, and Jeffrey Kenworthy: on urban density and car use, 40, and gasoline consumption, 47

Newness: of postwar cities, 10–11, 13, and detachment from local environment, 133. See also Homogeneity

Newton, Isaac: central to scientific revolution, 180

New urban environment. See Postwar city building

New York City: Battery Park City, large-scale development, 147; children afraid to leave homes in, 109; housing in, maintenance costs of, 63; large-scale development in, 154; self-help organizations in, 217–19; suburbs of, housing density in, 7; worker space in offices of, 7. See also Manhattan; South Bronx

Niagara Street: area of Toronto study, 15–16, 223

No-growth legislation: has little effect, 159–60

Noise: lowers property values, 46; in Spadina Avenue area, 24

Non-place urban realm: description of postwar city, 179

Normal: the local environment considered as, 132, the modern urban environment, 203–4, the physical infrastructure, 125. See also Amnesia; Awareness

Novick, R. Marvyn: on home as sanctuary for children, 106
Nowlan, David: on savings from building housing downtown, 51
Nursery schools: designed by children, 114

Oakland Technology Park: large-scale development, 151
Office space: demand for, from large firms, 141; per office worker, 7; in suburbs, growth of, 142
Office tower: as cathedral in North America, 169–70
Office workers: contribution to costs of services of workplace, 123
Oil: cost of, from Persian Gulf, 214; and urban transportation, use of, 47. *See also* Gasoline
Old buildings: and depreciation allowance, 150; destruction of, because of tax laws, 149–50; and new ideas, 67; in Ontario Street area, 22. *See also* Mix of old and new buildings
Olympia and York: Canadian developer of Battery Park City, 147
Ontario, province of: builder of infrastucture in Toronto suburbs, 61. *See also* Governments, higher-level
Ontario Housing Corporation: public housing in St Jamestown area, 21
Ontario Street: area in Toronto Study, 22–3, 225
Orange County, CA: example of industrial deconcentration and decentralization, 6; vertical disintegration in, 143
Organization: new approaches to, 214–21
Organizing: local level, problems of, 212. *See also* Alinsky groups, Community organizations
Orren, Karen: on legitimacy of corporation, 167
Owner-occupied housing: its separation from rented housing, 169; as source of cheap rental units, 64. *See also* Housing; Renters
Ownership: collective, as problematic, 185–6; defined as rules about transfer, 186; exclusive, and separation from nature, 186, and social concept of space, 187, and suburbs, motive for, 187, vs inclusive, 186–8; of land, and individualism, 187; and market system, 186; meanings of, 185–6; native peoples' concept of, 186; of property, redefined by Mrs Ivy, 203; relaxation of, and urban vitality, 201. *See also* Property

Packard, Vance: on mobility in Azusa, 108
Palos Verdes Estates: conformity to physical design in, 126
Paris: urban renewal in nineteenth century in, 56
Parking: land required for, 10, 42, 44
Parkinson, C. Northcote: on inexorable growth of bureaucracy, 193, 216
Parks: as interdependent with rest of city, 183; and public contact, 86
Parr, Alfred Eide: on intelligence and physical diversity, 76
Participation: cooperative, 214–21; in large organizations, discouraged, 213; political, in Levittown, NJ, 121, its low level, 116–17, and postwar city building, discouraged by, 126. *See also* Elections, local; Political interest
Pedestrian traffic: in Maitland Street area, 18; in St Jamestown area, 22, 41. *See also* Walking
Perin, Constance: on children, 106; on separation, of owners from renters, 168–9, of workplace from home, 169; on social conflict, 164; on suburbs and underdeveloped political skills, 130
Personality: as central to evaluation of neighbourhoods, 75. *See also* Psyche
Pessac, France: Le Corbusier's design modified, 121
Phoenix: mode of travel to work, 44

Physical determinism: fallacy, attributed to Jacobs, 84

Places: awareness of, 200–2; and local government, as concern of, 119; and politics, connected to, 118, instrumental view of, 123; for politics, special, 130; responsibility for, and land-use separation, 123. *See also* Space

Place Ville Marie, Montreal: large-scale project, its homogeneity due to scale, 4, 11

Planners: advocate, and citizens' groups, 176, and scientific approach, 176; as consultants, 172; and developers, employed by, 172, in contact with, 171; influence on social life seen as limited, 71; as idealists, 172; political role of, 171–2; and postwar city building, 171–7; on private vs public contact, 84–5; on social life and built environment, 83–4; their social-science training, 175–6; visionary, and views about society, 172–7. *See also* Land use

Planning: and architecture, indivisible, 173; by children, 113–14; for children, attitudes toward, 99–100; and cities that work, 221; departments, and citizen participation, 103, as facilitators of development, 172; Le Corbusier's ideas on, 173–4; process, and democratic politics, 176; Wright's ideas on, 172–3. *See also* Land use

Plans, land-use: preparation of, as function of planners, 171; role in land-use regulation, 159

Play: seriousness of, for children, 100

Playgrounds: private, seen as substitute for social life of children, 106

Pluralism: and planning practice, 176; political philosophy of postwar city building, 166–7. *See also* Ideology; Interest-group liberalism

Pointe-aux-Trembles: annexation by Montreal, 1983, 34

Polanyi, Karl: *The Great Transformation*, 186; on land market, 145; on land as a fictitious commodity, 145, 186

Police: as inexact source of crime rates, 91

Policies, public: and daily experience, non-obvious link with, 202; of Canadian provinces, and deconcentrated development, 151–2; and industrial development in sunbelt, 151; and postwar city building, 148–56; physical vs social, of local government, 161; pro-growth, of local government, 150, in Michigan, 151. *See also* Choices, daily; Fiscal policies; Housing policies; Taxes; Tax laws

Political activity: no public space for, 130; restricted to certain places, 124, 130

Political culture: North American, lacking in local dimension, 120; reflected in buildings, 127. *See also* Culture

Political efficacy: of working class, and physical diversity, 127

Political explanations: for decentralization, 143; for deconcentration, 144; for large firms moving to the suburbs, 127; for postwar city building, 148–68

Political institutions: of North America, and postwar city building, 191–8. *See also* Government, local; Governments

Political issues: and built environment, shaped by, 122–3; around instrumental view of place, 123; local, seen as technical, 121

Political legitimacy: of large corporations, 212–13

Political participation. *See* Participation, political

Political self-consciousness: local, absent in North America, 120, 207

Political skills: as casualty of suburbs, 73. *See also* Negotiation; Street-level government

Political system: and economic demands, facilitator of, 166; and power as control, 191; symbiosis with large companies, 116

Politics: authentic, as cooperation, 135, and daily life, 117–18, defined, 117–18, and places, connected with, 118, 200, and small-scale spaces, 118; beliefs about, expressed in postwar city, 199; of Broadacre City, 173; and cities, intertwined, 135; conventional, alienation from, 204, as conflict, 135, 194–8, defined, 115–16, as influence and power, 191, as power-over, 135, as unappealing to average citizen, 116; as cooperation and energy, 191; and economics, 115–16; of Howard, 175; informal, casualty of postwar city building, 129, *see also* Street-level government, Politics; local, interest in, discouraged by environment's unmanipulability, 121, in new cities, 120–1, *see also* Government: Suburban; seen as petty, 131, 132–3, concerned with places, 119, and technical issues, 121; passively consumed, 129; and postwar city building, 115–35; redefinition needed, 135; residence-oriented, 127–8; scientific, underlying postwar city, 181; and the street, pushed from, 129; of suburbs, 120–1; and urban design, 174. *See also* Government, local; Governments

Pollution: as cost of postwar city building, 47–9

Popenoe, David: on privatization, 110–11, 131

Porches, front: destruction of, as avoidance of social contact, 164; and street life, 88–9

Port Authority of New York: independent local authority, builder of large projects, 154, 157

Portuguese: in Niagara Street area, 15, 16

Postwar cities: expression of ideology of growth, 179; and scientific politics, 181–2

Postwar city building: and authority, expression of need for, 181; and children, uninteresting for, 101–2; and civic responsibility, discouraged by, 103; and crime, 90–8; and deaths of forests and humans, 49; economic costs of, 29–69; its features, 3–13; and government structure, 156–62; and juvenile delinquency, 109–13; political explanations for, 148–68; and political ideology, 162–8, 179; and politics, its impact on, 120–34; social costs of, 70–114 and vandalism, 109; and visionary planners, influenced by, 172–5. *See also* Postwar urban development

Postwar urban development: and authentic politics, destructive of, 117; and compliance, 126–7; legitimized by scientific approach, 176; as normal. *See also* Large-scale development; Postwar city building

Power: as control relationship, 191, *see also* Power-over; as creative, 191, in Alinsky groups, 215, of Pat Roy and Stewart Scriver, 210, *see also* Power-to; Dahl's ideas on, 191n; government, acquired through creation of functions, 216; individual, sapped by representative system, 215;

Power over: and conventional politics, 135, private property as, 185, 191–2;

Power to: as an attribute, 191, as a creative force, 191

Private life: vs public life, 88

Privatization: of American life in suburbs, 8, 110–11; encourages juvenile crime, 110; of urban space, 130, 131. *See also* Public contact

Problem-solving: money as poor tool for, 189–90

Production: separated from administration, in large firms, 141; system, of food, supported by personal choices, 116. *See also* Consumption; Distribution system

Profit: and economics, only criterion of, 189, *see also* Financial gain; in high-rise construction, 141; maximizing, as unconnected to success, 210

Progress: ideology of, as coming from scarcity, 182; preoccupation with, and postwar city building, 182. *See also* Boosterism; Policies, public: progrowth

Property: expropriation, and local state, 192; meanings of, 185–6; ownership, redefined by Mrs Ivy, 202; as political power, 185; as power-over, 191–2; private, and concept of space, 187, as economic institution underlying postwar cities, 185–8, ideology behind postwar city building, 164–7 and sanctity of, used by developers, 165; servicing and protection of, function of local government, 119; values, concern for, and physical homogeneity, 145, and suburban politics, central concern of, 120. *See also* Land, impersonal; Ownership

Pruitt-Igoe: St Louis housing project, destroyed by children, 95, 110, rejected by homeless, 162, short lifespan, 62
Psyche: influence of built environment on, 75–83. *See also* Personality; Psychological response
Psychological response: to the built environment, 73, 75–83. *See also* Personality; Psyche; Purity; Reality
Public contact: and collective action, required for, 200; and crime, discouraged by, 94, 95; Howard on, 84; in parks, 86; vs private, 95, as linked to the built environment. *See also* Acquaintances, casual; Face-to-face contact; Friendship; Neighbours; Politics, informal; Public life; Street-level management
Public domain: as meaningless in postwar city, 130
Public lands: called private, 186. *See also* Ownership; Property
Public life: and private, dialogue between, discouraged by urban design, 88; pushed off street, 129; of street, and front porches, 88–9, 164. *See also* Politics, informal; Public contact
Public policy. *See* Policies, public
Public spaces: lack of, for politics, 130; use of, discouraged by car, 88. *See also* Places; Spaces; Squares
Pullman: company town with fierce strikes, 144
Purity: the desire for, 73. *See also* Psychological response

Railway companies: created to get profit from suburban development, 168
Reagan, Ronald: policies toward central city, 148
Reality: creating our own, 196; as determined by observer, 184; physical, of interpenetrating elements, 183, nature of, and values behind, 180–2, new conceptions of, 182–4; as not a zero-sum game, 197. *See also* Nature; Psychological responses
Red-lining: in inner cities, supported by government policies, 151
Reed, Richard Ernie: on housing rehabilitation, 57
Rehabilitation: of housing, as cheaper than urban renewal, 57, as job-intensive, 57
Reisman, David: critic of suburbs, 71; *The Lonely Crowd*, 71
Relationship: as definition of a building, 183; as definition of a particle, 182
Renaissance Centre: Detroit, large-scale office complex, 4
Renner, Michael: on transportation as pollution source, 47–8
Renters: cultural bias against, 168; separation of, from owners, 168–9
Representative structure: of local government, and low participation, 161
Representative system: Alinsky's view of, 215; as natural one for large-scale entities, 117; its weaknesses, 117. *See also* Democracy
Residence: focus of politics on, 127–8; separation of workplace from, part of culture, 169, and politics, 127, 144, and urban transportation, 30, 41, 44. *See also* Home; Housing
Residential areas: exclusive, the desire for, 73
Residential development: deconcentration of, 7–10; densities of, in Canadian suburbs, 8, in the US, 7–8; large-scale, 4. *See also* High-rises; Home ownership; Housing; Large-scale development
Retail: and manufacturing, costs to, of postwar city building, 65–8; shoe stores, in Louisville, 197. *See also* Shopping centres
River Rouge Plant: large-scale development, 6, 146
Roads, Michael J.: on cooperation with nature, 196–7
Robina Avenue: area of Toronto study, 224
Rockefeller Centre: as prototype of downtown office complex, 3
Roncek, Dennis: on large-scale development and crime, 96–7
Rosedale: area of Toronto study, 226
Rudofsky, Bernard: on vandalism-prone schools, 109–10

Safety, feelings of: in Don Mills area, 20; in Maitland Street area, 17; in Niagara Street area, 15, 16; and physical diversity, 97; in St Jamestown area, 21; in Spadina Avenue area, 23

St Jamestown, Toronto: area of Toronto study, 21–2, 224; large-scale residential development, 4; walking habits of residents, 41

St John, Craig: on evaluation of neighbourhoods, 75

Sale, Kirkpatrick: on costs of high-rises, 65–6

Sandels, Stina: on children and traffic rules, 104

San Francisco: as special case in spending on infrastructure, 35, 50

Sargent, Charles: on land speculation and farmers, 144

Satellite cities: in Howard's plan for Garden Cities, 175

Satin, Mark: on creating our own prison, 199

Scale: of city, geared to adults, 100; and land-use homogeneity, 11. See also Large scale; Small scale

Scarcity: essential to market system, 182; fear of, and preoccupation with progress, 181, 182; and separation from nature, 181

Schattschneider, E.E.: on conflict as essential part of politics, 194–5

Schumacher, E.F.: on Buddhist economics, 189; on economics as subjective, 188–9

Scientific approach: legitimizing postwar city building, 176

Scientific method: applied to study of humans, 181; and planning, 176; and separation from nature, 180

Scientific revolution: ideology of, 180

Scott, A.J.: and deconcentrated industrial development, reasons for, 6; and incubation theory, critique of, 67; on need for firms to be in central city, 141; on vertical disintegration of firms, 143

Scriver, Stewart: owner of Courage My Love, 209–10

Security: economic, from home ownership, 144. See also Financial gain

Self-governance: frustrated by sprawl of suburbs, 130; in Garden Cities, 175. See also Self-management; Street-level government

Self-help: in South Bronx, 217

Self-management: block-level, and physical diversity, 131, 132–3. See also Eyes on the street; Politics, informal; Self-governance; Street-level government

Self-selection: hypothesis about built environment and behaviour, 85

Self-sufficiency: and Broadacre City, 172–3; and North American individualism, 162–3. See also Independence

Sennett, Richard: on avoidance of social contact, 164; on meaninglessness of public domain, 130; on purity of residential environment, 73; The Uses of Disorder, 73

Separation: of administration from production, in large firms, 141; from nature, and awareness of our links with it, 184, and from each other, 83, 181, and insecurity, 180, and prediction, 183–4; and values behind postwar city, 180–4; physical, of technologies, 125; of renters from owners, 168–9; of workplace from home, as rule of culture, 169, and politics, 127, 144. See also Fragmentation; Land use: mix; Land-use segregation; Land-use separation

Servicemen: guarantee of housing mortgages for, 149

Services, municipal: costs for high-rises, 62; for new development, 150; provision of considered administrative, 132. See also Government, local; Social services

Sewage and sanitation: spending on, by cities, 49–51

Shopping centres: in Levittowns, 5; raising costs to business and to consumers, 66–7. See also Retail

Short blocks: as determinant of vitality, 13; invite caring for neighbourhood, 133. See also Block length; Diversity, physical; Long blocks

Sidewalks: as places for informal politics, 130. See also Public contact

Simmel, Georg: on withdrawal from city, 200

Single-family dwelling units (SFDUS). *See* Single-family homes

Single-family homes: and deconcentration, 55, 145; and neurotic patients, 163; in Niagara Street area, 16; percent of housing, US and Canada, 8, 55; and privatization, 110; production of, as goal of growth coalition, 140. *See also* Housing, detached

Slum housing: as high-priced land use, 57

Small businesses: as creators of jobs, 68; as crime deterrent, 97; efficiency of, 213

Small scale: important to children, 101; spaces, as incubator of authentic politics, 118

Smith, Michael Peter: on determining role of large developers, 147

Smith, Rhys: on land monopoly in Calgary, 60

Social action: and urban design, 217. *See also* Collective action; Community organizing; Diversity, physical

Social contact: avoidance of, in North America, 164. *See also* Public contact

Social control: purpose of local state, 192. *See also* Power

Social ecology: on relating to nature and to each other, 83, 181, 220

Socializing: of children, discouraged by postwar city building, 105–9

Social life: and built environment, 71–2, 83–9, 105–9

Social process: of urban gardening, 207

Social sciences: training for planners, 175–6

Social services: ignored in favour of infrastructure, 121; of municipalities, taken over by higher-level governments, 118–19

Sociologists: and built environment, interest in, 72; and physical environment, concept of, 86; and private contact, focus on, 84

The Solar Tenement: cooperative housing and ecology, 218

South and West: cities of, annexations by, 33, elections, turnout in, 120, spending on street maintenance in, 36; and defence contracts, 151

South Bronx: New York City, self-help organizations in, 217–18

South End, Boston: as a result of building boom, 11

Space: awareness of uses of, 200–2; exclusive ownership and concept of, 187; impersonal, and homogeneity, 187, *see also* Land: impersonal; medieval and Renaissance views of, 180; temporary use of, and urban vitality, 201; unprogrammed, important to children, 101–2, and teenagers' socializing, 102; user-designed, 220. *See also* Places; Public spaces; Unmanipulability

Spadina Avenue: area of Toronto study, 23–4, 225; and Courage My Love, 209–10

Sparrows Point Plant: of Bethlehem Steel, inefficiency of, 213; large-scale factory on fringe of city, 6, 146

Speculation, land. *See* Land speculation; Speculators

Speculators: decried by Wright, 172; and housing costs, 58. *See also* Land speculation

Spencer, Herbert: and survival of the fittest, 195–6

Spending by cities: on sewage and sanitation, US and Canada, 49–51; on streets, US and Canada, 35–7; on urban Transit, US and Canada, 37–9; world-wide on urban transportation, 29–30. *See also* Expenditures

Spirn, Anne Whiston: on interdependence of built environment, 183

Sprawl: Broadacre City as prototype, 173; and detached homes, 8, 55; as inexact term, 13; self-governance frustrated by, 130; in Toronto area, and government policies, 152. *See also* Decentralization; Deconcentration

Spurr, Peter: on walk-ups as cheapest form of housing, 62, 63

Squares, public: as places for politics, 130. *See also* Public spaces

Squires, Gerald: *Unequal Partnerships*, 157–8

Stern, Martin: on cost of land taken by cars, 42–4; underestimation of costs of car, 43–4

Streetcar: as spur to building boom, 11

Street-level government: and physical diversity, 87–8. *See also* Negotiation; Political skills; Politics, informal; Public contact; Public life; Self-governance; Self-management; Street-level management

Street-level management: impossible in suburbs, 207. *See also* Politics, street-level; Street-level government

Street life: improved by front yards, 205; working-class, and built environment, 129. *See also* Street-level government

Streets: Spending on, in US and Canadian cities, 35–9

Stress: withdrawal from, and suburban dream, 163.

Suburban dream: desired by neurotic patients, 163

Suburbanization: central to growth of GNP, 140

Suburbs: advantages of, 79; as avoidance of social contact, 164; and children, not really built for, 113, stunting their social life, 106; choice to live in, and long-term effect, 202–3; and citizenship, as failure in, 73, 122; as communities, illusory, 207; and community organizing, 216; critiques of, 70; defended, against critics of, 71–2; energy needed for services to, 53; factory construction in, in South and West, 151; their heterogeneity, 13; and mobility, promoted by housing design, 108; and office space, as location for, 142; politics of, 120–1, attractive to large firms, 127, not street-level, 130; and privatization, of space, 131, and juvenile crime, 110; as refuge from dirt, noise, and crowds, 79; social isolation in, designed into housing, 109; social life of, unaffected by physical design, 71. *See also* New cities

Suffolk County: Long Island, land speculation in, 58; politicians and developers in, 155

Sully-Cinder: area of Toronto study, 226; juvenile crime in, 111–13

Sunbelt. *See* South and West

Support: for physical form of city, and personal choices, 208; for political system, decline in, 204

Surveillance: of children, and physical diversity, 111. *See also* Eyes on the street

Sweat equity: in self-help groups in South Bronx, 218

Synergy: reduction in, caused by cars, 43

Taylor, E.P.: developer on Don Mills, Canada, 5

Taxes: as reason for decentralization, 143

Tax laws: and large firms, encouraged by, 153; and old buildings, destroyed by, 149–50

Technologies: fragmentation of, and built environment, 124–5

Technology: anti-democratic nature of, 124; and decentralization, as reason for, 143; and deconcentration, as reason for, 143; as enslaver, 163; holistic, doer in control, 177; prescriptive, demanding compliance, 177; as saviour, 176; and separation of production from administration, 141

Teenagers: in Don Mills area, 20; and physical environment, 95

Thompson, Wilbur: on business innovation and old buildings, 67; on slum housing as high-priced land use, 57

Thorncliffe Park: area of Toronto study, 225

Toronto: Alinsky groups in, 215; atypical city, 3; construction freeze in, 160; downtown, housing and transportation costs in, 51, land devoted to streets and parking in, 44; density gradient of, 8; government of, approval of large-scale projects, 154; policies promoting sprawl in, 152; Harbourfront Corporation in, 158; its low-density development, 47; land monopoly and housing costs in, 61; lack of local autonomy, and large-scale projects in, 160; metropolitan government, not local, 118, and infrastructure, 152; the study, areas studied, 14–24, 223–7, on diversity and juvenile crime, 110–13, on evaluations by residents of density, 82, on evaluations by residents of neighbourhoods, 79–83, on land-use mix and walking, 41, on safety and physical diversity, 97, on social life and physical environment, 86–9; suburbs of, land speculation in, 58, politicians and developers in, 155; worker space in office buildings of, 7

Tower City Project: costly office project, Cleveland, 66

Traffic: in Don Mills area, 20; in Maitland Street area, 18; in Margueretta Street area, 18. *See also* Cars; Transportation

Transit: minimal use of land by, 43; in Howard's plan, 175; service, in US and Canada compared, 39; spending, by US and Canadian governments, 32, 37–9. *See also* Transportation technology; Urban transportation

Transportation technology: and building booms, 11; and deconcentration, 30–1; and land-use segregation, 30–1

Truce: postwar, between business and labour, 140. *See also* Growth coalition

Tugwell, Rexford: on dismantling cities, 84

Tunley, Roul: on juvenile delinquency, 102

Turner, John F.C.: on heteronomous housing, 61–2

Ukrainians: in Niagara Street area, 15, 16

Unmanipulability: of built environment, and children, 101, and interest in local politics, 121; of high-rises, 78, 126

Urban design: and politics, symbiosis with, 174; and social action, 217. *See also* Diversity, physical

Urban Development Corporation: New York State, developer of Hunters Point, 154, power as public body, 167

Urban renewal: costs of, in construction of expensive housing, 57–8, in destruction of housing, 57–8, in jobs, 56, in land prices, 56–7

Urban road mileage: built by state and federal governments, US, 37; worldwide, 40

Urban transportation: direct costs of, as user of urban land, 42–4, and land-use segregation, 30, due to postwar city building, 29–41; indirect costs of, due to postwar city building, 42–9; spending by governments on, 30–9. *See also* Cars; Expenditures; Spending; Traffic; Transit

Vancouver: lack of local autonomy in, and large-scale projects, 160; planning process in, 171; pro-growth policies of local government of, 154; worker space in offices, 7

Vandalism: as juvenile delinquency, 95; lessened in areas with community gardens, 217–18; its nature, as action against physical environment, 95; and physical diversity, affected by, 94–6; and postwar city buildings, teenagers' response to, 109–10; as sign of unhealthy street life, 94–5. *See also* Crime; Juvenile Crime; Delinquency

Veery Place: Don Mills, area of Toronto study, 224

Verrazzano Bridge: New York, built by Robert Moses, 157

Vertical disintegration. *See* Disintegration, vertical

Vienna: planning department's findings on single-family homes, 163

Vitality: economic, of Ontario Street area, 23; urban, decreased by cars, 42, nurtured by physical diversity, 13

Voluntary action: springing from awareness, 204

Vote: lack of significance, 116–17. *See also* Elections; Representative system

Walking: to workplace, Kensington Market, 209–10, percent in Boston, 44, percent in Phoenix, 44, in Toronto, 41

Ward, Colin: *Child in the Street*, 100; children killed by cars, 104; sensitivity to the environment, 100

Washington, DC: spread of urbanized areas around, 8
Water: cost, and postwar city building, 50–3; and urban ecosystem, 183. *See also* Sewage
Webber, Melvin: on the non-place urban realm, 179
Wellman, Barry and Marilyn Whittaker: on evaluations of high-rise dwellings, 77–8
White, David: on construction freeze in Toronto, 160
Whyte, William H.: on children in the city, 99; critic of suburbs, 71; *The Organization Man*, 71
Winnipeg: citizens' group in, 132; Market Square, as place for politics, 129
Withdrawal: passive, response to industrial city, 200. *See also* Autonomy-withdrawal
Wolfe, Tom: critic of modern architecture, 78
Women: suburbs built for, 113
Working class: homes, destruction of, in St Jamestown area, 21; neighbourhoods, physical design of, and politics, 129; political efficacy of, and physical diversity, 127; politics of, and street life, 128. *See also* Labour; Labour unions
Workplace: deconcentration of, 6–7; separation from home, considered normal, 208–9, in eighteenth and nineteenth centuries, 31, and politics, 127–8; services for, paid by taxes on commuters, 123
Wright, Frank Lloyd: dislike for politics, 174; great influence of, 174, 175; ideas on planning, 172–3

Yards, front: and civic street life, 205; giving to the environment, 205
Yeates, Maurice, and Barry Garner: on residential mobility, 108

Zeckendorf, William: developer of Place Ville Marie, 4
Zero-sum game: and conflict, 197–8; and love, 198
Zoning: as defence against unwanted industries and people, 11, 156; exclusionary, to keep out troublesome political issues, 122; functions, for landowner, 155; and land-use homogeneity, 119, 155–6; and insensitivity to the environment, 122–3; and local government, 119, 155; as money-making device, 155; and separation of land uses, 119. *See also* Planners; Planning